Book Self

7 auki Street.

363 TSC

Book Self
The Reader as Writer and the Writer as Critic

C. K. Stead

AUCKLAND UNIVERSITY PRESS

First published 2008

Auckland University Press
University of Auckland
Private Bag 92019
Auckland
New Zealand
www.auckland.ac.nz/aup

© C. K. Stead, 2008

ISBN 978 1 86940 412 3

Publication is kindly assisted by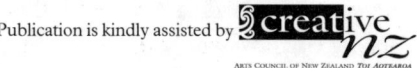

National Library of New Zealand Cataloguing-in-Publication Data
Stead, C. K. (Christian Karlson), 1932-
Book self : the reader as writer and the writer as critic /
C. K. Stead.
Includes index.
ISBN 978-1-86940-412-3
1. Stead, C. K. (Christian Karlson), 1932- 2. English literature—
History and criticism. 3. New Zealand literature—History and
criticism. I. Title.
820.9—dc 22

Cover design: Spencer Levine, Base Two

Printed by South Wind Production, Singapore

Acknowledgements

Some parts of the work on this collection were done while I held the Creative New Zealand Michael King Fellowship, 2005–06; and final work was completed at the Liguria Study Centre near Genoa where I held a Bogliasco Fellowship in Literature in 2007. I record my grateful thanks for both these awards; and especially to my colleagues and friends at Bogliasco, and to the generosity of the Foundation there.

I make also special and grateful acknowledgement to my two brilliant editors at Auckland University Press, the late Dennis McEldowney, who edited five of my books, and Elizabeth Caffin, who has edited eight.

My thanks are due to the editors of the following journals in which some of these pieces first appeared: in the UK and Ireland, *Areté*, *British Review of New Zealand Studies*, *Critical Survey*, *James Joyce Bloomsday Magazine*, *Leviathan Quarterly*, *London Magazine*, *London Review of Books*, *PN Review*, *Stand* and *Times Literary Supplement*; in Croatia, *Quorum*; in France, *Les Cahiers du CICLaS*; in New Zealand, *Christchurch Press*, *Landfall*, *New Zealand Listener*, *New Zealand Books*, *New Zealand Herald*, *Sunday Star-Times*; and to the editors of the following books: *A Passion for Travel*, ed. Tina Shaw; *Auckland Minds and Matters*, ed. Nicholas Tarling; *Katherine Mansfield's Men*, ed. Charles Ferrall and Jane Stafford; *Look This Way: New Zealand Writers on New Zealand Artists*, ed. Sally Blundell; and *Selected Poems of Eugene Lee-Hamilton (1845–1907): A Victorian Craftsman Rediscovered*, ed. MacDonald P. Jackson.

C.K.S.

Think, too, that of all the arts, ours is the one that co-ordinates the greatest number of independent parts: sound, sense, the real and the imaginary, logic, syntax, and the double invention of content and form – all this by means of that essentially practical, constantly changing, always dirty-fingered maid-of-all work the common language, from which we must draw a pure, ideal Voice capable of communicating... an idea of *self* miraculously superior to *Me*. – *Paul Valéry*

I would like to be Mercutio [. . .] the voice of reason amid the fanatical hatreds of the Capulets and Montagues. He sticks to the old code of chivalry at the price of his life, perhaps just for the sake of style, and yet he is a modern man, sceptical and ironic. – *Italo Calvino*

The ego is not master in its own house. – *Sigmund Freud*

Contents

The Function of Criticism

I am sixteen years older than Martin Amis, but when I find him writing, in his foreword to *The War Against the Cliché*, the following passage about himself when young, I feel as if we are almost contemporaries:

> I was very moral when it came to literary criticism. I read it all the time, in the tub, on the tube; I always had about me my Edmund Wilson – my William Empson. I took it seriously. We all did. We hung around the place talking about literary criticism. We sat in pubs and coffee bars talking about W. K. Wimsatt and G. Wilson Knight, about Richard Hoggart and Northrop Frye, about Richard Poirier, Tony Tanner and George Steiner. It might have been in such a locale that my friend and colleague Clive James first formulated his view that, while literary criticism is not essential to literature, both are essential to civilisation. Everyone concurred. Literature, we felt, was the core discipline; criticism explored and popularised that centrality, creating a space around literature and further exalting it.

Since I grew up in New Zealand, he in London, Amis's experience of this consensus was more sociable than mine, and more intense. But I remember a similar ambience, and how defining it seemed. It was, Amis suggests, the Age of Criticism. Working as a hospital orderly during one student summer vacation, and put to work in the Senile

ame after a stint in Infectious Diseases, which had been
one in the morgue), I used to spend my free time sitting
corner reading T. S. Eliot's *Selected Essays*. Already I was
arriving at ideas which a few years later would go into the chapter
on Eliot's criticism in *The New Poetic* (1964), my Bristol PhD thesis
which was to have a success beyond my, or anybody's, expectations,
becoming, I was told by a graduate student at University College
London, something of 'a cult book' there during his undergraduate
years in the early 1970s.*

But literary criticism, Amis goes on in that foreword, 'was inherently doomed. Explicitly or otherwise it had based itself on a
structure of echelons and hierarchies; it was about the talent élite. And
the structure atomized as soon as the forces of democratization gave
their next concerted push.'

> You can become rich [Amis continues] without having any talent (via the
> scratchcard and the rollover jackpot). You can become famous without
> having any talent (by abasing yourself on some TV nerdathon . . .) But
> you cannot become talented without having any talent. Therefore, talent
> must go.

In the Age of Criticism there was a canon of great writers and
great works. It was never, as later caricatured, an unchallengeable
orthodoxy, an unassailable fortress. If it had been, there would have
been nothing for literary criticism to do. The canon was a basis for
discussion, a beginning, constantly open to challenge and constantly
being adjusted. Its great usefulness was that it gave those who were
reasonably well-educated (which also required talent) common
ground for discussion.

The white-anting of the canon began, alas, in the universities. Where
once literary criticism had been taught and practised, literary theory,

---

* The student was Steve Ellis, now professor of English at Birmingham. He meant, of
course, only that it was fashionable among students of poetic Modernism. It was, and
remained so, selling more than 100,000 copies over several decades before I stopped
counting. Seamus Heaney, in *The Government of the Tongue*, has written how it taught him
to read Eliot's poetry and made Eliot available to him. It has been reprinted many times
both in England and America, most recently in 2005.

2

derived from France and vulgarised in America, began
Political worthiness dressed itself in a language only i
all, to the initiated, in order at once to assert its acadei
and to conceal its predictability and repetitiveness. Inge
serious thought, sociological measurement replaced pei ___. ___gage-
ment, ideology replaced sensibility. Writers and writing, once the
object of academic respect, were treated with a new arrogance. When
I took early retirement from the university in the 1980s, after twenty
years at the top of my profession, I went without regret.

Not, however, without fears for my future. It was like stepping off
a secure academic perch into nowhere. As a writer in my own country
I had no secure audience, nor the comfort of feeling myself 'one of
the chaps' among writers. Abroad, any credit I had was confused: was
I Christina Stead (who, when a computer once 'corrected' my first
name, Christian, to Christina, was credited with all my fiction as well
as her own in a list of books in print); or the author of *The New Poetic*
who wrote sometimes for the *London Review of Books*, the *TLS* and the
London Magazine; or someone else entirely, yet to make his name?

Because I learned my trade in the period of what was called the New
Criticism, and came to maturity when the dominant figure in English
studies throughout the Anglophone world was T. S. Eliot, it has never
at any time seemed to me that there is, or should be, a conflict or
disjunction between the role of poet and that of critic. The greatest
critics in English were, all of them, poets – Sir Philip Sidney, Dr
Johnson, Wordsworth of the Preface to the *Lyrical Ballads*, Coleridge,
Matthew Arnold, T. S. Eliot. Every poem (and every fiction, too, which
aspires to the quality of art) involves, in the writing, an unending
series of critical decisions. The choice of one word over another, the
sound of that word in relation to others around or near it, the tone of
voice, the degree to which 'meaning' is revealed and concealed for
effect and whether it can be enriched by doubleness or ambiguity,
the observance or avoidance of rhyme, of form, of metaphor and
imagery – these and innumerable other choices are being made and
remade, reconsidered and revised, in the course of composition. And
all this must be held together, must not fall into fragments. In fact

seem that so much is going on, control of the process must beyond consciousness – hence the idea of poetic 'inspiration' and the mythologies of the Muse. But 'inspiration', I became convinced, though real (nothing with such a strong tradition should be lightly dismissed), and often beyond the poet's conscious control, was only a speeding up of the process. It was not driving blind but, more likely, a kind of *super* vision. Its occurrence might be facilitated by certain private rituals, as the high jumper rocks to and fro before making the run-up, or the tennis champion bounces the ball again and again before serving. But these are not preparations for an act of will. They are a clearing the mind of obstacles. They are (in Eliot's pregnant phrase) 'a passive attending upon the event'.

It was the recognition of this (as I saw it) crucial fact of poetic composition that made me reconsider and qualify the New Critical approach, especially to T. S. Eliot, which tended to unfold and expound densely textured poems as if every effect was the result of deliberation and conscious choice. What I wanted my academic colleagues (who were often not poets) to consider was the proposition that choices made in the process of literary creation were not necessarily conscious at all; that they were, rather, rapid intuitive discriminations. It was not so much the intellect that was engaged as the sensibility, the sensuous eye, the quick (spontaneous, opportunistic) wit, the talent for tone (not unlike 'charm' in conversation), and the 'ear'.

That explains why, in doing my PhD at Bristol University, I paid such close attention to accidental, probably unintended, revelations, hidden in Eliot's critical writing, of his own processes of composition, and tried to show how different these were from what they would have been if his poems had indeed been the 'classically' organised structures he liked to pretend they were – poems whose obscurities were mere omissions of 'links in the chain'. Eliot, posing as the cool anti-Romantic, had wanted to be seen as one in whose work everything was where he meant it to be, the result of the 'frightful toil' (his phrase) of poetic composition. *The New Poetic* questioned this view and the critical approaches (Cleanth Brooks's, George Williamson's and many others) that had been built upon it. A whole methodology of dealing with Eliot (and everyone dealt with him in those days, in classes all around the world) was called in question.

4

It was probably the rediscovery of the lost manuscripts of *The Waste Land* in 1965, and their publication in 1971, that finally put paid to those confident explanations of the poem's 'meaning', and restored its mysteriousness. One thing that became clear was that Eliot had not been exaggerating when he gave generous credit to Pound for rescuing the poem. Pound's work on it had pulled *The Waste Land* together and determined its dominant tone and colour, cutting the satiric passages right down and giving prominence to the elements of Symbolist mystery.*

Apart from Eliot himself, names like Allen Tate, William Empson, John Crowe Ransom, I. A. Richards, and R. P. Blackmur are the ones that come to mind as most important when I think of twentieth-century New Criticism. Perhaps I learned something too from F. R. Leavis, whose much gentler and less absurdly dogmatic lieutenant, L. C. Knights, was my professor at Bristol and supervisor of my thesis. These men, reacting against the rather watery critical impressionism that had come before them, and wanting, commendably, to give authority and backbone to the literary criticism of the mid-century, seemed, however, burdened by what they saw as a consequent need to make definitive critical statements. If one was not to waffle impressionistically, one had better know good from better, and better from best, and be able to explain the difference by close readings of texts. There was a fear of relativism, a desire for firmness, even for absolutes, which in Tate's case (and that of his pupil Robert Lowell) was matched, at least for a time, by a search for 'God'.

For myself, while admiring, as Martin Amis did a decade or so later, the intellectual heat these critics generated and the new light their readings could throw on individual poems, I knew that no critical statement, however clever and comprehensive, was ever going to be final. I came to see literary criticism as a form of persuasion, a rhetoric, and I was soon telling my students that while some literary

---

* These matters are discussed at length in Chapter Four of, and in an appendix to, my *Pound, Yeats, Eliot and the Modernist Movement*, Macmillan, London, 1986.

judgements could be factually wrong, or so quirky as to be irrelevant and worthless, many different judgements could be 'right'.

Criticism was in fact not unlike the literary works which begat it. If it revealed intelligence, sensibility, clarity of mind, an engaged and engaging personality, then it would do its job, renew interest in the text under discussion, even return to it a life it had lost, and earn admiration, irrespective of whether the reader agreed with its particular judgements or not. Who 'agreed' any more with Dr Johnson's view of Donne and the Metaphysicals; yet who doubted his greatness as a critic, found him dull to read, or forgot his 'Donne for not keeping of accent deserved hanging'? Criticism was one half of a conversation, the other half of which was the silent reader. Leavis used to say that the right response in critical discussion was, 'Yes, but . . .' – the 'Yes' acknowledging the value of what had been said, the 'but . . .' taking it further, questioning or qualifying it. This was well said; but when Leavis himself engaged in debate the underlying tone had much more 'No, and . . .' than 'Yes, but . . .' about it.

If the literary theorists, who came after the New Criticism, brought something new and significant to academic critical discourse, it was a recognition of the sense in which it is true to say that the work of literature is not complete until someone has read it; and that, consequently, reader response is a part of what we mean when we talk about any poem or story. There can be no absolutes, no definitive critical statements, because the variations of time, place and individual temperament are as broad as history.

But characteristically the theorists took this recognition too far, denying those irreducible marks on paper which we know as *Hamlet* or *David Copperfield* their authority and uniqueness. The printed pages were merely the occasion of our freedom as readers, the dance floor on which we held our party. Barthes had announced 'the Death of the Author'. Writing was mere *écriture*, and whatever the reader made of it was 'criticism', and might even be 'art'. No work of literature was better or worse than any other until a reader had made it so. *Hamlet* or a bus ticket, it didn't exist until it was read and someone – preferably a literary theorist – made something of it. Further, deconstructive theory gave its practitioners a method for uncovering internal contradictions in language which undermined the writer's own intention and authority; a method, in other words, by which, again and again, the critic could be proved clever at the writer's expense.

By these means, the theorist-critic was elevated above the writer (who was 'dead' anyway). The academic worm had turned – turned against 'literature' itself, which was seen as a false and élitist category, supported by a canon which was racist, sexist, and classist.

The weaknesses in all this might have been more immediately apparent if the pronouncements had not been made in a language designed to be difficult and to sound authoritative and intimidating. Nothing was simply said if a way could be found to make it difficult. A wall was built around literary criticism. You had to be a clever climber to get in; and, once in, your job was to make the barrier higher and stronger. In fact the argot developed by these academic cultists was so repetitive, arcane and pretentious, so obfuscatory and oracular, they were soon being listened to only by one another, and by their conscript students who had no choice. But for at least two decades they were a dominant force in academic literary studies. It is a fashion that is passing – so fast that many of its once-practitioners (Terry Eagleton for example, a major exponent) write and behave now as if it was a foolishness they observed closely but never shared. Like Bill Clinton, they were present at those graduate seminars, but didn't inhale.

But damage was done, and some of it continues. During the period of Eliot's dominance – Amis's 'Age of Criticism' – university English departments, however imperfect, had at least aspired to practise literary studies at a level of intellectual sophistication, scholarly exactness and critical discrimination which kept them clear of, and uninfluenced by, the world of commerce, publisher promotions, best-sellerdom, literary prizes and the fame game. Under the regimen of Post-Modernism and literary theory, that aspiration towards something 'higher' was largely abandoned, along with the notion that 'standards of excellence' could have any meaning or authority.

I am no longer in the university and can't speak about what goes on there now, apart from observing that creative writing programmes seem to be flourishing at the expense of traditional literary studies. For three years in the mid-1980s I myself ran the University of Auckland's first such course, and I'm happy to claim some of its graduates who have succeeded in the world – Greg O'Brien, Andrew Johnston,

7

Chris Price, Tim Wilson. But I'm uncertain of the value of this trend because I know that the poets (past and present) whom one is able to take seriously, invariably turn out to be the ones who were best-read in the history of their art. I don't mean that studying literary history will make a poet. I do mean that someone who is to be a poet in a more serious sense than writing lines that don't go all the way to the edge of the page needs the help of the poets who have gone before. That is the nature of a tradition. That is a necessity of anything that calls itself an art.

There is no going back, especially here in New Zealand, where universities which once set stiff requirements for entry now advertise for students and compete for 'market share'. Yet the optimist in me says the critical instinct will find ways to assert itself, because even when fashion dictates otherwise, human beings in every aspect of social interaction, and especially in matters of language (which is what distinguishes us on our planet), do really know that some users are more skilled than others, and want to be shown how and why this is so; want to enjoy excellence, meet its challenges, and show it respect. As I said at the end of my introduction to *Kin of Place: Essays on 20 New Zealand Writers*, 'the recognition of difference, the discovery of excellence, and the understanding of where and how failure occurs, are the intelligent consciousness of literature itself, without which the book world is in danger of becoming only another branch of commerce, a brain-dead machine turning out objects for sale whose material just happens to be language'.

At intervals in this collection I refer to myself when young as a 'literary nationalist'. This was not quite a conscious doctrine; but it is a way of retrospectively describing, and perhaps explaining, my own behaviour. My mentors were Sargeson and Curnow. I felt keenly what Keith Sinclair meant when he wrote (with a characteristic awkwardness, no doubt, but the feeling is the point) 'I sing of our youth / and the fierce gladness of being in at the beginning'.* Of course it was not really the

* 'The Muses', written 1956, first published in *A Time to Embrace*, Paul's Book Arcade, Auckland, 1963.

beginning; but that's how it felt. I wanted to share in the excitement of 'making a New Zealand literature', shaking off the last vestiges of our colonial past. As I have also said more than once in this context, it is an ambition that no longer seems entirely meaningful. This is not to say that I now think it reprehensible; only that it belonged to its time, and that time is past. We are more secure in our collective identity – or at the very least more certain that we have grown up and left Home – and to make a parade of this now would seem needless and artificial. Yet we are all New Zealanders, and that fact, that identity, must in some way be present in what we write.

In an article in *Landfall* 205 (May 2003) John Newton attempted (if I understand him, looking, as far as I'm able, past the unfriendly tone) to 'place' me as a critic, and the place he found for me was in Curnow's pocket – his back pocket, I would say, or at best his fob pocket – an unswerving literary nationalist, more hide-bound even than my master. How could this be, when as a critic I have an identity outside New Zealand, and on subjects quite other than New Zealand literature? He must have asked himself this question. Here is how it is answered:

> Someone needs to take up *The New Poetic* (1964), on which Stead built his reputation as a critic of the modernist masters, and read it with an ear for colonial centre-margin ironies. For what this would show, or so I strongly suspect, is that this by-now thoroughly canonical account of the poetics of the metropolitan centre is first modelled, here at the margins, in Stead's formative encounters, not with Pound, but with Curnow himself.

I'm uncertain what 'colonial centre-margin ironies' might mean; but that aside, this is a major plank of his argument, and it is not only erected on an 'I suspect', it is simply (and this is something only I can say) wrong. I have made many acknowledgements of my debt to Curnow, both the poet and the man. To turn these against me as proof of a kind of subservience seems a good deal less than fair. Even as a student my critical theory (insofar as I could be said to have one) and practice were learned from Eliot and the New Critics, not from Curnow.

I admired Curnow's poetry, his lectures, his mind, and his critical writing. He stated the nationalist position brilliantly in his Caxton anthology of 1948 and '51; and restated it well, and more fully, in his Penguin of 1961. But by 1963, in his lecture 'New Zealand Literature: The Case for a Working Definition',* he was beginning to repeat himself defensively without adding much that was new. Later again he was less than pleased when, in my 'From Wystan to Carlos' lecture,† I turned the discussion of New Zealand poetry away from his own nationalist/identity terms to those of a much broader literary-historical perspective – that of the rise of international Modernism.

Curnow's critical range was narrow. He confined himself almost entirely to New Zealand subjects. He wrote hardly at all about fiction, and never on a broad base of knowledge. He shared with Glover and Fairburn an inability to take women writers entirely seriously. The only remark I ever heard him make about Katherine Mansfield was an irritable reminiscence about 'some fool' in Christchurch who had called her 'the only peacock in New Zealand's literary garden'.‡ He was loyal especially to his contemporaries (so we disagreed, for example, about Fairburn), and to a small group of friends. But my own critical scope and interests were always broader. That I was critically and intellectually his dependant was something not even Curnow would have wanted to claim.

But Newton has a further nail for my critical coffin. It is that I represent what he calls 'settler nationalism', a declaration of independence from the colonial Motherland which, however, fails to come to terms with the tangata whenua. Of course one cannot will oneself to be at another place in history, and there is a sense in which everything becomes 'out of date' even as it goes down on the page. As one gets older, and time seems to pass with increasing rapidity, one becomes even more conscious of this. I have described myself as someone who began

---

* *Look Back Harder: Critical Writings 1935–1984*, ed. Peter Simpson, Auckland University Press, Auckland, 1987, pp. 191–208.
† Reprinted in this collection, p. 406.
‡ This was when he and I and Denis Glover were on a panel discussion together. I interjected 'peahen', which Denis characteristically capped with 'Piha'.

10

when we were still in some degree a colony; and I have lived through (not resisting them, I hope) considerable changes in our social and literary landscape. When I was very young there would not have been an Ihimaera, a Grace, a Tuwhare or a Hulme, to argue about, and that is surely a change for the better.

The example of this failing of mine – this 'settler nationalism' – Newton offers is my review of Witi Ihimaera's *The Matriarch** in which, he says, I failed to show 'respect'. To satisfy Newton, it seems I would have had to show the work respect *because it was by a Maori*, rather than because it was inherently worthy of it. This strikes me as an example of what has been called 'reverse racism'. *The Matriarch* is a novel (a European form), and written in the English language, and I paid it and its author the respect of putting my best mind to explaining how and why it seemed to me to fail. If Newton disagrees he should attempt to deal with what I said, and with the novel I wrote about, but that is something he is at pains to avoid.

What strikes me about his article is that the word 'Maori' in it seems to exist almost as an abstraction, one which has more to do with morality and propriety than with real people. Newton doesn't discuss either Ihimaera or his novel. They are merely the instruments by which he deducts 'marks' from me and awards them to himself. Not for valour (certainly not!), but for virtue. This is not literary criticism as I understand it and have tried to practise it over many years. It is ideology; it is moralising.

I see the present book as a sequel to *The Writer at Work* (2000), but this one, while like the other in that it assembles a variety of pieces written for a number of journals in the United Kingdom and New Zealand, has been more narrowly conceived or, perhaps I should say, more purposefully structured. Forty years ago, embarking rather apprehensively on an article which would make 'the case against' the then widely admired and recently deceased A. R. D. Fairburn, I wrote this:

* See *Kin of Place: Essays on 20 New Zealand Writers*, Auckland University Press, Auckland, 2002.

11

'Literature' is a confronting of personalities occurring somewhere between the cold, immoveable words on the page and the living eye which perceives them; and perhaps criticism is rightly only a form of biography, not of the poet's life, nor of the critic's, but of the life generated in successive confrontations. It is no science. It proceeds from feelings before rational analysis has anything on which to work, returns to feelings for its final sanction, and though it may be 'better' or 'worse' it can never be 'right' or 'wrong'.

Around the same time I complained more than once of criticism written, it seemed deliberately, without personality, as if composed by God, or a committee – with that kind of (as I saw it) bogus authority.

Quite a few years after the Fairburn essay, writing about John Mulgan, I described my own personal connections (in terms mainly of place, Auckland and the suburb of Mt Eden) with the writer who was my subject, and whom I had never met, quoting, by way of explanation for this way of proceeding, what Allen Tate wrote in a critical essay on Edgar Allan Poe, a fellow Southerner:

in discussing any writer, or in coming to terms with him, we must avoid the trap of mere abstract evaluation, and try to reproduce the actual conditions of our relation to him. It would be difficult for me to take Poe up, 'study' him, and proceed to a critical judgement. One may give these affairs the look of method and thus deceive almost everybody but oneself. [. . .] This is the recognition of a relationship almost of the blood, which we must in honour acknowledge. [It is an] obligation [. . .] of loyalty to one's experience: he was in our lives and we cannot pretend that he was not.

In a later comment on this approach to Mulgan,* I conceded that it wasn't altogether successful in that 'my own presence in the article became intrusive, and gave to those who wished to refute it something to attack'.

What is clear to me now is that this has been an on-going pre-occupation. I have always believed that the reader of a piece of literary criticism should feel in the presence of a particular person, a personality, who is reading and commenting on the work in question.

* See *Kin of Place: Essays on 20 New Zealand Writers*, pp. 195–6.

But how did you make your presence felt (which I saw as a kind of honesty) while keeping that self subsidiary to the work under discussion? It is this question of the presence of the critic in the critical statement that lies behind the structure of the present book.

The first section, Shelf Life, contains pieces which are literary reminiscence or autobiography, together with social commentaries written in my own person as writer-critic.

The second section, Third Person, contains pieces written almost entirely in the neutral persona of the literary critic. These will, I assume, have my fingerprints all over them; and just occasionally, when a personal reminiscence or anecdote seems helpful, or where (as in the case of John Mulgan) my own work is part of the critical history, I haven't hesitated to use or refer to these. But my self, my identity or persona, is not a necessary part of what I have to say in these pieces, and the opinions expressed would stand without them.

The third section, First Person, is (or seems to a person of my temperament) the riskiest part of the venture. This is the section that goes further 'inside' the life of the writer-critic, offering two personal interviews and a series of journal extracts in which he is writing mainly to, of, and for himself, recording aspects of his daily personal and professional life. Here the ego is exposed – not quite naked, but now and then with its shirt off.

The final section, Lit Crit and Lit Hist, offers three examples of myself as literary historian and literary critic. 'From Wystan to Carlos' has been referred to and discussed, often heatedly, probably more than any other essay I have written, but it has been printed only once, in *In the Glass Case* (1981). The article on Marvell's Horatian Ode, published long ago in an academic journal, is offered as an example of the (rather youthful) mid-twentieth-century New Critic at work. The other, on Eugene Lee-Hamilton, is more recent. I hope these will stand, not just as examples, but in their own right, to engage and to entertain as 'essays', 'pieces of writing'.

My intention, then, in assembling the book in this way, has been to raise a larger question, to which there is no one answer, but which revolves endlessly around a phrase Eliot (that indelibly personal poet-critic who liked to pretend to 'impersonality') used as the title of one of his most famous essays: 'the function of criticism'.

Part One Shelf Life

Fifty Years Ago

Some Images of the Young Poet and his Elders: Brasch, Curnow, Sargeson*

The Hocken Lecture has recently become the Michael King Memorial Hocken Lecture – and of course the convention is that one first pays tribute to the person named. This, if taken too literally, might sink the ship, there would be so much deserved praise, so many good things to say – so we will take most of that for granted and I will be brief.

Michael King and I had what I think of as a very proper literary relationship. We always got on well and enjoyed one another's company; we reviewed one another often, and always with the greatest respect; and we had one or two quite fierce and very public disagreements. Michael dedicated his penultimate book to me as follows: 'To C. K. Stead who, like an execution, concentrates the mind' (a slight misquotation, probably deliberate). When his cancer was diagnosed and spoken about publicly, Chris Cole-Catley put together a little book of tributes, which she ended with a quotation from a letter I'd written to Michael and which he had copied to her. Part of what she quoted said:

* The annual Hocken Library/Michael King Memorial Lecture, delivered at the University of Otago, 11 October 2006.

Your interview with Kim Hill this morning was *so* good. You always do these things well, but this one was exceptional – such good things said, and such perfect tone and pitch . . .*

'Such good things said, such perfect tone and pitch'. From someone who considers himself a musician manqué, that's no mean tribute, and I'm happy to let it stand for the volumes that might be spoken if Michael were in fact my subject tonight.

When Stuart Strachan phoned inviting me to give this lecture it happened I had just exchanged e-mails about Charles Brasch and Frank Sargeson with Margaret Scott, who is transcribing the Brasch journals; so those two late luminaries were in my thoughts. Stuart said the lecture usually had some historical aspect, and as I thought about that, what came to me was a formulation something like this: 'Half a century ago is certainly "history"; it just happens I was there at the time!'

I remember many years ago there was a lecturer in the History Department at Auckland University who wrote, I thought, very readable and intelligent articles but whose work, I discovered, was not greatly admired by his colleagues. When I asked why, I was told, 'He doesn't interpret. He just writes narrative.' 'But,' I protested, showing my ignorance of modern historiography, 'a narrative *is* an interpretation.'

I still suffer from this defect of understanding; so what you are to hear this evening will have the same limitation. It will be essentially a fragment of autobiographical narrative – recollection, supplemented by a look back into some surviving documents. The Hocken librarians have helped by supplying copies of my own letters to Charles Brasch; and other materials have been sent me by Margaret Scott, and by the Turnbull Library.

Discovering myself in the past has been interesting though not uniformly comfortable. The young poet – *this* young poet – half a century ago was naïve, unsophisticated, romantic, egotistical, competitive, combative, and often just plain silly. But he did have, as a

* *A Small Book for Michael*, the Sargeson Trustees, Auckland, 2003.

17

writer, a couple of saving graces, the most important of which was that his interests were powerfully grasped by things – people, events, animals, scenes – *outside* himself.

It did not, however, occur to him, not until the time I'm speaking about was long past, that living in the moment was also, from time to time, living in history. There should have been a warning: 'Anything you say may be taken down and lodged in the Hocken Library' – but of course there wasn't.

A look through my letters from Charles Brasch reveals that I first offered poems to *Landfall* in July 1951 when I was eighteen. I didn't at that time own a typewriter, so they were submitted hand-written – an elegiac sequence about my friend Ian Lamont, killed in a motor-cycle accident. I don't have the poems any more because they went into one of those periodic burn-ups young writers have to have, and which they later half-regret; but I do remember how the sequence ended:

> Earth you are frozen now
> The dead-cold centre of a doom-darkened winter;
> Yet from this spiny row
> Of waxen, wasted willow-sticks must grow
> New life in spring.
> The sun will be warmer then
> And velvet leaves will spin
> A net of new-born comfort round old signs.
> Persistent sapling-shoots in lines
> Of contradicting green
> Will not admit
> That dead-brown death has ever been.

Charles declined the sequence but said he admired its 'freshness', particularly a poem called 'Fragments of a Saturday Night' which I remember was about roaring along Dominion Road Extension with my friend on the fatal motorbike, the concrete strip 'unfolding like a toilet roll'. In his tiny handwriting, on the bottom of my letter (addressed to 'The Editor, Dear Sir', and surviving in his files), he wrote, 'odd combination of conventionality (one sonnet on only two rhymes all through) with unexpected freshness; but uneven'. He also wrote 'file, meet' – so clearly his interest was aroused.

18

I had at this time no assistance from seniors, no guidance about how one went about 'being a poet', finding outlets, dealing with editors. But there was a small group of students at Auckland University College (as it then was) who wrote poems and met to read them to one another and to talk about such matters. The periodical shelves at the library, and to some extent the bookshops, particularly Progressive Books in Derby Street, showed us where poetry was taken seriously and gave us addresses and editors' names.

For two years and nine months after that first offering to *Landfall* I sent Brasch poems on eight occasions. Some were declined in a single sentence; others with some encouragement to try again. The comments he wrote for his own reference only were mixed, and show some signs of irritation. One was simply 'N.B.G.'

In April 1954, however, two poems were accepted, and then a third. I was now 21 and in the interim I'd had poems in the student literary magazine *Kiwi*, the *Listener*, the *Poetry Yearbook*, and the Australian annual *Jindyworobak Anthology*. Because it had been difficult, acceptance by *Landfall* made me feel as if I was in some sense launched. I felt as Wilfred Owen did when he wrote to his mother in 1917, 'I go out of this year a poet [. . .] I am held peer by the Georgians; I am a poet's poet. I am started.'

In the exchange of letters now there was a change of tone. Brasch was a good editor, always helpful, sometimes admonitory, conscientious in making up his mind and letting you know his decision. In June 1954 he came to Auckland and suggested we should meet. I remember very clearly that I found myself acting in a way that was quite false, playing the part of what would be called now a 'jock'. This impulse was triggered, before I had set eyes on him, by his phoning and saying that we should meet in the foyer of the Auckland Art Gallery, and that he would be wearing a purple tie. Linguistic sensitivity can operate in very peculiar ways. Before two people know one another, an innocent verbal solecism, a genteelism, a wrong note, can loom very large. In the case of Charles it was a genteelism, and a manner of speaking. 'I shall be wearing a purple tie.' I think the 'shall', combined with a voice I would have thought of as 'prissy' or 'fruity', and perhaps even the colour purple and a whiff of Oscar Wilde, must have been too much for me. I couldn't pretend to be the kind of poet it seemed to imply and require, so, being young and insecure, I would have to pretend to be something else. I wore a lot of clothes and a large overcoat, and sat opposite Charles in the famous Somervell's coffee bar hunching my shoulders and talking bullishly about my role as centre forward (striker it would be called now) for the university.

His journal entry recording this meeting is brief – and his reaction is expressed in visual/physical terms.* I'm described as having 'a long narrow vertical pale face with roman nose and rather ugly projecting chin and jaw'. It was all very unflattering, though he does add, 'But I might revise my impressions if I saw him again.' Before our conversation had gone very far, however, he records that 'we were interrupted by Allen Curnow, who had been writing at another table and took charge'.

I mention my own absurd behaviour, and Charles's reaction to it, and to me, and ask you to keep these in mind, because they perhaps explain his surprise when we met for a second time sixteen months later – a meeting I will come back to.

In the meantime the life of the young writer had been continuing. In May 1954 I invited Frank Sargeson to come and read to our student literary society, a meeting which I chaired, and which Margaret Mahy, a couple of years behind me as a student, still remembers vividly.† A day or so later Frank wrote saying he had seen work of mine in the *Poetry Yearbook*, and suggesting I might try poems on John Lehmann who had recently terminated *Penguin New Writing* in favour of the new *London Magazine*. Ten days after that, writing to thank me for the fee I'd sent, he said his idea of the Second Coming was 'a sort of Ibsen [. . .] big enough to force recognition from our provincial public, [. . .] prove to it that a poet with his pencil can be as good or better than Hillary with his oxygen and nylon rope'. (It was, of course, just a year since Hillary had famously 'knocked the bastard off' as a sort of present to Her newly crowned Majesty.) Without telling me that he was himself writing a play, Sargeson went on: 'Let's have the poetry – but I do hanker after the long poems and plays (Ibsen called all his

<hr>

* I am grateful to Margaret Scott for supplying this quotation, and another later in the lecture.
† Bill Pearson and Keith Sinclair, lecturers in English and history, were also in the audience. I think but am not certain, that Maurice Gee – doing his MA that year – was also there.

20

plays poems). It's up to some young poet to take the hint from Curnow and Cresswell – I mean *not* wait until the first fine careless rapture is all over, before getting round to what they should have been attempting in the hay days.'

He also wrote that it was better to have poets and writers visit universities than have them 'permanently on the premises – probably bad for them, and bad for pupils who show signs of brilliance and originality in excess of their masters'.

About Curnow, Sargeson was always delicately poised between grudging acknowledgement and irritable dismissal, so these side-swipes, one direct, the other oblique, were something I would get used to later on. For the moment I was simply excited to have a hand-written two-page letter from the man who was already a literary icon – one who had a publisher in London and yet remained right here, writing in, and about, New Zealand.

And in any case nothing was going to alter my view of Allen Curnow, whose work I'd rated above all the rest even before arriving at university. Since then Curnow had been my second-year tutor; and over the period of my student years was gradually becoming what I suppose would be called, these days, a mentor.

I also knew Fairburn reasonably well – he too rather dismissive of Curnow, devoted, at that time, to the poetry of the American Edgar Lee Masters, and inclined to wonder aloud why no one read or talked about A. E. Housman any more. Ron Mason was to be seen occasionally, reading his wonderful early poems very badly, so they sounded as if they'd been written by Madge Allsop.* Mike Joseph was one of my teachers in the English Department, and Keith Sinclair in History. James K. Baxter visited Auckland now and then to combine poetry readings with drinking and pontificating. Kendrick Smithyman was in and out of the university library and his name sooner or later turned up on the borrowing card of every collection of modern poetry, English or American. His wife, Mary Stanley, had just published her first (and only) book, *Starveling Year*.

---

* Dame Edna Everage's New Zealand bridesmaid. Fairburn, Mason and Joseph were respectively A. R. D., R. A. K. and M. K., as Yeats, Eliot and Pound were W. B., T. S., and W. H., and as I have always been C. K. – something now so out of fashion I am often asked about it as if it requires explaining.

In other words, there were poets everywhere – poets you could take seriously, admire, hope to emulate; and *Landfall* published them all.

Baxter's visits were memorable. Having, I suppose, a view of Auckland's weather that had been formed in Dunedin, he wore what I liked to call his 'Presbyterian raincoat' together with galoshes. He was still at that time a short-back-and-sides man and considerable alcoholic, and, once in the hands of Bob Lowry, with whom he liked to stay, his behaviour became unpredictable. Lowry was as famous for his parties as for his work as a printer; and he liked to take visitors out to the Henderson Valley where signs that said 'LICENSED TO SELL TWO GALS' meant not girls but gallons; and not 'up to two gallons' but 'not less than two gallons'. I have a vivid memory of wondering why Allen Curnow and Rex Fairburn were pressing so close on either side of Baxter as they came down the aisle of the university hall to give a public reading, until they were past me and I saw from behind that the galoshes were not touching the floor.

Baxter was the young man who, a few years previously at a writers' conference, had offered a high-toned paper in which he famously said the poet must be 'a cell of good living in a corrupt society'. I'm sure, if challenged, he would have argued that there was no contradiction: that a man carried drunk on to the stage to read his poems might indeed be, in the special sense he meant, a cell of good living – and I wouldn't have wanted to disagree. What I enjoyed was not the moral question, argued one way or the other, but simply the comedy of it, and the challenge it represented to social norms. It's difficult to overstate how repressive and conformist Cold War McCarthyite New Zealand felt, and how liberating it seemed that our writers ruffled feathers – social feathers, political feathers, moral feathers.

On one of his visits Baxter extracted from those Presbyterian pockets a small pink paperback edition of *The True Confessions of George Barker*, which was supposed to be shocking, and which he pressed upon me, with the understanding that having profited as a poet from reading it, I would send it back to him in Wellington. The poems made no great impression, but, shamefully, and forgetting my obligation to be a cell of good living, I kept the little book as a memento.

I got to Wellington, not as a poet but as a soccer player, representing AUC at a winter tournament there, and a year later passing through on my way to another at Christchurch. I'd heard there was a pub where the Wellington literati met, and I went in the spirit of a bird watcher, or a sight-seer. Thinking I recognised one of the drinkers as Alistair Campbell, whose photograph I'd seen in *Landfall*, and whose 'Elegy' series had made a strong impression, I went up to him and asked, diffidently probably, or just possibly adopting my sportsman persona, whether he was indeed the poet. When he confirmed that he was, I was unable to think what to say next. After a moment of embarrassing silence I asked whether he could tell me where I might find Jim Baxter. He looked less than pleased, understandably, and said he didn't really know. However, many years later I saw a reminiscence of those years in which he recalled the young poet Stead, wearing a long 'Varsity' scarf and carrying a hockey stick, paying some kind of homage to him in a Wellington pub. He was wrong about the hockey stick; and he must have intuited the homage, because I don't believe anything of the kind was said – but that indeed had been the intention.

On one of those Wellington visits I called on Louis Johnson, taking with me another Auckland student poet who went at that time by the name of John Kay. Johnson, I thought, looked like a cross between Mario Lanza and a dance band leader of the 1940s. He used a lot of Brylcreem on his hair; and there was something lubricated, even lubricious, about his voice – a remembered impression that was confirmed for me when I heard his reading (an otherwise very good reading) on the recently released CD of New Zealand poets in performance.

Johnson was living in an exceedingly dreary suburb of Wellington and was engaged on what he called 'peopling the landscape' of New Zealand poetry, setting himself in opposition to what he and his cohort liked to call 'the South Island Myth' and 'the Mountain Mysticism School' of Curnow, Holcroft, Brasch and Glover. As this developed into a war and, strangely, began to take on something of an Auckland versus Wellington character (Baxter riding shot-gun for Johnson), I threw my support on to the Curnow side – not because I was too absolutely positively pro-Curnow's regionalism and anti-Johnson's internationalism, but really because I thought Curnow was such an important poet, and because I could see at close quarters how sensitive and pained he was by a fight which spectators – admiring his well-aimed blows – probably imagined he enjoyed.

But in those student years the battle was only brewing, and I was grateful for the fact that Johnson had welcomed me, encouraged me, and published my work.

After my visit he wrote me an amusing letter in which he referred to John Kay, the student poet I'd brought with me, as 'the wee Narcissus'. Kay was indeed small. He soon changed his name to Kasmin, which did nothing for his physical stature, but may have helped in other ways. He later became, and probably remains, one of the most successful art dealers in London, the one, I think, who first promoted the work of David Hockney. When I walk past his mansion in Warwick Avenue, as I sometimes do when I'm in London visiting my daughter, the phrase 'the wee Narcissus' always floats into my head. This Narcissus had evidently been interested in a beauty beyond his own.

Still in 1954, first with my friend Rob Dyer, and then on my own after Rob went off to Oxford on a scholarship, I edited an issue of AUC's literary annual *Kiwi*, which Bob Lowry printed for us very beautifully but belatedly in 1955. The standard was pretty high. There were poems by the editors, of course. I included the talk I'd persuaded Sargeson to give to the Literary Club. John Kay was there under his new name, Kasmin. There was work by Lily H. Trowern, Sue Renshaw, and Geoff Fuller whose poems were beginning to appear in other places; poems by Paul Temm who went on to be a High Court judge; a story by Kenneth McKenney who now, I believe, lives in Spain writing thrillers; and a story – one of the earliest to be published, possibly the first – by M. G. Gee who would soon shed the initials in favour of Maurice. I like to claim, anyway, that I was Gee's first publisher.

I speak of all these things, I suppose, in an affectionate, semi-comic tone that won't surprise anyone old enough to look back on his or her youth from such a great distance. But I'm not unaware that the comic tone doesn't do full justice. It was a time of life full of mistakes, absurdities, embarrassments; but under all that there was a deadly – and I think a proper – seriousness. Literature mattered. I had no patience with T. S. Eliot's formulation that poetry was, after all, 'only a superior form of entertainment'. I considered that an affectation – only a snootier version of my own occasional pretence that I was really just a tough-guy sportsman.

I completed my BA at the end of 1954 and enrolled for an MA. In

January 1955 I married Kay Roberts, who worked in the university library, and we went to live in a flat (hardly more than a glassed-in veranda with attachments) on Takapuna Beach. Kay earned, I think, £7 10s a week. I had a bursary worth £75 for the year, and probably as much again saved from vacation jobs – work which each year had varied between wool stores, freezing works, the Post Office, a metal foundry, and the Auckland Hospital. So we had in total at least £10 a week and, with rent of only £3, that seemed more than enough. There was no harbour bridge and we went to and from town each day by ferry across the harbour.

The year 1955 was for us a sort of *annus mirabilis*, which, many years later, with much misrepresentation and comic exaggeration, and with a shift back in time to 1951 so it could include the waterfront dispute as background, would provide the substance of my novel *All Visitors Ashore*. Frank (as Sargeson had now become) was living within easy walking distance, and his routine was unvarying. In the early morning he read the great classics of English literature, poetry and prose. After breakfast, and for the remainder of the morning (during which no visits were permitted) he read and corrected his previous day's page ('a page a day' was his formula) and wrote the next. In the afternoons he did gardening, chores and shopping. In the evenings he read contemporary work, listened to the radio and entertained any of his literary friends who chose to call. The gardening was especially important. It gave him his own vegetables and fruit, with some over for sale or trade, and for gifts to his friends. It was an essential part of the ambience of 14 Esmonde Road.*

This is the life as described, so to speak, 'officially' – and it's true: that's how it was. But his anxieties about his writing, about his lack of progress, about how little he had to show for all the dedication and fuss he had made about 'the literary life', were really weighing on him in

---

* The house is now preserved without its garden. The back of the section has been sold off, and also a wide strip to give access to the new house. The space occupied by the army hut, where Janet Frame wrote *Owls do Cry*, is gone. A great fuss was made in an attempt to preserve the frontage when the road was recently widened. Though I understand how all this came about, and was party to it when I was a member of the Sargeson Trust, I feel now that it might have been better to let it all go, and leave the written record to speak for what it once was.

the decade of the 1950s, and he needed the companionship of younger people to maintain faith in himself.

Soon Janet Frame was occupying the army hut in his back garden, writing *Owls do Cry*. 'She is', Frank wrote to Brasch, 'one of the most remarkable persons I have met. I have taught her chess, and she is too good for me after half a dozen games. Her typewriter taps away all day.'

Kay and I now saw Frank and Janet together, and the close friendship was formed which Janet has described very beautifully – indeed lyrically – in *An Angel at my Table*. We were a strange quartet: Frank in his early fifties with an irregular but committed homosexual life that was not secret from his friends, but not seen; Janet in her early thirties, recently released from the latest of her decade-long series of incarcerations in mental institutions; and a newly married, very innocent young couple in their early twenties, full of literary appetites and idealism. For a period of about a year we made for one another extraordinary, idiosyncratic, and sparky company.

I now felt as if I had two educations running simultaneously. At the university I was doing seven MA papers – Shakespeare, Milton, the Victorians, Twentieth-Century Poetry, the History of Criticism, Selected Minor Authors and an essay paper on poetic drama in the nineteenth and twentieth centuries. Frank didn't mind helping me now and then with my studies. There was even an occasion when I had more reading to do than I could manage, and he read and took notes for me on two books about Milton. But his view of the university was almost entirely negative. From him I was learning what he saw as the proper alternative – the living world of writers and writing, the interconnections national and international, the gossip and goodwill, the solidarity and the bitchiness and competition, how it all worked and could be a way of life. The problem was of course – and I knew this perfectly well – you could not in those days live as a professional writer in New Zealand. You could only be full time at it if, like Frank, you lived a subsistence life and had no dependants. I needed a degree, because I would need employment.

Janet was very shy, but once that was overcome, she was clever, witty, and with an underlying sense that nothing was stable, and therefore nothing could be taken either for granted or entirely seriously. She uttered our collective pieties with, I'm sure, complete sincerity, and yet always as if she was on the brink of laughter. As high intelligence tends to be, hers was anarchic.

Frank was interested in everything, and in all the varieties of human behaviour, social, religious, and especially sexual. He asked questions one was not supposed to ask, and got away with it because the questions made you feel that you were interesting, that someone really wanted to hear what you thought, what you felt, what you did.

Recently I re-read his (I think neglected) three-volume auto-biography, and there's a passage towards the end of *Once is Enough* in which the young Sargeson is facing the bitter truth that he will never write poems like his hero, John Keats. But then he reads in the poet's letters a passage describing a very old Scottish lady being carried on someone's back causing Keats to wonder what the life of such a person had been; and all at once Frank seems to see a way forward for himself. He goes on:

> I was moved at last to such a state of heart-knocking excitement I felt driven from my room to the streets outside where I walked for hours which I am never likely to forget – because I began with the thought that the wonderful poet the world had received could hardly be reckoned a gift when he had had to be paid for by the loss of a novelist who might have been reckoned no less wonderful: and I returned to my lodgings with the conviction that I was going to repair the loss by writing the sort of novels which the poet might have written.

It's not the day-to-day Frank who speaks there; but it's the man who was just beneath the surface. Under all the jocularity, wit, impropriety and irreverence – and, as I've acknowledged, the occasional bitchiness – the serious purpose was there, mostly undeclared, but potent. It was something one absorbed almost without knowing it.

These locations, 14 Esmonde Road, Takapuna and Princes Street, Auckland, were two worlds that were, for me, one world, and Allen Curnow was a bridge between. Allen I considered, not only our major poet, but also by far the most rewarding of my teachers. But you had to listen carefully and wait patiently for the moment when the valuable *aperçu* arrived, because there might be only one in the course of an hour, and it would come in the midst of a relatively unstructured reading of a poetic text. Often it would seem to take the man himself by surprise and then be gone in an instant. Curnow was not by nature, or not primarily, a conversationalist. His talent, like Coleridge's, was for monologue; and there were times, then, and during the years that followed, when I would come home drained and tell Kay I'd been captured again by 'the ancient mariner'. But, like Coleridge, when the wind was in the right quarter, the monologue could be studded with gems. Even in small classes he didn't really encourage direct engagement with his students; and when someone dared to plunge in with an unsolicited comment, Allen would do his lizard blink, and frown as if he'd been inconveniently disturbed in a private meditation.

Allen had only recently met Jeny Tole who was to be his second wife, and the love affair had set him writing new poems that seemed to take him a step beyond anything he'd done before. One of my most exciting memories of that year is of sitting in the university 'Caf' with a group of students when Allen came in with the typescript of a new poem – 'Spectacular Blossom'. He handed it to me and asked whether I would mind, when I had a moment, reading it and letting him know what I thought of it. Imagine being the first, after the poet himself, to read lines like

> All over the dead hot calm impure
> Blood noon tide of the breathless bay.

It seemed – and indeed it was – an extraordinary honour, and an act of trust. It was the start of something that would go on for the remaining 45 years of his life. I was flattered; but I think it's also true that he was astute. He knew I could read; or (as Auden says of his best readers) that I could rune. And I think he also knew that I would want to prove myself useful – and that would require more than platitudes and flattery. He was putting us both to the test.

Somehow, in conjunction with all this, my writing life and the interchanges with Charles Brasch were continuing. In January, a week or two after moving into the Takapuna flat, I sent Charles a new poem, a verse letter to Rob Dyer. Charles told me he liked it and would use it in *Landfall*. Later, after discussing it with Allen, I rewrote it, cutting the pentameters down to tetrameters, and again Charles accepted the revised version, agreeing that it was better.* Also, during these early months of the year, I wrote a verse play, based on Racine's *Andromaque*, but giving the events a modern setting. *Andromaque* had been a set book during my last year doing French; and this was a time when T. S. Eliot was trying to write verse drama that would work in the theatres of the West End.

I remember going for a walk with Allen, scrambling around the inner-harbour foreshore at low tide, and telling him that an almost insuperable problem was 'motivation' – how to make modern characters say and do what they said and did in Racine. But this – new plays for a New Zealand theatre – was what Frank, who was struggling to get his Kendall play finished, had urged on me – and it was an interest of Allen's as well. When I read the play to Frank he wrote at once to Charles about it.

Dear Charles, [this was dated 18 March 1955]
I must mention to you my delight that young Stead has written a five act play. I and his young wife listened while he read [it], and perhaps I am all wrong but it seems to me something new in New Zealand. He is devoted to Racine – hence he has produced something very lucid and logical. [. . .] I couldn't help thinking of almost any novel by Ivy Compton-Burnett. Classicism, I suppose. The verse a sort of not-verse, but responding beautifully where the heightening demands it.

He said he'd suggested I send the play to Charles, and he hoped it would read as well as it had sounded.

* I have long since lost the earlier version, but now, fifty years on, find it preserved among Brasch's papers!

Sending the play on 8 April I told Charles of the difficulties it had given me and said I was 'sick of the sight of it'. 'Characters, setting, and hardest of all, motives, had to become twentieth century – the heroic motivations debased into a modern coinage – physiological and psychological.' 'I have all sorts of doubts,' I went on, 'but thought it was good while I was writing it.'

A month later Charles wrote that he'd 'read the play once and been carried along compellingly, but I'll have to read it a couple more times before I know what I think of it'. In the interim, Frank thought, he would be having it read by Rodney Kennedy, whose opinion was professional and would be crucial.

The verdict, when it came early in May, began encouragingly. He praised 'its concentration and bareness, the way in which you've got down to the bones [. . .] so that the people are presented almost naked. This – your consistency in it – is impressive; it is from this that the play gets its power.'

But from that point on, in what was quite a long and typically conscientious letter, the message turned irremediably negative. In the stripping process I'd 'got rid of time and place'. There were 'no climaxes [. . .], no heightening and intensifying'. The story was not worked out 'in strictly dramatic terms'. The language was flat. The characters' feelings were not engaging, not convincing, and didn't develop. The play wouldn't work on the stage . . .

I don't think this verdict can have been altogether a surprise. Frank tried to soften the blow; and it's obvious from what he wrote to Charles on 9 May that he wasn't altogether persuaded:

> You may well be right in the great majority of your points – the only general thing I am doubtful about is whether or not you may be expecting the play to be what it is not. Taken as the kind of play that it is I was so impressed by the reading that I fancy I should like very much to *see* it performed.

What impresses me now, at this great distance, is the patient attention both men gave the play; and also, the insuperable nature of the task I'd undertaken. How could you ever make those pairs of conflicting passions – Oreste for Hermione, Hermione for Pyrrhus,

Pyhrrus for Andromache – believable in a modern setting? No wonder I went on about the problem of motivation.*

I was now at the end of the first term, with only six months to go until it would be time to sit those seven papers. So there was only spasmodic traffic, a few poems offered, a little news back and forth with Dunedin, until November, when Charles announced that he was coming to Auckland, and Kay and I invited him for a meal. He came the day after I'd sat the last of my seven papers. I was pretty sure I'd done well, but probably didn't say so. I wasn't wrong, however, and the consequences would follow fairly quickly. By February 1956, after a brief spell as an Auckland postman, I would be lecturing in an Australian university; and from there I would go on, in August 1957, to take up a scholarship in Bristol and London. An academic career was opening up; and though I was determined to return and write in New Zealand, and turned down offers to stay and work in English universities, I think it was a disappointment to Frank that for so many years I wasted my energies (as he saw it) on academic work rather than on what he always called 'works of the imagination'. Charles perhaps agreed, and was offering me a way out when, towards the end of 1960, he suggested he and I might begin preparing for me to succeed him as editor of *Landfall*. I was flattered; but I knew that would be only frying pan and fire, and I declined. Frank wrote to Charles that he was 'disconcerted' by my decision, and thought I should have been more 'adventurous'.†

But I want to conclude by bringing you back to that meal – 12 November 1955, the day after my MA exams were completed. This was only the second time Charles and I had met, and more than a year

---

* My good friend Craig Raine attempted, more successfully, the same exercise in his play *1953*, which uses the structure of Racine's play (he calls it a 'version'), setting the events in Italy in the year of the title, but in a 'parallel universe' in which Hitler and the Axis Powers have won the Second World War. It was published (Faber, London, 1990) but, it seems, never performed.

† Charles had raised the question, first in conversation, then in a letter, late in 1960. My reply, dated 1 December, which I showed to Frank before posting, was grateful, but firm in its refusal. Frank wrote to Charles, 'Such a remarkable person, a powerful mind and wonderful sensibility – and yet it does seem that back in the twenties and thirties we could be somewhat more adventurous.'

had gone by since the first meeting, when I'd put on a large overcoat and played the role of butch sportsman.

The flat itself – the glassed-in veranda, more like a railway carriage than a room – seemed to us, and perhaps also to Charles, primitive but rather lovely. Somehow we'd got hold of matting from the bales of bananas that came down from the islands and used it to cover the white weatherboards that formed the inner wall – so there was a distinctly Polynesian flavour. There was a bookcase in pale pine, a divan with bright cushions, a small table with a radiogram, and on the wall a very fine painting from Louise Henderson's Cubist period which she'd given us as a wedding present and which hangs now in Parnell alongside a McCahon, not in any way diminished by its illustrious companion.

The long line of the windows looked out on a small white courtyard with a cabbage tree at the centre; and you had to cross that to reach the bathroom and lavatory shared with another small, whitewashed flat on the other side. That was rented by the violinist Felix Miller and his soprano wife, whose architect-designed house had recently burned down in a domestic dispute, and who took turns to use the bathroom for solo practice. Finally, the little table where we dined looked out, across a few yards of green lawn flanked by pohutukawa, to Takapuna Beach, and beyond it, straight across the Hauraki Gulf to Rangitoto, the whole expanse, including distant reaches left and right of the island, one of the most beautiful views imaginable.

When I remember that meal, however, there's one thing that stands out for me above everything else because it was so embarrassing. I'm taking you back, remember, half a century to what was not only an Anglo-Saxon beer-and-whisky culture, but (as Frank would call it) a wowser one as well, where pubs still closed at 6 p.m. and restaurants were fined and put out of business if they tried to sell alcohol with meals. As students we drank beer when we drank at all (which wasn't often). Or, if there was some kind of polite party and young women were to be present, there might also be strange alcoholic concoctions with names like Pimm's Number One Cup, and Honeymoon Cocktail. Out at Henderson, where Kay grew up, there were the rough beginnings of a wine industry; and those signs 'LICENSED TO SELL TWO GALS' signalled that you could buy what was known as 'Dally plonk', not in bottles but in bulk. Even Frank, who admired, and aspired to, European culture, served only a cheap citrus wine called Lemora, which everyone who ever drank it there agrees tasted awful.

In other words, Kay and I knew nothing at all about wine, except that, being readers of modern novels, we'd picked up that to serve it with a meal was the civilised thing. But what wine to choose? I knew (again from reading) that port was posh; so, wanting to do our best for the eminent editor, I bought a bottle of port and we served it with what was almost certainly the Elizabeth David-style pan-fried rice and oysters Frank had taught us.*

Charles must have been faced with a dilemma: did he educate the young couple, or did he save them embarrassment in the interests of a happy occasion? I'm sure I would have chosen the latter. He, being Charles, decided to educate us. Port, he explained, didn't go *with* a meal; it came *after* – often, at least in England, after the women had withdrawn to allow the men their cigars, and where it was always passed to the left around the table. We were intensely embarrassed. I felt glad to have learned the lesson, but faintly resentful of the teacher.

A few days later Charles wrote thanking us for the good evening we'd given him and saying it was a pity we couldn't meet more often. To Frank he wrote, 'I felt a bit concerned that Karl was not looking very strong, but perhaps he was simply exhausted after exams.' More interesting, of course, and only available now, through Margaret Scott's transcription, is what he wrote in his journal. There's no description of the flat, and not even of the view, despite the fact that one of his best-known poems was called 'A View of Rangitoto'. Even more surprising, there's no mention of the port wine solecism and the necessary lesson in culinary proprieties. He records that we talked about my play, and that I was thinking of writing a novel. And he records in some detail the conclusions I'd come to while studying nineteenth- and twentieth-century verse drama. He says, 'For me it was a happy evening; we talked freely, constraint evaporated, & I felt there was confidence on both sides.'

---

* Poor Charles might well have had the same meal, plus Lemora, with Frank the night before! See *Once is Enough*, Reed, Wellington, 1973, p. 29, for the recipe.

But by far the largest part of the entry is once again taken up with physical appearances – first how I'd appeared to him sixteen months before – 'loosely built but wiry with a long strong jaw [. . .] an out-of-doors young man well able to meet the world' – this image then contrasted with the one that now confronted him: 'a tallish but slight figure with small well-kept dark-red beard on a long head, the skin very pale, grey pensive noticeable eyes & delicately formed high thin birdlike nose, hair pale and rather thin; the whole head suggesting both a very refined Viking figurehead on a ship's prow, & a hollow-cheeked fasting Christ from some rococo Italian or Spanish painting or majolica statue, too pure & sensitive and melting-eyed.' He concludes that he had found my 'want of robustness disquieting'.

No such anxiety about Kay. She 'by contrast looked warm-blooded and rich with life – dark skin, full bright eyes & generous mouth; quiet, but alert and responsive'.

Gone was the strong-jawed sportsman, replaced by the aesthete, 'pure and sensitive and melting-eyed', possibly ill, and contrasting with the wife, 'warm-blooded and rich with life', who should really, of course, have been married to the sportsman.

Looking back on all this through the imperfect glass of memory, and through the also (but differently) imperfect glass of written records, I recognise how much was extraordinary in what I received from these men who were two and three decades my senior. Frank's conversation, by the social norms of the time, was outrageous; but it was lively, fascinating, and full of intelligence. He made the whole business of 'being a writer', the mystique of it, exciting. And already he was treating me as a colleague, suggesting we might write a play together. Allen I was to get close to slowly, over many years, as colleague, fellow poet, neighbour and friend. But already, in addition to giving me, as teacher, the benefit of one of the finest literary intelligences I would ever encounter, he was also reading and commenting on my poems, and inviting me to do the same with his. And finally Charles, somewhat prim and repressed compared to the other two, was the painfully conscientious editor – the man who read my play three times before writing at length to explain why it wouldn't do – and who five or six years after that first comic encounter in Somervell's, was suggesting he might hand on to me the editorship of *Landfall*, the journal which was his own creation, and which had become, over the years, the single unifying platform for New Zealand's serious writers.

It's a very different world our young writers have to cope with now – much more commercial, more conformist and awards-conscious, more in the public eye, semi-official, Government-sponsored, education-oriented. Perhaps, after all, Fairburn's warning that the mushroom grows in the open field, the toadstool under the tree, had a point – but who would want to go back? None of us – then or now – chooses the world he or she is born into. We simply learn to cope with whatever it happens to be – whether in an army hut in Frank Sargeson's garden, or in Bill Manhire's 'International Institute of Modern Letters' funded by a millionaire with headquarters in Las Vegas.

Brasch, Curnow, Sargeson: I have sometimes tried to stand back and take the large view, seeing them – and myself – fifty years ago as provincials in an outpost of a world empire at a time when power was diminishing at the centre. There ought to be a Roman analogy, but I don't know enough to suggest what it might be.

I hope I've made clear how conscious I am of a debt to each of them. If I have anything to blame them for it could only be for giving me such a positive idea of what it would mean to 'be a New Zealand writer' – saddling me with a romantic literary nationalism which, in our altered circumstances, is no longer meaningful. There was a kind of apostolic blessing in what they did for me – something I was not aware of, and they would not have intended, but which determined that I would return to New Zealand committed to living out my life as a writer here. This requires no 'interpretation'. It is 'what happened'. It is 'history'.

Janet Frame[*]

When I try to focus as exactly as I can on Janet Frame as I knew her, what I always think of first is humour – her jokes, and her response to jokes. But these were not just any old 'funnies'; they often had to do with language and with perception, and were full of dangerous intelligence. It was as if the whole of human existence was a joke – a black one perpetrated by the gods. Here we were 'on earth', destined to live (good), but also to die (bad), and with nothing certain 'beyond' except extinction, and nothing that alleviated the starkness of this fact except our own inventions. That's why the inventions – which we could make only because we had the gift of language – were the most important expressions of our humanity. There was truth and there was fiction; but in a way everything was a fiction, because it seemed we had no choice but to go on behaving as if everything was for ever. We had to pretend our social structures enshrined absolutes. We had to pretend that there were universal sanctions, not because we could see that there were *really* (as children say), but because there ought to be, otherwise we were inhabiting a universe without justice. Janet's presence, when I first knew her, had the feel of a self-recognising fabrication. It was tentative, an offering, as if she were saying 'This is quite absurd but – *under the circumstances* – what else can one do?' Later that presence

* This obituary for Janet Frame appeared in the *New Zealand Listener*, 7 February 2004.

would become the voice of her fiction – equally tentative, but strange and brilliant, as if she and her readers were required to walk on water, and somehow, by the magic of language, contrived to do it.

Apart from this darkly comic scepticism, there was, however, another aspect to her personality and her work, not a contradiction, but an addition, which came largely from her periods in mental hospitals and from her memories of childhood. She had no consistent 'message'; but she had suffered and seen suffering, and she did not want it to be overlooked. She knew it continued everywhere, mostly unseen, mostly inside people's heads, and she felt a moral responsibility to acknowledge that it was there. It was this sense of responsibility that produced some of the most vivid recollections and recreations in her writing; it gave purpose and authority to the uses she made of that part of her life experience which was exceptional, and exceptionally dark. On the other hand it could also sometimes trap her into characterisations which equated misfortune with virtue and luck with vice. Her novels tended to be uncomprehending and unforgiving of those who were comfortable and at home in the world, and this could at times undermine the quality of the fiction, making it seem programmatic.

Janet (by her own account) grew up with a sense of shame, of being unwashed, with bad teeth, badly clothed, poor. But it was a household rich in poetry and stories, and the sense of magic that went with them. Literature transformed reality, redeemed it, even superseded it. So there was a way out for her, an escape through books, first in reading, then in writing. But the shame of poverty remained. Many others from such backgrounds have simply asserted their talents and have been able to leave deprivation behind. She could not – she brought it with her – and the reason for that, I suppose, was something genetic, bio-chemical, a social incompetence springing from extreme, almost morbid shyness, made worse by incarceration in mental hospitals at the time when a young adult needs to be out in the world learning social skills. Janet never quite lost the look of someone who was socially 'disadvantaged'. Her body language was seldom confident. In public she appeared to be either in retreat, or held against her will. When she faced an unexpected camera the head and torso seemed to be dragged to face it while the feet and legs were already turning, or tending, away. Yet (one of so many paradoxes) on the very few occasions when she consented to read in public the effect was sensational. Her voice was light, bell-clear, almost childlike, but compelling. It matched her writing perfectly – a *kind* of innocence, almost ominously clever.

In private, with family or a few trusted friends, she could be quick, witty, articulate, entertained and entertaining, capable of everything, not excluding malice. She had her bad days; but at her best she sparkled and shone like her own writing.

In addition to the deprivations of her early childhood there had been a sequence of tragedies visited upon the family that would not have looked out of place among the curses and plagues of the Old Testament. Of the five Frame children Geordie, the brother, was seriously epileptic. One sister, Myrtle, had a heart seizure and drowned at the age of sixteen. Ten years later Isabel, aged 20, died in exactly the same way. Janet fell into suicidal depressions in her late teens and spent most of a decade in mental institutions. That left only June, the sister on whose companionship and support Janet relied, especially during the latter part of her life, the only one of the group to marry and have children, and now the only survivor. Not a fortunate family, one might say, except that it had produced a writer whose work, even when it was less than perfect in execution, seemed to shine with the unmistakable quality of genius.

As Janet's work became known in literary circles certain myths grew up around her. One (which I believed until it was dispelled by Michael King's biography) was that she had been incarcerated against her will for a period of ten years. In fact her medical history was not so simple. There was a certain amount of coming and going. Janet retreated into mental hospitals, at times voluntarily. On the other hand there were quite long periods when she was simply locked away, and in danger of remaining there for life. Even worse, there had been the threat of a lobotomy – an operation to sever the frontal lobes of the brain – which would almost certainly have destroyed her personality and her creativity. Her mother had been persuaded to sign the authorisation for this to be done. Only the publication of Janet's first collection of stories, *The Lagoon*, and the award of a prize for it, saved her. Someone in the medical fraternity thought to stop at the last moment and ask,

'Why are we about to make a major alteration to a brain that can produce prize-winning fiction?'

Frank Sargeson took her in, gave her the use of the old army hut in his garden to live and work in, looked after her, encouraged her to believe in herself. In letters and conversations he liked to dramatise her – 'the madwoman in my garden'. But his interest in her was selfless, entirely humane and literary. He treated her exactly as he treated all his friends, and for her, used to brutality from some and cloying concern from others, that can only have been salutary. He was brisk, practical, entertaining; he cooked for her, brought her cups of tea, made sure her working routine was protected, made practical arrangements for her, helped her to find a publisher. She in turn knitted him 'an enormous sweater' and made a patchwork quilt for his bed. They played chess, talked about books (Frank was a mine of gossip about other writers, both in and beyond New Zealand); they wrote comic poems together, and Frank told ribald stories.

This was the period when I knew her best, when she was writing *Owls do Cry*, her first novel – the time she writes of with such gratitude in *An Angel at my Table*, the second volume of her autobiography. In the social bleakness of the 1950s Frank's presence was liberating to all of us who were his friends; but how much more so for Janet after years of confinement and hopelessness.

Her behaviour was still erratic. There were episodes when she locked herself away for a day or two and refused to come out. She sometimes took a job and then almost at once handed in her notice. Frank encouraged her to think of herself only as a writer. That was her work, her identity, her *raison d'être*, her future. She said of him, 'Frank Sargeson saved my life.'

But he also grew weary of caring for her. Wanting after more than a year to escape from what he called in one letter 'the Janet situation', and believing in any case that a New Zealand writer must experience Europe, he began to encourage her to go abroad. He helped to gather money for the fare from friends, and to get her a grant from the New Zealand Literary Fund. By March 1957, when she was ready to depart, £125 had been paid for her fare (in a six-berth cabin) and there was a further £300 for her to live on when she got there.

From London Janet travelled to Ibiza, off the coast of Spain, where she lived for some time. There was new fiction, her first (perhaps her only) real love affair, and a pregnancy which miscarried. She returned to London and settled, but felt herself failing to cope and admitted herself to the Maudsley psychiatric hospital. In 1958 (I was by then a post-graduate student in London) I was asked to talk to Dr R. H. Cawley who was to be her most understanding and helpful physician. Cawley wanted to meet someone who had known her in New Zealand. I soon recognised that he was exceptionally intelligent; but I remember that he surprised me at first by asking had I ever thought Miss Frame was 'mad'. I said no, not in the least. A shy person recognises shyness. Here was simply – and by a mile – the worst fellow sufferer one had ever encountered.

Cawley told me that the medical staff considered her their most interesting patient. They had all taken an interest in her, and were divided more or less evenly between those who accepted the New Zealand diagnosis of schizophrenia, and those, like himself, who thought she had no classifiable mental illness but was suffering from what he would later describe as 'an existential dilemma – an identity crisis; something very real and alarmingly elusive'. He also told me that he thought the number of ECTs (shock treatments) that had been forced on her in New Zealand was 'barbaric'.

This division of opinion about her 'illness' is not quite the story she tells in her autobiography, which seems, throughout, motivated by the wish to clear her name of the slur of 'madness' – an odd and old-fashioned motivation, it now seems, at a time when we are encouraged (quite properly) to understand that mental health, like physical health, is a spectrum, or scale, up and down which we all move at different times. Janet's movements up and down were more extreme than is common. There was something unusual about her brain, which (I don't think it's too much to say) caused her at times to be partially disabled socially, but which was also no doubt connected to her brilliance and creativity.

After the Maudsley I think there were no further hospital episodes, though her contact with Dr Cawley, and her reliance on his support, whether near at hand or at a distance, continued. She dedicated a number of her novels to him, and also the third volume of her autobiography.

Her life was now focused on her writing, but involved a great deal of moving from place to place. She had been a failure as a sea-traveller, confined to bed, and even to the ship's hospital for most of that first journey to Europe; but once air travel became affordable she made frequent use of it, moving in and out of New Zealand, spending periods in America (where she found new admirers, and even rich patrons), and back in England. In New Zealand she changed addresses often, usually following her sister June and June's family, but also sometimes in search of silence. She had a Proustian horror of noise, and I remember a visit to one of her many homes, I think it was in Levin and probably in the early 1980s, when she had piled a great deal of furniture into the middle of the sitting room, leaving only a narrow path around it, and had had the front wall of the house covered with hideous tiles meant to shut out the sounds of what was, after all, a very quiet suburban street. Janet never gave the impression of having much sense of style when it came to appearances.

And all the time there was new work being written and published. *Owls do Cry* had established her as a brilliant new star of New Zealand writing. She had strong publishers' backing in England and America. There was academic interest in her work, and studies of it written. In New Zealand her books were set in English courses. She was a success. Prizes were won and honours awarded. She must, over the years, have received every conceivable honour New Zealand could confer, culminating in the ONZ. New Zealand PEN wrote at intervals to the Swedish Academy nominating her for the Nobel Prize for Literature, and in the late 1990s it was rumoured, I think on good authority, that she was among the very small group whose names were being seriously considered. Last October [i.e. 2003] it was reported that she was once again in the running, but I doubt that at that time the picture had significantly changed for her. There had been no new work since 1988, and her chances in Stockholm had receded.

In fact that flurry of renewed attention, though I'm sure it can't have been entirely unwelcome, came at a bad time. She was seriously ill; and she e-mailed me, after it had been announced that the South African, J. M. Coetzee, had won: 'Vampire-fashion I have to have blood transfusions until "the end", and the day I was receiving phone calls about the ignoble prize I was in a hospice learning of my

41

curtailed future.' 'Curtailed future' was characteristic of her, as her reply had been when asked by a journalist what she would do with the money if she won: 'I'd buy back the railways'. Later she e-mailed me a photograph of herself in hospital receiving a blood transfusion. She was reading a review I had written for the *Listener*, holding it so the heading could be seen.*

Public success didn't of course mean instant and reliable happiness; but I think it steadied her. Her sense of self no longer depended solely on what was happening in her head. It existed partly outside herself, even beyond her control. Perhaps that was the biggest award of all – a secure identity; and yet it was something which, being the person she was, she was partly embarrassed by and wanted at times to escape from. When she was beginning to be widely known she changed her name. The name on the published work would remain Janet Frame. That was the public person, the one upon whom the honours were conferred. But her name in law became Janet Clutha.

Her work is quirky, original, experimental, structurally discontinuous, very uneven, full of surprises and, at its best, dazzling. Its special genius is in the language – simple, direct, with glittering clarity (something she shares with Katherine Mansfield), and full of brilliant images. She was a poet of prose (she perhaps lacked the sense of form necessary to be a poet of poetry), and I think it was because her primary appeal lay in language rather than in her characters or subject matter that she was, as Joy Cowley said, 'a writers' writer' – or anyway a writer for sophisticated, literary readers.

Janet Frame's novels have never quite been best-sellers, either in New Zealand or abroad; but she has always earned huge respect. The broader public has been more interested in her life than in the subtleties of her writing. She came from poverty and deprivation, through family disasters and her own suicidal depressions and mental breakdown, to become New Zealand's best-known author. It was an extraordinary story, and when she wrote it as fact, rather than just quarrying it randomly for the material of fiction, she reached beyond her established readership. The three-volume autobiography, followed by the Jane Campion movie *An Angel at my Table*, gave her a much

---

* It was the review of O'Sullivan's biography of John Mulgan. See p. 239.

wider, less literary public. That public was interested in her as a phenomenon, a victim of the medical system, a mysteriously brilliant author whose novels serious readers revered, the woman who looked like a housewife of the 1950s and was said to be admired overseas and even a candidate for the Nobel Prize! So she was at one end of the scale a writer whose work presented a challenge to high-powered literary and academic minds, and at the other a suburban success story, a Dame Edna of Letters.

I find it hard to imagine how a Janet Frame would be seen or would behave if she were just arriving now into a literary scene so commercialised, democratised, homogenised, in which so many emerging writers are so keenly aware of what may and may not be said, and so willing, even eager, to be smoothed out and schooled for the marketplace. There was one British publisher in the early 1960s – Mark Goulden – who tried to teach Janet how to write 'books that would sell'. He failed of course, and she went her own way. We have to be grateful for that.

I think what is essential and durable in her work is a tragi-comic vision, bleak in its implications but full of life, courage and humour in its expression. New Zealand has lost an icon but we have not lost the books she wrote nor the letters and records of an exemplary life. The life and the work together are reminders of how unpredictable, uncontainable, unmanageable – how rare and mysterious – real talent can be.

Discovering Poetry[*]

During the Second World War my sister Norma, two and a half years my senior, acquired a 'pen-friend' in Rugby, England. I don't recall the friend's name, but we sent her family food parcels – it was something that was done to 'help the war effort'. After the war, when I was fourteen, she sent my sister a copy of *The Complete Poems of Rupert Brooke*, because Brooke came from her home town and attended its famous public school where our national game had its beginnings.

My sister had no special interest in poetry. My own was at an early stage – a distinct quickening, a prickling excitement in response to poems in *The Golden Treasury of Songs and Lyrics*, which was a school text, and to the language of scenes from Shakespeare that came up in third- and fourth-form English. I 'borrowed' the Brooke collection and it was never returned. I have it still, with my sister's name in it.

This was the first time I'd sat down with a book of poems by a single poet and read them right through, randomly, then in sequence. I returned to them often, getting a sense of Brooke's personality – an English poet who had even come to our part of the world, and who had died young and romantically, a soldier in the First World War. I looked at the frontispiece photograph of him with the poetic hair and the large loose poetic tie. More interesting to me was the holograph of

[*] Written for the Imprints series, *New Zealand Books*, December 2006.

his most famous poem, 'The Soldier', which I committed to memory. There was even what must have been a last-minute alteration in the manuscript. The opening phrase of the sestet – 'Think, too, . . .' had been scored out and replaced by 'And think . . .' This was an exciting reminder that poems were not delivered from the gods, set in stone, complete. They were made by human beings, worked on, changed, improved.

It had probably not yet occurred to me that one poet could experiment with many forms – and Brooke, without being dauntingly adroit, was a good craftsman. Reading him I began to learn about poetic forms, how they worked, what to look for, what to listen for. I can see from the poems I gave a special tick at the top of the page that it was not the ones for which he was best known that appealed most. 'The Old Vicarage, Grantchester' got no tick – and nor, I now know, would he have wanted it to. 'The Soldier' was moving and well made, but among the war poems 'Safety' was better. There was a certain rigour about it which, many years later, I would recognise as showing the influence of Donne, even to containing a phrase from 'The Anniversarie'.

But I think what interested me most was the sense of a young man engaged in a series of erotic adventures, with all their inevitable complexities, pains and contradictions. They were, many of them, 'I' and 'you' poems, which seemed to invite an adolescent to put himself in the picture and to fill in the spaces.

> Somewhile before the dawn I rose, and stept
>> Softly along the dim way to your room,
>> And found you sleeping in the quiet gloom . . .

He could rise to a high rhetoric –

> Shall I not crown them with immortal praise
> Whom I have loved, who have given me, dared with me
> High secrets . . .

– and then seem to mock himself for it. He could make light of religion, as in 'The Fish', without losing his balance or sense of humour. And were poems which had a strange nightmare quality – the 'Lust', for example, that began

> How should I know? The enormous wheels of will
> Drove me cold-eyed on tired and sleepless feet.
> Night was void arms and you a phantom still,
> And day your far light swaying down the street.

I'm sure this kind of thing must have lain behind some of my own earliest poems (all later burned) one of which began, I remember

> No light there was, no sound nor sense,
> No moving shadows broke the night.

In the school library I found a copy of the collected poems with a memoir by Edward Marsh. There I discovered more about Brooke's visit to the South Pacific, his falling for the romance (and one or two women) of the islands, and the fact that he had passed through New Zealand as an indirect route from Suva to Tahiti. This was of special interest to me because my mother had spent much of her childhood in the islands, and our house was full of photographs of sailing ships, coral reefs, palm trees and beautiful people with brown skins. One of my great-grandmothers was buried on Ocean Island, and my Swedish grandfather in Noumea.

I learned also that Brooke had died of blood poisoning (rather unromantically induced by a mosquito bite) as a young naval lieutenant on his way to Gallipoli; and that our own Bernard Freyberg, who would earn his VC there, and who was still very much in mind as CO of New Zealand forces in the more recent war, had been one of the party that carried Brooke's body to its burial place at the top of the Greek island of Skyros.

Most of one's adolescent reading belongs to its time, stays there, and is returned to, if at all, as to a foreign country. But the case of Brooke for me was different. He had got me started as a poet; and in time I would have to go back to him. He interested me greatly; but he didn't take possession of me in the way that Keats and Wordsworth did a year later; and then Donne a year or two after that. And over this

46

same period, during all of which I was writing poems of my own my discovery of Eliot and the Modernists, and of our New Z poets, especially Curnow, Fairburn and Baxter.

By the early 1950s, when I was a student, there was a very clear orthodoxy, throughout the international world of English studies, which bundled Brooke together with the Georgians into the bin labelled 'poetic nobodies'. Brooke was described by F. R. Leavis as having 'energised the Garden-Suburb ethos with [. . .] the vigour of a prolonged adolescence' and of manifesting 'something like Keats's vulgarity, but with a public school accent'. His soldier sonnets were unfavourably compared with the work of Wilfred Owen and Siegfried Sassoon, who had gone into battle, looked at war's realities squarely, and written poems that were at once true records and impassioned protests. No one wanted to be a Georgian any more; and when (I offer this example to show how the term was used and abused) Alistair Campbell wanted to argue that R. A. K. Mason had been overvalued by Curnow, he set out to demonstrate that he was 'really a Georgian'.

For a time this was an orthodoxy I accepted, or didn't think about; but when I came to write a book called *The New Poetic* (this was in the late 1950s), a large part of which was twentieth-century literary history, I had to look carefully at the Georgians, and what I discovered was that they had been innovators, 'modern' in their own time, Brooke no less than the others; and that if you wanted to recognise what they had achieved, it was fairer to compare them with what had gone before rather than with the Modernism that followed.

There is no case to be made that Brooke was a major poet, or that he was likely to have become one had he lived; but technically he was at least the equal of Owen and Sassoon; and there were rough drafts, written just before he died, suggesting a new cool realism that might have led on to something different, fresh and original.

> I strayed about the deck an hour tonight
> Under a cloudy moonless sky, and peeped
> In at the windows, watched my friends at table
> Or playing cards, or standing in the doorway
> Or coming out into the darkness. Still
> No one could see me.

I would have thought of them
– Heedless within a week of battle – in pity,
Pride in their strength and in the weight and firmness
And link'd beauty of bodies, and pity that
This gay machine of splendour'ld soon be broken,
Thought little of, pashed, scattered . . .

Only always
I could see them – against the lamplight – pass
Like coloured shadows, thinner than filmy glass,
Slight bubbles, fainter than the wave's faint light,
That broke to phosphorus out in the night,
Perishing things and strange ghosts – soon to die
To other ghosts – this one, or that, or I.

What in the end went against him, and prevented his talent from being critically and fairly recognised, was fame, the cult of Brooke, 'the handsomest young man in England', the soldier-poet whose 'corner of a foreign field' would be 'for ever England'. He had become the proud possession of those whose interests were not primarily literary at all.

The Sweetshop Window

One New Zealand Writer's Engagement with French Language, Literature and Society*

My title is derived from some lines in which Yeats represents Keats as a schoolboy, his 'face and nose pressed to a sweetshop window'.† I'm suggesting that for me France is the sweetshop, and the glass is the French language. The glass doesn't prevent me from seeing; but it's an obstacle to touching and tasting.

This is not because I'm ignorant of the language. *Au contraire* I know it rather well. I've spent many, many hours labouring over French *proses*, memorising irregular verbs (*faire, faisant, fait, je fais, je fis, je ferai; être, étant, été, je suis, je fus, je serai; avoir, ayant, eu, j'ai, j'eus, j'aurai; prendre, prenant, pris, je prends, je pris, je prendrai* – and so on); and preparing (often with pleasure) translations into English of 'set books' – Racine, Molière, Corneille; Daudet, Hugo, Merimée; Loti,

---

*   This was the opening keynote address at the New Zealand Studies Association's annual conference held at the University of Paris, Dauphine, in June 2006, and published in *Les Cahiers du CICLaS*, No. 8, November 2006.
†   His art is happy but who knows his mind?
        I see a schoolboy when I think of him,
        With face and nose pressed to a sweetshop window.
'Ego dominus tuus', *Collected Poems*, Macmillan, London, 1952, p. 180.

Flaubert, Camus; and poems by Lamartine, Verlaine, Rimbaud, Mallarmé and Apollinaire, two or three of them later revised and published. I can still quote French poems memorised long ago. I can still make my way through a Simenon with enjoyment and only occasional help from a dictionary. A newspaper can sometimes be difficult precisely because it goes nearer to spoken French. On the one hand you have the assistance of knowing already what subjects are in the air; on the other, spoken idioms can be deeply puzzling except when they derive from English – *le weekend, le foot, mon jour off.*

But that implacable plate glass of the French language remains; and a good deal of the little I have to say about it will be true for many English speakers. In the case of a New Zealander, however, the difficulties are made worse by distance – we can't step across the Channel for a refresher course.

The problem is one of learning the language off the page rather than by ear. Yes this is obvious. I think we all know it, and yet we don't recognise how extreme a case, how absurd even, it is. I know teaching languages has improved since I was young. But there's still this radical difference – that as an infant you learn by hearing; as an adolescent you're taught from a printed page. We know that whole societies, including the Maori, have existed without written language. We know that children blind from birth learn to speak perfectly, and that profoundly deaf children don't. We know that the commonest kind of dyslexia is phonological, where the person can't make a sound out of the symbol – can't 'hear' the words on the page. We know, in other words, that the ear is primary in language, the eye secondary, and even unnecessary. No one would think that holding large printed words up to the child in its cot or cradle would be a useful way of promoting linguistic development. But once the victim is past a certain age and can read, out come the books. We Anglophones are – or we were (and how much has it really changed?) – taught French as if it were Latin: as if it were a dead language.

'As if it *were* a dead language.' There's a subjunctive. It came to me quite naturally – I'm sure I was never taught when and how it's proper to use it in English. I think I only know it's a subjunctive because I learned French, and French grammar. But if I were (there

50

it is again) to use a subjunctive in French I would have to think, 'The rules require it here', and then try to remember how the subjunctive of that particular verb is formed, and which tense was appropriate – calculations of the kind one used to make in writing those weekly French *proses*. No aid at all to fluent speaking or quick comprehension – in fact an inhibitor.

It was only when I was making my first visit to France that I recognised one major indicator of the linguistic damage that had been done to me by my schooling. Assailed by a torrent of French, and uncertain of the meaning of one important word, I would have to visualise it, see the word as it looks on the page, before I could recall what it meant. By the time that was done, the torrent had rushed on and I was lost. This is the exact opposite of what I do in English, which is to take sense from sound; or in the case of written texts, to translate the word on the page instantly into sound and then apprehend meaning *as if* by ear. I read in English by ear; in French by the eye.

At school I was taught by men who I'm sure had never been to France and probably never encountered a native speaker. Their pronunciation was so far from what it ought to have been, they avoided, as far as possible, actually speaking the language. At university it was different, and better, but not much.

I should explain to those of you who are from England that in New Zealand we had at university what I think is, or was, the Scottish system. You took your first degree in more than one subject – roughly, four subjects in the first year, three in the second, two in the third. And something I noticed, comparing levels of success among my contemporaries, was that those who did exceptionally well at French or German didn't do particularly well in English – and vice versa. I remember being puzzled by this because it seemed logical to expect that if you were talented at your first language, you should be talented at your second. I also noticed that the teachers of French were good grammarians, but remarkably unsophisticated, even primitive, when it came to what we called 'lit crit'.

So this was university French. Not living French, but French the dead language, the grammarian's exercise yard, the academic 'subject'. It had for me what Yeats (who couldn't spell in English let

51

alone French, and whose French was said to be execrable) calls 'the fascination of what's difficult':*

> The fascination of what's difficult
> Has dried the sap out of my veins and rent
> Spontaneous joy and natural content
> Out of my heart.

Those lines could be a description of myself labouring over those weekly French *proses*.

On the other hand, doing translations into English I felt like Samson with his strength restored. I could take my time over meanings, and then what mattered, what made the translation better or worse, was my skill in my own language – finding the right, the most felicitous, English words.

Two illustrative anecdotes: The first is recent, finding myself with a Portuguese labourer in a village in the Languedoc. He was explaining things in French with a confidence and fluency quite beyond my powers. The pronunciation was entirely approximate, even comical. He avoided the distinction between *le* and *la* by using the Portuguese *lu* for every noun. And none of the verbs was conjugated – he simply used the infinitive. It was crude but effective – he could communicate as I could not.

The second is slightly more complicated. It's a memory of being, first, in a French café with an English painter, Ken Gill, and his German companion, Monika Kemper. This was in Cancale in Britanny, where the couple had lived for about a decade. They were at home in the town and in the language, speaking French which I could recognise was rough, corner-cutting stuff, but fluent and effective. I, on the other hand, contributed the odd phrase, and missed a lot of what passed back and forth at high speed. Ken had been doing a series of paintings of a black moon, which he'd thought was something new – his own invention. But recently he'd been given an occult document that seemed to show it was a symbol with a history, even a tradition. Back

---

* 'The fascination of what's difficult . . .', *Collected Poems*, p. 104.

at their studio they showed me this document, which neither could make very much sense of. To their surprise, the linguistic incompetent from the café understood it and translated it for them.

So much for my linguistic failures, and my excuses for them. This is perhaps the moment to make a couple of positioning statements for myself, speaking as a Pakeha New Zealander of mainly British descent.

The first is to emphasise that when I talk about my education I'm looking back across a period of more than half a century to a time when New Zealand was still, if not a 'colony', at least somewhat (or more than somewhat) 'colonial'. As a schoolboy I would have been offended by that description; I would probably have denied it; and later, as a young writer, I was one of a group who did everything we could to make it not so. But the strenuousness and the denials were necessary because it *was* so. For that reason New Zealand literary nationalism in the 1940s and 1950s was important. Some kind of a break with our British past had to be made; an independence had to be asserted. Now it's less important, or unimportant, because a degree of genuine independence has been achieved.

For most of my childhood, from the age of six to the age of twelve, the Second World War was being fought, in which France figured on the whole either sadly, or badly. There was the invasion, the astonishing and rapid capitulation, and the image of Hitler on the Champs Élysées. There was Dunkirk where, as a French friend once put it to me, Britain celebrated a retreat as a victory. There were stories, I suppose somewhat mythical, of the Resistance. And there was the Liberation. That was France as it figured in the news during my childhood. 'Our war', New Zealand's military contribution, was elsewhere – in the Middle East, Greece and Crete, then Italy; and belatedly in the Pacific.

France figured for me in primary school as part of the history of Britain. The year 1066 was ambiguous – a defeat; but then the Normans stayed and became English, so the long view neutralised the 'Conquest', and made England if not the English the winner. Trafalgar and Waterloo were victories; Wellington was a great British soldier, and Nelson a great British hero, and these two gave names to two of our

New Zealand cities. France, in other words, came to me through a British filter.

Where France and its history became real and touched us directly was in stories of the First World War. It was hardly more than a battle site, but New Zealand soldiers fought there after the disaster at Gallipoli. My great-uncle was killed in France, and is buried here. My grandmother, who lived with us when I was a child, still wept at the memory of her own folly in encouraging her only sibling when he decided he wanted to 'join up'. I have the beautiful bronze plaque she received that says 'he died for Freedom and Honour'.

But there was another France that had actually touched New Zealand's shores, and I don't remember that it figured much, if at all, in my consciousness as a child. It was only later I learned about Bishop Pompallier in his purple robes upstaging the Anglicans in their black at the Waitangi signing, and heard of the Akaroa settlement and the race to claim New Zealand before the French did; later again that I came upon the plaque marking the place where Surville stepped ashore on the Karikari Peninsula. That was an aspect of local history that was absent from my schooling.

So even before I encountered that pane of glass, the French language, there was what I've called the British filter. France for me was in the first instance a British colonial construct. Later it was something else – an intellectual and literary construct – something it still is, at least in some degree.

We all, I think, should have another linguistic world than that of our first language. Mine – because there was no other in my education – had to be French. I don't say that in a tone of lament. France always seemed a region of romance, just as, I suppose, from the other side of the pane of glass, the South Pacific has been for French writers and painters. It's true the French had capitulated, lamentably or wisely, at the start of the Second World War; but the myths of the Resistance followed and made it more or less 'all right'.

And then soon after the war came a series of French movies which helped to reinstate France in its own eyes, and in the world's, as the place it had been before – home of the café society, of left-wing intellectuals like Sartre and Beauvoir, of the courageous and tragic voice of Edith Piaf, and of 'La vie en rose'. A few years ago I recalled the most memorable of those movies, *Les Enfants du Paradis*, in a poem whose tone both appreciates and (I hope delicately) mocks it:

Les Enfants du Paradis

Garance! Garance!
Come back!
She rides on in her coach.

This is the final scene.
The mime-artist
jostled by the Mardi-gras crowd
is losing her for ever.

The villain
with his villainous moustache
the contemptuous Count
the brave thespian –
each has loved her
after his fashion.

It's the mime-artist she loves
and he loves her
but Fate has determined . . .
(and so on).

Garance
with your round eyes
and your beautiful smile . . .

Garance!

I'm not sure how these transferences occur, but somehow a literate young New Zealander of those mid-century years inherited, along with everything else that was British, the idea of France in general, and

Paris in particular, as romantic, elegantly immoral, a place where style mattered, where cooking was important and beautifully done, where the language gave to love and death barely distinguishable nouns, so that each contained an echo of the other. Who but the French would have thought of calling the orgasm *la petite mort*? It helped that my girlfriend, in my first year or two at university, had a French mother and that French was her first language; and that she told me she thought it would be wonderful to die at the moment of consummation. There was in fact to be no consummation, so not even a little death; but she added intensity to French studies, and to the sense of failure or insufficiency which is part of my subject today.

Quite early in my university education I became conscious of a significant difference between French and English prose. At school I'd loved the density and comedy of Dickens and Fielding, and the upholstered eloquence of Sir Walter Scott; and I recall bristling at a short story by Baudelaire in which Scott is referred to as 'A tiresome writer. A dusty unearther of chronicles.' But in French – first in Daudet and Mérimée, and later in Flaubert – I discovered simplicity, clarity and elegance, compactness, and often a shimmering quality that you find also in Chekhov, who possibly himself learned it from the French. These were qualities found in Katherine Mansfield too, on whom French literature had made a significant impression. And so my interest in France was reinforced by its connection with another early influence, our one writer at that time who had made a significant reputation beyond New Zealand – not only in England but in France where for some decades she had a considerable vogue.

I can recall, very early in my attempts to write fiction, a sort of argument going on in myself between two kinds of prose – one clear, simple and tending to subtleties and elegance; the other rich, dense and syntactically complex. It would be wrong to describe these as belonging, one to the French language, the other to English. Each was a kind of English. But clearly French helped more with the first than with the second.

And I think I can see the end products of those two directions much later, in the early 1980s, in my second and third novels. *All Visitors Ashore* has density, long running sentences, complex syntax, even Germanic compound nouns; *The Death of the Body* has structural

56

complexity but a much more lucid and transparent prose. Of the two of course it's the latter that was translated into French.*

In poetry French was of less direct use. When I did feel I was learning something – from the French Symbolists, for example – it was more theoretical than stylistic; or if it was stylistic, it came indirectly, through T. S. Eliot, whose early poems owed so much to Laforgue and Corbière. The important theoretical influence came in the form of the idea that poetry should have a certain mysteriousness; that it should never yield up its meaning entirely; that it should not be easy, or, as Paul Valéry says, easily 'used up'. This was very important for a person like myself, over-anxious about being understood. Temperamentally, I was a Parnassian; by intellectual preference, I was a Symbolist. The study of French literature helped me recognise these oppositions within myself; and the Symbolists gave a licence to be less than crystal clear in poetry – a rationale, indeed, for the mysterious, the opaque, the arcane.

In my last year doing French at the university Racine's *Andromaque* was a set book. I felt, not indifferent to the rhetoric, but resistant. The high-flown alexandrines with their caesura rigidly cutting the lines in half, their mute 'e's given full measure to keep the syllables marching in step, and their rhyming couplets, were so far from the linguistic variety and unpredictability of Shakespeare, it was hard to take them seriously.

> Hélas! Pour mon malheur, je l'ai trop écouté
> Je n'ai point du silence affecté le mystère:
> Je croyois sans peril pouvoir être sincère;
> Et sans armer mes yeux d'un moment de rigeur,
> Je n'ai pour lui parler consulté que mon coeur.
> Et qui ne se seroit comme moi déclarée
> Sur la foi d'une amour si saintement jurée?
> Me voyoit-il de l'oeil qu'il me voit aujourd'hui?
> Tu t'en souviens encor, tout conspiroit pour lui:
> Ma famille vengée, et les Grecs dans la joie,
> Nos vaisseaux tout chargés des dépouilles de Troie,

* *Je ne suis pas ce corps*, POL, Paris, 1993, translated by Anthony Axelrad.

Les exploits de son père effacés par les siens,
Ses feux que je croyois plus ardens que les miens . . .*

And so on . . . The psychology was no doubt acute; but the expression seemed so artificial it was as if there was not only the shop window between me and the goods; there was an iron grill over it as well.

I did, however, admire the structure and balance of the play, and its overall shape; and in my spare time while doing my MA in English, I wrote a verse drama, putting the characters and situation of *Andromaque* into a modern setting. I remember telling Allen Curnow, one of my teachers at the time, that the problem was motivation: how did you give modern characters the motivation to say and do what the characters said and did in Racine. That was an intelligent anxiety. Recently, however, I found the finished text; and I can report that neither that problem, nor the one of how to make spoken verse fit modern realistic settings, had been solved.

Racine is to French what Shakespeare is to English. Valéry says of him, 'Of all poets, it is Racine who bears the most direct relationship to music – Racine, whose periods suggest recitatives only a little less singing than those of musical composition.'

Since this is a music I can't honestly pretend to hear, I could choose to take comfort in knowing that Rimbaud said of Racine, 'Tout est prose rimée' – it's all rhymed prose – forgetting that Rimbaud had his

---

* The passage comes from Act II, scene I, and the speaker is Hermione. I suggest the following translation:

> My misfortune was that I paid him too much attention,
> Never kept silent in order to seem mysterious,
> Didn't see how vulnerable my sincerity made me
> Nor protect myself, even for a moment, with cool glances,
> But asked only my heart what I should tell him.
> And who would not have given herself up
> In trust to a love so solemnly sworn?
> Did he look upon me then as he does today?
> You'll remember how everything conspired to suit him –
> My family avenged, the Greeks rejoicing,
> Our ships laden with the spoils of Troy,
> His father's great deeds surpassed by his own,
> His love seeming more urgent even than mine . . .

own axe to grind. The reason I don't accept that easy comfort has to do with Shakespeare. I know the French can't 'hear' Shakespeare's music; so why should I think I can 'hear' Racine's?

There was one occasion when I saw why this transference of great poetry across languages doesn't occur – or how it fails to occur; and this was the one time when I think it could be said that unusual circumstances had put me through the glass and inside the sweetshop. It was some time in the early 1980s, I was in Paris, and I went to a performance of Shakespeare's *The Winter's Tale* in French. This was a play I'd lectured on for a number of years; I'd taken the part of Leontes in a reading of the play; I knew every word, every subtlety, every ambiguity and dark corner of the text, silent and spoken. I also knew the French language well enough to follow the translation effortlessly. This was an experience entirely different from, for example, seeing a French movie with sub-titles. I knew the meaning before I heard it, and so there was none of that visualising of words before understanding them. For once I was apprehending French by ear, instantly. What I heard was a Shakespeare that had lost its edge, its richness. I don't think it was a bad translation. The *meanings* were all there. But the vocabulary had shrunk, the sounds were smoothed out, the loss of texture was immense. It was no longer a language you could chew on. Without the English language Shakespeare was not Shakespeare, and never could be.

One other example of influence on my writing before I leave academic French behind: this was another set book from my student years, Victor Hugo's *Les Travailleurs de la Mer*. Years after I'd studied it, what I chiefly remembered, apart from the general sense of a tone of voice pitched constantly too high, was that it ended in a way which seemed to me absurd and, indeed, not possible. The principal character, Gilliat, a sort of super-fisherman, or fisher-Superman, who at one point wrestles with a giant octopus and prevails, loves a beautiful woman, Déruchette, who I suppose is above and beyond him. I'm remembering from long ago, but I don't think the love is even declared. At the end of the novel she leaves the island and sails away. Gilliat, who has selflessly assisted her to marry another man, stands on a rock in the sea and, with the incoming tide gradually rising over him, watches her ship fade into the distance. At the moment when it vanishes from sight, the waters close over his head. 'À l'instant où le navire s'effaça à l'horizon, la tête disparut sous l'eau. Il n'y eut plus rien que la mer.'

It's a very romantic suicide. But it's also impossible, and especially ridiculous in a novel which makes so much of the sea as a force – its shaping power, its unceasing movement. Human beings are not rocks, and you could not stand like one, quite still, while the tide crept up and over your face and head. Even on an unusually calm day you would float. As you became buoyant, you'd be pushed this way and that by the movement of waves and tide. Of course you could drown. But the way Gilliat dies simply couldn't happen. It suggests to me that although Hugo spent a number of years in political exile on Guernsey, he never ventured into the sea; never learned how seawater behaves and feels when you're in it.

That's all I remembered of *Les Travailleurs de la Mer*, and the idea that it might in any way have influenced my own writing would have seemed quite ridiculous – until, that is, not many years ago, I found a copy of the novel in a friend's house in France and went straight to the final chapter to re-read the ending. It was as I remembered it, and quite as absurd. But what precedes Gilliat's placing himself on the rock in the sea are the pages where he walks and runs along the shoreline, following the departing ship until he can go no further; and as I read that section I recognised that the end of my novel *All Visitors Ashore* – though it doesn't end in Curl Skidmore's death – does end with him running along the shore in just the same way, following the ship in which his girlfriend, who's leaving him, is sailing away from New Zealand. In other words more of Hugo than I knew had lodged in my imagination, waiting to be used.

My ending, you could say, is a sort of comic correction to the humourless romantic pitch of Hugo; but it's also an example of the ingratitude of authors. I remembered what I'd thought ridiculous about the novel, without consciously remembering what I would later steal from it.

I am in all this – and I do understand this perfectly well – a product of my time and place, and an oddity: a person rather well-schooled in the past literature of a language I can speak only well enough *pour faire les courses*; and scarcely schooled at all in what has been written in that language in my own lifetime. Apart from the odd *policier*, French literature in the French language pretty much ended for me with the end of 'set books' – the latest I read in French was probably Camus. When I got around to bits of Sartre, Beauvoir and Genet, and later Robbe-Grillet and Marguerite Duras, and later again the French literary theorists (about whom I'll have more to say in a moment), I took the easy path and read them in translation.

In 1972, like roughly 35 New Zealand writers since, I held the Katherine Mansfield Menton Fellowship, and since that time I've been in and out of France almost annually. Menton is not quite France – but then, what is? It's the down-market end of the Côte d'Azur, but with one foot in Italy to give it its special character. Paris is Paris. Britanny is rugged and Celtic, the Wales of France. Northern France, with its alternating black graveyards and white graveyards, is for me the region of battle zones and sad memorials and the burial place of my great-uncle. Périgord, for a twentieth-century poetic Modernist, represents the troubadours and Ezra Pound. The Dordogne is becoming an English county – a nation of retired shopkeepers, to misquote Napoléon only slightly.

But Uzès and the countryside and towns of the Languedoc, where I've spent one or two months every year of the past ten, has become what I can call 'my France'. This is Roman France (Nîmes, Arles, Orange and the Pont du Gard), Papal France (Avignon), Huguenot France (the Cévennes), and modern France (*partout*). It's France of the mistral, ferocious floods, and the garrigue that can seem so barren, a sort of dead zone, until you experience it in spring with wild flowers and the smell of thyme. It's productive France of cherries and apricots, wheat and wine, olives and sunflowers. To me it's one of the human world's most beautiful and inexhaustible regions, and I understand what Racine meant when he was sent there as a young man to spend time with his uncle, and wrote 'Ici nous avons des nuits plus belles que vos jours.' Those are the nights Van Gogh painted, when the stars shine out of a sky which retains an extraordinary dark blue long after the sun has gone.

A number of these different versions of France have figured in my fiction and poetry. Menton almost became my second novel until I gave up on the project and reduced it to a novella called 'The Town'.

Britanny and Brantôme figure in different parts of my one (very literary) attempt at a thriller, *Villa Vittoria*. In *Mansfield*, my novel covering three years of Katherine Mansfield's life, France comes and goes as she visits and revisits during the period of the First World War.

There are also two of my fictions that show the French sensibility exposed to, or exposed in, the world outside France. One is *The Death of the Body*, in which Natalie, the first wife of Harry Butler, comes with Harry to New Zealand encouraged by romantic notions of 'ze sous seas' – notions which the narrator suggests might have been corrected if only she'd looked more carefully at Gauguin's representations of the Polynesian Pacific.

Everything begins well. It's summer, she enjoys the beauty of New Zealand, the bush, mountains, sea. 'But', as the chapter goes on [p. 33] we're told, 'it wasn't going to work and it didn't.'

> To her it seemed the houses of Auckland were always open but the people were shut. The accent was unfamiliar and her problems with the language got worse. Summer passed and it seemed it was always raining. Harry worked long hours. He grew anxious and irritable. She missed her loving parents and the stone house and the twice-chiming clock. It was said of her, as it's said of most immigrants, that she was difficult, complained too much, wasn't grateful. (The descendants of settlers have buried the trauma of transplantation and don't want it dug up again in every generation.) And in addition Natalie was French. At first that was an advantage. It was chic. But as people got used to it they grew impatient of the Gallic inflexibility.

This is only a retrospect in the story. It has happened in the past, and the marriage is now over. But I recall that the French translator of the novel, who in fact had lived some years in New Zealand and was abandoned there by his French wife or partner, told me that passage seemed, when he first read it, like a direct transcription of his own experience.

The other, very different, example of the French temperament seen outside France occurs in a story called 'Sex in America' where a young New Zealander in San Francisco, in a moment of extravagance, shows interest in buying a Miró lithograph displayed in a dealer gallery. He soon finds himself in company with, and before long in bed with, the Frenchwoman art dealer. She talks about Paris and tells him stories about her days as a student there, including an occasion when she made hasty love with a baker as a way of earning a big cake for her boyfriend's birthday, 'and came home with puffs and handprints of flour on her quickly-lifted skirt'. She and the young New Zealander seem to be having a very nice affair until he tells her he can't really buy the Miró.

'That's final, Cathérine. It has to be.'

It was as if she had been shot out of the bed by the release of a spring. Naked, her face set hard in an expression he had not seen before, she fumbled to put on her bra. 'So it was all a lie.'

'What was a lie?'

'All this.' She waved a hand at the bed that was like a battlefield.

Silence, until he said in a voice that sounded strained and weak, 'You mean you fucked me so I would . . .'

She was not listening. She had found her underpants. Now she dragged her skirt over them. The face was still hard but there were tears. 'You are not a man of honour.'

'A man of . . . Jesus. Did you think I was the baker?'

Silence. She had dragged her shirt on and was tucking it in, roughly so there were creases and lumps. She went to the mirror to look at her tears and touch them with her finger.

He's so angry he calculates what she would have made on commission if he'd bought the painting and offers her a cheque, as if paying for the sex. It's meant to shame her. To his great surprise she takes it, reads the figure, tucks it into her handbag and goes.

This, you might say, is a very cynical view of the French temperament, whether at home or abroad. In defence I could cite Balzac, whose major characters seldom do anything without counting in money terms either the profit or the loss. But there's perhaps a better defence in the way the story concludes, and I quote the last paragraph, where the young Kiwi, flying out of San Francisco, is writing a postcard to his brother:

In small neat spider-letters he wrote on the card, 'Have just spent three nights with a beautiful French mercenary. Won't see her again. Thought I was after (your phrase) *sex in America*. Feel now as if I'm in love. Can you explain that, *mon vieux*?'

Ambiguity, you see, which I hope the story in its complexity justifies and makes intelligible. She has turned out to be a 'mercenary', a tough realist. He's shocked, and yet he knows exactly where he stands, and to his surprise he thinks perhaps he has fallen in love with her. One might even risk suggesting that this is not untypical of the way the temperaments that go with the English and French languages relate to one another.

Early on in this talk I mentioned that France was for me at first – and to some extent has remained – an intellectual and literary construct; and I think it was *that* France I was writing about in the 1980s, in the long poem called *Paris*, which was published as a little book, with illustrations by Gregory O'Brien; also in 'Paris, the End of a Story', and in the French sections of the long poem called 'Yes, T.S.' This is both an abstract France, recognisable to anyone of my Anglophone literary background; and at the same time it's the France that is unique to oneself, 'The Paris of Paris that's nobody's dream but your own.' To write about *that* France is really to say something about poetry itself, and the life of the mind.

But France as subject has also become for me simply – and you might think more mundanely – the setting for whatever a poem finds itself wanting to say; which I suppose is a way of saying that France has become, almost, 'real' to me. It has shed some of its glamour, and most of its sinister challenge, and permits me now and then just to be myself, and my poetry to be itself. Here's an example – a poem written only two or three weeks ago near Uzès. (If technical matters interest you, it's written in not quite strictly observed thirteen-syllable triplets.)

La Sainte Famille

The donkey stands
head bowed ashamed
of her enormous

ears, while the foal
who certainly loves
her tugs at her

udder. Their friend
the black ram with curled
horns who secretly

believes he's
Joseph to her Mary
shares with them

the shade of over-
hanging trees. Today
the mistral

gusting down the
corridor of the Rhône
is beating

the last of the
poppies to bits. No
green is greener

than these spring
vines, no grey greyer
than olives in

flower, nor blue
bluer than the
windswept skies of

Provence that will
make you at evening
the gift of stars.

My encounters with France, direct and indirect, on the page and in reality, have happened over many decades. One of the most interesting occurred a dozen years after the Menton experience – in fact on 10 July 1985. My wife and I were in Parnell, Auckland – as far from France as it's possible to be. Just before midnight we were drifting off to sleep when we were disturbed by the sound of a considerable explosion that seemed to come from down at the wharves. About ten minutes later there was a second, even louder. In the morning came the news that the *Rainbow Warrior*, the Greenpeace ship that had been just about to set off again to monitor French nuclear tests in the Pacific, had been sunk, and one of the crew was dead. I didn't have any doubt the French had done it. Of course this was denied; equally 'of course', it was soon proved to be the case.

What emerged in the days and weeks that followed was that the DGSE underwater team that did the job had got away by yacht, I think to Noumea, but two of the back-up team, Alain Mafart and Dominique Prieur, were caught. They were charged, convicted of manslaughter, and sentenced to ten years' jail. France then subjected New Zealand to remorseless economic bullying in order to rescue their agents. After a year or two Mafart and Prieur were sent by agreement to serve the remainder of their terms in French Pacific territories. Once out of New Zealand, the agreement was broken and they were quickly repatriated and honoured at home. And meanwhile the bomb tests continued, damaging atolls, polluting the ocean, and bringing ill health to Pacific Islanders.

Inevitably this was a subject that found its way into my writing; and the form it took was a poem in which I managed, quite unfairly you might think, to make a connection between the act of sabotage and the work of modern French critical theorists, Barthes, Derrida, Foucault, Saussure and the rest. Those theorists were very fashionable in English departments at the time, and I was entirely out of sympathy with the fashion. I thought of them rather in the way bio-security teaches us these days to think of alien weeds and insects and funguses – organisms that have a place in their originating environment, where the balance of Nature keeps them in check, but which, when exported are likely to run wild and do serious damage.

So the poem, which appeared first in the *London Review of Books*, was called 'Deconstructing the *Rainbow Warrior*', and it played on the disconnection the theorists seemed to insist on between literature and the 'real'. I'll read the poem, but I should warn you that the false name Mafart and Prieur were arrested under was Turenges – M. et Mme Turenges – and that gave me the opportunity for a pun which those among you who hate puns (there always are some) will find it hard to forgive.* Here's the poem:

Deconstructing the Rainbow Warrior

In my game (and yours, Reader) it was always the Frogmen
had the clever theories. We did the dirty work

using the English language like a roguish trowel.
Tonight, two rubberised heads have set their Zodiac on course

from Okahu Bay. Past the container port,
around Marsden Point, they're ferrying a transitive verb

called Bomb. In a hired campervan a man and a woman
smoke, check their watches, and bicker.

Turenges don't make it right, and anyway
the names are false, like their Swiss passports.

Half of Auckland, Dominique argues, has taken their number.
She's exaggerating of course. He refuses to panic.

A beautiful night. You can see the lighthouse light
on off Rangitoto, and an undercover moon

casual among clouds over North Head. Here come
the rubber boys, back in their puttering Zodiac.

---

* '[S]he loves language to the point of enjoying bad puns and doing a good deal of unrepentant punning herself, the pun being a model of the natural instability of language.' Frank Kermode, reviewing Christine Brooke-Rose in the *London Review of Books*, 6 April 2006.

Remember reader, poems don't deal in fact.
This is all a bad dream in the Élysée Palace.

Now scatter! It goes like the Paris Metro, according to plan.
Soon you will hear explosions. Someone will die.

More than a ship will founder – and the theory? Ah the theory!
Dig a hole for it with your English trowels.

The poem works on an opposition between French as the language of theory ('it was always the Frogmen / had the clever theories'), and English, which is represented as doing 'the dirty work' of realism. The frogmen's Bomb is only a 'transitive' verb; and in describing the event, the poem adopts the voice of one absolving himself of responsibility, reminding the reader that 'poems don't deal in fact'. If the poem is, as Barthes would say, only 'écriture', then the bombing it refers to has to be a purely theoretical event, an act of the imagination. But critical exercises in deconstruction (in which the theorist is always seen to be cleverer than the author) commonly demonstrate that the author has done the opposite of what he or she intended. So contrary to what the poem asserts, we finish with a ship *literally* 'deconstructed', a man literally dead, and two French agents learning Weet-Bix and Vegemite in an Auckland gaol.

The poem is, I suppose, a case of *faire d'une pierre, deux coups* – killing two birds with one stone, and both birds are French.

The *Rainbow Warrior* incident had to be mentioned in this address because it does represent something significant about France in our region. But I should add that when I think of France and New Zealand in political terms now I prefer to remember, and celebrate, that both our countries declined to join what George Bush was pleased to call 'the Coalition of the Willing' in Iraq. French fries for me are still *pommes de terre frites* – they are not Freedom Fries.

I've spoken at length about the considerable inconvenience of the French language to an ill-educated English-speaker such as myself; but there is of course a whole range of French culture we receive without benefit of the language. The classical repertoire would be poorer without French music; and what would the history of Western art be, particularly in the century from 1850 to 1950, without the French? Can't we acknowledge even, as good New Zealanders, that without the example set by the panache of *les Bleus*, rugby might still be the static and often rather boring game it was thirty years ago.

In fact, for all the difficulties posed by language, one's whole intellectual, artistic and imaginative life has been significantly, perhaps profoundly, affected by France – French literature, French thought, French music, art, politics, movies, cuisine; and by France itself, the place where French people go about being French, apparently without effort. French is my second language, and France is host to a second self – the clumsy one, the socially inept, the linguistically incompetent, the foolishly romantic. If I didn't have that French self I might not have understood quite so clearly how it is that even failures can enjoy themselves.

I'm happy to have this opportunity to pay tribute to France, not from a distance of 20,000 kilometres, but right here in Paris where so many of the debts have their source.

A Poet's View*

When Dennis McEldowney invited me to contribute to this series of lectures I hesitated, and I've gone on hesitating ever since. My brief is first to adopt, of all the roles I might and do adopt from time to time, the role of the poet; and second, to speak of Books and Writers in New Zealand as this poet sees those things. It's not an easy task because I'm not invited quite to take an objective view – the view of the historian or the scholar or even the critic – but the more personal view of the writer of poems. This is to be an overview which somehow keeps the viewer, a poet, in the picture. The two reefs between which I'm to steer, or the two stools between which I'm invited to fall, are those of literary autobiography and literary history. No doubt by confronting the problem I've made it larger than it need be; but I want it clear from the beginning that I will be trying – no doubt trying and failing – to steer a middle course. I will in fact be trying to make literary history of literary autobiography.

Let me first place myself historically, as others in this series have

* This is the text of one of the 1974 series of Winter Lectures at the University of Auckland delivered under the general title of 'Books and Writers in New Zealand'. Other lectures were delivered by Keith Sinclair ('A General View'), Maurice Shadbolt ('A Novelist's View'), Wystan Curnow ('A Critic's View'), Dennis McEldowney ('A Publisher's View'), Simon Cauchi ('A Librarian's View') and Michael Noonan ('A View from the Media'). My text has been revised.

done. I was born in 1932. That means I remember learning at school that the population of New Zealand was one and a half million and that we were part of the British Empire, an Empire on which the sun never set. Before I'd turned seven 'the War' began. Six years later when it stopped the headmaster of Balmoral Intermediate School told me to ring the school bell and keep it ringing – for as long as I liked it seemed. I didn't know, and I don't suppose he did either, that the bell was tolling for fifty million people who had died violently in those six years. I remember enjoying ringing the bell, but wondering, and even worrying, what 'Peace' might be like.

One other memory places me pretty exactly. It's the memory, a little before the bell-ringing episode, of my sister reading out of the *Auckland Star* that an 'atomic bomb' had been dropped on a Japanese city called Hiroshima, and of myself, about twelve years old and never having heard the word 'atomic' before, correcting her and saying it must have been an automatic bomb. There may be an apt irony in the fact that this incident stuck in my memory, not because I understood what had happened at Hiroshima (big bombs had been falling on cities for years), and how significant it was historically, but simply because I was embarrassed at being wrong about a word.

What was happening on the New Zealand scene during those years when the fifty million were dying violent deaths and I was passively enduring the interminable fathomless boredom of primary school? Could anyone have been finding words to fill the enormous gap between the unremarkable and the unspeakable? Poetry is limited to what the human imagination can assimilate. It can't deal with death in millions, but it can deal with one. Here's Allen Curnow:

> Weeping for bones in Africa, I turn
> Our youth over like a dead bird in my hand.
> This unexpected personal concern
> That what has character can simply end
>
> Is my unsoldierlike acknowledgement
> Cousin, to you, once gentle-tough, inert
> Now, after the death-flurry of that front
> Found finished too. And why need my report

Cry one more hero, winking through its tears?
I would say, you are cut off, and mourn for that;
Because history where it destroys, admires,
But O if your blood's tongued it must recite

South Island feats, those tall snow-country tales
Among incredulous Tunisian hills.
                    'In Memoriam, 2/Lt T. C. F. Reynolds'

In Christchurch during those war years Curnow was writing the poems for which he's possibly still best known. In Takapuna Frank Sargeson was writing stories which in their way represented a fictional parallel to Curnow's poems. Both were to go on to very different and less obviously public work. But at the time they must have seemed like literary cartographers, each charting new territory – Sargeson with his scoring of the cadences of the vernacular; Curnow with his witty and finely structured questioning of our history; both with a capacity to catch, as no writers before them had done, the distinct physical quality of what lay around them.

It hardly needs saying that as a child at primary school I didn't hear of either, but it was of great consequence that they should be there. What the subject 'Books and Writers in New Zealand' conjures up is something altogether more substantial than it would have been without them.

My initiation as a poet came a year or two after the end of the war. New Zealanders sent food parcels to Britain and my sister, Norma, corresponded with the daughter of a family in Rugby to whom ours had been sent. This 'pen friend' sent my sister a copy of *The Complete Poems of Rupert Brooke* – one of Rugby School's most celebrated Old Boys. Norma didn't read the poems, but I did, and I was soon writing Brookish imitations. The effect was immediate, compulsive and long-lasting. My long boredom was over and I could say, I suppose, that I've never looked back.

There was still as far as I was concerned no local literary scene. Secondary school pupils now seem at least to be made aware of the existence of New Zealand books and writers. In the late 1940s we read *Macbeth* and Keats's 'Ode to a Nightingale' and Wordsworth's 'Tintern Abbey' and Milton's 'Sonnet on his Blindness' – and much else from the Great Tradition – and I'm glad we did. But there was no mention of New Zealand poems or fiction. Literature and life were separated by 12,000 miles of water. There was what Maurice Duggan called 'a discrepancy between the real and written'; and Duggan catches it beautifully in his story 'Along Rideout Road that Summer', where the teenage rebel, Buster O'Leary, driving a tractor over farm paddocks shouting Coleridge's 'Kubla Khan' above the noise of the engine, is suddenly aware of a girl, Fanny Hohepa, with her ukulele. Does she compromise the poem's vision of the damsel with a dulcimer? Or is she a materialisation of it?

> Almost happy, shouting Kubla Khan, a bookish lad, from the seat of the clattering old Fergusson tractor, doing a steady five miles an hour in a cloud of seagulls, getting to the bit about the damsel with the dulcimer and looking up to see the reputedly wild Hohepa girl perched on the gate, feet hooked into the bars, ribbons fluttering from her ukulele. A perfect moment of recognition . . . in spite of the belch of carbon monoxide from the tin-can exhaust up front on the bonnet.

That 'discrepancy between the real and the written' continued for me – it didn't bother me, but it was a fact – until I was sixteen, when I read my first New Zealand book,* *Man Alone*. That was a powerful experience and set me writing one or two Mulganish short stories. I discovered a few Sargeson stories in the same year, and some Mansfield stories then or earlier. But I was also, by now, reading new stories and poems in the *New Zealand Listener* edited by M. H. Holcroft, and reading reviews there of new work. So by the time I came to this university as a student I had at least some idea of what was going on in the local literary world.

---

* Apart from (I think it was) A. H. and A. W. Reed's *Maoriland Fairytales*, which retold traditional Maori myths, legends and stories, owned by my sister and me, and read when we were at primary school.

Suddenly exhilaration
Went off like a gun, the whole
Horizon, the long chase done,
Hove to. There was the seascape
Crammed with coast, surprising
As new lands will, the sailor
Moving on the face of the waters . . .
                    'Landfall in Unknown Seas'

If you can see me for a moment as the literary sailor moving on the face of the waters I mean those lines of Curnow's to catch the excitement I felt arriving at Auckland University College (as it then was) in 1951. In the library of the old Arts Building there was a room – not a large room – which housed English literature. English literature seemed of manageable proportions. But more significant, there was a case for which the key could be obtained from the lending desk, which contained the work of New Zealand poets. (I don't suppose many people who are let into the air-conditioned closely guarded room which is called the Glass Case in the new library know that the name has been directly transferred from what was once literally a piece of furniture.)

And finally, as if the existence of the books wasn't enough, some of the poets could be seen walking about. Allen Curnow had just given up his job on the *Christchurch Press* and come to lecture in Auckland. An absurdly youthful looking and very emphatic Bob Chapman, who published poems in those days, was my Stage One tutor in history. Keith Sinclair, whose poem 'Strangers or Beasts' I used to quote to girls at parties with varying consequences, was a lecturer. M. K. Joseph in the English Department was just beginning to be known as a poet. Rex Fairburn had transferred from a tutorship in English to a lectureship in the history of fine art, and he, like Frank Sargeson, put in occasional appearances at Somervell's coffee bar. R. A. K. Mason was a more remote, but not unapproachable, figure. And later there were others – notably Kendrick Smithyman and Maurice Duggan.

This is not meant to be an exercise in nostalgia. My subject is Books and Writers in New Zealand, and I'm trying to suggest the particularity and vividness with which they materialised for me in 1951. I studied the books in the glass case more closely even than anything set down as texts in the courses I enrolled for. They were, mostly, finely printed, put out in small editions; and if they had one quality in common it was a kind of freshness in the writing. The voices were distinct, the subject matter stood out sharp and clear. Nobody was aiming for a commercial, or foreign, or academic, market – there were no such markets for New Zealand work. Maybe they were writing for one another, or for the future, or to please themselves. Whatever they thought they were doing, the predominant qualities seemed to be confidence, excitement, and sharpness of definition. What I was discovering, I suppose, was the wave of literary energy that had begun to move in New Zealand in the 1930s, had gathered momentum and achieved remarkable work in the 1940s, and was to fade – replaced by another – in the 1950s.

For myself at eighteen and nineteen, publishing my first poems and having them sometimes noticed by these people, it felt like a good beginning. I was accepted into a literary world as intimate, as personal, as compact and comprehensible as I imagine the London coffee-house scene might have been in the eighteenth century. And in addition there was a periodical, *Landfall*, edited by Charles Brasch in Dunedin, which provided a forum for new writing from all over New Zealand. Without *Landfall* as a centre of gravity, as a platform, and even as a target, the literary scene couldn't have produced and sustained the body of work it did during the years of Brasch's editorship. Writers need a periodical as much as actors need a stage.

For a moment now I'm going to put aside the role of the poet and speak as the literary historian.

The significant literature of Western Europe has seldom been unconnected with the great political and social movements of its time. In this century war, depression, revolution, and short of revolution the political surges to left and right – these have all influenced, or incited, or provided subject matter for, or found correspondences in, literary developments, particularly developments in poetry.

The First World War not only prodded a number of talented young men into poetry before killing them off; it seems also to have liberated the survivors (mainly American) into literary experiments which were radical and successful to a degree unmatched in the poetry of the English language since the Romantic revolution of a century before. The 1930s, the Depression, and the Spanish Civil War, set off secondary shock-waves of Modernism, closely associated with hopes for a socialist revolution. The 1940s brought the war, which had its own intensities and reverberations. The post-war decade brought intellectual and cultural exhaustion, the Cold War, the Korean War, McCarthyism, an inevitable shocked withdrawal, as the body count went on, from everything new and fresh and exciting that the twentieth century had seemed to offer.

Poetry needs a head of steam. It lives off euphoria. If I had been able to adopt the role of the literary historian in 1951 I might have shaken my head over the emerging young poet and told him not to expect much of himself, even if he was talented, because talent is never enough. Soon the English literary heroes of the decade would begin to appear – Kingsley Amis, John Wain, John Osborne, Philip Larkin. Who could sustain for long the excitement that each of them at first produced? Weren't they just what the literary historian might have predicted – an expression of the directionlessness of the time? And in New Zealand, where 1949 saw the defeat of Labour, and 1951 the Waterfront dispute and the defeat of the unions, for a new 'new broom' we had Louis Johnson.

As the decade went on there was some recovery of the political idealism of those pre-war years, but not enough to shake the predominant conservatism. Towards the end of the decade I was in London when Harold Macmillan won an election on what must have been the most blatantly unidealistic slogan of the century: YOU'VE NEVER HAD IT SO GOOD!

I remember someone saying, when she was asked why she wouldn't try marijuana, that she didn't need it; she was 'auto-euphoric'. To survive the 1950s I think a poet had to be auto-euphoric. Of the seven or eight very talented students who used to meet and read poems to one another when I was an undergraduate, I think I was the only one who went on writing.

I've sketched two opposite impressions of the poet stepping on to the scene in 1951 – as it seemed to the poet himself, and as it seems in retrospect to the literary historian. Everything is relative. To emerge in

1951 from the silent wastes of the volcanic suburbs on to an intellectual scene had to be exciting, even if the intellectuals themselves were in retreat and political and literary radicalism was exhausted. I didn't see then what I see now: that I had no great subject; that 'the age' was not 'demanding' poems of me as it had seemed, for example, to demand them of Ezra Pound; that consequently I had no obvious material to work on but myself, a self that was unformed, provincial, uncultured and erratically educated.

These were the things I *didn't* see, and of course not seeing was as necessary to keeping going, as keeping going was to finding where I would 'end up'.

Allen Curnow and his contemporaries had imbibed from the wider world of the 1930s the feeling that poetry should reach out towards public statement; and Curnow in particular found his themes during the 1940s in our history, the voyages of discovery, the sacrifice of blood on which the new nation was founded, and the gap between the colonial dream and the post-colonial fact. Stylistically he and fellow poets owed most to the Auden group in England. Like that group they set themselves against what were seen as the stylistic vices of their Georgian predecessors. They spoke with firmer voice, replaced whimsy with wit and romantic nostalgia with a disciplined candour. A cloud of sentiment was rolled away and New Zealand appeared almost for the first time *plausibly* in our poetry.*

Such an exercise wasn't to be repeated in the 1950s, and in the post-war years the only poet on the New Zealand scene who had any kind of new programme, the only one who ran up a banner under which younger poets might gather, was Louis Johnson. Johnson proposed to 'people the New Zealand scene'. His subject was the suburbs which, he argued, being like suburbs everywhere, were 'universal'. The new subject was to be, not what was (in Allen Curnow's phrase) 'peculiarly New Zealand's', but what was *typical* in New Zealand. It was to be the world, or the Western world, as it's found immediately to hand.

---

* It was however, a distinctly masculist movement, as the proportion of male to female contributors in Curnow's two anthologies will show when compared to the proportion in earlier anthologies like *Kowhai Gold*. Curnow, Fairburn and Glover were all reluctant to take women writers – particularly women poets – seriously.

Expressed in that way Johnson's programme doesn't seem absurd, and I suppose wasn't absurd. It made a kind of sense, and I can see now, although I couldn't see then, why a poet as talented as James K. Baxter seemed to rally to it. But I preferred the measured affirmation, the element of deliberated nationalist assertion, in the best of Curnow's poetry, to the international suburban drabness of Johnson's. There was a ring of authority, of authenticity, I suppose of sheer talent, one looked for and didn't find in Johnson. Certainly I favoured Curnow in that protracted argument. But I knew there was no point in trying to repeat what Curnow had done; and in any case my own temperament, and the particular bent of such talent as I possessed, was bound to take me off in another direction.

A damsel with a dulcimer
In a vision once I saw:
It was an Abyssinian maid
And on her dulcimer she played
Singing of Mount Abora.
Could I revive within me
Her symphony and song,
To such a deep delight 'twould win me
That with music loud and long,
I would build that dome in air,
That sunny dome, those caves of ice!
And all who heard should see them there,
And all should cry, 'Beware! Beware!
His flashing eyes, his floating hair!
Weave a circle round him thrice
And close your eyes with holy dread
For he on honey-dew hath fed
And drunk the milk of Paradise.'

Those are among the great lines of English lyric poetry. They're from the end of Coleridge's 'Kubla Khan' and they are the lines Duggan's Buster O'Leary is shouting above the noise of the tractor. And it has to be admitted that if Buster were driving his tractor somewhere in Somerset where Coleridge wrote the poem, rather than in New Zealand, his sense of there being a 'discrepancy between the real and the written' would be just as acute; because although the lines do create their own reality, it's a reality of a peculiarly inward and visionary kind.

'Kubla Khan' is usually discussed in terms of its symbolic structure, or in terms of the sources of its imagery in Coleridge's reading, and the peculiar circumstances of its composition, a drug-induced inspiration interrupted by a knock at the door and a visitor from Porlock. But if any critic really tried to come to grips with how the poem works, he or she would have to confront the element of poetry that's seldom discussed in any depth or detail because it's at once too elusive and complex: that is, the element of music.

If I say the music of poetry is the prime vehicle of feeling and the true fabric of imagination, I mean, by 'music', not merely the way the words are gathered into groups to create a texture of sound; not merely how that texture moment by moment is relating to an overall sound structure; but in addition, how those sound patterns affect, and shape, and space out, and regulate, our rational apprehension, and our visualisation of images placed before us word by word, phrase by phrase, line by line. The whole business is too dense and simultaneous to be entirely conscious in the doing (hence the need for 'an ear', and even the notion of 'inspiration'); and too complex ever to be fully 'scored'.

I've described myself as a young poet in the 1950s who lacked both culture and a great subject. What I did have was an erratic, but usually acute, sense of the music of poetry – a sense of the poem as *composition* and of myself as composer. So when, in London in 1958, I wrote a long poem called 'Pictures in a Gallery Undersea', it seemed to me I'd done something quite unlike any other New Zealand poem, and that the outcome was 'musical', 'scored', in the way I've described. Just how I had done it – or how it had happened to me (which is nearer to how it felt) – wasn't clear. I knew there was a debt to Pound, and a larger one to Eliot; but it felt, and still feels, my own – something instinctive, 'inspired', mysterious and unrepeatable. It had sprung out of the exhilaration of being in London, feeling I was at the 'centre' of a world which for the first 23 years of my life had existed vividly, but only in the printed word. In due course I would have moments of uncertainty about the poem, nervous that it owed too much, and revealed its debts too openly; but in the lines themselves, whenever I went back to them, I discovered no such unease. *I* might be uneasy but the poem was not. It was, if you like, the supremely *colonial* poem. But how often did you find the colonial voice sounding so clear, so confident and unashamed of itself; so perfectly in key and on the note?

And it brought me success. I had at first to twist Charles Brasch's arm a little to persuade him to take it for *Landfall*. But then it won an award voted on by subscribers to the magazine for the best poem published there in its first fifteen years. Meanwhile Allen Curnow had selected it for his new Penguin anthology of New Zealand verse; it was noticed favourably in reviews* and went into other anthologies.

If, then, it can be said that I added anything new to our poetry in those years, my contribution was technical, in the realm of poetry as an art rather than poetry as a bearer of tidings. So much of the argument about our poetry had been about 'subject matter'. Should we write about mountains or people, scenery or suburbs? Should we aim to be 'local' or 'universal'? Should we keep always in mind the (as Curnow described it) 'regional thing, the real thing'? 'What can I take that will make my song news?' Brasch asked himself, as if the poetic equivalent of a 'scoop' might be the making of him. In 'Pictures in a Gallery Undersea' I had demonstrated to myself what I knew anyway, that the distinctive poetic element was not in the 'subject'; that in fact, as Mallarmé had said, poetry is not made of ideas, or subjects, it's made of words.

> Each day He dies to do me good.
> I sign a protest, join a march,
> What Wolf began, Eagle accomplishes.
>
> Minerva had a mouse in mind.
> It was a weasel, tore her beak.
> What Owl began, Eagle accomplishes.

---

* For example, 'one of the best poems in the book [Curnow's anthology] and a remarkable poem by any standard.' Anthony Cronin in the *Daily Telegraph*, 30 December 1960.
  Recently (i.e. 2006) I found the following in Frank Sargeson's correspondence. Writing to Brasch on 19 July 1959, he said, 'I've had the advantage of an exegesis of [Stead's] Landfall poem. I find it his best thing so far, but *not* a poem to be written by anyone who has made the mistake of returning to this country.'

Eagle bears the Snake to die.
Up there it twists about her throat.
Out of the sun they fall like brass.

I signed a protest, joined a march.
Today he dies to do me good.
What Eagle began, Serpent accomplishes.

Poetry is made with words; but during the middle and late 1960s a very large *subject* forced its way into my poems. Ever since the Korean War, being angry at American foreign policy and at what I saw as our own slavish involvement in it had been a more or less constant state of mind. But in 1965 when Lyndon Johnson contrived an excuse* to begin bombing North Vietnam and simultaneously put half a million American troops into South Vietnam, the ineptitude and brutality of that policy was all at once exposed and magnified. The movement of protest one had looked for and failed to find, began – first in America, then in Europe – and developed rapidly. By 1968 it had broadened to become something of a minor revolution in Western society.

By now I had children. My family and the war seemed to grow together, and that made the war seem more real, nearer, more intensely felt. The deaths weren't abstract as they had been when I was a child. They were a dark stain over everything, and correspondingly the political commitment I felt was deeper and more implacable. I learned from that how people must have felt in the 1930s, and in fact at any time when a great wrong seems about to precipitate radical change. Because as well as horror there was a compensating excitement. So much was going on at an emotional level one was very largely relieved of the burden of reason; and, however dangerous such a state may be, it has, as well as force, its own kind of purity.

All this feeling got into the poems I wrote during those years, which are domestic poems, suburban New Zealand poems, but in a context of world events, with Roman overtones.

How important, then, is 'subject' in such poems? This is difficult to answer, because the 'subject' is an abstraction. Perhaps we can say

* The Gulf of Tonkin incident.

81

that what gets into poetry, when it works well, is not the piece of history that may seem to be the 'subject' but rather the poet's feelings about it; and it's those feelings which remain durable and vivid while the events themselves fade. Milton felt strongly about certain 'slaughtered saints' whose bones lay 'scattered on the Alpine mountains'. Only a history book, or notes to the poem, will tell us who they were, and how their bones came to be scattered, and why Milton was concerned. There are numerous instances of this, from Horace's ode on the defeat of Cleopatra, through Marvell's celebrations of Cromwell, to Auden's poem on the Spanish Civil War. Time takes the heat out of every cause, blurs the memory of the most memorable events, and dulls even the colour of blood. But the feelings remain intelligible, because they are constantly renewed in the present; and it's the feelings, not the events and causes, which survive in the verbal music – as in Curnow's sonnet:

> Weeping for bones in Africa, I turn
> Our youth over like a dead bird in my hand . . .

We talk of turning something over in our minds; of a bird in the hand being worth two in the bush; and those casual colloquial phrases are gathered into the elegiac cadence and played upon. The pathos, the loss, are there in the lines – more durable than the fragment of 'history' that brought the poem into being.

What does the poet so far presented to you see when he looks around at the literary scene as he finds it in 1974? It's always difficult to be clear about what's happening *now*, and I'm going to try to arrive at an impression of it by reminding you of some of the things Keith Sinclair and Maurice Shadbolt said in their lectures, and then attempting both to confirm and to qualify their views.

Keith Sinclair's lecture was for me one of those rare occasions when one is made to see and to recognise one's own society in a new and dramatic light. His image of the uncovered floors, the kerosene lanterns, the butter-box larders, all in living memory, was a reminder of how close the colonial bare boards are to us all, how they lurk in our consciousness, and how, correspondingly, our intellectual and cultural life is one which has only recently emerged from a state of colonialism. His lecture also revealed the degree to which a kind of cultural oppression, or cringe, has lingered in New Zealand and hampered our intellectual growth.

I think Sinclair is right, that the colonial lack of confidence has pretty well gone in literature as in everything else. But while losing it we have also been losing the distinctness that gave colonial life an inherent sharpness of definition. Life in New Zealand has become more like life everywhere in the West – the same mix, but milder, the same colours, but paler, the same sounds, but quieter. Our physical environment still offers great opportunities – but they are to be taken or left. They don't press upon us as necessities.

In 1961 Keith Sinclair and I were among the contributors to a winter lectures series on the effects of remoteness on New Zealand. Less could be said on that subject today. The ease of air travel and its cheapness relative to earnings means that a very high proportion of New Zealanders are able to travel abroad if they want to. There are also the effects of television and the growth of cities.* In 1961 Auckland was still just recognisably a South Seas port. Today it looks like a modest city in the Great Nowhere of Western affluence. Buildings, motorways, domestic interiors, immigration – the whole visible fabric of our lives is becoming increasingly anonymous.

And that brings me to what was chiefly celebrated in Maurice Shadbolt's lecture – the advent of literary professionalism. Shadbolt's narrative went something like this: Twenty years ago fiction writers in New Zealand were part-time amateurs who soon gave up in despair. Today our fiction writers can live by writing. That phrase 'live by writing' begs a lot of questions. They live by writing journalism, advertising copy, television plays, guide books, even university lectures. I can think of only two who have lived for any significant period of their lives by writing *fiction* and they are Barry Crump and Ngaio Marsh.

* Postcript, 2006: And since 1974, the cheapness and speed of telephone links and the growth of e-mail and other electronic links mean that most kinds of business, and equally research, can be conducted as easily from within New Zealand as anywhere.

But I accept that on the whole Shadbolt is right. Literary profession-alism is coming, along with motorways, television, tall buildings and national confidence. It's also true that the necessities of professionalism cut through a lot of preciousness and pretence. Nevertheless I see it as a mixed blessing. The professional is answerable in the first instance, not to the traditions of an art, but to public taste and the state of the market. Occasionally public taste accords with what is meritorious and durable. At others (and often), what is successful in the marketplace is of dubious quality, while something that goes unheralded and unread except by a few devotees proves to be of permanent value. I wonder for example whether some of the smallest and finest work in that original Glass Case would ever have got into print in a time of literary professionalism.

So I offer two cheers for professionalism, as E. M. Forster offered two for democracy. But I believe it needs to be accompanied by a criticism which is not destructive but which reserves its most careful attention and fullest celebration for those various excellences which the study of literature teaches us are always rare and never impossible.

The national confidence Sinclair celebrated I celebrate too. Without it we would labour under the old crippling illusion that the excellence which is rare here is abundant somewhere else. It's rare everywhere, but never and nowhere altogether absent.

Ebullience, energy, eloquence, wit – and perhaps something beyond all that which the French call *réalisation* – realising in the sense of making real, bringing to life, so that the literary moment is lived through by the reader, and retained like a piece of real life: these are the qualities to be striven for and celebrated.

Of course there's no need to see the professional and the artist as belonging to different camps. They may occupy the same skull. But it is in the consciousness as artist, not as professional, that the writer achieves these qualities; and that is a consciousness reaching back, not 12,000 miles to a European marketplace, but centuries back into the European past.

Colin McCahon*

My introduction to 'Modern' (i.e. abstract) painting was in the early
1950s, my first years at university, when I went about with Diane,
daughter of French-born Louise Henderson (1902–94). I saw Louise's
paintings in her studio and at her house, where I met at various times
John Weeks (a revered figure with whom Louise was studying), Rex
Fairburn, Eric McCormick, Dennis Knight Turner, Theo Schoon; also
Eric Westbrook, just then converting the Auckland Art Gallery from
the Victorian mausoleum it had been in my childhood into a modern
gallery. I attended openings of shows – particularly of the Thornhill
group, where Louise's work was displayed along with that of Weeks,
Charles Tole and Alison Pickmere. It was during this period that I first
heard about Colin McCahon.

In 1952 Louise went back to Paris, I think for most of a year, where
she worked in the studio of Jean Metzinger, a minor but significant
figure among the early Cubists. After her return McCahon, who came
to live in Auckland in 1953, wrote an article in *Home and Building*
praising her work. Now employed in the Auckland Gallery, he included
her in the first show he curated there, along with work by himself, Milan
Mrkusich, and one or two others. In writing about Louise, McCahon

* Commissioned for *Look This Way: New Zealand Writers on New Zealand Artists*, edited by
Sally Blundell, Auckland University Press, Auckland, 2007.

was writing partly about himself, enunciating basic lessons he had extracted from Cubism. The receding lines of traditional perspective were artificial; the frame should not act as an encloser, dividing viewer from painting; in Nature there were 'no empty spaces'. . . . And so on.

I don't recall which of McCahon's paintings were shown then; only that my view of his work was influenced by Louise who, though she respected him as a force, and was grateful for his support, felt, I think, that his work was inclined to be heavy-handed, lacking finesse. My view had also been influenced by finding some reproductions of his work in early issues of *Landfall*. These included *The Angel of the Annunciation* and *The King of the Jews* (both 1947), works done in a style somewhere between Rouault and a classic comic. Since all the distinction these paintings possess, at least for this viewer, is in the richness of their colour (involving at once boldness, vivid contrasts and often also gradations within a single colour), it can hardly have been a favour to McCahon, nor enhanced his reputation, to reproduce them, as *Landfall* did, in a muddy black and white.

I was married in 1955 and spent most of four years, from early 1956, outside New Zealand, returning at the end of 1959. By this time Eric Westbrook had moved to take over the National Gallery of Victoria, and Peter Tomory was in charge of the Auckland Gallery, where McCahon had established a place for himself. What I remember most vividly from this period is the shock of seeing some or all of his Elias paintings; and then the Gate series, including his homage to Mondrian. These were shown in Auckland at a private gallery in Symonds Street. At once my feeling about him changed, and I could measure this by the fact that I now wanted very much to own one of his pictures. I remember also, however, a certain nervousness, not only because we had come back from overseas with next-to-nothing, so the idea of buying a painting seemed an extravagance; but also because this was repressive mid-century New Zealand when it was still possible to have a member of the City Council (it was Tom Pearce, father of Sandra Coney) complaining that a Barbara Hepworth bought by the Auckland Art Gallery looked like 'a cow's buttock', and when anything at all by McCahon was fair game for public ridicule.

It was at this period, the early 1960s, that Colin, together with Hamish Keith and Peter Tomory, promoted the idea that an 'Art of the Pacific Basin' might be identified – a style common to Auckland, Sydney, San Francisco, Vancouver, and possibly even Asian cities bordering on the Pacific. It was, I think, an attempt to make a break with colonial New Zealand and with Euro-centrism, without retreating into insular nationalism or faux-Polynesia – a not unworthy aspiration, but abandoned when the exhibition meant to illustrate it showed, rather (as I think one might have expected), little regional commonality except that which sprang from cultural roots, European or otherwise.

Over the next two decades Colin McCahon became, for me, simply a part of the intellectual and artistic life of Auckland, someone I knew reasonably well, saw at not infrequent intervals, whose shows I attended and whose work I admired – a colleague, a friend of friends. He worked at the Art Gallery. He taught for a time at Elam. He worked with Chris Cathcart and Frank Sargeson on set designs and handbills for Frank's plays. He painted a mural in Maurice Shadbolt's studio at Titirangi. I thought of him as sombre, inward, warily determined, but there was also something charming and innocent about him.

It was through the lawyer Peter Williams and the Howard League for Penal Reform that I became briefly involved in visits to long-term prisoners in Mt Eden jail. Twice I accompanied Colin visiting the 'lifer' Ronald Jorgensen (of the Bassett Road machine-gun murders) who was attempting to develop his talent as a painter. I saw my role only as encourager and conversationalist. I remember telling Jorgensen, through the screen that separated us, that a painting he held up of a coat hanging on a peg on the back of a door was 'very good'; and then how fatuous that seemed as I listened to Colin analysing the picture, giving 'Ron' exact advice about what he was doing well and (mainly) what he was doing badly.

Colin at this time was expanding his range beyond landscapes, and the Elias paintings were among the first of what was to become a central aspect of his work, the use of texts, mainly biblical, as material, or 'subjects'. I became a complete convert to these paintings while remaining relatively indifferent to the messages they carried – which means I was probably not the kind of admirer Colin was happiest with. For him, the words were of critical importance. Yet the fact that I could have so positive a response, while hardly noticing, or while remaining indifferent to, the 'message' (who was Elias? – I had no idea), is an indicator of what I think must be unarguable – that the power came, not from 'story', or text, but from the use of paint, the application of colour, the filling and balancing of spaces. Archibald MacLeish's 'A poem should not mean / But be' was for me a mantra at that time, and I felt the same should be true of a painting. The intensity of Colin's feeling for those texts no doubt affected, even determined, how the paint was applied. But for the viewer, or for this viewer, an entirely different text, a quite other faith (or doubt), might have had the same effect. I was responding, not to a statement, but to a painting; not to a 'meaning' but to a 'work of art'.

Colin had a studio now at Muriwai on Auckland's west coast, and was learning the landscapes of the north, which I thought of as 'my New Zealand'. The first McCahon I bought was one of his Helensville series (PVA on board) done in 1968, a pale sky, a severe dark green landscape with a wide area of black shadow between foreground and horizon. The sky glares; the land frowns but doesn't blink – just absorbs the glare, darkly. Colin described this region as 'shockingly beautiful', but added that it was the area the Maori spirits passed over on their way from life to death, and that he 'didn't recommend it as a tourist resort'.* When I collected the painting from the Barry Lett Gallery I found that the reverse side was also interesting. Colin had painted the back in black (the brush marks are very clear) and then, over that, in large yellow letters, 'Colin McCahon / 8B / Helensville / July '68 / P.V.A. / No. 8 of a series / of 8. A & B'. This fills the space (600 x 450 millimetres), and seems, if less than a 'painting', rather more than just a statement of fact.

My next purchase, once again from the Barry Lett Gallery, followed soon after. In October 1969 Colin displayed a series of works done on rolls of wallpaper, each with a text. He called the series 'Written Paintings and Drawings', but they have become known as his 'Scrolls'. The one I chose I bought within minutes of seeing it – a text in its New English Bible version: 'All mortals are like grass, all their splendour like the flower of the field. The grass withers, the flower falls away. But the word of the Lord endures for evermore'. The words – mainly in black

* Gordon H. Brown, *Colin McCahon, Artist*, Reed, Wellington, new edition 1993, p. 109.

with red shadows or echoes, and one crucial word, 'Lord', in red – seem to hang in the air above an orange-reddish desert landscape. Here I can't pretend to be indifferent to the text, nor to the fact that I see the landscape as biblical. But still the magic of the painting, its inexplicable character, has everything to do with colour and space, and in particular with the way the landscape seems to recede without reaching sky or horizon, so that we must be looking down on it from a great altitude – a God's-eye view; and the words are magically imprinted, in Colin's unmistakable hand, as if on an intervening glass.

In 1976 I won the New Zealand Book Award for poetry. The prize was $1000, and I went to Colin's next show, 'Rocks in the Sky' (acrylics on paper), intending to buy one. They were $450 each, and I bought two. They were compositions of the numbers 1 to 14 (sometimes Arabic, sometimes Roman) against an abstract Muriwai landscape and seascape. There was a lot of black and white, dark and light, glare and shadow, laid out predominantly in horizontal lines, which is what you see looking westward on that coast. I confess to my ignorance at the time of the fact that the numbers represented the Stations of the Cross; but I recall thinking that the number 1, sometimes entombed below ground, at others rising into the heavens, represented Christ, or Colin, or more likely both – C suffering, C triumphant. My first and determining response, however, was intuitive, not analytical. That I could see landscape/seascape in it was part of the experience, but it was not, for me, its end, or object. And as for the numbers – they were arcana. They were mystery. They were the presence of the artist – Colin being Colin – permitting me to be myself in what I made of them.

There was one work in this series, the one I liked best and bought immediately, that was not black and white. Working down from the top of the picture: the sky is dark overhead but the number 1 is up there in an orange box, distinct; declaring itself; absolute. Across the middle of the picture there is a broad orange strip, suggesting the setting sun glaring out, as it can do on that coast, under black brows of cloud. The near-to-middle distance is (as I see it) dark sea, echoing the dark cloud. And in the immediate foreground there is another horizontal section, this in paler orange and containing the numbers 8 to 14. I have heard or read that this foreground is an abstraction from one of Muriwai's lagoons, and perhaps it is. But because it is cut off so emphatically and squarely, close to the right-hand edge, I see it as part of a human structure – a veranda rail for example, over which, the artist is looking out at sea and sky.

There is also (possibly only to my eye) an echo in this painting of Sydney Nolan's Ned Kelly series, the square box at the top of the picture remembering the mounted bush-ranger's head looking down in its protective helmet. This is a painting I saw once, at about this time, exhibited at the Auckland Art Gallery, which means that Colin too had seen it there.

Why (possibly uniquely in this series) are Stations 2 to 7 missing? My guess is that they were meant to go across the orange band I've interpreted as a sunset, and that that band, as it was done, looked too vivid, too strong just as it was, to be spoiled by numbers. If that should be right, it's a case of instinct winning out over intention. Also 1 followed by 2 would have been unambiguously the numeral. Isolated as it is in the picture, and painted as a single stroke, the number 1 can as easily be read as the capital letter, I – first-person singular; precursor to the big I AM. One could also choose to see that foreground strip as one arm of the Cross, in which case the other arm would be off to the left, out of the picture, and that's where the missing numbers would have to be.

In 1973 I had a note from Colin telling me an essay I had written about James K. Baxter was 'so real – I jumped for joy'. Along the bottom of the note he wrote in his big lettering, GOD, IT WAS GOOD. Then he added a postscript about my suggestion that Baxter's Christian theology was turning, at the last, into Zen Buddhism: 'The Lord, or God', Colin wrote, 'is found in the end only – and reality. Tough tough hard and beautiful – all the time. As the body dies God is discovered. I find I can take it all really. Finally.'

Colin was not humourless, but it's proper to acknowledge that the deft touches, the wit, the (to borrow Julian Barnes's adjectives) 'playful, companionable' aspects of twentieth-century Modernism, were outside his range, or his interests. That postscript is moving in its way – intense, serious, high-minded, typical of Colin in life and in all his work. It is also slightly incoherent; and by the time it was written everyone who knew him knew that alcohol, which had always been something of a 'necessary protection', was beginning to do serious damage.

The last time I saw him must have been a year or two before his death in 1985. I had heard that he was no longer able to paint. He was in the street in Parnell, wearing trousers that were too short for him, and pink socks. He knew that he knew me, and that there was a reason for goodwill, but I suspect could no longer remember why or in what connection. His smile was innocent and seraphic. I don't suppose it was typical of his last years (or perhaps it was), but all the wariness and pain seemed to be gone.

Ken Gill in Cancale*

The first time I drove into Cancale, on the western side of the Baie du Mont Saint Michel in Britanny, I had an impression of some kind of natural disaster – one of those earthquakes perhaps which realign the seabed and radically alter the tidemark. It appeared to be a seaport without a sea. All across the broad bay dinghies, yachts, launches lay dead on the mud; even quite large fishing boats sat on it – though the fact that these, at least, had not fallen on their sides gave the clue that they were built to cope with the absence. The height of the promenade and sea wall above the harbour floor suggested depths of at least two fathoms close in shore. Yet the sea was nowhere in sight. If it was out there, it was lost in the June haze beyond the many hundreds of acres of black frames for oyster farming.

Cancale, however, gave every sign of life and none of disaster. In fact the tourist car parks on land reclaimed along the foreshore, and the many bars, cafés and restaurants, are lamented by some who remember the town, as recently as ten years ago, as a simple fishing port. That was when Kenneth Gill, sometime plumber and pub-keeper, more recently dealer in antiques and expert in Oriental art, gave up England at the age of 47 and moved to Cancale with his German companion, Monika Kemper, to make a full-time profession of painting.

* *London Magazine*, October–November 1995.

The first of his paintings I saw were in a restaurant, La Vague, on the sea-front. When I admired them (there were two) I was shown more from the same series in a room upstairs, and I was told there was another in a café along the street. These were from a wonderfully colourful series, nostalgic and exuberant, using images from those old drinks advertisements that were once to be seen on the gables of French houses along highways that passed through small towns and villages – BYRRH, DUBONNET, ST RAPAHEL, SUZE – in the jazzy commercial lettering typical of France in the 1930s and 1940s. Some of these fading advertisements can still be seen, or could until quite recently.

In Gill's paintings the lettering and commercial images are quite recognisable; but they are also appropriated, broken up and re-disposed into interlocking and overlapping patterns which are the painter's own. It is difficult, I think, for an artist to create images which both record something quintessentially French, and at the same time register and celebrate the fact that it is seen with a foreigner's eye. That is what these paintings do.

By the time I had eaten a lunch of the local seafood, admired the paintings, exchanged a word with *le patron*, Thierry Raoult (an admirer of Gill's work), and looked again out at the bay, the natural disaster had turned itself around. The sea was advancing so fast you could watch it pick up one craft after another, dust it off and, so to speak, set it on its feet again. This was the same extraordinary tidal flow which, 10 miles along the coast between St Malo and Dinard, is harnessed four times daily to generate electricity – twice as it races into the estuary of the Rance, twice as it races out again. The volume and force of water through the *barrage* there, which the coast road crosses, is a terrifying sight.

At Cancale's Bar du Port I was told that Ken Gill lived just around the corner, that if I looked down the little rue George VI I would see a house with a Madonna inset in stone and the name Gill painted in large letters on the green front door. That name seemed to invite one to knock; and the white wine that had gone down with my solo lunch, together with the very real interest that those 'lettering' works had aroused, set aside my customary reticence. The door was at street level, I knocked, and a bearded face wearing red-framed spectacles looked out from the first floor window and invited me to come around to the door at the back.

For almost ten years that room at street level has been Gill's studio. Above it, the first floor is living space and kitchen; the top floor, bedrooms and bathroom. Recently, however, he has acquired a barn 10 kilometres out of town. There he has been able to work on large metal sculptures, the most recent series of which, eight pieces, commemorate the storm of 1987 in which many trees across Britanny were broken or blown down. If current negotiations with the *mairie* are successful these will be set up by the town for a trial period of one or two years as a sculptural promenade.

Gill's earliest work after moving to Cancale were attempts to catch its essence as a fishing port. There were portraits of fishermen, exhibited together in the town's fish hall. One of these now hangs in Gill's sitting room. Another series, of which I have seen only photographs, were of fishermen in the local bars – brightly coloured, stylised representations, suggesting action, energy, aggression, inebriation. In a note on Gill's work the poet Adrian Henri suggested these were 'in an idiom perhaps owing something to Gauguin's Breton period at Pont-Aven'.

In 1993 Gill returned to the fishing port theme in an entirely new way. Eight canvases, 195 x 165 centimetres, were stapled out flat on the decking of the jetty where the boats unload their catch. From the boxes where ink fish are first emptied, a few preliminary splashes of the ink the fish eject were scattered over the canvases. Then, in the hour or so it takes to unload two boats, and watched by a crowd of onlookers and photographers, Gill moved from canvas to canvas, like a player of simultaneous chess, working up patterns in black and white while the fishermen were encouraged to go on with their work as they would normally. On some of the canvases the lines of the planks they were stapled to show through, together with tyre- and boot-marks. One painting was done using an ink fish for a brush.

These abstracts, subsequently displayed in the Cancale fish hall, and in London, have the energy of action painting, but their randomness is focused on, and confined by, the functions of the jetty. Gill had found a way to celebrate what is Cancale's oldest, and enduring, *raison d'être* while escaping the traps of the merely picturesque.

His current works, a series called Moon Paintings (Bartley Drey

94

Gallery, 62 Old Church Street, Chelsea) are in two groups, oil on canvas, and smaller works of oil on Japanese paper. Each of the canvases has a central image of one, sometimes two, moon shapes, some white, most black, against a background of roughly geometrical shapes. Although there are elements of colour – very pale greys, browns, yellows – the effect is black and white; or, more precisely, darkness and light. These are images of the night, which is essentially colourless.

But in the oils on paper Gill's love of colour again asserts itself. A calm grey-blue moon, ringed with yellow, hangs over a symbolic sea of stormy blue waves. A thin sickle yellow moon almost encloses the black circle of an eclipse against planes of blue, green and grey. Moons in various stages of waxing and waning sit on pinnacles of red, blue and green.

Gill has been fascinated to discover, since embarking on the series, that the black moon, which he thought his own invention, has a strong astrological and occult history, representing the subversive, instinctual, socially denying self out of which come crime and/or creativity. A French text setting out some of this tradition and citing Groddeck for partial authority has been given to him and will be translated to accompany the show in London.

For myself however, the very real excitement the work generates is something less grandiose, at once precise, particular and elusive. It comes especially from its subtleties, the way one element or shape or colour seems to come through another without either one being eliminated or even diminished. The canvases are unframed and have something of the feeling of the Japanese visual tradition, not so much Japanese painting, but the fine materials and the effects at once subtle and austere of Japanese interiors.

There is also a strong intellectual continuity from his past work. In Cancale, it might be said, moon almost as much as the sun is the source of energy and life. It brings those huge tides, releasing the fishing boats on which the town's economy still depends; and in the twentieth century the same tides produce the region's electric power.

Gill's work is shown in alternating years in London and Munich.

On Reading and Writing[*]

What one has to say about reading is necessarily determined by age and individual temperament. I am 73, which means I grew up when reading as an activity had only movies ('going to the pictures'), and the outdoors for competitors. My temperament is essentially literary and intellectual. That will give me a lot in common with others of like temperament, whatever their age. My age, on the other hand, will put something of a space between me and people of my children's generation; an even bigger space between me and those the age of my grandchildren. I have to accept these gaps and not grumble about them or say they shouldn't exist. It may be largely an illusion to think that the world improves; but that it changes over time is beyond dispute.

I don't want to resist those changes; but I do see it as my proper role to speak up for the literary culture I grew up with and which still seems to me of great and permanent importance. Language – spoken and written – is power. Our social structures depend on it as surely as our physical structures depend on mathematics. If as a society we want to be effective in the world we need large numbers of people who are both articulate and literate; and the best promoter of those talents is literature itself.

[*] *Christchurch Press*, 15 July 2006.

Literature is also a source of comfort and of learning. In reading we learn from virtual rather than actual experience – living through, in imagination, experiences we haven't had to live through in fact. We learn from others' mistakes – from Othello's jealousy, from Macbeth's ambition, from the pride of Coriolanus. Sometimes our literary experiences can be more real to us than our own. We forget most of the detail of our own lives but remember a story. Narratives give shape to a shapeless world.

I did not grow up in a particularly literary household. My mother was a music teacher, and I think what talent I have for the literary arts was inherited from her. My father, a post-office accountant, was a self-educated man, a senior official in the Labour Party, a trade union secretary, and my image of him in the evenings is either of a man with a Gladstone bag going out to a meeting, or a man in an armchair smoking and reading. He seldom read novels, and I'm sure he was astonished – perhaps disconcerted – when his son turned out to write and publish poetry. He didn't own a large numbers of books, but I remember that his shelves included things like Rousseau's *Confessions*, Pepys's *Diaries*, a popular version of Cook's *Journals*, Marx's *Das Capital*, Spengler's *The Decline of the West*, books on the History of the British Navy, and a large collection of Left Book Club volumes in red covers published by Victor Gollancz and bought by subscription, dealing with problems of contemporary history and society. My parents were members of the Fabian Society and went regularly to hear speakers of the intellectual left and to take part in the discussions that followed.

When I was five my father read me R. L. Stevenson's *Treasure Island*. That was memorable, and important, but unusual. Our household was notable mostly for music and politics. Literature I discovered for myself at Mount Albert Grammar, partly in the school library, partly in the English classroom. It was a gradual and entirely normal (for the time) advance through public school stories (British) and books like *The Last of the Mohicans* (American), to R. D. Blackmore, Fielding, Sir Walter Scott, Dickens and Brontë in prose; and in poetry from Rupert Brooke, to Wordsworth, Keats, Shakespeare and Donne. The poets taught me what language could do above and beyond simple narrative.

Though I would not at the time have been able to formulate it as an idea, I perceived in reading certain passages of poetry (the fifth and sixth stanzas of Keats's 'Ode to a Nightingale', for example) that poetry was important beyond mere prettiness. It was not just another kind of decoration. Language was what really distinguished us from the other occupants of the planet; and poetry was like the distilled essence of that difference. It demanded more and gave more than any other form of language. It was not everyone's cup of tea, but it would be mine, and for life.

I received, as everyone did at that time, a British education – no bad thing in itself, very good in fact, but strange given where we were in time and place. There was scarcely any mention of, or attention paid to, New Zealand writers. We were colonials – though I would have resented and resisted the word; and I was in time to become one of the writers who asserted New Zealand literary nationalism – an important phase, no longer necessary.

I had to discover New Zealand writers by my own initiative – Mansfield, John Mulgan's *Man Alone*, Sargeson's stories and our poets as represented in Allen Curnow's Caxton Press anthology of 1948. Those writers became special to me, because they were the first to show me literature at work on what I knew at first hand, elevating it, intensifying it, making it real to me, and more than real.

At this time my father subscribed to the British *New Statesman and Nation*, which kept him abreast of world politics from a leftist perspective; but it also gave me, in its review pages and its poems, my first insights into a larger world of contemporary writing and publishing.

Whatever I have made of my life since follows from those beginnings. I studied English at university, was taught by Allen Curnow who became a lifelong friend; got to know Frank Sargeson and Janet Frame; travelled overseas on a scholarship where in due course I turned my back on offers of employment and came home like a good literary nationalist to help – as it seemed to me then – in the establishment of a 'New Zealand literature'. I was a serious young man – probably self-important; but there was a goal in all this which was at once ambitious and beyond ambition. I believed in the power and importance of literature; I believed in New Zealand – and I suppose I believed in myself; or I was able to behave as if I did. My 'career path' (as people say these days) was fixed.

New Zealand writing now has official recognition, figures in schools and universities, has its own publishing industry, its generous awards and prizes. Writers are public figures, acknowledged at home and (sometimes) abroad. I have just come back from giving the opening paper to the New Zealand Studies Association's annual conference, held this year in Paris on the theme of New Zealand and France. In November I go back for the launch of my new novel, *My Name was Judas*, in London. By e-mail I have word of translation rights bought by Polish, Spanish, French and Brazilian publishers in advance of publication.

These are all healthy developments and one would not wish it otherwise. But most blessings are mixed; and along with this public recognition goes an inevitable commercialisation of literature which is, potentially at least, inimical to the pursuit of literary excellence. As a writer one has to keep constantly in mind that the goal is not to please anyone but oneself. My job is to set myself high standards and try to match them. Of course I want to please readers, and hope there will be many of them. But to try to please them, to try to guess what will be popular and provide it, is a recipe for failure.

As a writer of fiction your reading becomes very particular and often narrowly focused on the next work. I no longer try to 'keep up' with what is being written. I am a writer first, a reader only second. When the writing seems to slow up and become sluggish – something that sometimes happens in the middle of a novel – I often read Dickens or Shakespeare, not because I want to write as they do, but to be reminded how various and energetic the English language can be. The effect can be like a shot in the arm.

Poetry is more mysterious. It comes and goes more or less like a welcome but unpredictable visitor whose length of stay is its own choice. But it continues for me to be the most demanding and most satisfying of literary forms, and not popular enough ever to be vulgarised by fashion or commerce.

On Teaching English*

David Hill's article on language is not an untypical example of Mr Facing-Both-Ways. On the one hand he wouldn't be found dead with an ungrammatical sentence in his head, or on his page, spells impeccably, knows all the right linguistic distinctions and traps to be avoided (and lets us know that he does), but on the other hand wants to show that he's a democrat, one of the lads, up with the play, 'modern'. This is the intellectual equivalent of the upper-class chap who lets you know he's upper-class but insists he can mix with anyone, and does; or the clergyman who likes to get down among the sinners, but never to sin.

Hill's argument is based on a false either/or: either you believe in a hard and fast set of rules for language use, or anything goes. Since it's easy to show (and he's right in this) that language is constantly changing and over time will break out of any set of rules we make for it, the logical conclusion seems to be that anything goes, and that those who insist that one usage is 'correct' and another 'incorrect' are silly old stick-in-the-muds fighting a battle they can't win.

I hope I will be excused for referring to my own recent book, *The Writer at Work*, and an essay there called 'English in our Schools' which deals at some length with schoolteachers who promote this

* *New Zealand Herald*, 10 April 2001.

kind of argument as an excuse for teaching no grammar, being casual about spelling (including their own), and treating any attempt to improve children's written or spoken language as a cruel attack on their confidence and 'sense of self worth'.

There is a middle point between rigidity and chaos, and that is what ought to be aimed for. To take an example Hill offers: usage is changing, so 'disinterested', which once meant 'objective', is being used so often to mean 'uninterested', it seems likely that will soon be its predominant, or even its only, meaning. I agree there's no point in attempting to stop this process – though there is no need either to hurry it along. However, a good teacher will *teach* that this is an example of a shift in usage, perhaps also remarking that an educated person knows that the change is happening, watches it happen, and makes a conscious choice to use the word in one or other of its two senses, while an uneducated person manifests the change in ignorance. David Hill seems to be promoting ignorance – for others, of course, not for himself.

Teaching grammar, spelling and pronunciation according to an agreed set of current conventions is a way of aiding good order and easy communication. It is not the same as asking that those conventions be set in stone.

Nor is it damaging children, on the contrary it is helping them, to point out that certain uses of language will signal to those who have power in our society – and even to the nice Mr Facing-Both-Ways who reserves the right to have a good 'chuckle' (his word) at those who make mistakes – that the speaker or writer is an ill-educated or uneducated person. This is a fact of our society, and it is surely part of the work of teaching English to make it known.

On the subject of spelling David Hill gives the example of 'Aprylle showrs' which, he tells us, is how Chaucer spelled it. He suggests some of the elements – fashion, trial and error, personal preference etc. – which brought about the change over centuries, and points out that the same forces are at work in the present. 'Presumably', he goes on, '14th to 19th century columnists also fulminated against them.'

I suppose he knows that there were no fourteenth-century column-ists because there were no fourteenth-century newspapers, though if he does it's a puzzle why he should refer to them. What he doesn't seem to know is that no one in the fourteenth century would have complained of any of the three different spellings of that phrase I can find in editions of Chaucer on my shelves, because English spelling was not standardised until the early eighteenth century. It was standardised for convenience, precisely because it made pages of printed text more immediately and unambiguously meaningful, a convenience which David Hill believes others – young folks, not himself – should feel free to abandon.

As for his advice that rather than complaining about the decline in standards of written and spoken language we should laugh at verbal howlers it brings about: well of course one does laugh. But it seems strange to present oneself as a liberal humane defender of 'the young, the illiterate, the deprived', and then suggest that the mistakes we give them licence to make will provide us with first-class entertainment.

Poetry and Politics (and a beating)*

In 1965 I was in London on a Nuffield Travelling Fellowship. I was 32, had published my first collection of poems at home in New Zealand, and in the UK my first book of literary criticism, *The New Poetic* (in subsequent editions *The New Poetic: Yeats to Eliot*), and I was now back on sabbatical leave intending to work on what were my two obsessions, poetry and politics – in particular on how they mixed and didn't mix in the work of Auden and his confrères in the 1930s. But I was also hoping to recover my own ability to write poems, which had seemed to vanish under the weight of work as a lecturer in English at the University of Auckland.

I enjoyed being back in London with my wife and first child, enjoyed the work on the Auden group, and meanwhile waited for any faint stir or twitch that might signal that poetry for me was not dead but had been in hibernation. Some months passed and then, as I recall it, very quietly, the poems began to write themselves. This was the year when Lyndon Johnson was making his wrong decision about Vietnam. It was get out or bog in time. Like Anthony Eden with Suez, and like, much later, Tony Blair with Iraq, Johnson thought he had reasons for going in but felt they weren't good enough, couldn't be made to sound

* Published here for the first time.

necessary and legitimate, and so had to concoct another, something more urgent, a trigger. So the Gulf of Tonkin incident was invented – an attack by North Vietnamese gunboats on a US navy ship. Senate and Congress responded with outrage as required, and the president was given the authorisation he needed to make war. Half a million troops were committed, and soon a new word (language serving the need of the hour) began to be heard – 'escalate'. There would be no way back now until seven or eight years had passed and tens of thousands of Americans, and many hundreds of thousands of Vietnamese, were dead – and nothing gained. I felt the drama of it almost moment by moment. Some of this got directly into the new poems; but mostly it was there obliquely.

There is always something mysterious about poetry. It takes its own path and often, especially in its early drafts, has little to do with deliberation. One day, sitting in a downstairs study at the back of what were at that time flats for Nuffield Fellows along the north side of Prince Albert Road, I found myself writing lines about a caning I received as a fourteen-year-old. They were flat and factual, though with the kind of heightening assonances and alliterations that the mind seems to discover for itself when it is composing out of obscure but deep feeling:

> I was caned often at school.
> Only once so it mattered.
> His name was Tammy Scott.
> I never knew him use a cane
> Except just once – on me.
> He taught maths,
> Promoted a small pianist
> Who grew to be a big one,
> And painted bowls of roses
> In a fine, dead style.
> He used the names and dates
> Of the school's two hundred war-dead
> To make a book,
> One fine laborious painted page
> For each dead old-boy.

All this was true. The small pianist promoted by the maths teacher had become a concert performer on the international circuit; and the memorial book was still to be seen in a glass case in the school library. There had even been a time – I didn't know whether it continued – when a page was turned each day, revealing another name in scrolled letters, another elaborately worked floral decoration, another face belonging to an Old Boy killed in the Second World War. Tammy Scott's memorial to the school's war dead was also his own.

I look at the poem now as if it had been written by someone else; and in a way that was how it seemed at the time – as if I had been taking dictation. Everything thus far suggested gentleness, art, reverence. But in the lines which arrived next there was a hardening of tone:

> I used a pen-knife,
> Hacked my impertinent name
> On the top of a desk: STEAD.
> Was it the bald style
> Of a life inscription
> That so distressed him?

The verb 'used' ('he used the names and dates' / 'I used a pen-knife') connect the two kinds of inscription, but as opposites. If the one on the desk was 'a life inscription', then the ones in the memorial book were death inscriptions.

Now I had to deal with the caning and my recollection is that that was the only part of the poem that didn't simply 'write itself'. I tried to describe it as it had happened but, when I did that, the beating became the subject, and that was not quite the direction the poem wanted to take. So I went quickly past it, except for a passing reference to its violence:

> Nothing had prepared me
> In that empty cloakroom
> For Tammy's violence.
> He went. When he came back
> I was still where I'd stopped
> My forehead sweating
> Against the panelled wall.

By this point a very slight element of fiction had entered. The caning took place in an empty classroom, not a cloakroom. My memory of the event is very particular, so why the change? I can think only that this was something determined by the ear. The hard syllables in that line, and particularly the double k sound following the double p in the line before, suited the feeling better than the softness of 'classroom'. The poem had also minimised the pain inflicted, and omitted the sense I experienced at the time that I was alone in a room with a man who, once he began beating, lost all control and couldn't stop.

And it had maximised my crime. In fact I had not used a pen-knife. I had impressed my name in pencil. It was an act deserving, by the rules of those times, a caning; but mine was one name among many. It could only have been found by a person who went hunting for it, could easily have gone unnoticed or been overlooked, and certainly didn't deserve what I got.

Again these slight shifts of emphasis to the facts did not have the feel of conscious decisions. They were – or seemed – more like following instructions, as if a voice in my head was saying 'Not that . . .' 'Not that . . .' 'Yes, that's more like it . . .' The poem was 'using' Tammy Scott's name as he had 'used' the names of the school's war dead; but it had its sights on something more than the beating. It was interested in war and peace, death and life, and even in kinds of art – the death art of the memorial book contrasted with the life assertion of the name carved on the desk.

So it concluded:

> I think of Tammy
> Who meant no harm
> Labouring among the dead.
>
> I walked past him, and out.
> I looked at him, not 'daggers'
> But truly without feeling.
> He might have been a desk-top.
> My pride was exact.
> I would not go down
> In Tammy's book.
> He would go down in mine.

I called it 'With a Pen-Knife'. It was an anti-war poem, and in the poetry readings of the time the assertiveness of those final lines always resonated, caused a stir of approval, got a round of applause. But the poem was also an act of revenge, and I remember that Kay, my wife, hearing me read it in public, felt uneasy, while a former English master* who took an interest in my literary career was distressed by it and told me he wished I hadn't written it. Tammy Scott was long since retired. Whether he ever saw or heard the poem I have no idea, but I would not have wanted to protect him from it. There was more than a little bit of hate in me towards him which is still there, and which is a part of my subject now.

The poem is truthful when it says I was caned often at school. Not as often as some, and only for misdemeanours. I was a civil and sensitive child, not significantly rebellious, and certainly without criminal intent; but I was full of bounce, jokes, smart remarks. I was not consciously disrespectful, but I sometimes neglected – forgot – to show due respect. I deeply disapprove of corporal punishment now, not because of the incident described in the poem, but because I believe it wrong, even when controlled and used moderately; but as a boy I accepted routine school beatings (at primary school it had been the strap on the hand) as a fact of life. Like most things at that time it was neither good nor bad. It just was.

Tammy Scott's beating was not routine. It was severe – more severe than any I ever saw inflicted on anyone else in five years at the school. Canings usually took place immediately and in front of the class. That could be humiliating, but it was also a control against excesses. He had chosen a classroom somewhere in the upper part of the school and told me to meet him there during the lunch hour.

The first strike was so painful I yelped and stood up thinking it was over. I was told to bend over again – and again, and again. I could just see behind me his torso swinging into the blows and hear him grunting with the effort. He was working himself into a frenzy that had nothing to do with my crime, and no foreseeable end. The air was charged with something frightening and poisonous. Each swipe got harder – and harder to bear, and finally impossible.

* Mt Albert Grammar's famous 'Butch' Brown.

After five strikes I couldn't take any more. I would have needed to be tied to a post. I ran between the desks until I came to the back wall of the classroom. That must have checked his frenzy. I heard him leave, banging the door shut. Perhaps twenty minutes later he came back. I was exactly where I'd stopped, standing, leaning forward, my forehead against the wall, still seething with astonishment and pain.

He said, 'Get out.'

He was standing at the door and I had to go past him. Perhaps he expected me to cower. I know that all my outrage and contempt for him was in my face. He felt it, and for weeks afterwards he watched me in his maths classes, not, I'm sure, out of fear of consequences, but with an unmistakable anxiety. I had seen something about him that was normally concealed. I knew his secret. But did I know I knew it? That, I think, would have been his fear.

The pain continued for some days. I told no one. My parents would not have known what to do; and in any case the thought of their doing anything was alarming. I was fourteen, not fully grown and very thin. The wounds – bruises, corrugations on the buttocks, broken skin on the flanks where the cane had flicked around and cut – healed slowly.

For many weeks Tammy Scott got nothing out of me but the coldest necessary courtesy. And then, slowly, it became possible for me to behave almost as before; or rather, it became difficult – artificial – not to. I stopped showing him what I felt; but I hadn't stopped feeling it. Perhaps he thought I'd come to accept my punishment; that I'd 'taken it like a man'.

Recently in an Auckland newspaper a man aged, I should think, in his early forties wrote a piece about his loss of Catholic faith which had begun when, as an altar boy, he had been sexually abused by a priest. He was the son of a man who had lectured in English when I was a student at the university, and I sent the piece to a friend, living in Melbourne, who had been my fellow student, saying I was sorry there was not in fact a Catholic heaven in which our former lecturer, who had been a sexual puritan and determined proselytiser for his church, could now be reading what his son had written.

My Melbourne friend, who is Jewish, wrote back saying she'd felt rather more sympathy than I had for our former lecturer (now deceased); that she was becoming weary of the public spilling of so many beans, and found it hard to respond with sympathy to a tone of fashionable reproach and self-pity among the growing army of the abused.

I understood what she meant. There is, no doubt, a lot to be said for silence and a stiff upper lip. All I could reply was that when this thought arose and I remembered the only kind of abuse – relatively minor – I had suffered (by which I meant the caning), I felt what I supposed these people felt: outrage for the younger helpless self, as if for a child not oneself.

In Vietnam the war went on and on, always 'escalating'. There were the triumphant 'body counts', in which the ration of ten Vietnamese to one American seemed standard and acceptable, and in which every dead Vietnamese not in the uniform of North Vietnam counted, man, woman or child, as 'Vietcong'. There was the napalm, the burning of villages, the Agent Orange used to destroy rice crops and forest cover, the bombing of the North, the assaults into Cambodia and Laos only extending the area of conflict. Australia had bogged in enthusiastically, even sending conscripts. New Zealand hung back but, visited by bigger and bigger wigs until the president himself came, was persuaded to send some of its tiny regular army. No end seemed possible, either that America could accept defeat or that there would be an end to the resistance in the southern countryside or from the North.

For five years and more that war was for me a commitment, an obsession. I wrote about it, was involved in protest and caught up in the sense of a social revolution that accompanied it. It found ways into my poems. It also gave me the subject of my first novel, *Smith's Dream*, a political fantasy which has never been published outside New Zealand and Australia but which was later (1977) made into a movie, *Sleeping Dogs*, directed by Roger Donaldson, with Sam Neill as Smith. Donaldson's first movie, and also Neill's, and shot by Michael Seresin who was also to become famous, it would probably look very creaky now, but it was the beginning of serious commercial movie-making in New Zealand.

Some time around 1968, the year of the Tet Offensive and of Lyndon Johnson's announcement that he would not stand for a second term, I was involved in preparations for a march. A man turned up – one I hadn't seen before at these rallies. He brought some banners he had made, and also a large box-like arrangement to go on the roof of a car. They were beautifully painted. He looked familiar and reminded me that his name was M and that during our fourth-form year we had sat side by side in maths classes, which happened probably five times a week.

At school M had been a brilliant representational painter. He was a good-looking lad, tall, lively and full of good humour. We hadn't been close friends, but during those classes we had enjoyed one another's company and laughed a lot. The two desks were side by side right at the front of the room.

When the protest march was over we went for a drink together, exchanging information about our lives since leaving school. Quite late in our conversation I told him – off-hand, not making anything special of it – about Tammy Scott's caning and that I had written a poem about it.

There was a moment of awkward silence, and then he told me his story. Tammy Scott had taken special interest in him because of his skill as a painter. He had invited M to his house one weekend. They had painted together. Then Scott had told him it was 'time to take a shower'. M was puzzled, reluctant, but, in the way 14-year-old boys do, or did, when instructed by a schoolmaster, he took his clothes off and got into the shower. Scott joined him there and made some kind (I didn't ask for details) of sexual assault on him. Horrified, distressed, M went home and never went back. He had never told anyone.

To me there was something both horrible and satisfying about this information, because it made a 'story' of what had happened to me, provided an explanation for it; and also because I had written my poem without knowing it. Or rather the poem had written itself, telling me what it knew and I did not.

Fill out the story for yourself, in whatever way makes best sense. Mine, I'm afraid would be trite, banal, but vicious too. What else, so many years later, could I make of what I now knew than that Tammy Scott had fallen in love with M and had been jealous of the boy who sat beside him and could be seen, day after day, enjoying his company and his friendship.

A Portait of the Artist as a Young Man Reading *A Portrait of the Artist as a Young Man**

I read James Joyce's *Portrait of the Artist* in 1951, when I was eighteen, and when I went back to it more than two decades later I was surprised at what I'd remembered and what had slipped out of sight. I remembered vividly the priest's account of the interminableness of eternity, but little of the pains of hell as he detailed them – and I think that may have been because eternity, like infinity, is something the young mind wrestles with constantly, whereas, lacking the benefits of a hellfire and brimstone education, the infernal torments struck me as comic strip. (The Steads were Catholic Irish, but my father, whose mother was Protestant, had lapsed, and my mother was Protestant, which in her case meant nothing at all.) I had already proposed for myself the mantra 'consciousness is contrast', so the idea of extreme and unvarying pain without even a few moment's vacation must have been deeply unconvincing.

I remembered also very clearly the section that comes late in the book when Stephen composes a poem – a villanelle. I was a young poet myself, and the process of composition, and the fact that the poem was

* *James Joyce Bloomsday Magazine*, 2004.

associated with a beautiful girl, a Muse figure, was deeply satisfying. When I glance over that passage now, with an elderly and disciplined eye, it strikes me as somewhat overwrought, and the villanelle as something less than brilliant.

The scene I remembered most vividly, and one which I still especially treasure, is the argument, at the Dedalus Christmas dinner table, about Parnell and the role of the priests in his downfall. At the time I knew little about Irish history and nothing about Parnell (that would come later when I studied, and wrote about, Yeats), but you need to know no more than the scene itself provides, and that is part of its brilliance. The movement of feelings, the way they surge up, clash, come back under imperfect control, and then flare up again, is brilliant comic writing, wonderfully detached and exactly observed. This is one of those scenes (there are a number also in *Dubliners*) where I feel Joyce taught twentieth-century writers how 'modern' (or Modernist) fiction was to be done. You read it and you knew that in some sense you had to do likewise. It looked plain, though it wasn't. What was gone from it was 'literariness', the nineteenth-century and Edwardian elaborations, inversions, locutions and decorations that had kept the language of fiction separate from the language of speech. It was like Wordsworth a century before choosing to shed 'poetic diction' in the *Lyrical Ballads* in favour of 'the language really used by men'.

When I go back to the *Portrait*, what seemed (and was) so original looks now, at first glance, stylistically unremarkable. The writing is as clean and fresh and intelligent as ever; but you have to think back in order to regain the sense of just how new it tasted after a diet of conventional pre-Modernist fiction. The other thing I notice now is that the writing, especially towards the end of the novel, is in its own way surprisingly elaborate, even in places over-charged. Joyce was a very complex and contradictory master: one who taught plainness but in a style that was itself anything but simple.

He was also a master of the ringing phrase, the commanding and memorable sentence. A number of them took root in this reader's memory and, half a century later, remain there. 'Silence, exile and cunning', for example: I thought, and still think, it's the perfect formula for writerly self-protection, although I have myself failed on all three fronts. And for the New Zealand writer in the 1950s – a time for us of literary realism and quite intense literary nationalism – there were those wonderful concluding statements: 'Welcome, O life! I go to encounter for the millionth time the reality of experience and to forge in the smithy of my soul the uncreated conscience of my race.'

At the age of eighteen it even pleased me, in a Joycean, ego-centred way, that the book's last sentence ended with my name: 'Old father, old artificer, stand me now and ever in good stead.'

An Academic Colleague*

Although I was twenty or thirty years younger than Elizabeth Annie Sheppard, and less the committed scholar and academic, I think she respected my intelligence and liked me well enough for us to have been closer friends than we were. But I avoided overtures, accepted invitations but didn't return them, and behaved towards her (or so it now seems to me) in an evasive, self-protective, way. This was not because I didn't find her an interesting colleague – on the contrary, she fascinated me and had my fullest respect. But I was a young man trying to be critic and academic teacher, poet and fiction writer, husband and father of a young family. Dr Sheppard (as we all called her) deserved the attention and support her behaviour often signalled she needed, and there would have been reward enough in getting to know her better; but I was not the person to offer these in any degree that would have been of use.

No one who knew Elizabeth would imagine the above paragraph to have been written in a tone of condescension. Like everyone else, I could be made to quail in her presence. But there can be no doubt that I was able to manage and control my professional life in a way

---

* This was written for a memorial booklet prepared by Dr Sheppard's family and then revised for *Auckland Minds and Matters*, ed. Nicholas Tarling, the University of Auckland, Auckland, 2003.

114

that she was not able to manage and control hers. She was a brilliant woman and a formidable one, but in some fatal sense unfocused; and she didn't go as far academically as her talents deserved. Why this should have been so is a question everyone who knew her must at some time have tried to answer.

She ought at the very least to have been appointed to the University of Auckland's Chair of English Language, but she was not. It would be easy to argue that this was simply a matter of sexist discrimination. That is how she would probably have seen it, but I don't think it's a sufficient explanation. There is no way around the fact that Elizabeth was temperamentally difficult – dauntingly formal, meticulous in the observance of social forms which seemed almost to belong to a past age, and yet at the same time franker than most people find acceptable in professional interchange, less inhibited in going on the offensive, sharper tongued.

She was a person who might have sprung from the pages of her beloved Henry James, with a talent for dramatic entrances and exits he would have relished. I remember her appearance, angry and red-faced under her wimple-like head scarf, at the door of the old common room in Princes Street, used at that time (the early 1960s) by all departments. The conversation fell away and in a moment it became apparent that I was the person at whom the beam of her wrath was directed. Into the silence her small clear bell-like voice delivered its accusation. She had discovered that I had borrowed from the library certain works by Henry James. Didn't I know, she asked, that *she* was at work on James? And didn't I understand that there was a convention among academic colleagues that they didn't poach on one another's territory?

It should have been flattering that she should think of me, a new member of the Department and very recently her student, as a potential rival; but my instant reaction to an angry challenge was an angry rebuttal. Didn't *she* know that academics sometimes borrowed books to read, not to 'work on'. But she should know also that if I chose to 'work on' Henry James with a view to writing about him (I had in fact no such intention) I would do it without consulting her.

No doubt she raced off to be consoled by Professor Musgrove, or M. K. Joseph, or J. C. Reid – whichever of the Department's senior triumvirate was for the moment serving a reluctant term as her protector. Or she might have gone outside the Department to Eric McCormick – a friend she often quarrelled with, but a serious and dependable colleague, one of those rare scholars whose standards matched her own, and a person who from time to time could console her.

When it came to marking students' essays and examinations, Elizabeth's academic standards were high. She was the most meticulous 'marker' in the Department, but not always prompt in getting the work done, and there were times when, the term, or even the academic year, over, she would go about Auckland in a taxi (she never drove a car) from address to address, delivering work that should have been marked and returned long before.

In my first years as a lecturer in the English Department, while my head was still clear and my confidence high, I tended to side with her in demanding more rigour from fellow markers. But there were lengths she went to in the name of high standards which, if not absurd, were certainly comic. I have the clearest recollection of a Department examiners' meeting – there would have been no more than six or seven of us at that time, including Professor/HOD Sydney Musgrove, poet Allen Curnow, novelist Bill Pearson, poet and novelist M. K. Joseph, critics J. C. Reid and Thomas Crawford, bibliographer Bill Cameron, and me – and Elizabeth arguing before this impressive tribunal that a student who, according to our preliminary count, had passed by the skin of his teeth, must be reconsidered and failed. So, reluctantly but conscientiously, the reconsideration was done. It took time. Answers were re-read and re-marked, arithmetic checked, a total arrived at, and . . . the result was the same. It was close, but the student had passed.

There was a brief silence, and then suddenly Elizabeth's small frame rose from its chair as if propelled by some force other than simply muscular. Small hands clasped into tight fists on either side of a face blazing under white hair, eyes raised imploring to the heavens, she cried out, 'Fail him! I implore you – *fail him!*' We were all acutely embarrassed. If she had been asking for money we would all have clubbed in at once. But could we fail a student just to make her happy? No, we couldn't.

Elizabeth was sometimes absurd in her suspicions, wayward in her loyalties, excessive in her negative judgements, extravagant in expressing them; yet it was possible to sit down with her and analyse the state of the English Department, the psychology of one or several of its members, or equally the current state of New Zealand or world politics, and be impressed and delighted by the breadth of her knowledge, the range and penetration of her intelligence, and the fullness of her comprehension. She was an intemperate person who was also a wise one.

My view is that despite all the difficulties she gave her colleagues, and sometimes her students, she probably should have had her Chair. I also believe that a man as frankly intolerant of what she liked to call 'cant' as Elizabeth Sheppard was would also have been denied it. If the University of Auckland is to blame in any way in this, it is not for sexism, but perhaps for lack of courage. Her case was undoubtedly a difficult one; but she deserved more reward than she got for the high standards she set in her teaching and research.

Most of her teaching life was spent on Old and Middle English texts; but her one published work was her study of Henry James's *The Turn of the Screw*, delivered first as Macmillan Brown Lectures and subsequently expanded. In her last years, after retirement, she worked on an edition of the letters of Frances Hodgkins, work which came her way, no doubt, through the good offices of Eric McCormick, but which was far from completion when she died. In those years she was immensely helped by the patience and goodwill of Dennis McEldowney, editor of the university press and himself a writer of distinction.

Elizabeth Sheppard was a woman of rare quality of mind; yet when I think of her honestly, without (to use her word) the cant of commemoration, I think of someone whose life had in some way gone wrong – who was brilliant, unfulfilled and unhappy. Was it simply the case of a professional woman who had sacrificed too much of the biological self in a time when women couldn't 'have it all', but were forced to choose? If so, then we must be thankful for the changes that have occurred in the ninety or so years since she was born. Or was it, as I felt it must be, something else – something more?

Very early on, perhaps while I was still a student, I had heard it said that Elizabeth when young had been a marvellous pianist – potentially a concert pianist – and had had to choose between scholarship and a life in music. But this was not a fact offered on good or certain authority; and since it was never repeated, and not mentioned by her, I discounted it as myth and forgot it. After her death I discovered it was true. It was something which made her seem at last more nearly intelligible – more than ever a Jamesian figure, one who (as I now chose to see it) early in life had made a wrong choice, and had lived among books and ancient texts which as time went by gave her less than the satisfactions which music had once seemed to promise.

History as it Happens[*]

What would a book launch be like in Zagreb? Kay and I were in Oxford for two terms, where I was Senior Visiting Fellow at St John's College. There had been a summer holiday in rural France and winter visits to Paris and Stockholm. It was January 1997, an exceptionally – wonderfully – severe English winter, in which the rivers in Oxford had frozen over, and the fountain outside the Radcliffe Infirmary had gradually vanished, first behind the curtain, then under the pile-up, of its own self-created ice. We were close to returning to New Zealand when the message came. A translation into Croatian of my novel *All Visitors Ashore*, which had been in train for some time, was ready for publication, and we were invited to come to Zagreb for a few days at the publisher's expense.

I had no idea what to expect. I knew about the recent Yugoslav war – who could not? – but it seemed such an unhappy and typically human mess I had averted my eyes from its complexities. I was vague about Serb and Croat, Croat and Muslim, about Belgrade and Zagreb and Sarajevo. My thoughts were basic, and superficial. How safe was Air Croatia? How safe were the streets of Zagreb? Would we be holed up in a dingy Eastern European hotel, afraid to go out? A friend who

* Written for *A Passion for Travel*, ed. Tina Shaw, Tandem Press, Auckland, 1998.

had been behind the Iron Curtain both before and since the collapse of communism advised that we should take our own loo paper.

One forgets that as well as communist austerity for the many there used to be communist opulence for the few. Some of each survives. I was an official writer, and therefore, it soon became apparent, to be accorded the status that role used to imply in the communist world before the brutal truths of the marketplace began to be enforced. We were met by my publisher and taken by chauffeur-driven Merc to a hotel, the Esplanade, the lobby of which had enough marble and staircases to suggest, at the very least, a Cecil B. DeMille movie set.

Our suite was very grand indeed, all maroon and grey stripes, and with its own interior corridor. There were flowers and fruit on the tables, and white bathrobes, his and hers, in the marble bathroom. Our windows looked out past noble pillars and down over a vast snow-covered square with a fountain at the centre, where people, mostly shabbily dressed, waited for blue trams, and equestrian statues from various *époques* made their historical and political statements in the cold misty light.

The Esplanade is, I suppose, a hotel of the old Austro-Hungarian Empire days, preserved under communism for the *nomenklatura*, and preserved now by the new Croatian nationalists the old socialist internationalists have become. Visually, Zagreb is that same mix – empire grandeur, some of it falling into disrepair, along with worker-state drabness.

Two women were partly responsible for our being there – the translator Ljiljana S., and the editor Jadranka P. They had, they said, fallen in love with *All Visitors Ashore*; indeed the book can never have had two more ardent admirers; and they had encouraged the publisher in his plan to launch it in style.

For the next few days we were showered with gifts and entertained lavishly in the best restaurants, which were very good indeed. There was a press conference in a book shop. There was a meeting with the Minister for the Arts, Božo Biškupić, shown that evening on national television news. The launch itself was held in a jazz club, B. P.'s, where it seemed all Zagreb's intelligentsia had gathered. There were clever speeches, and a reading from the Croatian version of the novel by a professional actor. There was good jazz, good food, good booze and good jokes. Everyone who came was given a copy of the novel.

I was struck by the scale of the thing, its generosity, and also its oddness. It was as if we had stepped back into a world of privilege – not the old privilege of empire, but the more recent one of communism, which had survived communism's demise. The CP and its doctrine were gone, but the habits were not. Only a publisher with official Government backing could have spent so much on a book that was so distinctly 'literary' and unlikely to make big sales. Yet this was also a publisher who wanted very much to make his way, and prosper, in the new environment of free enterprise and open markets. Of course I was grateful, and enjoyed every minute of it; but I couldn't blind myself to the ironies of history it seemed to encapsulate.

Before we arrived there had been news in Britain of marches in Zagreb in support of the one remaining independent radio station, which had been critical of the Government of Franjo Tuđman and was now threatened with closure. At some point during the evening of the launch I was approached by a young woman saying she represented that station and asking whether I would agree to be interviewed. I said yes and was taken at once to a sort of cupboard under a stairway. There, in almost total darkness, she taped an interview, thanked me, and was gone. It was my visit's only unofficial public moment, and it too felt like a throwback to the days of the Wall and the Iron Curtain.

In between the official engagements and meals, Ljiljana and Jadranka took Kay and me for walks in Zagreb – up to the old town, to the cathedral, the market, the cable car, the parks and squares – and once, in Jadranka's noisy but dependable Škoda, out of the city to a charming coffee shop in the village of Samobor. There, in the late afternoon as darkness fell, we encountered by chance a local winter folk carnival – people dressed as animals making a variety of hoots and wails, roars and whistles and squeaks, as they paraded along the road.

We were learning all the time about the recent war, the complexity of its politics, the cruelty of its enactment, the pain and fear and anger it had left. Every dinner and every conversation added to one's knowledge and increased one's curiosity and one's sense of how people inherit their history almost as an aspect of personality. On our last night there we met a poet and editor who had remained in exile through all the years of communism, still writing in his own language, and who, on hearing news of Croatia's declaration of independence, had bought a revolver and come home to defend his country. Already, of course, being an honest and forthright fellow of high intelligence, he was in conflict with the new Government that had welcomed him home as a national hero.

Every writer is a scavenger, and one reaches an age where every new experience presents itself both for what it is and for what might be made of it. By now all these riches were beginning to merge in my mind with thoughts I'd had long before about a novel that might make something of New Zealand's historical links with Croatia, links which no one growing up in the north can be unaware of. I had recollections of farmland still pock-marked by the grave-like holes made by Dalmatian gum-diggers, and of rusty spade-handled gum spears they left behind. And Kay (like Maurice Gee) had spent her childhood among the orchardists and wine-growers of the Henderson Valley west of Auckland. It was a rich furrow, only made richer by the recent war.

The following European summer, the novel taking clearer shape in my mind, I returned to Zagreb.

I stayed with Ljiljana who lived with her aunt in an apartment in central Zagreb. My days were spent there, or walking about the city. Then, each evening, Jadranka, who owned a modern flat in the suburbs, came in her Škoda and took me to a café or restaurant, or for a walk in a park, or to a movie. The plan was that towards the end of that week the three of us would travel to an area on the coast where many New Zealand Dalmatians had come from.

I began to see Ljiljana and Jadranka as representing two separate, even opposed, Croatias which the recent war had pushed into unity. Ljiljana's parents had been communist *nomenklatura*, the father a lawyer and diplomat; and in her student years Ljiljana had been a serious Young Communist. The idealism hadn't lasted; but neither had the world view it implied been entirely discarded. She still tended to see the wealthy nations as having gained their advantages by imperialist exploitation rather than by economic efficiency; and philosophically she was, I'm sure, a rationalist.

122

Jadranka, on the other hand, was almost certainly from a right-wing Catholic family of the kind that had long ago prospered under the old Austro-Hungarian hegemony, and had suffered least under the Nazi occupation. She represented (if my speculations were right) the Croatia for whom the communist federation of Yugoslavia had been particularly unfortunate.

Neither was entirely frank on political matters – or I felt they were not – and given the history of their lifetime (they were aged 40 and 36) that is not surprising. My feeling, however, was that there was an important underlying difference, like a crack in a wall that is none the less solid. The wall was their common loyalty to Croatia. Like most Croatians, they had resented the dominance of Belgrade in the old Yugoslavia, and the preponderance of Serbs in army and police; and they were indignant at what that army, which had become the army of Serbia, had done to Croatia in its attempts, ultimately unsuccessful, to hold the federation together.

But there had been another, more important, determinant in Ljiljana's life. When she was twelve, living the life of a privileged child of senior communists, both her parents were killed in a car accident. She was returned to the Zagreb apartment where her aunt and uncle occupied one bedroom, her grandmother and grandfather the other. The only remaining space was a small kitchen, a bathroom, and a sort of cupboard room into which, as she grew older, a bed was put for her.

Ljiljana had lived there until she left to be a student in Dubrovnik. Now, after a number of years working for large corporations, during which time both grandparents and the uncle had died, she was back with the surviving aunt, attempting to make a living as a free-lance translator and, it seemed, succeeding.

On the fifth floor of a grim, grey-faced post-Second World War block in a street of such blocks, the apartment was reached by means of a dark stairway of cracked and stained concrete. There was no lift. The blue trams banged away in the street below. A small balcony off the kitchen looked down into an inner courtyard echoing with the voices of many families. To reach the room where Ljiljana slept and worked, you went through the bathroom, where the one tap over the handbasin was cold, and the bath-shower, hidden by a curtain on a wire, was served by

123

an old-style gas calafont. The kitchen was minimal, with space for only a small supply of utensils and equipment. The refrigerator was kept in the hallway, just inside the front door.

I slept in the cupboard room listening to the summer-night voices echoing around the shaft-like courtyard, shouting, singing, arguing and murmuring in Croatian. I relished the flavour of it, the richness, the sense that this was like a short ride back into Central Europe's recent past. I had loved the opulence of the Esplanade hotel, but this was better!

Rebecca West records her impression of Zagreb as a kind of gymnasium of the intellect, and Ljiljana was that formidable person, a Central European intellectual, her room full of books and heavy with smoke. At all hours of the day we smoked (I reverted briefly to the habit) and talked books, politics, movies, music – and then books again. Around two p.m. each day the aunt, whose name was Kristina and who spoke no English, called us to the table, barely big enough for three, in the tiny kitchen where she had cooked lunch. There was a particular food style which I suppose must be typical of the region, and distinct from the Dalmatian style I was yet to experience. I remember especially delicious stews, with stuffed peppers and marrows, rich in garlic, and a thick tasty soup-like juice.

Kristina seemed to enjoy her role as Ljiljana's mother-figure, and as hostess to the 'famous visiting writer', about whom she held daily news conferences for inquisitive neighbours on the apartment stairs.

Later in the day came the change of gear which my evenings with Jadranka represented. Jadranka, Ljiljana assured me, was 'the real intellectual'; but since her English was imperfect and my Croatian non-existent, communication at that level was impossible. Jadranka laughed a lot, and used the English language recklessly, like a drunk at the wheel of a powerful car. Once, in a restaurant, she recommended that I have the lamb because I came from New Zealand and was 'used to eating ships' (plural of sheep). Another time, attempting to explain the meaning of a restaurant's name, she told me that the first word meant 'forest', and the second meant . . . There was a pause while she tried to remember the word in English that would follow forest. 'Vell,' she said. 'It mins . . .' And then with a rush. 'It mins a middle-aged house for knits.'

It took some time to work out that she meant a house for knights of the middle ages, and the word she was seeking was 'court'. The restaurant's name in English was Forest Court.

In a cinema, when the movie suddenly stopped and the theatre went dark, she got up and made her way to the back. A minute later she shouted something from the projection room, and the audience broke into laughter. When the movie started up again and she returned to her seat I asked her why the laughter. It was because she had called out to let everyone know what she'd found there – the reel finished and needing to be changed, and the projectionist sound asleep.

The day came for our trip and the three of us set off in the roaring, shuddering Škoda, smoking, laughing, arguing, listening to tapes of a Croatian ballad singer whose name on the copy I have appears to be Renzo Aboré, and whose songs, atmospheric in themselves, still conjure for me the strangeness and richness of that journey. I had seen many images of the war that had taken place in the countryside. There was a time when they had been a daily item on television. So the shock I felt at my first sights of the destruction was itself a shock. Television is not what it seems – 'reality' – and by that I don't mean that it misrepresents; only that, for whatever reason, the impact of the image and of the real are different, chalk and cheese.

I think we can't have been more than 50 kilometres south of Zagreb when we encountered the first of the war zones – burned-out houses, collapsed roofs, pock-marked walls, shell-holes, abandoned crops, tiny villages entirely emptied of their inhabitants. Now and then there was a single family living in the ruins of what had been their home. In one place a very small child standing in the doorway of a burned-out house was the only living thing I saw in a wrecked village.

These shocks were to continue at intervals all the way to the coast. I wanted to stop and take photographs, but I was conscious that this might seem insensitive, and I raised the question tentatively. Jadranka's response was not encouraging. Sometimes she drove on as if she hadn't heard. Other times she suggested there could be an armed madman about in the ruins who might take a shot at me; or that there might still be mines laid along the road's edge.

Perhaps she was genuinely afraid for me, or wisely cautious. What I couldn't determine was whether or not a political element came into it. Certainly whenever I asked whether a destroyed village was Croat or Serb she answered that it was Croat – another example of Serbian barbarism. I knew that although this must often be true, it couldn't always be so. Croats had also engaged in 'ethnic cleansing', especially in the Serb-dominated Krajina region around the city of Knin.

Ljiljana said nothing during these exchanges (tentative on my part, crisp on Jadranka's); but later, alone, she confirmed my supposition. Not every ruin we passed was the work of Serbs.

Quite early in this passage through the war zones there was a pause, a change of circumstance and mood. About 120 kilometres south of Zagreb, as the road took us through a forest, Jadranka pulled into a car park outside what looked like a hunting lodge. We had coffee there; but this was in fact an entrance to the national park of Plitvička Jezera, a region of woods and interconnected lakes, rivers and waterfalls, so beautiful it seemed unreal, or super-real. We walked there for more than two hours but could, it seemed, have gone on all day without exhausting it. Our route took us down into deep gullies, around small deep lakes, along the edge of streams, the water everywhere an astonishing pale blue, the woods crowding overhead an intense green, while out of holes in rock-faces waterfalls plunged, sometimes five or six into a single deep clear pool, where fish hung suspended like balloons or kites in an upside-down sky. A ferry took us across a small lake, after which it was time to climb back to the lodge and continue our journey.

Now it was the lovely countryside again, and at intervals the burned-out villages. Once Jadranka stopped to hunt for something in a handbag and I got out, risking the wildflowers that might be mined at the road's edge, and the concealed madmen among the ruins, to get my pictures. Jadranka wasn't pleased. 'Vas that *destroyed* enough for you?' she asked.

The landscape was changing now as we climbed a mountain range, leaving behind the lush pastures, the crops and woodlands of the plain. These slopes were littered with loose white stones, the trees low to the ground and widely separated. We stopped for coffee at a bucolic restaurant, enjoying, through gaps in the walls that appeared to have been blasted by artillery shells, wide views of the passes below.

As we came down the other side of the range the familiar Mediter-ranean/Adriatic colours and patterns began to appear – a landscape of vines and olives, pines and cypresses, orange-red roofs and yellow-orange walls, with the intense pale-into-dark blues of the sea a recurring background. Now we were in Dalmatia, still with evidence from time to time of the recent war, but the coast, or this part of it, seeming to have returned pretty much to what it had been before the fighting began.

Zaton, where the mother and aunt of one of Jadranka's friends had said they would look after us, is a small fishing village not far from the town of Šibenik, at the end of an estuary into which three rivers flow. As you come in from the coast road you look down the estuary and see, perhaps 3 or 4 kilometres away, the white church at the centre of the village, and the yellows and oranges of the buildings clustered around it. As you get nearer you see its cafés, a few shops, a restaurant perched over the water, and many small brightly painted fishing boats. On the hills behind the houses are small holdings, vineyards, vegetable gardens, olive groves.

Since I no longer remember their names I will have to call the two elderly sisters who, separately, welcomed us to Zaton, Aunt A and Aunt B. They were of peasant stock, widows, partisans (along with their husbands) during the Second World War, communists who had prospered under Tito's Yugoslavia, but now, it seemed, loyal Croatian nationalists. Aunt A told me (through Ljiljana's translation) that when she first married she moved into a modest house occupied by 24 members of an extended family. She and two other young wives of three brothers took turns to cook for the whole household. The meal was prepared in a cauldron, and the family sat around it and ate from it. Every summer as many as twenty, or even thirty, children from the village, mostly babies and infants, would die of diseases that seemed to arrive with the hot weather.

Jadranka wanted to know how anyone in those circumstances had found a way to get pregnant. Ah, the old lady said, her expression for a moment happy at the retrospect, they had gone out into the fields and the woods for that. Later, when we visited Aunt B, she showed us a very small room, reached by a ladder through a trapdoor from the floor below, in which, in those pre-war days, a family of two adults and four children had lived.

Now Aunt A had her own pleasant house in Zaton. In her late seventies, she was still a big strong healthy woman who each day climbed the hill behind the house to tend her goats and hens, her vines and vegetables. Aunt B, who had been a schoolteacher, owned several rooms opening off an enclosed lane in the village, and also an apartment in Šibenik, her principal dwelling place.

Aunt A greeted us with the traditional welcome of the region – a dish of almonds, and small glasses of her own plum brandy, colourless and with a kick like a mule. Later, when we were washed and rested, there was a meal she had prepared for us – three kinds of fish, straight from the boats, each cooked in a different way, with courgettes and kale, rich in garlic, and her own red wine taken (as was the habit of the region) with water. That, however, was not to be the end of eating. There was, Jadranka explained, a certain rivalry between the two widowed sisters, and Aunt B had also cooked us a meal which politeness demanded we should not refuse.

The day had been hot and humid and while we prepared to move on, the air seemed to press down until rain began to fall – warm, heavy, drumming on the vine leaves outside the open windows, with sudden forks of lightning, very near, and thunder like the snapping of huge branches. Under umbrellas Ljiljana, Jadranka and I made our way down into the village, sloshing through the warm flooded streets to Aunt B's and another heroic engagement with food. My recollection is that it was chicken, with a cucumber and tomato salad, very good but of course too good, and too much; and because I was male and (it was agreed) not quite as fat as a successful man of my age ought to be, the onus of doing justice to it fell on me.

That night, back at Aunt A's, I slept well despite waking at intervals to an extraordinary conjunction of summer night noises – a snoring giant in a nearby house, a chiming clock loud enough to suggest it belonged to the giant, roosters crowing at the moon, the clatter of goat-hooves, and loudest of all (there is surely no other sound in nature quite like it) Aunt A's donkey practising his scales.

Next day Ljiljana, Jadranka and I took a ferry from Šibenik, two hours' brisk chug to the island of Prvić, from which, I was told, so many had gone to New Zealand it had sometimes been referred to locally as Zealandia. There was a small village, not exactly flourishing, but still inhabited. But in our walk around the foreshore, and later, after swimming off a stone jetty, when we made our way 'inland' and got lost among vineyards and olive groves mostly abandoned to weeds and blackberry, we encountered only three or four people.

Back on the mainland we swam and lay in the sun among smooth white stones, or in the shade of pines; and in the evening found ourselves a restaurant – a small courtyard, open to the sky and enclosed by an ancient wall of white stone out of which a single fig tree grew, hanging leaves and fruit over our table. Jadranka and I had a sea-food risotto and salad, with wine, while Ljiljana, who always lost her appetite in public places, sat smoking. When we came out it was almost dark and a full moon was rising.

It had been very jolly in the restaurant until Jadranka had noticed her watch was missing. She valued it especially because it had been given by her sister, and I wanted us to return to the beach and look for it, but she refused, insisting the loss was a 'sign', a reminder, a punishment for happiness. 'I vas not meant to be happy,' she assured me.

Back at Aunt A's house, announcing an intention to greet the full moon by getting drunk, she downed two good glasses of the welcoming plum brandy, and suggested we walk into the village. The three of us set off, brayed away by the donkey. On the narrow road below the village graveyard Jadranka stopped to pray at a wayside shrine to the Virgin. Ljiljana and I looked past one another, down at the ground and up at the night sky, while Jadranka knelt on the hard stones, her dark head bowed to the plaster Madonna, her hands clasped. The sceptic in me couldn't believe it was so much a prayer as a piece of theatre. And whatever it was, in that region where the murderous divisions call themselves ethnic but are really religious, I would not have been surprised to discover in myself a feeling of impatience. But it seemed I'd entered a world of comedy. Maybe, unlike Jadranka, I 'vas meant to be happy' – sometimes, anyway.

Zaton under the big moon was unbelievably beautiful, the fishing boats set in glass, the tables outside the two cafés full of fine handsome people and, by a stroke of luck, a *klapa* group, six male singers in white shirts, dark trousers and embroidered waistcoats, entertaining the village with traditional Croatian songs, sometimes accompanying themselves on mandolins, guitars, zithers, sometimes unaccompanied, always in three- or four-part harmony. The music, passionate, primitive, full of pain and full of hope, was like an indicator of Dalmatia's location – Greek-Italian, or Italian-Greek, between the two, with something of each and something that was neither. Love songs, songs about war, songs about immigration – Ljiljana translated for me. I wrote out the words of one, thinking of the Dalmatians who had come to New Zealand from this beautiful region and climate, and whom too easily we expected to be simply happy, grateful for their good fortune: 'In vain my mother told me / The sea never returns what you give it / Not the people and not the ships. / In vain she told me / In vain she cried / The sea was stronger / And my ship sails tonight.'

For a long time, while we sat drinking, smoking, singing, moon-bathing, Jadranka remained sober. Then, suddenly it seemed, the alcohol won. Helping her home we had to restrain her from diving into the harbour.

A few days later, driving back to Zagreb, she took the route through the Krajina region which she had avoided on the way down. It was as if she had inwardly relented, or ceased to feel defensive, or had decided to trust me. We drove into the town of Knin and stopped for coffee. Where were all the people? There were a few about; but this was an ordinary working day, and it was as if we had gone into Hamilton, or Dunedin (I mean a town of that size) early on a Sunday morning.

'Yes,' Jadranka admitted. 'The Serbs are gone.'

I wanted to know how they had left.

On foot, she said. They had been given the chance to go, and they had gone.

I tried to imagine the scene – the victorious Croatian army, fine young men like the *klapa* singers, but grim, silent, heavily armed, watching as people who had lived there all their lives filed out, carrying what they could, knowing they were leaving their homes and their region for ever.

That was bad enough. It was best not to dwell at all on the worse things that had been done in this region in the name of an independent Croatia – the work of the 'Autumn Rains' unit, for example, whose luckiest Serbian victims, I had heard, were the ones killed with a single bullet to the forehead.

To think like that, putting Croatia in the wrong, was to forget all the wrongs which had brought that action about – all of Serbia's murderous ethnic cleansing, practised against Croat and Muslim alike. But then, did one fact excuse another? – and the fact that confronted me was a once-flourishing town now emptied of the larger part of its population only because they were not Croatian.

All at once I understood more clearly why Jadranka had not wanted me to see certain things, nor to ask certain questions. Laying blame is so easy, especially at a distance. But our history is not of our own making or choosing, and whatever it happens to be we have to live with it and make the best of it.

Trying to be 'philosophical' I said something to the effect that war was, perhaps, only life intensified.

'Intensified?' They didn't understand.

'Sped up,' I suggested. 'The bad things happen faster.' (I was struggling.) 'Sooner.'

'Oh my god,' Ljiljana said, smiling and patting my hand indulgently. 'You're beginning to sound like one of us.'

Postscript, 2007: Clearly some parts of these visits went into my next novel, *Talking about O'Dwyer* (1999). I returned to Croatia in May 2007 for the launch there of *My Name was Judas*, my fourth novel in Croatian, the third translated by Ljiljana and edited by Jadranka. Ljiljana was now living in America, where she had married and I think divorced. After seeing me off at Zagreb airport for my return home, Jadranka received a message that Ljiljana had committed suicide.

Men and Mansfield in *Mansfield**

I had the words 'a novel' added to the title *Mansfield* to make it clear what I was doing; and I put a note at the front to indicate the rules I had set myself. It said:

> None of the characters is invented, and all major events, occasions and relationships are as near to documented 'truth' as I could make them.

But there was also a warning:

> This is a work of fiction, and therefore employs imagination, guesswork and contrivance. Like every historical novel, it fills as best it can – and sometimes also is glad to exploit – gaps in the record.

So if I have done my job as intended nothing in the novel should conflict with what is known. What I was interested in exploring, however, was the area beyond what is known. The biographer takes us up to the limits of what's recorded and verifiable, and, now and then, will speculate beyond: 'We may suppose . . .' 'It is surely probable . . .' 'It seems likely . . .' The fiction writer, on the other hand, has to pretend to *know*. He was *there*, heard what was said, word for word; knew what

---

* A lecture in the series 'Katherine Mansfield's Men', put on by the Katherine Mansfield Birthplace Society, Wellington, in 2004.

at least one of the characters was feeling. Fiction needs 'fact'. It needs the contingent, the circumstantial, the texture of the 'real'.

We all know that this is the difference between fiction and biography; but you have to do the exercise to discover what a large space remains beyond the record for imagination to work in. That was what made it a truly interesting exercise. These were real people, and a very large amount has been written about all of them – in letters, journals, biographies and autobiographies. But what was this or that one feeling at particular important moments in their lives? What did they say to one another? What happened during the minutes, or days, or weeks that went unrecorded?

The other rule I made for myself was that each chapter should be written from inside the head of one character (what's called POV in film-making – point of view) and this would be indicated at the head of the chapter. It would be mostly Katherine's POV; but other's would also be represented. There's one chapter to each of Jack, Leslie, Frieda Lawrence and Dora Carrington; and two to Fred Goodyear. The remaining seven are Katherine's. She of course is present in every chapter. It's her story – but not told solely from her point of view. We see her from the outside as well as from within.

Mansfield is a novel about relationships. It's about Katherine's struggle to find love and companionship; and about her effort to balance the duties and demands of human attachments against the consuming ambition to write what she called 'a new kind of fiction'. That was my subject; and if it was to have density I knew it should not be spread over too many years. That was another way it would differ from biography.

I chose the three years from 1915 to 1918 partly because that was the period in which she began to see her way through to the kind of fiction she aspired to write – a way that would take her back to her New Zealand and family material previously rejected or set aside. Also because she was in reasonably good health during those years (I didn't want to write a novel about a dying woman); and it was the time of her most intense engagement with an extraordinary cast of characters on the English literary scene: John Middleton Murry, D. H. and Frieda Lawrence, Lady Ottoline Morrell, Bertrand Russell, Dora Carrington, T. S. Eliot, Virginia Woolf, Aldous Huxley.

The other hugely important fact for me was that those were war years. At first Katherine behaves as if nothing will be much different. She comes and goes between London and Paris. She pursues her affair with Francis Carco as if the war and its dangers only add the salt of the picturesque to the sugar of romance.

But gradually the darkness and horror of the war close down on her and on her friends. Her beloved brother is killed. Bertrand Russell is engaged in an heroic public campaign against the way in which victory rather than compromise is being pursued, with the consequent huge cost in human life. Fred Goodyear is killed. When she makes what is (in the time scale of the novel) her final dash to the south of France the war has cast its ugly shadow over everything.

As a novelist I find I'm not usually satisfied with having characters in the foreground. This is a temperamental thing, something I've come to recognise in what I write rather than the outcome of a decision or strategy. I like there to be a larger narrative, political, social, historical, going on behind the principal characters, of which they are in some way representative. My characters and their doings are like a sub-plot of a larger history which is not being recounted in detail but is going on there in the background. In this sense *Mansfield* is really a war novel.

My task today is to talk about Katherine's relations with men as they figure in the novel, and I will take four examples, and say something about each, because in each case the way I dealt with the relationship was different from the other three. The four men will be her brother Leslie; John Middleton Murry, with whom she was mostly living during the period the novel covers and whom she married soon after the novel ends; Francis Carco; and Bertrand Russell.

The most delicate subject is the relationship with her brother. It's generally acknowledged that the time they spent together in London before he went to France, and their reminiscing about their childhood and family, gave her the wish to write the New Zealand stories which are commonly said to be her best. His death intensified this wish; she used it almost as a goad to force herself to persist with the story she called first 'The Aloe' and later 'Prelude'. She had promised him she would do this so it had to be done; the method for it had to be found.

What struck me when I looked into the documents was an intensity between brother and sister which seemed to go beyond what you would call a normal sibling love and to have about it even a whiff of incest. The incest taboo is very strong; but I suppose it's less uncommon as a phenomenon between brother and sister, and less absolutely frowned upon, than between father and daughter. It's common in literature and mythology of course. In Wagner's *The Ring* the lovers Siegmund and Sielglinde are brother and sister, and the hero Siegfried is the child of their illicit love. (I can think of only two instances of it in New Zealand writing, but there are probably many more. It occurs as a minor sub-story in my novel *The Secret History of Modernism*; and it's there in Maurice Shadbolt's novella 'Figures in Light'.)

In her journal entries after his death Katherine addresses Leslie directly in her journal entries. Here's a sample: 'Nobody knows how often I am with you . . . I will never be away from you again. You know I can never be Jack's lover again. You have me. You are in my flesh as well as in my soul . . . .' What she asserts there is, at the very least, surprising. You could say it's simply an example of her capacity for extravagance and theatricality on paper – and perhaps it is. But she was extravagant and theatrical in life too. She often acted out her fantasies, urging herself to 'Risk! Risk anything! Care no more for the opinions of others. Act for yourself.'

When I got copies of Leslie's letters from the Turnbull Library, I found one or two expressions of similar intensity – one, for example, in which he tells her that he loves her 'as no other living soul could' and that the relation of their bodies and their minds was 'one of the most beautiful works of God'.

This was a case where I did not want to imagine very far beyond the known facts, but I did want the possibility that seems to lurk in the known facts to be visible. A certain rather difficult tact seemed to be called for. So I wrote a brief scene in London in which Katherine comes in the night and lies down with Leslie after he's gone to bed. There's a strong suggestion of something sexual between them, but it's not clear whether Leslie is dreaming or this is something that happens. That was as far as I was prepared to go. It seemed to acknowledge the peculiar intimacy between the brother and sister without deciding what it meant. It was for the reader to imagine and for the reader to decide.

In a later scene, after Leslie's death, I have her turn to Murry in bed,

135

wanting him, and seem to see her brother lying there. This is derived from an entry in her journal; and I connect it with the writing of the poem, based on a dream, which ends with the dead brother offering her berries and saying, 'These are my body. Sister, take, and eat.'

In the course of my research I made one interesting new discovery. In every biography of Katherine Mansfield you will read that the mortally wounded Leslie's last words were, 'Lift my head Katy, I can't breathe.' The sole source for this is a letter Katherine wrote to her friend Koteliansky. How could she have known what her brother said as he was dying? Well, there is a letter to her from someone who was present, a fellow officer, James Hibbert, and one can see that it's the source for Katherine's account. Hibbert records Leslie repeating 'God forgive me for all I have done', and then saying, 'Lift my head. I can't breathe' – but no 'Katy'. It's quite clear that Katherine added the 'Katy'. She so wanted to believe that her brother's last thought was of her, she simply – and characteristically – made it up! She wrote it in her letter to Koteliansky, and each of her biographers has assumed it must be true!

In the chapter in which Leslie comes to London, stays with Katherine and Jack, goes to France and is killed, I represent him as a rather simple, innocent good-hearted fellow, much less brilliant and sophisticated than his sister. The fact that the chapter is his POV and goes up to the point of his death means that it has to end with the closing-down of consciousness of a wounded and dying soldier:

He was lying on the dry ground staring up at the sky. He could hear nothing but a buzzing shriek, intolerably loud, like a mechanical saw close to his ear. He was aware of himself as if it was another person, another's body. The body was damaged in some way. Beyond repair perhaps. The thought came to him like that; and then the further thought that his mind was still working, so perhaps things were not so bad. He knew he was groaning, couldn't stop himself, but couldn't hear the groans. Heads came in sight looking down at him and then were withdrawn. He tried to move the arm that had held the grenade, could not, and thought possibly it was no longer there. He felt no pain. What he felt was not numbness either; it was a kind of rapid vibration within himself. It was as if he longed for pain but could feel nothing that was appropriate, nothing that was not horrible, terrifying.

He thought he might be dead, and then thought, No, not dead. Dying.

Now there was fear – fear of death, of what might lie beyond. He remembered there were ways of dealing with this. He began to say over and over, 'God forgive me for all I have done. God forgive me for all I have done. God forgive me . . .' Though he could not hear the words he could feel them in his throat and mouth. On his tongue. There was blood there too.

The words – or the blood? – choked him. He found it hard to breathe. He was losing something – losing everything. He needed to breathe. His friend Jamie Hibbert was there, crouching over him. He was speaking but Leslie could not hear him; could hear nothing but that continuous grinding buzz.

'I can't breathe,' he said. 'Lift my head, Jamie.'

He didn't hear his own voice but Jamie must have heard because his head was lifted. He saw better now the men, standing back. That was horror in their eyes. He recognized it. He must look bad. Wrecked. And yes, dying, certainly. Over and beyond their heads he saw leaves, and blue sky. He saw a black dot rising and falling in the blue that must have been the lark. Though he could not hear it, he tried to fix on it, as a test, and to take his mind off this lack of breath.

It became two dots, then four . . .

In some ways the characterisation of John Middleton Murry – Jack – was easy. So much is known about him. I represent him as well-meaning but not really up to the task. She was too brilliant for him to match, and too demanding for him to satisfy. I feel sympathy for him, but also sympathy for her, and understanding of her impatience with him. I think the most revealing chapter about Jack is Chapter Four – not just because it's his POV, but because he's seen here reacting to stress.

This is immediately after Leslie's death and Katherine's behaviour is extreme. She insists a dinner party must go ahead and there's to be no mention that her brother has been killed. She refuses outwardly to grieve or shed tears, while at the same time showing signs of great suffering. She demands they go away from London, yet she won't talk about her brother's death. In fact she hardly talks to Jack at all. It's as if he's to blame. They're travelling together, heading for the south of

France, but they're estranged. Jack begins secretly to read her diaries – something he hasn't done before – and he discovers those things she's writing about her love of Leslie, and about how he, Jack, is not important any more.

We know they went to Bandol together, and that Jack left her alone there with her grief and returned to London – something which Lawrence reproached him for. But what happened between them? This is a case where the novelist has to use his imagination. The tension comes to a head in a scene which is, of course, wholly invented:

Next morning after breakfast they walked in silence. The waves lapped gently at the sea wall. The sun shone and the sea that had been churned up and opaque during the storm was once again clear, concealing nothing. White pebbles, chips of marble, old broken tiles still with traditional patterns as if preserved from Roman times, could be seen bending and stretching under the brightly moving water. They clambered down on to brown shiny rocks at the far end of the bay and walked on, holding on to one another for balance when the ground was uneven. At last they stopped to look away into the distance where sea-blue became sky-blue, a division less and less well-defined as the day warmed and the heat blurred it.

It took Jack courage – or he felt it did – to speak the forbidden name, but at last he came to it: 'Darling, why do we never talk about Leslie?'

She shook her head. 'No, please. I don't want to.'

He persisted. 'Leslie's dead and we're alive. It's sad but it's the fact you have to come to terms with, Tig. We've got to get on with the business of living.'

'No.' She put one hand to her eyes, half-turning away from him, waving the other behind her as if to keep off an attacking dog.

'We do,' he said. 'We must.'

'*We* don't have to do anything. What *you* have to do is your business.'

He adopted a reasoning, caressing tone. 'I know how you're feeling at this moment . . .'

But she turned towards him, eyes cold. 'You know nothing about feelings – mine or anyone's.'

He bridled. 'I'm tired of hearing that. You're the one who seems to lack feeling. You have none for me.'

'Is that your complaint? That I'm neglecting you?'

138

'I think you're behaving extravagantly.'

'You expect me to behave normally when my only brother . . .'

He interrupted her. 'No, no, no. Of course I don't. But we can't go on like this. We'll go mad.'

'I'm mad already. I don't have to *go* mad.'

He was losing his grip on himself. He heard the bitterness in his own voice as he said, 'You ask too much.'

'I ask nothing from you, Jack. Nothing. I don't need you.'

'Katie . . .'

'Don't call me that. That's not your name for me.'

'Oh for heaven's sake! Tig, then. Listen to me. It's Leslie who died. I think you should let him have that all to himself. It's his, not yours.'

'What do you mean?'

'Stop appropriating his death.'

She stared at him. He could see the reproach she wanted to deliver caught up and impeded by the recognition of what he had said – the hard truth of it. And then, as if there was no way out of a trap, like a child denied something she wanted very much, she began to weep. The tears streamed. She reached out to steady herself and he helped her as she sank down to sit on an outcrop of stone that formed a natural seat. All the grief that had been dammed flooded forth. She sobbed. She bent forward over her knees. Her whole body shook.

He had expected this – this weeping. Sooner or later it had to come. And he'd thought that when it did, *then* he would feel a more complete sympathy for her, the kind of pity anyone who lost a dearly loved son or brother in this horrible war deserved. He had been sure that at this moment his love for her, which had seemed frozen during these past days, would surge out to comfort her. But it wasn't happening. Not at all. It was anger he was feeling, anger and jealousy. As her grief was released, so too was his rage. He wanted to beat her.

'Are you going to carry a dead man with you for the rest of your life?' He heard his own voice, cold and harsh. The sound only made him angrier. It was the voice of a man who had right on his side. Was that himself, Jack Murry, confident he'd been wronged? He began to shout: 'Carco was bad enough, but at least he wasn't a corpse.'

She looked up at him, an expression of astonishment recognizable through the wet shine of the tears: 'Carco?'

'Your French soldier-boy. Have you forgotten him? Your cocksure would-be novelist. Your grubby little *amour*?'

She sobbed one more time, like a gasp for breath, looking down at her knees, swallowing and widening her eyes as if gathering her thoughts and her strength. Her inner storm had passed, or was passing. 'At least,' she said, almost casually, 'Francis Carco is fighting for his country.'

'Oh thank you for that! A white feather. My first – and it comes from my wife.'

'I'm not your wife, Jack. Had you forgotten?' She brushed her skirt and stood up. 'And is Carco a would-be novelist? His novel was published – something you have yet to achieve.'

He absorbed that. Shocked by his own moment of rage, he had begun to take control of himself.

After a moment she spoke quietly: 'You were jealous of Leslie.'

'That's nonsense.'

'You don't care if he's dead. Why should you? He was not clever, not literary, not D. H. Lawrence. He hadn't read Dostoevsky. He was nothing to you.'

'For heaven's sake, Tig, stop this. You know what Lawrence would tell you. Stop wallowing in it.'

'What does it matter what Lawrence would say? He doesn't like the war because it's going on without him. What right have all these foolish young fellows to die and take the world's attention away from *him*?'

But these were only words. They didn't any longer come like flaming swords.

The fire had gone out of both of them. Soon they were walking in silence. He felt shame. Did she? Possibly, but he couldn't be sure.

That evening, over their supper in the hotel, they talked. The air had cleared. They were not close, not intimate, but franker than usual. The distance was marked by something faintly formal, an absence of the jokes and verbal nonsense that filled their conversation when they were together and happy. They were calm, almost honest, like two old friends who led, or were about to lead, separate lives.

I think that's probably the only moment in the novel when Jack really asserts himself. She has driven him beyond the end of his tether. Later of course they come together again – and they go on coming together right through to the end. But I think the view the novel implies is of a relationship that might not have endured under normal circumstances. She's questing always, straining at the leash, wanting more of Jack than he can give, looking for alternatives. Lawrence advises her to learn to be alone; to stop seeking always to be 'in love'. She says 'But I want to be in love', and Lawrence says 'Yes and children want sweets'.

Now, an example of another, very different way I went about dealing with one of Katherine's relationships: the case of Bertrand Russell. The writing of her story 'Psychology' coincides pretty closely with the time of her intense friendship with Russell, and I've always assumed that that was its source or provenance. So what I did with one crucial scene between her and Bertie was to read her fiction as if it were fact, and take over the structure and some of the elements of the story and put them into my novel.

'Psychology' is a story about intellectual friends, a man and a woman, who have decided they shouldn't spoil their beautiful mind-relationship with the sordid and complex business of bodies and emotions. But their conversation keeps running into silences, and it becomes obvious that they are flouting their own natures by this prohibition on instinctual behaviour. After one of these gaps in their talk she suggests perhaps he's keen to leave and that she's holding him. He reacts as if he's been told he's outstayed his welcome, and rushes away. When he's gone she has a silent frenzy of regret – and then the doorbell rings. She thinks – and so does the reader – that the friend has come back; but no, it's an elderly, usually unwelcome, lady bringing her a bunch of violets. She hesitates, and then wraps the visitor in an embrace. Clearly, this is what she should have done to the man, and the thwarted impulse has been unleashed on the astonished and delighted old lady. Having released her frustrated feelings in that way, she goes indoors and begins to write him another artificial intellectual letter. The fault in their relationship is to be continued.

The story's title is the clue – 'Psychology'. The incident it describes is a perfect illustration of what the newly fashionable Freudian psychology would have called repression and sublimation.

I took the framework of this story and, using, of course, completely different dialogue – dialogue about the war in fact – I made it happen between Katherine and Bertie Russell; and then I made the visitor – the one who comes to the door and receives an unexpected embrace – her devoted friend and lifelong slave Ida Baker.

Ida was standing on the top step somehow signalling in her expression, and in the way she held herself, that she was already leaving, not there on a visit, had no intention of coming in. [. . .]

Katherine smiled. 'Ida, darling, it's so late.'

'I know, darling. I'm not coming in. I'm staying with . . .' Mumble mumble. There was a name Katherine didn't catch. 'We're just down the road – at the YWCA. I was passing and saw your light. I thought, I *can't* pass without saying goodnight. Is that too foolish, darling?'

Why would she be 'just passing'? She must have come out hoping . . . Snooping . . . Perhaps she'd been lurking in the shadows and had seen Bertie leave . . . Ida wavered there on the top step, cringing from the rejection she fully expected – perhaps even wanted – knowing that Katherine was likely to be at her most brutal when there was a man in her life.

Katherine stepped forward and wrapped her in a hug. 'Of course not, silly thing. Goodnight, darling. Goodnight, dear friend. Now hurry back to Mumble before they lock you out.'

'Oh,' Ida said. '*Oh!*' It was almost too much for her, this kindness, this embrace. She wasn't used to it, certainly not from her 'best friend'.

'Go,' Katherine said, kindly but firmly. She fluttered a hand in the gap, and closed the door.

She stood a moment in the passageway hearing the steps recede. She congratulated herself. The hug had been a *tour de force*. That was how she should have treated Bertie – wrapped arms around him. Smothered the little fellow.

She felt again a surge of pleasure and affection for this famous absurd great man. She went to her desk, took out a sheet of her best notepaper, and sat thinking. She would write as if she'd let a day go by, and wouldn't post it until tomorrow afternoon.

'I meant to write to you immediately after you left me on Friday night to say how sorry I was to have been such cold comfort and so useless to lift even ever so little of the cloud of your fatigue . . .' [Which is indeed how one of Katherine's letters to Bertie begins.]

This then (if my assumption about the provenance of Katherine's story is right) is a case of real life made over by Mansfield into fiction and then taken back by me into faction.

Different again is what I've made of her relationship with Fred Goodyear. This is the one in which I've imagined most and had the fewest documents to go on. The intimacy with Goodyear, as I represent it, and their looking forward to what they might do together after the war, is based on hints that lie in the record; but what I make of those hints is guesswork. Was it really as my novel represents it between her and Goodyear? I don't know. All I can say is that it might have been, and if it was, she was acting in character.

But the Goodyear episodes are very important in maintaining and intensifying the war as the force of history that reaches beyond itself to affect and determine even the characters' emotional lives. Here, for me, the challenge was not simply to invent action and dialogue but even to become Katherine Mansfield writing a long letter to Goodyear – a letter which can't, of course, survive and is therefore lost, blown away with his leg when he falls victim to a shell.

Finally I'm going to look at one further case where so much is already there in the record you might think there was nothing left for the fictional imagination to do. This is the matter of her affair with the French writer Francis Carco. Katherine wrote about it in her notebooks while it was happening; she wrote a story about it, called 'An Indiscreet Journey'; Jack discusses it in his autobiography; and Katherine's biographers recount it. So what is there left to say?

First, what do we know? We know that things were not going well between her and Jack; that Carco was Jack's friend and that she hadn't been especially struck by him when the three of them spent time together in Paris; that the two corresponded and gradually the letters turned into love letters. He was in the French army, not a fighting soldier but postman to a bakery unit. (And it occurs to me that only the French army would have a bakery unit large enough to need a postman.) Not in the trenches, but nonetheless in the war zone, where ordinary citizens from outside the zone were not allowed to go. Between them Carco and Katherine concocted a plan by which she would get through to him and they would spend some days together as lovers.

We know that she got through, that they had their brief affair, that it had its good moments, and that she came back (according to Murry) 'disillusioned', and never spoke of it again. So what happened? What went wrong? Here, even in the midst of something so amply documented, there's a crucial question to be answered – something needing to be 'made real' to the imagination. Here's the crucial scene:

They were in the barn again, their favoured, indeed their only, restaurant ('*sympa*', he called it), where the boy who ran about doing little jobs, and the woman who waited on the tables, and the chef who appeared at the door to the kitchen, late, when the rush was over, all greeted them, on some French principle that three days established a 'regular', with the favoured tone reserved for such customers.

Somewhere between the *plat du jour* and the day's variation on *crème brûlée* that was to follow, she asked did he love her and he said (of course – what else?) that he did.

She asked what it meant and he said it meant she was very dear to him.

But what did *that* mean she asked, and he asked what did it mean to her.

She said it might mean something about the future, and he cast his eyes to the ceiling and sighed.

If he had only sighed – sighed and (for example) looked down at his hands on the table – it would not have mattered; it might have suggested sadness – as if to ask what, in such times as these, could one say about the future? But eyes cast towards the ceiling – that was quite another matter. That spoiled it all; ended the idyll. She could not forgive his eyes – would never forgive them.

'You are bored with me,' she said.

He said he was not, but it was spoken without conviction.

'Your voice,' she said.

'My voice?'

'Bored. Exasperated. I know that voice.'

No. He insisted not.

She said, 'You can tell me the truth. I'm not a child.'

He said, 'A man is what he does. You can see what I am. I am a man who loves you.'

'In the night – in bed.'

'In the night and in the morning and in between.' He smiled very nicely. She should have left it there, but she couldn't. 'Please, Francis . . .'

'These inquisitions,' he said. 'Why do women do it?'

Women. To use that word was a mistake, almost as unforgivable as the eyes cast towards the ceiling. It meant (or so she argued) that for him she had passed already into a category. She was a woman, one of many. One of his women. Yes he was bored.

The quarrel, or debate (because at times it took an intellectual turn) went on through the night. They half made it up, made love (and not half-heartedly – rather well in fact), and returned to it. In its latter hours he dozed in the long intervals when she was talking. Finally he was answering in his sleep.

Next morning she planned to say just one thing to him. It was something that had come to her in the dark, bitter hours of his sleep: 'To me, Carco, you have been a drug, a poison. Fortunately you are also the antidote.'

But – whether because it was unjust, or too studied – in the full light of morning she decided against it and in favour of silence. It was he who spoke. '*Ecoutes*, Kathérine. I am sorry that I have disappointed you. I want to say that you have not disappointed me.'

She'd resolved that she would not speak to him again – not ever; not in this life or the next – if there should be a next, and if they should find themselves in the same place, which she allowed herself to think unlikely. That was how she'd put it to herself as the sun had begun to pick out the flowers on the clock face – and she stuck to it, but with difficulty. 'Your little speech was very charming,' she wanted to say, with heavy irony; but she only thought it – and reproached herself. He had made her a very nice compliment, which almost made up for the fact that he had not fallen in love with her.

Katherine was living the 'free life' and that meant 'free love'. Lacking the pill and antibiotics which protected the new free women of the 1970s and 1980s, she suffered damaging consequences – unintended pregnancies, venereal disease (which in turn lowered her resistance to TB). But one thing that neither the pill nor antibiotics could have protected her from – any more than they protected the new free women of the pre-AIDS era – was falling in love. As I represent her, the adventure with Carco had engaged deeper emotions and this had not been part of the plan. That he had stuck to the plan was what she couldn't forgive. She would take a revenge later by representing her 'little corporal' extremely negatively in her brilliant story, 'Je ne parle pas francais'.

It became fashionable in the 1980s, and to some extent remains fashionable, to refer to Mansfield as 'bi-sexual' – sometimes even as 'lesbian'. Claire Tomalin in her otherwise excellent biography took this line; and in fact the jacket blurb took it further, describing Mansfield as 'bi-sexual, with a husband, a wife, and lovers of both sexes' – a clear and quite extreme distortion of the facts.

Nothing in the record seems to me to justify this view. Prompted partly by her reading of Oscar Wilde, and partly by teenage crushes, she had her early (and surely not unusual) single-sex experiences; but as far as I can see, once the first heterosexual experience had been had, there were no more homosexual ones. My impression is of a person who reacted to every male in her life in some degree sexually. That's why even her brother became, briefly, a 'sex object'. Whether in reality or imagination, when Leslie became intensely important to her he became in effect another lover.

If you compare her letters to women with those she wrote to men, you see at once how differently she related to the male. (Strangely, but perhaps not so strange, Lawrence is the one important male in her life with whom her interactions seem to have been sexually quite neutral.) Her letters to Carco clearly made him think there could be sex – and there was. Her letters to Russell gave that impression. Her letters to Koteliansky seem designed to make him feel their relationship was potentially sexual, even when it wasn't. Even her interactions with strangers could have sexual overtones – and that's how I represent her encounter with the eight Serbian officers at Marseilles on her second visit to Bandol. This is no more to be deplored than the Tomalin view of her would be if it were correct. It's simply a fact of her life and character – one which has been quite severely misrepresented; and I think we should try to get our facts, and our factions, as nearly correct as possible.

Two Parochial Pieces and a Postscript

1. A 'Corridor' for Auckland*

Like the three tenors, our two mayors, Banks and Curtis, sing the same song, though it sounds like something written by a tuneless PR man with little concern that words should mean anything or that facts should be verifiable. In answer to Professor Hazledine's article questioning the $4 billion cost of the proposed Eastern Corridor our mayors claim that 'the benefits to Auckland's economy over time are huge' and will justify the expenditure. These 'benefits' as they describe them, however, are so vague and generalised as to be meaningless: 'an investment for securing sustainable growth'; 'the benefits, including social multipliers, could reach $46 billion'; 'urban transformation and economic development' – these are phrases meant to persuade, but what do they mean in real terms?

The idea that a motorway dressed up as a 'transport corridor' is magically going to send New Zealand up the OECD ladder, and that Auckland therefore has a responsibility to build this dinosaur for the good of the nation – these are catch-cries, without economic or intellectual substance, and not to be taken seriously.

* *New Zealand Herald*, 22 March 2004.

There are many ways of measuring costs. The 'Eastern Corridor' is a proposal (and it should be remembered it is no more than that) which would cost us not only in dollars but in damage. Auckland is a beautiful city, rating high on international surveys. That it attracts tourists is very important. Much more important is that those of us who live in it love the place and want to preserve its attractions for our children and grandchildren. Short of massive aerial bombardment a motorway is the most destructive modern weapon against an urban environment, blocking access on either side, dividing communities, destroying residential housing, waterways, parklands and areas of natural beauty, creating both air and (even worse) noise pollution, and in the long term making worse the traffic problem it is supposed to solve. This latter point cannot be repeated too often, since our civic leaders seem unable to learn the lessons even of very recent history.

I am old enough to remember when Grafton Gully was a piece of charming bushland, with old graves and a stream running down towards the harbour. When it was proposed as the route for a motorway we were assured by the planners that only a thin strip would be taken and that otherwise its natural beauty would be preserved for future generations. It is now a maze of concrete. That is a mistake that can't be undone; but there is no need to repeat it along the waterfront, and through Hobson Bay, the Orakei Basin, and Meadowbank.

Never unwilling to make themselves ridiculous Mayors Banks and Curtis predict 'land value rises'. Are we to expect real estate advertisements reading 'Come and Live by the Motorway!!'? What is most likely in fact is the development of a wide ribbon of low-grade living and industrial degradation, a no-go zone.

Those of us who prefer to use the car (and I include myself) have to be disciplined, or at the very least have to learn the facts of urban life, one of which is that, if you live in a city of a million or more and insist on using your car during rush hours, you must be prepared to spend some time in it going nowhere. If billions of dollars are wasted in an attempt to defeat or disprove this basic fact of modern living, the relief will be short-lived, the cost and the damage enormous, and in a very short time the problem will have recreated itself. There are no exceptions to this rule; but there is a way out – public transport; and that is where, if only we had talented and visionary public leaders, all our efforts would be now be concentrated.

Mayor Banks favours making motorway- and harbour bridge-users pay. That is reasonable, but only if the money gathered goes into public transport. If driving your car is a pleasure at public expense, then it is a pleasure that should be taxed. To make bridge-users pay for the Eastern Corridor would be wrong. To make them pay for a cheaper ferry service, on the other hand, would be fair and reasonable. Similarly, if private cars are taxed for using existing motorways, the money gathered should go to subsidising public transport. Systems of this kind are working in European cities, and now in London.

'We have been around Auckland's incomplete roading network problems for at least 25 years,' the mayors tell us. If that is so they must bear some of the responsibility for the failure to get on with the kind of public transport system that Mayor Robinson was calling for back in the 1960s. Now they are rushing to solve the problem by adding a 'highway' which runs parallel with the existing motorway and eventually converges with it.

One of Auckland's problems in the past has been a centralised bureaucracy in Wellington, run largely by civil servants who saw to the capital's needs before they gave any thought to New Zealand's largest city. It was noticeable a few years back when Auckland had its power crisis that we had four main cables into the city while Wellington had ten. Similarly, the old NZ Railways (though I lament its sale into the hands of asset-strippers) made sure that Wellington had a viable commuter rail service while Auckland's remained relatively undeveloped. These are facts of our city's past that have to be recognised and met. We are a long way behind in the provision of public transport, and should have maximum help from Government in correcting the deficit.

The west coast of North America, which has been through all this before us, offers lessons we should learn from. To the north is Vancouver, a city of sails like Auckland, of a comparable size, with the ocean to the west and the mountains rising behind – a city which has recognised that motorways solve nothing, and that there are values and qualities to be preserved for the future. Vancouver has spent money on public transport, including its excellent skytrain services, and is reaping the benefits.

To the south is Los Angeles which preserves a few havens of comfort and beauty for the rich (Santa Monica, Brentwood, Beverly Hills, Bel Air) and is otherwise a network of clogged motorways with their attendant smog, low-grade commerce, dingy housing and industrial wastelands.

These are the futures Auckland must choose between. Our two mayors are pointing us in the wrong direction.

Postscript (and salutary lesson): Mayor Banks was defeated at the next election, and Mayor Curtis's majority was shaved to within an inch of its life. Although Banks was re-elected mayor in 2007, it was on a promise that the plan for the Eastern Corridor motorway would not be revived.

2. Our 'Arts Capital' and What it Costs Us*

When I hear that Wellington is the 'Arts Capital of New Zealand' my response is to ask how, given the disproportion of public money that Wellington's arts community receives, could it be otherwise. This is a matter the new Government should give urgent attention; but it will have to be approached rationally, and probably slowly.

Blind local loyalty and naked competition won't help us sort out the problem. There is, however, one indisputable fact. More New Zealanders have chosen, and continue to choose, to live in Auckland than anywhere else; but because Wellington is the capital, all the major arts institutions are located there, as are the funding bodies. That's where the cake is divided; and that's where the largest slice of it is eaten.

The New Zealand Symphony Orchestra has a history which illustrates the problem. It was founded after the Second World War, when our total population was one and a half million. It was our first, and at the time our only, orchestra – 'the *national* orchestra' – and a significant

* *New Zealand Herald*, 2 February 2000.

part of its work was to tour the country bringing great music to the nation.

It made perfect sense then; it makes none now. Yet the orchestra still sits in Wellington providing great music to Wellingtonians and touring only enough to justify or excuse the huge input of Government money that keeps it going. Meanwhile the Auckland Philharmonia (now, I believe, New Zealand's finest) and other regional orchestras struggle to survive.

The NZSO is an anachronism. As one who has subscribed to it for forty years, and has had immense enjoyment listening to it, I acknowledge this reluctantly. But how long can such a historical anomaly be allowed to persist?

I am not suggesting that it should be disbanded, or take a sudden and possibly lethal cut in funds. What is needed is a long-term plan which will slowly redistribute Government support for orchestras, bringing it into line with the size of the population served and the size of audiences that are attracted to listen. Probably there should be one orchestra in each of the major cities, perhaps with some extra subsidy to offer concerts in surrounding regions. This could be achieved over a five-, or if necessary a ten-, year period. There is no need to rush it; but a policy needs to be declared and a movement in that direction begun.

For our national museum there is not the same historical excuse. Nor is there the defence of excellence that can be applied to the NZSO. Te Papa* is visually distressing, governed by a commitment to populism which springs from a fear that large expenditures can't be justified where there is any hint of 'élitism'. It is a monument to the vanity of politicians who promoted it and the intellectual shallowness of those who planned and run it.

Recently I visited the newly refurbished Auckland Museum, not having seen it for several years. Here is an institution which has brought itself into the new century without compromising its serious purpose of informing us about the space we occupy; one which manages at once to be entertaining and educative, and which is everywhere tasteful and pleasing to the eye.

---

* Said in the *New Zealand Herald* on 20 October 2006 to have cost the nation $394 million.

Yet it is the Wellington institution which takes huge amounts of Government money to run and is asking for more, while Aucklanders have very largely paid for their own museum and continue now to pay at the door.

Again it seems to me a long-term plan is needed. Te Papa should be gradually made over as a gift from us all to the city of Wellington, which is said to be 'absolutely positively' proud of it. Thereafter as an institution it should get its share of Government money, as should the other major city art galleries and museums around the country – but no more than its share. It should either cease to be a national museum, or become only one of several.

This picture of disproportionate funding is repeated right across the arts. A few years ago writer Stevan Eldred-Grigg published a study of grants to writers over some years by Creative New Zealand which revealed that those based in Wellington had a considerable, and on the face of it an inexplicable, advantage.

Last year I accepted appointment to the Board of Creative New Zealand (I resigned after one meeting) and was astonished, going through the papers for the meeting, to see how much more money had gone in one year to theatre productions in Wellington than to theatres in other centres. The disparity was breath-taking. After I resigned from the Board I wrote asking for statistics, which I know exist, showing the proportions of arts funding to the various regions. My request, though made several times, received no reply, and it's clear this is a set of facts Creative New Zealand would prefer remained hidden.

Helen Clark's dual role as Prime Minister and Minister for the Arts, her appointment of Judith Tizard to keep a watch on Auckland's interests, and her own commitment to what she called her own region, seemed to give some hope that these matters might begin to be corrected. Despite my huge respect for Ms Clark I can't see any sign that change is happening, and I think now that unless the push comes direct from Aucklanders, it won't happen.

Because Wellington is the capital its citizens know where to go, which doors to hammer on, and that, in dealing with politicians, a lot of noise is likely to produce a response. Also, the civil servants who advise ministers are themselves Wellingtonians with local loyalties.

If we don't, here in Auckland, begin to clamour and complain, demanding that some serious movement towards a fairer sharing of arts money should begin, there will be only cosmetic changes. The long-established inequities will continue.

3. A Brief Postscript, September 2006

In his reply to this article in the same newspaper, Peter Biggs, at that time chairman of Creative New Zealand, seemed uncertain whether he was defending Creative New Zealand or the city of Wellington. On the one hand he seemed to say that Wellington didn't get more than its share; on the other hand that it did because (or when it did it was because) more 'arts' went on there, and rightly, because 'after all it is the capital city and the seat of Government'.

My concern was not only with Creative New Zealand but with the larger picture. Government arts funding might almost be said to come in two blocks. There is funding for the whole country, of which Wellington gets more (sometimes grossly more) than its fair share. And then there is additional funding for Wellington as 'the Capital'. Under the latter heading come the NZSO, Te Papa, the Royal New Zealand Ballet, and a good deal else, largely administrative. This adds up to a massive disproportion, and one which I was arguing the new Government (as it then was) should give serious thought to. This has not happened.

I still have the notes I made as I went through my papers in preparation for a meeting of the Arts Council in March 1999,* where I noticed, for example, that Council spending on the theatre in the previous year was as follows:

Auckland	$390,000
Wellington	$1,154,000
Christchurch	$556,000
Dunedin	$340,000
Palmerston North	$290,000

* See the journal entry for 1 October 2006, pp. 330–2, on this subject.

The difficulties of dealing with the problem would have been considerable, because of a genuine (and often hurt) incomprehension that emerges from Wellington as soon as these delicate matters are raised. I have vivid recollections of the problems faced by a group of Auckland writers when we began the effort, ultimately successful, to make NZPEN (now the New Zealand Society of Authors) a genuinely national body, rather than a club of Wellington writers lobbying Government principally on behalf of themselves, though in the name of the nation. The officers of that body were elected in Wellington and all its decisions were made there; and the moves to open local branches and to require the national body to listen to them were resented and resisted.

The Institute of Economic Research has recently calculated that Aucklanders pay $3.8 billion more in taxes than they receive back in Government expenditure. While it's inevitable that a city the size of Auckland will pay more than it receives, this disproportion seems excessive, indeed extraordinary, amounting, one commentator calculated, to an annual donation of $5823 by every working Auck-lander – quite the reverse of the popular notion south of the Bombay Hills that Auckland is in some way a drain on the rest of the country. The region, with 34% of the population, pays 35% of the Government's revenue, and receives back 31% – and this disparity is repeated in every aspect of our lives, including (my special interest) the arts.

I note that the NZSO's prospectus for 2007, just released, offers eighteen subscription concerts to Wellington, sixteen to Auckland, seven to Christchurch, and assorted smaller numbers around the rest of the country. How are these figures explained or justified? It is hardly value for the huge subsidy given to the orchestra, while the APO continues to be starved. Once again I ask the question: why should this outdated concept of a 'national orchestra' persist?

As for Te Papa: a few years back Brian Rudman wrote in the *New Zealand Herald*: 'Te Papa in its first year, just ended, after allowing for depreciation lost $1.7 million. It plans to do even worse over the next year, and the next, and the next. Over this period it is forecasting losses of $4.7 million, $5.17 million, and $6.99 million. That's after allowing for $8.4 million in depreciation in each of these years. [. . .] It makes you wonder what the Government is playing at. At the same time as it

154

is insisting that every local authority account for the true costs of any project it enters into, it is sticking its head deep into the sand over the real costs of its own great and expensive cultural extravagance. [. . .]

'This Disneyland approach Te Papa has adopted will require constant and expensive renewal.'

As, indeed, it has, and does, and we Aucklanders shrug and go sailing.

Christianity and Culture*

LQ Symposium invited eight writers to comment on the following passage from T. S. Eliot's *Notes towards the definition of a culture*: 'I do not believe that the culture of Europe could survive the complete disappearance of the Christian Faith. If Christianity goes, the whole of our culture goes.'

'If it is true,' LQ asked, 'more than half a century after Eliot's misgiving, that the Christian Faith is indeed disappearing from many parts of Europe, what are the most serious implications for European culture?'

The 'complete disappearance of the Christian Faith' seems improbable, even so many years after Eliot made these remarks; but a lessening of its hold on the European mind has occurred and will surely continue. Science has progressively eroded its literal foundations, leaving it an insecure metaphorical or symbolic story with a psychological or therapeutic function and little or no rational base. The human capacity for irrational belief (usually as a form of comfort in the face of death) is the weaker side of the creative imagination, and will persist; but as the Christian church loses intellectual respectability and social privilege, that capacity can be seen taking new forms and new directions,

* *Leviathan Quarterly*, no. 3, March 2002.

while Christianity itself, forced to be tolerant of variations, becomes fragmented and diluted.

These changes are only aspects of larger developments within Western culture, which has a broader base and much longer history than Christianity, and will continue with or without it. Christianity has played a part – often not a creditable one – in the history of the culture; but the statement 'If Christianity goes the whole culture goes' is absurd. It is just one of many examples of Eliot's personal anxieties projected out upon society at large.

I can see no 'serious implications' for European culture in this – or none that is gravely negative; certainly none that compares, for example, with problems of over-population, or with the difficulty of bringing our genetically inherited tendency to territorial self-protection into line with our technological ability to kill one another in ever-larger numbers. The developments that gave poor Tom Eliot such anxiety were, and are, simply part of the on-going cultural history of the human race, and might even, without too much risk, be called 'Progress'. Human societies are on the whole better off without false faiths and their accompanying prejudices, discriminations, repressions, hypocrisies and ineffective rituals of propitiation.

Letter from New Zealand*

In New Zealand (as in Ireland) anything, even the weather, can get tangled in politics, and a large part of politics here involves race.

Our millennium celebrations ('beamed to the world' we'd been promised, as no doubt most of the world had been promised theirs would be) were disturbed if not ruined by La Niña, the weather pattern which (I think) follows El Niño – the same warm winds and wet squalls which, as I write, are giving the challengers for the America's Cup a hard time in the waters of the Hauraki Gulf. At Waitangi, where in 1840 the treaty was signed by which Maori ceded sovereignty or (depending on who is reading it) governorship to the Crown, a waka (large war canoe) went aground on rocks in rough weather. There were women and children on board as well as the warrior paddlers, practising for the millennium. No one was drowned, but there was an embarrassing rescue, involving police and helicopters.

A few days later a smaller waka was overturned in bad weather on Lake Rotorua. The rescue boat tried to save the waka, and left the men to swim to an island. One, an asthmatic, drowned. It emerged later that the paddlers were Maori prison inmates learning Maori custom and culture, a programme (of which there are a number) intended to build a sense of identity and self esteem.

* *Areté* (Oxford), Spring–Summer 2000.

Public argument followed. New Zealanders spend a lot of leisure time on and in the seas and rivers. In a country where almost everyone learns to swim, and to be confident in the water, there is inevitably a disproportionately high rate of drownings. It was argued that life-jackets, like seat belts in cars, should not just be recommended; they should be required by law.

Maori hui (meetings) followed and the idea was rejected as far as waka were concerned – and one could see why. It was a matter of appearance, and in that it seemed to characterise a lot of the Maori element that permeates our lives. Those ceremonial waka are carved with steel, not stone, tools. The smaller Rotorua one had a fibre-glass hull. The warriors wear underpants beneath their grass skirts. Their moko (facial tattoo) is, with a very few exceptions, painted on and washed off. They speak to one another in English, which in almost every case is their first, and in most their only, language. But put an orange life-jacket around the shivering office-pallor warrior torso and the illusion that this is a genuine cultural survival rather than 'dressing up' is destroyed. If what has become in recent years our way of dealing with these problems is adhered to, we will very likely have a law about life-jackets in boats which will exempt ceremonial waka, but with an understanding that children will be excluded. It's not a bad sort of compromise. Yet all the time one wants to be allowed to say, 'We're pretending, of course.'

I did say it some years ago in what I considered to be my own domain: poetry. Reviewing *The Penguin Book of New Zealand Verse* edited by Ian Wedde and Harvey McQueen in 1985 I said that the inclusion of poems in Maori by two editors who didn't know the language was a wishful rather than truthful representation of our literary history. I also quoted some of the translations provided, which were banal in the extreme, and remarked:

> It may be that the Maori behind these verses is fine, noble, striking, inventive or beautiful. If it is, the translations haven't done justice to the originals. On the other hand, if the translations match the quality of the originals, then they might be better left unexposed to the comparison. Either way the loss is to the mana of Maori.

This was construed as an attack on Maori language, Maori culture, Maori; and Michael King, historian and biographer, joining the chorus of disapproval, accused me of advocating 'the ethnic cleansing of New Zealand literature'.

King had been somewhat provoked. He was in those days a solemn purveyor of the complete liberal package – as I tended to be myself, except that, like the bored child in the classroom, I found myself occasionally erupting in rebellion when Virtue went too long unchallenged. King had written somewhere about New Zealand's Old Boy network. I had responded in a column suggesting that he represented the Good Boy network which had replaced it.

King had made himself expert in Maori matters; had written biographies of two notable Maori women, Princess Te Puea, and Whina Cooper; also the text for a book of photographs of old Maori women whose faces still bore the genuine moko; and an autobiography, *Being Pakeha: An Encounter with New Zealand and the Maori Renaissance*. More recently he has turned to literary biography, first of Frank Sargeson, and now of Janet Frame; and since I and my letters figure in both, he and I have got used to dealing with one another. There has been a wary closing of the gap.

King's dealings with Maori have not all been plain sailing. In 1989 he published a book on the almost forbidden subject of the Moriori – the people who occupied what are now called the Chatham Islands, 600 miles east (and now a part) of New Zealand. In 1835 a Maori tribe, the Te Ati Awa, displaced from their favoured homeland region by warfare with a tribe from the Waikato region, decided to take the Chathams. They either forced or bribed the captain of a British ship (he claimed afterwards his ship had been taken over by them) to sail them there in two batches. The local population, the Moriori, who had no tradition of warfare, and indeed a protocol against it, were dispossessed. Hundreds were murdered and eaten straight away; the remainder were made slaves, forbidden to use their own language, worked to death, starved, beaten, traded or killed at will – a situation which remained unchanged for twenty years, during which most of the surviving Moriori died out.

The facts are not disputed; but King's making them widely known was frowned upon by some of the Maori who had previously considered him an ally. When our recently completed Museum of New Zealand, Te Papa, opened and it was noticed that its Moriori display omitted all mention of the massacre, four professional historians (King was not one of them) wrote complaining.

'The truth of this event is not in question,' they wrote, 'and its relevance to contemporary affairs in the Balkans and Rwanda is painfully obvious.' They went on to point out that the museum's manager, challenged about the omission, had said that a revelation of the truth would constitute 'a return to a view of history which has overtones of racism'. This, the historians remarked, was tantamount to saying that 'it was "racist" to reveal truths which show Maori in a bad light'.

Towards the end of last year King gave a lecture in which he cited this and other omissions, and argued that Maori history had sometimes been less scrupulous than Pakeha history, and that the standard of scholarship should be the same for both. He mentioned in particular a recent tendency to introduce New Age ideas into the treatment of Maori history, denying current scholarship which holds that Maori have been here for less than one thousand years, and positing instead an ancient race still possessors of secret knowledge 'hidden in the land, in the trees and in the stones'. He quoted from a Maori student's examination answer in a course he taught at the University of the Waikato:

> Though you have taught that Maori were migrants to this country, I
> and my iwi [tribe] do not accept your bullshit. According to my tipuna
> [grandparent/s] my nation were always here and no amount of talking or
> writing or publication on your part is going to convince me otherwise.

What King was exposing here is the kind of self-serving mythologising that begins to replace fact when the race who are the object of study see themselves only as victims. Whatever they say about themselves goes, and it's all good. Furthermore, others should not represent them without permission and a vetting of what is said.

King's lecture was given in the Waikato, heartland of a tribe which has recently received $170 million cash and several large parcels of Crown land in recompense for land confiscated after the tribe went to war with the Crown in the 1860s – money and property which the tribe are, it seems, at least for the moment, squandering and mismanaging. The lecture was greeted by a Maori walkout.*

King rang me afterwards to tell me what had happened. We agreed that we live in interesting times.

But some elements of Maori culture do survive in New Zealand society and we are the better for them.

Last year my older sister died. She had been progressively disabled by multiple sclerosis, and the death was an occasion for relief as well as great sadness. In the final hours she was unconscious, but the struggle for breath, a protracted and terrible death rattle, was hard to watch, even harder to listen to. One of her daughters is married to a Maori and he insisted that the grandchildren should be called to the bedside. The rest of us were doubtful, perhaps secretly appalled, but it soon became apparent that we were wrong. It was distressing to be there, but not more so for the children than for the adults, and if we could take it, so could they – and they did.

After the death she was taken to her son's house. His partner is also Maori, and Maori protocol prevailed. The family were expected to spend time with the body. I called at the local school where my son and daughter were each picking up their two children. Told where we were all going, my oldest grandson, aged nine, let out a histrionic wail, put his hand to his brow, and said 'I don't want to see a dead body. It'll ruin my day.' He was told he didn't have a choice.

On the front veranda of the house in South Auckland we all re-moved our shoes and went in. My dead sister was laid out in her coffin, surrounded by photographs and mementos of her life. The life of the household went on around her. We talked across her, one of her daughters sometimes stroking her brow, or even speaking to her, as the conversation went on. The children stared at first in awed silence, until their eyes began to stray towards the television. I have never known a death in the family which was so normalised, so absorbed

---

* The lecture, 'A Fraction too much Fiction', can be found in King's *Tread Softly, For You Tread on My Life* (Cape Catley, Auckland, 2001), where the walkout is mentioned. The same book, p. 116, records the protest by four professional historians at Te Papa's refusal to mention the genocide of the Moriori by Te Ati Awa in their Moriori display.

into full consciousness and acceptance. There was nothing dark and mysterious about it. It was sad, and it was appropriate.

Almost twenty years ago a gang of four at Auckland University – the historian Keith (later Sir Keith) Sinclair; a young political science lecturer, Helen Clark; a secretary, Joan Anderton; and I – used to play badminton together. Keith is now dead; and Joan, divorced from Jim Anderton who is our new Deputy Prime Minister, is an assistant to Helen, who is our new Prime Minister.

Among the many political repair jobs Helen Clark had to achieve to get Labour back into a winning position was to regain the confidence of Maori voters. That puts her in the position of being in some degree beholden to the largest and strongest single pressure group in the country. It is not an easy position to be in; but I have enormous faith in Helen Clark. She is, I think, the best educated, the most sophisticated, the most lucid and intelligent person to have held the post in my lifetime. She is thoroughly professional; and she has a heart.

As for that Old Boy network that gave King and others such anxiety: in a country where the Prime Minister, the Leader of the Opposition, and the Chief Justice are all currently women . . .

Part Two Third Person

Michael King's History
of New Zealand*

If it were possible to subtract the Maori element from New Zealand history then the story would be remarkable only in an entirely unremarkable way, offering yet another illustration of the human capacity for hard work, optimism, endurance, adaptability and (on the whole) triumph against odds. It's a very British story, though with a slightly larger proportion of Celt than in the United Kingdom. The hard work (principally turning forests into farmland) brought affluence, especially after the invention of refrigeration. It has also been recognised more recently that it did ecological damage. Topsoil is washed away; fertilisers promote weeds which choke lakes and rivers; our grazing herds (Michael King notes) produce animal wastes equivalent to a human population of 150 million, and animal flatulence contributes to global warming on the scale of industrial cities. But problems of that kind are only a challenge to further adaptation; and Britain did its reluctant-to-cut-loose child a favour when she went into the EC and forced New Zealand to diversify the uses made of farmland and to discover new markets in unlikely places. For a New

* *Times Literary Supplement*, 11 June 2004. This was written while King was still alive, and appeared after his death in a car accident. A few words were added to acknowledge his death.

Zealander of my generation, who once carried a passport that said 'British Subject, New Zealand citizen', there was in the 1980s no more salutary reminder of where we now stood than to wait at Heathrow in the long line of 'Others' while former Luftwaffe pilots went straight through on their EC passports. New Zealand was now where, as a young 'intellectual' in the 1950s, descendant of settlers who arrived in the 1830s, I had argued it ought to be – independent and self-directed; yet by education and profession I was culturally much more closely aligned to British ways and mores than those New Zealanders whose mindless loyalty to the British Crown I had found embarrassing and demeaning. These were, I suppose, standard ironies and contradictions of a transition from colonial to post-colonial.

That queue at Heathrow also represented what I think was the largest single alteration to New Zealanders' view of themselves. The settlers who travelled three and more months to reach their new home felt they had truly gone to the end of the earth, and for most there was no way back. They had gone to escape poverty, urban squalor, constricted lives and the limitations of the class system. Most had few regrets. But there was, nonetheless, a sense of being cut off, remote, isolated. Our nearest neighbour was 1200 miles away; and the 'real' world, where 'important' things happened, was unattainably distant. Many of the men who volunteered for one or other of the world wars did so partly because it was a way of experiencing what was otherwise, for ordinary working people, unreachable. Even as late as the 1950s, when modern liners took almost five weeks to reach the UK, the sense of remoteness persisted. Now one can fly Auckland – Los Angeles – London (or the other way, via Singapore or Hong Kong) in just 24 hours, and airfares are relatively cheap. This, together with fast phone and e-mail services, has made a profound difference to the feel of life in New Zealand. It is no longer just the affluent who travel. Most young New Zealanders have their period of 'OE' (overseas experience); none has that sense of appalling distances which sea travel used to instil.

Post-Second World War transitions also meant a switch in defence and foreign policy – from New Zealand as loyal British family member to New Zealand as Uncle Sam's Little Helper in the Pacific. In the war our troops had fought on bravely in Greece, Crete and the Middle East, and then all the way up the Italian peninsula, while the Japanese were inching down the Pacific towards us. New Zealand in those years had been defended, not by the Royal Navy, whose claim to maritime supremacy had proved to be just another empty imperial boast, but by the US army, navy and marines. So when the post-war call came for troops, first to Korea, then to Vietnam, we sent some, but (unlike the Australians who were conscripted in large numbers) only a few regular force volunteers, offered by a Government that never sounded entirely convinced of the need. After Vietnam New Zealand began to show real independence. We declared ourselves 'nuclear free', excluding both British and American warships from our waters if they were nuclear powered or nuclear armed. In the past two decades we have withstood repeated complaints from Australia at our refusal to arm ourselves in ways that would suit our larger neighbour's defence plans; and, most recently, New Zealand has refused to be part of the 'Coalition of the Willing' in Iraq. It is not certain that this degree of independence will be sustained; but there is a reasonable hope that it will. The nuclear-free policy, for example, which came in under a Labour Government, proved so popular that the National (Conservative) Party, which had opposed it, felt unable to remove it when it became the Government in the 1990s. And probably nothing helps to sustain this independence more than to have, as now, a US president manifestly ill-equipped for the job, and a British Prime Minister inexplicably compliant to his whims.

New Zealand has also earned, over the past 150 years, a reputation, partly deserved, for liberal social policies. On the basis that Maori land is held collectively, all Maori men had the vote by 1867 while Pakeha had to qualify by owning land as individuals. The vote became universal in 1893 – the first modern state to give votes to women, as it was among the first in which women graduated from universities. (In recent years, and in varying combinations, our Prime Minister, Leader of the Opposition, Attorney General, Chief Justice, Governor-General, and mayors of our four largest cities have all been women.) Unionism was encouraged by the Liberal Government as early as the 1890s, and an old age pension introduced. By 1935 Labour was the dominant political force, became the Government, and was able to introduce a full Welfare State. This was the period (it didn't last) when New Zealand was called 'the social laboratory of the world'.

National ruled for most of the 1960s and 1970s, but introduced nothing new, made no radical changes to the order of things established under Labour. By 1984, when a new Labour Government was elected, the country had dropped some way down the OECD economic table and was mired in regulations, controls and subsidies. So it was Labour which turned us back in the opposite direction, towards the then fashionable forms of Friedmanite monetarism. This produced at first a feeling of liberation. The effect, King writes, was 'to reduce inflation dramatically, bring down national debt and increase economic growth'. Unfortunately a great deal of the 'family silver' was also sold off, and remains unrecoverably and profitably in private (usually foreign) ownership. New Zealand's most remarkable reform of this period, following a referendum, was the change of the electoral system inherited from Britain to MMP – a mixed member proportional system based on the German model. At present, under this system, we have a Labour-dominated coalition led by Helen Clark, a popular leader and I think our most intelligent and capable Prime Minister since the Second World War.

That is how it seems if you leave out the Maori element which is, however, the most complex, intractable, interesting and on-going part of the story, and the part Michael King, a Pakeha, biographer of two Maori leaders, who has learned Maori language and custom, is well-qualified to deal with.

Prior to eighteenth-century European discovery, the country now called New Zealand had been, to its settler-occupants, their whole world, beyond which there were only mythical places and beings. There is no evidence of human habitation earlier than 1350; but where they had come from (eastern Polynesia) had receded into mythology – a homeland called Hawaiiki, to which the way back, if it had ever been known, was forgotten. Since there was no one else in the world but themselves they had individual and tribal, but no collective, identity. The word Maori meant normal, ordinary, and did not take on its present racial meaning until some time after the arrival of Europeans. Similarly there was no word for the country as a whole (Aotearoa is a recent adoption), since the country was the known world. There were no native land mammals apart from bats, and the islanders had soon wiped out several species of flightless birds and of seals, and had burned off a great deal of the southern island's forest. They remained quite well supplied with protein (fish and birds), but extremely poor in fruit and vegetables, and in fact could not have survived but for the sweet potato brought from Polynesia which, King says, grew only to the size of a human finger.

The tribes fought wars with one another, had no projectile weapons, only clubs and spears, took no prisoners except as slaves, and usually cooked and ate the enemy dead. At times (King notes) whole tribes were expunged and their oral record died with them. Life was short (few lived beyond their late thirties), ruled by mana, tapu (sacred proscriptions, taboo) and utu – the latter, the restoration of a balance of mana, meaning, most often, simply revenge. They had no wheel, no method of casting metals nor even of baking earthenware, no written language; and their inter-tribal meetings were governed by ferocious challenges, of which the haka was a part. These ceremonial 'welcomes' on to the tribal marae, protracted while the peaceful intent of the visitor is gauged and accepted, are among the torments we inflict on official visitors to New Zealand – necessarily – in the name of good race relations.

There is a present tendency to romanticise pre-European Maori life, but current knowledge as King summarises it suggests rather (though he doesn't say this, or spell it out) that the Maori were a Polynesian race who were hanging on with some difficulty in colder latitudes. Their total population at the time of Cook's visits is thought to have been around 100,000, and this number was reduced by at least twenty thousand during the 'Musket Wars' – the intertribal slaughter that followed the acquisition of European weapons.

In 1840 the British Colonial Office, prompted by concern at the colonising intentions of Edward Gibbon Wakefield's New Zealand Company, appointed William Hobson Lieutenant-Governor with instruction to negotiate the transfer of sovereignty from Maori, as indigenous owner-occupiers, to the Crown. A treaty was drawn up in English, and Hobson called as many tribal leaders together as it was possible to draw to Waitangi in the Bay of Islands where there were already European missionaries and settlers. The treaty was hastily and imperfectly translated into Maori, debated throughout one day and on the next, as rain began to fall and food was running out, was signed by the chiefs, each of whom received a blanket before departing. (It has always seemed to me fitting that the Governor, who had been mistaken about the arrangements and had to arrive in haste for the signings, wore informal clothes but put on his ceremonial hat.) Later the document was hawked around the country for more signatures; and then, before the South Island had been covered, and as the French showed signs of interest in a claim of their own, New Zealand was declared a British colony.

It is not surprising that this ramshackle document, the Treaty of Waitangi, an ambiguous agreement between Maori and the British Crown in which European settlers had no role and no voice, was declared by one judge in the late nineteenth century 'a legal nullity'. It is not surprising either that by the end of the twentieth century, it had been resurrected as a sacred covenant between Maori and Pakeha, our nation's 'founding document', the seal of a 'partnership'. That the Treaty means one thing to Maori (that they have special status and rights) and another to conservative-minded Pakeha (that all New Zealanders have equal rights) rather reduces the force those engaged in this revival process want it to have; but the Treaty has become a fact of our lives, a necessary piety to be observed and, more than that, something stitched into recent legislation requiring, often, consultation of 'Maori interests' as distinct from simply 'public interests'.

New Zealand does not have a bad history, as such histories go, in dealings between indigenous people and settler descendants. But whatever those chiefs understood by the treaty they put their marks to, one thing seems certain: they had welcomed Europeans for their trade, their tools (including guns), and their technology, but surely cannot have envisaged settlement on the scale that was to occur. There was, and there is still, plenty of land (New Zealand is roughly the size of the British Isles and has now four million people); but an invasion on tip-toe was about to happen, and the Maori must soon have felt they were being swamped. By the 1860s some tribes showed signs of resisting; but there was not a Maori nation that could speak or act with one voice. When one tribe opposed, another took the Pakeha side. They could win battles but never the war. And in addition, European diseases, to which they had poor resistance, were killing large numbers. By late in the century the Maori were being described (wrongly) as 'a dying race'.

King doesn't avert his eyes from the damage, but prefers to stress the positives. The Maori population has increased and in recent years there has been what is referred to as a Maori renaissance – a reassertion of pride, language and culture. But the fact remains that, considered collectively, they have taken a huge hit and are still at the wrong end of most social statistics: health, education, employment, crime. Improvements are being made. The Waitangi Tribunal, set up in 1975, has sat in more or less permanent session, hearing (largely unchallenged by the Crown) claims for compensation for past wrongs. Large payments have been made to individual tribes ($170 million to Tainui, the same to Ngai Tahu). Maori collectively have been awarded rights to, and returns on, 20 per cent of the country's huge fishing industry. There is acknowledgement of customary rights exclusive to Maori; there are positive discriminations, special scholarships, Maori health initiatives, 'cultural safety' courses, re-education programmes for puzzled, uncomprehending or otherwise reluctant Pakeha. Out of all this is emerging a Maori middle class who sometimes seem, however, as indifferent as their Pakeha counterparts to that significant percentage of Maori who remain fixed at the bottom of the heap.

One of the difficulties is simply the question one is not supposed to ask, but in a society with so much intermarriage is in the end unavoidable: what is a Maori? I have Maori (it is considered insulting to say 'part-Maori') nieces who have special rights and no more need of them than my Pakeha nieces. 'Logically' that is wrong, and easy for a politician like the current leader of the National Party, Dr Don Brash, to exploit. Yet the outcome of these policies does, over all and over time, seem to be very slowly correcting imbalances – and in the meantime we are not harming one another or coming to blows. Perhaps Andrew Marvell's wisdom is relevant: 'For Men may spare their pains where Nature is at work, and the world will not go the faster for our driving'.

The Hoaxers Hoaxed

Ern Malley's Poems*

Ern Malley's collected poems, sixteen of them, were concocted in Sydney in 1943 by James McAuley and Harold Stewart and accepted for publication by Max Harris, editor of *Angry Penguins*. There have been, and continue to be, two opposite views of them: (1) that they were worthless, and therefore an entirely successful hoax exposing the folly and self-deception of poetic Modernism in the 1940s; (2) that McAuley and Stewart, in writing Modernist pastiche, liberated a brilliance not otherwise apparent in their work, and thus that the hoaxers hoaxed themselves. Though I don't accept either of these views unqualified, I lean towards the second.

If you read the Malley poems straight through you will most likely, despite moments of admiration for their shafts of careless brilliance, wonder how Harris and his associates could have failed to notice the dead patches and the fakery. But it has to be remembered how much the poems were of their fashion and time, and how lines and whole poems from magazines of the 1940s, including some by deservedly established poets like Dylan Thomas and George Barker, looked back

* A review in the *London Magazine*, June–July 1995, of *The Ern Malley Affair* by Michael Heyward (University of Queensland Press, Brisbane/Faber and Faber, London, 1993).

at now can strike one similarly. Fashion is something we are all partly deceived by all of the time.

Also relevant is the fact that these poems came to Harris from a person claiming to be the poet's sister, and reporting that Ern had recently died aged 25. Recognising extraordinary talent in the poems, as Harris rightly did, it would surely have seemed churlish to pick and choose among a small body of work which the young man, pronounced incurably ill, had stoically prepared for posthumous publication. Harris was hoaxed as much by the fiction surrounding the poems as by the poems themselves.

The Ern Malley story, well-told as it is here, reveals truths about personalities and facts about current Australian cultural life. Under the pressure of the revelation that he had been deceived, and the subsequent absurdity of a criminal trial for publishing obscene work, Max Harris emerged as a young man of quite unusual courage and strength. He insisted on taking full responsibility for the decision to publish; and he stood up well to public ridicule, as he did to days of cross-examination in the court, where the criminality of the poems appeared to lie more in their lack of clear meaning than in their 'obscenity'. Yet when it was all over he seems to have collapsed. His confidence in himself was deeply shaken. A literary career which had had a very promising beginning came to a premature end. Harris acquired a new and lifelong identity as the publisher of Ern Malley. Harris the poet and fiction writer faded from sight.

McAuley was surely driven by the hoax further than need otherwise have been the case into the neo-classical cage which he defended thereafter as the sole and proper frame for poetic expression. As a Catholic convert and right-wing Cold Warrior, he argued tirelessly that poetic Modernism (Pound, Eliot, William Carlos Williams, Marianne Moore, Wallace Stevens, et al.) was a dead end, a delusion, the literary aspect of a larger moral and spiritual decay. He was thus intellectually, and by an act of will, committed to denying himself any further exploration of those relaxed moments of poetic free-wheeling which had given Ern Malley lines more memorable, and now more widely known, than any McAuley was ever able to lay claim to.

Just off-stage, but acting as party to the hoax, A. D. Hope was similarly committed, at least in literary matters, and has continued to attack what he has called the 'shuffle' and 'vomit' of Modernism,[*] writing as if it were at once the product of very meagre intelligences and a plot of devilish cunning. It is, I think, a measure of the low level of literary debate in Australia over several decades that these two men should have wielded as much influence as they did; and no recommendation to the academic life there that both should have occupied Chairs of English.

Harold Stewart emerges from Heyward's book as a less repressed and repressive character; but he long ago left Australia for Japan where he lives the life of a devoted Buddhist. He has put his homeland behind him, we are told, as if it belongs to another incarnation, and will never return.

It is of course only one way of viewing the affair, but not unsupported by the facts, to say that Malley seriously damaged the four men closest to his conception and promotion, and has survived them all.

I read this book in Sydney and was struck by the fact that since my last visit large bronze plaques have been set around Circular Quay to form what is called a Writers' Walk. The thirty-odd writers chosen by the NSW Ministry for the Arts include eight non-Australians – Darwin, Twain, Trollope, Conan Doyle, Kipling, Jack London, Conrad and D. H. Lawrence – there for no better reason than that each of them passed through and uttered something (all but Lawrence's *Kangaroo* quite inconsequential) on the subject of Australia. The Australians include expatriate media persons Clive James, Germaine Greer and Barry Humphries, but not (at this date) the stay-at-home poet Les Murray. They include the Booker Prize-winners Carey and Kenneally, but not Xavier Herbert who might in the long term prove more significant than either. Oodgeroo Noonuccal (formerly Cath Walker) is there, along with C. J. Dennis (author of 'I dips me lid') and Dorothea Mackellar ('I love the sunburnt country'), but not Australia's great short-story writer Hal Porter. There is no sign of Hope or McAuley, Stewart or Harris. A plaque for Ern Malley,

* See his *The New Cratylus: Notes on the Craft of Poetry*, Oxford University Press, Melbourne, 1979.

the great Australian Modernist, would surely have rounded out the absurdity of the exercise and truthfully recorded something deeply uncertain at the heart of Australian literary identity in the twentieth century.

I would have chosen, for the quotation to be engraved, the Malley line that still seems to me wonderful and which I quote from memory (remembering not a single line of McAuley or Stewart):

I am the black swan of trespass on alien waters.

O'Harashbery!*

I remember the pleasure of my first reading of Frank O'Hara's *Lunch Poems* when it came out in 1964 in a City Lights edition uniform (except that it was blue and red not black and white) with Allen Ginsberg's *Howl*, *Kaddish* and *Reality Sandwiches*. Two years later O'Hara was dead, killed by a dune buggy at an all-night party on Fire Island. There was something Keatsian about his poetry, its vividness and particularity, and its spontaneity, though there might be difficulties for anyone wanting to argue, as Matthew Arnold did when he tried to rescue Keats from the aesthetes, that 'there was flint and iron in him'.

In Keats, thought and poetry were neither identical nor simultaneous. Contemplation preceded composition, which replaced it and was a kind of action. Poetry had to come 'as naturally as the leaves to the tree or it might as well not come at all'. There's a difference in process, and consequently in product, between hard work poems such as Yeats's were almost without exception, and the headlong tradition in which Shakespeare (who, his contemporaries and collaborators record, 'never blotted a line') and Keats are pre-eminent. It is not a question of method, nor of density, but I think of pace. If you read

---

* A review of *Selected Poems* by Frank O'Hara (edited Donald Allen, Carcanet, Manchester, 1991) and *Flow Chart* by John Ashbery (Knopf, New York, 1991), *London Review of Books*, 23 April 1992.

attempts by nineteenth-century English poets (Byron is something of an exception) to write poetic drama, and compare their lines with Shakespeare's, the difference is all the more surprising because it's so clear that Shakespeare is their model. Their lines seem static where Shakespeare's are dynamic. There's an ambulant feel, one foot placed in front of the other, deliberately. In Shakespeare, even at his most clotted, his eyes and his mind, like those of a runner, are set well ahead of his feet.

Many poets work sometimes in one mode, sometimes in the other. The parts of *The Waste Land* that survived Pound's surgery had been composed in blocks, usually straight on to the typewriter, and the 'frightful toil' Eliot spoke of was not composition but disposition – disposing. In *Four Quartets* Eliot went over into the mode of deliberation, thus completing his accommodation on a British literary scene where, for most of the twentieth century, hard work was considered proper, and the other ('Romantic') tradition of how poetry happens was ignored, discounted or disbelieved. Consequently, among American poets, Lowell and Berryman, whose work shows in every line, have had the attention they deserve while William Carlos Williams and Allen Ginsberg have been slighted.

Frank O'Hara, like Eliot, inherited two traditions, one American, the other French. Although he says, half serious, 'of the American poets only Whitman and Crane and Williams are better than the movies', O'Hara, unlike Ginsberg, couldn't use the rolling self-importance of Whitman – any more than Keats could use the 'egotistical sublime' of Wordsworth. Like Keats, he rejected poetry that had 'a palpable design on us'. But he could learn from Williams's relaxed intimacy with places and things; and he found his own voice in Pierre Reverdy, as surely as Eliot found his in Jules Laforgue:

My heart is in my
pocket, it is Poems by Pierre Reverdy.

The other influences were music (he trained as a concert pianist) and painting. He was assistant curator at New York's Museum of Modern Art when Jackson Pollock, Willem de Kooning and Robert Rauschenberg were making Action Painting famous; and he and John

Ashbery, his friend and contemporary, must have felt their poetry belonged in tandem with that school. O'Hara's 'Why I am not a painter' doesn't tell us why he is not a painter, but shows how the process of making a painting and making a poem can be similarly oblique. The painter begins with sardines, but these get painted out, remaining only in the title; and in writing a poem, which becomes twelve poems, about 'orange', the poet never finds a way to mention the colour except belatedly, by giving his sequence the title 'Oranges'. But what distinguishes 'Why I am not a painter' is its tone of camp inconsequence, subverting all the notions of the sublime which attach themselves to talk about writing poems and painting pictures.

There are two O'Haras, one intelligible and still popular with anthologists, the other the composer of the kind of poem Ashbery writes, in which every sentence has a meaning but is designed, by discontinuity and lack of placement, to frustrate understanding. With diligence one could tease a sort of sense out of such poems, but that would not be a profitable exercise and is not, I'm sure, how they are meant to be read. O'Hara's 'In Memory of my Feelings' begins

> My quietness has a man in it, he is transparent
> and he carries me quietly, like a gondola, through the streets.
> He has several likenesses, like stars and years, like numerals.

A fleeting impression of sense is intended here; but to read it as if it were another kind of poem: the 'man' is not the poet (persona), since 'he carries me'; but he is 'in' the poet's 'quietness', and himself moves 'quietly'. He is like stars, years and numerals, specifically in having 'several likenesses'. This must mean that stars, years and numerals are alike in having 'several' (in fact innumerable) stars, years and numerals which are like them, but distinct; and this is so also of men. So 'meaning' in such writing tends to be an abstract and tautological circuit, denied connection with anything that precedes or follows; and the 'poetry' exists in tone, colour, flavour rather than sense – a flow of language disconnected, if not from reality, then from any particular reality. It is a pattern, a model, a blueprint of how language works, rather than language at work. This is the mode in which Ashbery has made himself famous and much honoured.

In a review of Ashbery in the *London Review of Books* 2–15 September 1982 and subsequently included in a Yale collection of essays on Ashbery edited (and one third written) by Harold Bloom, John Bayley sees the critical question 'in terms of the contrast between Englishness and Americanness in the contemporary poetic voice' – the 'English voice' dealing in 'robust reality' (which he concedes can sometimes be 'a fatal overpresence'), while Ashbery 'avoids definition as America does'. And Bayley quotes some Ashbery lines which he suggests describe the poet and his American quality:

> Behind the mask
> Is still a continental appreciation
> Of what is fine, rarely appears and when it does is already
> Dying on the breeze that brought it to the threshold
> Of speech.

My difficulty here is that I can't see how Ashbery can represent more than one branch (sub-branch) of contemporary American poetry. It's true he is somewhere down the track that leads off from Wallace Stevens; but Stevens can't be held responsible for the distance Ashbery travels there. And O'Hara, who began where Ashbery began, showed that theirs was a point of departure which could lead into the thick of time and place as readily as away from it:

> It is 12:20 in New York a Friday
> three days after Bastille day, yes
> it is 1959 and I go get a shoeshine
> because I will get off the 4:19 in Easthampton
> at 7:15 and then go straight to dinner
> and I don't know the people who will feed me
> I walk up the muggy street beginning to sun
> and have a hamburger and a malted and buy
> an ugly NEW WORLD WRITING and see what the poets
> in Ghana are doing these days
>   I go to the bank
> and Miss Stillwagon (first name Linda I once heard)
> doesn't even look up my balance . . .

The strangeness comes cumulatively from a deliberate overload of 'robust reality' – detail undifferentiated and unstructured.

An illustration of the two paths – one towards realism, the other away from it – can be seen in two O'Hara poems with the same name, 'On Rachmaninoff's Birthday'. One ('Quick a last poem before I go . . .') is Ashbery's territory, but with O'Hara's unique dash of charm. 'Rachmaninoff' here is a word, not a man, leading to other works ('off my rocker') and thus to a frame of language. In the other ('Blue windows, blue rooftops . . .') Rachmaninoff is the composer, imagined as O'Hara's piano teacher.

In Bloom's Yale collection of essays on Ashbery, Helen Vendler, with typical forthrightness, considers the question of the poet's 'subject matter': 'it is popularly believed, with some reason, that [his] style is impenetrable, that it is impossible to say what an Ashbery poem is "about".' Professor Vendler argues that, for all their evasiveness, his poems do have subjects and make statements; but she makes a case only by not letting it be seen that all such passages as she quotes are placed in such a way as to give them no support fore and aft, so that any general resonance they may have in isolation is diminished in context. Worse, her argument forces her to isolate what seems most commonplace in Ashbery, and might be taken as a measure of the lack of real distinction which his obscurity obscures – for example:

> But I don't set much stock in things
> Beyond the weather and the certainties of living and dying:
> The rest is optional. To praise this, blame that,
> Leads one subtly away from the beginning, where
> We must stay, in motion.

Or again:

> People
> Are either too stunned or too engrossed
> In their own petty pursuits to bother with
> What is happening all around them, even
> When that turns out to be extremely interesting.

181

Is this significantly different from the kind of pretentious pub chat that has you glancing at your watch?

But it is Professor Bloom who has made out the most determined case for Ashbery. I respect Bloom's passion, his intellectual energy, his seriousness, his knowledge.* What I distrust in him is something like taste; and, more to the point (but not unconnected), I wince at the damage he does to the language of criticism. Here is the centre of his argument for Ashbery, with some of the weeds pulled out:

> A strong poem, which alone can become canonical for more than a single generation, can be defined as a text that must engender strong misreadings [. . .] Texts that have single, reductive, simplistic meanings are themselves misreadings of anterior texts [. . .] Confronted by Ashbery [. . .] the weak reader is defeated by the energy of the Sublime [which is] available only to the agonist striver, not to the reductionist [. . .] Strong, canonical, Sublime poetry exists in order to compel the reader to abandon easier literary pleasures for more difficult satisfactions.

I set aside the fact that some poems seem to survive by their simplicity, and concede, at least in part, what I think Bloom wants us to understand: that 'difficulty' is not always an obstacle to poetic survival, and may even aid it. It's reported that chimpanzees in the Auckland zoo have enjoyed their lunches much more since keepers began to hide the food instead of just handing it out; and 'the fascination of what's difficult' operates for readers as well as for Yeats and the chimps. The bardic mode favoured mysteries. Traditions attaching themselves to words like oracular, Orphic, Delphic, arcane, hermetic are reminders of how much the human primate likes secrets, puzzles, hints, tricks and magic. They should remind us also of how open this aspect of the mind is to deception, and self-deception.

---

* Though I have to say a man who sets out the whole literary Western canon, from the beginning to the present, as if he knows it all, and well enough to pronounce critically upon it, including what should and shouldn't be there (even from Australasia!), is suffering from some kind *folie de grandeur*. I think we are better to have a canon, for the advantage of common ground and common discussion points, even though it will always be imperfect, and argued over. But it must be received over time, and constantly changing, not laid down and delivered as if by Moses down from the mountain.

Bloom's exaltation on reading Ashbery is clear enough, and genuine. That the same lines when I read them engage one part of the mind, leaving the rest free to wander and think other thoughts (ultimately a sleep-inducing division) is only of interest if it makes a critical point. I suggest, then, that Bloom's mind also wanders, and that in doing so it creates the half of the poem which Ashbery has left uncomposed. A needs B which is why B is exalted; and the poet's brow is wreathed in the donated sweat of his critic's labour.

Poetry claims its pre-eminence among the verbal arts by using to the full all essential functions of language, one of which is to point beyond itself – to name, to designate, to describe, to make real. Whether what it brings into being was already in some sense there, in history, like Keats's Hampstead garden or Wordsworth's Tintern Abbey, or was conjured like Coleridge's Xanadu, is unimportant. That prime function of language is one half of an equation, the realist half, which in the finest poetry is matched and to a degree opposed by the stamp of uniqueness that belongs to the particular poet – an eye, an ear, a voice, a style, an imagination. It is the object part of this subject/object duality which Ashbery declines to use. His language is half-language, and by this measure his poetry is half-poetry. He has made what others do now and then his sole trick, his stock-in-trade, as if fearful of exposing his limitations.

> The startling freshness of it blinkered me
> opposing me to many angles of lights
> that fell before the door frame. A weathered quince
> asked to be included. Round shrubs duly unwrapped
> after winter and how do you get hold of these? Sipping a
> > glass of brandy
> my mother high above the city shooed
> inset chimes to their places; how far
> and how many balloons see the light of morning each time
> > this year
> and one must have a peg to hang it on, and something to
> > walk upon,
> yet it got no worse,
> the time between the horse's lazily but abruptly twitched

183

                                        tail to
the flies from off the stable:
fellows who hurry by you,
they are taking you, out of the catalog, to
obnoxious rendezvous. Meetings. Was it ever a catbird that
                              called thus,
got us late after school, how much we were loving it,
                          instant
in each other's arms, and one thin called down, that was
                              a wave of air
to take the place away.

'Shadwell', Dryden tells us, 'never deviates into sense', and neither does 'canonical' Ashbery. There are 213 pages to his *Flow Chart*, and it is the randomness from one passage to the next, the refusal of firm designation, or continuity, structure, narrative, which makes each passage even more obscure and abstract-seeming in context than out of it. There is consistency of tone and language, but the language is seldom distinguished by compression, or wit, or eloquence. I can see no reason why Professor Bloom should admire this book less than others by Ashbery he has praised – or more; nor why I should be won over. By what measure such stuff better or worse?

As for O'Hara: no doubt he belongs to his time. There had to be some kind of break-out from the egg-bound neo-Metaphysical academic poetry that went with the coldest years of the Cold War; and at a time when Ginsberg and the Beats were making the running, O'Hara showed a way which managed to be personal but not confessional, free but not unconfined. He is perhaps a minor figure, but I think an important one. For me the charm and vivacity, inventiveness and humour, of his best poems persist.

Robert Lowell – History as Happening[*]

Robert Lowell died in 1977 at the age of sixty. Ten years earlier there had been a sudden alteration in his poetic pacemaker. From being a poet one might describe as a Modernist Metaphysical, a hard work poet, a poet of tight forms, dense textures, complex symbolism and slow production, he'd all at once broken out – or had seemed to break out – into a sequence of rapidly composed, free-running, unrhymed sonnets. This outburst, or outpouring, continued for six or seven years during which he published probably more lines of poetry than in all the rest of his working life.

Poets, Ezra Pound said, are the steam-gauges and voltmeters of society. Perhaps a better image in this case might be a seismograph. Lowell's behaviour in those years registered a social and political shift in the society of the West, involving sexual liberation, social protest and something close to political insurrection. He was engaged in all aspects of this upheaval, the largest single element being the agitations brought about by America's participation in, or, more accurately, America's precipitation of, the war in Vietnam.

An eastern seaboard Brahmin, bearer of a distinguished name, Lowell had been expected by his family to graduate from Harvard.

---

[*] A lecture given to the English Faculty, Oxford University, 5 December 1996, during my tenure as Senior Visiting Fellow, St John's College, and published in *PN Review*, May–June 1997.

Early signs of the manic-depressive illness that would blight his life appeared, however, during his first year as a student, and led his mother to put him into the care of Merrill Moore, a psychiatrist-poet who wrote sonnets, only sonnets, innumerable sonnets – never fewer than one per day; a doctor who liked to refer to his place of work as a sonnetorium. This was 1937; and I'm not aware that anyone has looked into a possible connection between Moore's poetic practice then and Lowell's thirty years later.

But the immediate importance of Moore was that he was a Southerner, and rather than attempting to persuade the young Lowell back to his studies at Harvard, he suggested he might find it more productive and congenial to go south to Nashville, Tennessee, where a formidable group of poets and critics had gathered around John Crowe Ransom and Allen Tate. Along with Randall Jarrell, Lowell became Ransom's pupil at Nashville; and when Ransom moved to Gambier, Ohio, where he started up the *Kenyon Review*, his two brilliant students went with him.

The influence of Tate and Ransom on Lowell was immediate. Lowell said in one interview, 'I became converted to formalism and changed my style from frail free verse, all in a few months. And everything was in rhyme.'*

Tate and Ransom's New Criticism grew out of Modernism, and was an aspect of that larger movement. Taking a good deal of its tone and substance from Eliot, it presented itself as conservative, anti-Romantic, in revolt against the nineteenth century; and it denied any absolute rift between the role of critic and that of poet. The writing of poetry, these men would have said (agreeing with Eliot), was at every moment a critical act – a matter of discriminations and choices. That was why the great tradition of poetry in English included all the names of the greatest critics. Eliot came at the end of that line of major poet-critics.

There were, however, contradictions in poetic Modernism, and these are most simply illustrated in Eliot's own work. On the one hand there was what he inherited from the Metaphysicals, the seventeenth century and what was called 'the line of wit' – everything that made

---

* Robert Lowell, *Collected Prose*, ed. Robert Giroux, Faber, London, 1987, p. 257.

him seem an intellectual poet, a poet of subtlety and shock rather than of passion and imagination. On the other hand there were the late-Romantic, shadowy, floating, surreal and musical elements inherited from French Symbolism. One can see these two strands very clearly by studying Pound's work on the manuscripts of *The Waste Land*. The manuscripts show Eliot wavering between eighteenth-century satire and late nineteenth-century Symbolism; and what Pound's editing did was to dilute the satirical edge and let the Symbolism dominate.

Of these two strands the New Criticism drew predominantly from the first – the line of wit – hardly at all from the second. It's in this sense that it could be seen as the conservative, or, to use Lowell's word, the formalist side of the Modernist literary revolution.

Ian Hamilton quotes Lowell saying 'The kind of poet I am was largely determined by the fact that I grew up in the heyday of the New Criticism. From the beginning I was preoccupied with technique, fascinated by the past and tempted by other languages. It is hard for me [. . .] to imagine a poet not interested in the classics.'*

By the mid-1950s Lowell was established in America as a major – probably *the* major – poet among the younger Modernists; but he was not entirely satisfied with this position. He was keenly aware of a division in contemporary American poetry between those, like himself, who tended to be academic, complex, tightly controlled, Eurocentric and deriving from Eliot and Pound, and another school, or several schools, that looked to William Carlos Williams, and even back to Walt Whitman. The work of the latter groups was more open and colloquial, informal, immediate, less intellectual, closer to the bone, or the knuckle, of experience. They were also felt to be more genuinely American.

Lowell had been aware of William Carlos Williams all along. In fact he'd been writing, without much success, Williams-like free verse before his move south and his conversion to the New Criticism. But although he admired Williams, he wasn't able to write the Williams kind of poem – neither then, nor at any time in his career. He had the wrong kind of ear – not essentially a musical ear, as Williams had (and also Pound and Eliot). He was like Yeats, a poet of rhythm and image rather than of music; of percussive measure and of structure rather

* Ian Hamilton, *Robert Lowell: A Biography*, Faber, London, 1983, p. 57.

187

than of ear and instinct; of the form imposed from the outside rather than generated from within.

It's clear that he felt in some ways constrained by his own mode; and the desire to open his poems out to the world was intensified by the sense in the 1950s that the poets of those alternative schools – the Beats, the New York school, the Black Mountain group, and so on – were claiming to be the new avant-garde; or that claim was being made for them. Lowell was by now at a dangerous age, almost forty, when poets begin to fear they may be losing the gloss, not just of youth, but of *modernity*.

This feeling became clearer in 1957 when he made a reading tour of the West Coast where audiences were used to hearing the poets published by the City Lights Bookshop in San Francisco – Ginsberg, Ferlinghetti, Frank O'Hara, Gregory Corso, Kenneth Patchen. These young audiences liked directness, immediacy, dramatic effects; and Lowell was forced to recognise that the density and complexity of his style created a barrier. He describes trying to simplify some of his poems in the course of reading; but on the whole there wasn't much to be done about it. The barrier was there; and he might, after all, have contented himself with the thought that a poet can't offer both 'the fascination of what's difficult' and at the same time the rhetorical immediacy of a Ginsberg, or the charm of an O'Hara.

But it was William Carlos Williams whose poetry really troubled Lowell. He'd already proved to himself that he couldn't simply imitate – that Williams was inimitable. But that made the question of why he was the important poet Lowell felt him to be all the more teasing; and when Lowell wrote about him in 1961, the tone he adopted was one of puzzled reverence.

> The difficulties I found in Williams twenty-five years ago are still difficulties for me. Williams enters me, but I cannot enter him. Of course, one cannot catch any good writer's voice or breathe his air. But there's something more. It's as if no poet except Williams has seen America or heard its language. [. . .] When I say that I cannot enter him, I am almost saying that I cannot enter America. This troubles me. I am not satisfied to let it be.*

* *Collected Prose*, pp. 41–42.

In the same tribute he writes of 'a seemingly unending war' between Williams and his disciples on the one hand, and the disciples of the New Criticism on the other. He represents himself as 'standing uncomfortably in the middle'. As a reader he may have stood in the middle, but as a writer he was distinctly not of the Williams school. He would have preferred to be closer to it, but he had found no way to achieve it.

The first really significant loosening of Lowell's style occurs in the collection he calls *Life Studies*. In the late 1950s he had given himself a rest from writing poems, working instead on what must have been disconnected pieces of prose autobiography. He found a 'prose voice' in doing this, and then proceeded to transfer it back into poems.

Long ago, writing of the Modernist revolution in poetry, Ezra Pound said, 'To break the pentameter, that was the first heave.' By the middle years of this century, even in formal poems with rhymes and stanzaic patterns, the basic unit in English had become a measure of five speech stresses rather than five iambic feet; but it was still a pentameter. Modernism had made room for other measures, or non-measures – Pound's and Williams's open forms, Marianne Moore's syllabic verse, Charles Olson's breath-measure, and so on; but the pentameter was still a strong recurring fact of poetic life.

Lowell tried to make for himself that 'first heave' by transferring not only the subject matter of his autobiographical writing, but the rhythms and the tone, back from prose into poetry. Looking back on the experiment some years later he said the autobiographical poems in *Life Studies* were in a style he thought he'd discovered in Flaubert. 'When I didn't have to bang words into rhyme and count,' he went on, 'I was more nakedly dependent on rhythm.'* 'Count' is the operative word there. Clearly it means either counting formal iambic feet, or counting speech stresses.

What he achieved in *Life Studies* is a more relaxed, less 'difficult', less intense kind of poem than he'd written before, with more human interest and less symbolic weight and portentousness. These poems are user-friendly. The poet persona is more accessible, capable of what Helen Vendler calls 'a fitful tenderness'.

* Hamilton, p. 233.

Most of the friends and fellow poets to whom Lowell sent samples of the new work were enthusiastic; but not his old mentor, Allen Tate: '[. . .] *all* the poems about your family, including the one about you and Elizabeth, are definitely *bad*', Tate wrote. He acknowledged some brilliant passages. But 'by and large, and in the total effect' the poems were 'composed of unassimilated details [. . .] which might well have been transferred from the notes from your autobiography without change'. Tate continued, 'Your fine poems in the past present a formal ordering of highly intractable materials: but there is an imaginative thrust towards a symbolic order which these new poems seem to lack.'*

Tate, however, was pretty much a lone voice. *Life Studies* was praised by friends and reviewers; it won a National Book Award; it sold better than any of his earlier books, and remained a favourite. To Lowell it must have seemed, at least for a time, that he had made a significant advance. In his speech accepting the National Book Award he described contemporary American poetry as divided between the 'cooked' and the 'raw'. 'There is a poetry that can only be studied, and a poetry that can only be declaimed, a poetry of pedantry and a poetry of scandal.' He was gently mocking of both kinds. The 'cooked' was 'expert and remote', designed for 'graduate seminars'; the 'raw' was 'like an unscored libretto by some bearded but vegetarian Castro'.†

This was amusing and it made a point. If Ginsberg and the Beats were raw, and early Lowell was cooked, the implication seemed to be that in *Life Studies* he had found, or hoped he had, a way of standing between the two; and that was where he might be expected to stand henceforth. That was why he valued (possibly overvalued) the poetry of Elizabeth Bishop. Bishop's work had seemed to offer a middle position between cooked and raw; or (to change the metaphor) between black tie and beachwear.

But no problem of poetic style is so simply resolved. In particular, where did that crucial figure of William Carlos Williams belong on the contemporary map of the cooked and the raw? The Book Award

---

* Hamilton, p. 237.
† Hamilton, p. 277.

speech was a public statement. In private Lowell was not so sanguine. To Randall Jarrell he'd written only a short time before:

> One wants a whole new deck of cards to play with, or at least new rules for the old. Maybe it's the times, or maybe it's being well into one's forties, or maybe it's all a private thing with me: but I feel so wrung with altered views and standards – more than I can swallow.*

Allen Tate had been too severe about *Life Studies*. He had overstated the negative case. But the fact remains that the new style Lowell had used in his poems about his family solved no fundamental problem in poetics. Those prose rhythms remained precisely that – the rhythms of *prose*; and in his two succeeding books, *For the Union Dead* (1965), and *Near the Ocean* (1967), we find him retreating from them. The clamps go on again. At first he writes what he later called a modification of the style of *Life Studies* – 'free verse stanzas . . . more ornately organized'. Then he stepped back even further: these were (again in his own description) 'metrical poems, more plated, far from conversation, metaphysical'.†

In terms of poetic form, poetic technique, he was back pretty much where he'd been before *Life Studies* – 'in harness' (to use his own phrase). And one might ask, Why not? He was at the height of his powers, and this was the kind of writing he seemed to do best. Form in Lowell is always interesting; and the fact that it gave him problems doesn't make it less so. But there was, thus far, no 'new deck of cards', no permanent escape from 'banging out rhyme and counting'.

The point of all this is not to suggest that there is, in any absolute sense, a right and a wrong mode of poetry, or even a better and a worse mode. Any mode can be well or badly done. What is of interest here is Lowell's tentative steps towards, and then his drawing back from, more open forms. Clearly he'd been searching around for a new mode, a new tone or register, a new speech which, while not being anything like an easy ride, would give freer expression, not just to the manic-depressive cycle of his private life, but to the life of the nation, of the

* Hamilton, p. 277.
† *Collected Prose*, p. 269.

191

times, of the West – and in due course to that ragey *Zeitgeist* of the 1960s. Auden says somewhere 'We are lived by history', and it's that sense of the collective life going on in each of us that Lowell wanted to get into his work.

But the harder he strove for it, the less sure he felt that he was achieving it. In some lines cancelled from the final version of 'Waking Early Sunday Morning' he describes himself as sick of his own rhetoric, of his own 'endless self-imitation', and of the 'gross confidence that shone / in meter and iambic line!'*

By the time we come to the 1967 collection, *Near the Ocean*, it's clear that Lowell is running out of steam. There are 43 pages of poetry, only 17 of his own poems, the remaining 26 of translations from Latin, Italian and Spanish; and the translations had been done in the two years from 1965 to 1967, when he'd been unable to write anything new of his own. 'O to break loose' is the first phrase of the first poem in the book. He returns to it in the twelfth stanza:

> O to break loose. All life's grandeur
> Is something with a girl in summer.

And the final lines in the book, although they come from a translation, seem to express the same wish and the same sense that there's something still poetically beyond his reach.

> The hours will hardly pardon us their loss,
> Those brilliant hours that wore away our days,
> Our days that ate into eternity.

The breakthrough came for Lowell in the summer of 1967 when he wrote a fourteen-line poem for his daughter Harriet. He must have intended it as a formal sonnet, and the scraps of rhyme can still be seen in it, surviving from that original intention. But it turned into something more open, informal, impressionistic. It was followed at once by another – and then another.

---

* Quoted by Paul Mariani in *Lost Puritan: A Life of Robert Lowell*, W. W. Norton, New York, 1994, p. 337.

It's clear he didn't first have the idea of a sonnet sequence and then proceed to write it. He simply found himself doing it and then, one assumes, puzzled over how to proceed. And the recognition of how this unexpected fluency might be exploited came to him, not from the Beats or the Black Mountain – those poets whose temperaments were radically different from his own; nor did it come from Elizabeth Bishop, whose manner so influenced *Life Studies*. It came from the work of his contemporary and competitor, John Berryman, a poet even more erudite than himself, with a similar combination of intellectual force with a tendency to mental and emotional breakdown and consequent riot.

In his sequence of eighteen-line poems, *Dream Songs*, Berryman had projected himself, with a kind of staccato brilliance, in the character of a poet he called Henry, a fiction, but one almost indistinguishable from himself. At first Lowell hadn't liked the *Dream Songs*; but now he saw there was something important to be learned from them – not only from their form, but from the particular way Berryman had used his own life as material.

This was the essential shift Lowell had to make: to write out of the centre of his own experience, no less than before, perhaps more directly and frankly than ever, but to do it as if he were himself a fictional character.

It might be asked what difference that could possibly make. It makes one fundamental difference. The poem and not the truth (in the sense of 'what happened') is the final determinant of what goes in. Professor Calvin Bedient of UCLA has written a brilliant article in which he catches Lowell out repeatedly, in these late sonnets, writing one thing and then, in revisions, reversing it for effect. Lowell, Bedient complains, is 'ready to say almost anything, then take it back and replace it with its opposite'.*

But it is really a matter of critical choice, or critical emphasis, whether one sees this as irresponsible, a lack of seriousness, or, quite the opposite, as evidence of the seriousness of the *poet*, his sense of a primary responsibility to the needs of the *poem*. 'What happened' in

---

* 'Illegible Lowell (The Late Volumes)', in *Robert Lowell: Essays on the Poetry*, ed. Steven Gould Axelrod and Helen Deese, Cambridge University Press, Cambridge, 1986, p. 144.

reality, what was seen, or heard, or thought, or felt, provides a huge amount of the material; but what *really* happened, what was *really* seen, heard, thought or felt, is less important than its poetic potential, its aptness, its rightness in relation to something which stands outside autobiography. If the primary fact can be reversed to good effect, then why not? This is poetry, not history; and though the context in which Wilfred Owen says 'The true poets must be truthful' makes that statement meaningful, it's equally meaningful for whoever it is in Shakespeare to say 'The truest poetry is the most feigning.'

In an eloquent chapter on Lowell, Helen Vendler says of the sonnets, 'what fixes us in admiration of this poetry is the continual presence of Lowell himself'.* I can assent to that only if I take 'Lowell' to mean a persona not identical with, or indistinguishable from, the author. In my reading of these poems, the poet is at last subjugating himself to poetry; subjugating intellect and ego to artistic instinct. He gets the ego out in order to make more room for the talent to get in. For that reason I think it's not altogether satisfactory to read these late sonnets as simply 'confessional' – a term, I should add, which Vendler also rejects.

The other great benefit for Lowell in this development was that it didn't require him to try again to break the hold of the pentameter on his poetic ear. There had been a good reason for Pound to break it: he had a new music (sometimes a new cacophony) to offer in its place. Lowell did not. 'I wrote in end-stopped lines,' he says of these poems, 'and rewrote to keep a sense of line.'† He departed often, sometimes radically, from the five-stress measure, but he always returned to it; and just occasionally, as if to remind his reader, or himself, of the long history of English poetry that was being carried forward in the work, there would be a pentameter of pristine iambuses – as in the line of the sonnet on Ezra Pound, where Pound asks,

> And who is left to understand my jokes?

Whether this happened consciously or not, it strikes me as a nice irony to put a perfect pentameter into the mouth of the man who broke

---

* *Part of Nature, Part of Us*, Harvard University Press, Cambridge, Mass., 1980, p. 130.
† *Collected Prose*, p. 271.

it. And it's noticeable that when Lowell revises the line a few years later – I should think because in speaking one doesn't say 'who is left', one says 'who's left' – it's revised in a way which preserves the iambic measure –

Who's left alive to understand my jokes?

Reading what Lowell said in 1971 about the writing of the sonnets, one gets the sense of excitement, freedom, a significant breakthrough, the poet suddenly finding fluency of a kind he'd envied in nineteenth-century poets but which the constraints of his training in the New Criticism had seemed to make impossible. Instead of working away at one poem, adding, subtracting, refining, revising, going at it very slowly over a long period and often digging himself into a deep hole, he could move to and fro among groups of poems, dropping one when it became difficult, moving to something else, and something else again, while still with the sense that this was a single unified work. The result is what Alex Calder has called a 'process poem'* – a long poem carried through without any preliminary design or blueprint, and without any developing narrative or argument, its shape and direction only discovered in the course of the writing, influenced by random day-to-day pressures. Other examples, obviously, are Pound's *Cantos*, Williams's *Paterson*, Charles Olson's *Maximus* and Berryman's *Dream Songs*.

Explaining that he worked hard at the sonnets, making many revisions in the course of writing, Lowell goes on,

Words came rapidly, almost four hundred sonnets in four years – a calendar of workdays. I did nothing but write; I was thinking lines even when teaching or playing tennis. Yet I had idleness, though drawn to spend more hours working than I ever had or perhaps will. Ideas sprang from the bushes, my head; five or six sonnets started or reworked in a day. [. . .] I wished to describe the immediate instant. If I saw something one day, I wrote it that day, or the next, or the next. Things I felt or saw, or read were drift in the whirlpool, the squeeze of the sonnet and the loose ravel of the blank verse.†

* *Axelrod and Deese*, pp. 117–38.
† *Collected Prose*, pp. 271–2.

My own recollection is that one felt this excitement in the writing when the sonnets first appeared; and it was greatly increased by the fact that those last years of the decade were so exciting, absorbing, dramatic and horrifying – in America and in the world. It really did feel like a time of insurrection, deeply upsetting and even repellent to some, but to others a time when they could echo Wordsworth's 'Bliss was it in that dawn to be alive / But to be young was very heaven'.

Lowell's new form not only allowed him to range about freely, reflecting as an observer on what was happening; he was himself visibly engaged in it. He became a figure in the anti-Vietnam war protest, first when he publicly declined an invitation to the White House, incurring the wrath of President Johnson; and then when he joined the leaders of the Pentagon march against the war in October 1967. He wrote sonnets about that march, and appeared as a character in Norman Mailer's *The Armies of the Night* – a book which also used self-fictionalisation as a way of separating Mailer as author from Mailer as character. The following year Lowell became an aide to Senator Eugene McCarthy during McCarthy's campaign for the Democrat presidential nomination.

Nineteen sixty-eight was the year of the Tet Offensive, which effectively put an end to America's chances of ever winning in Vietnam. It was the year of the assassination of Martin Luther King, and later of Bobby Kennedy. It was the year when Lyndon Johnson was more or less locked in the White House, unable to appear in public, until he dramatically announced he would decline re-nomination for the presidency. It was a year of Black riots and student protests in America, of student and worker uprisings in Paris and Berlin, and of the Democrat convention in Chicago when the police brutally quelled Eugene McCarthy's brigade of young supporters. It was, as Stephen Spender called it in the title of one of his books, *The Year of the Young Rebels*. It might even have been the year when the student Bill Clinton smoked dope and didn't inhale.

Lowell's sonnet was not only flexible enough to deal with many public events more or less as they happened; he could also range back in time, dragging up recollections of friends, famous literary people, books he'd read, characters out of history. So the *Notebook*, as it was first called, was not just an aggregation of discrete items. Each fourteen-line unit was somewhere between being a poem in its own right, and a stanza of a long poem.

There was a rough-hewn quality about the writing, and quite a lot of obscurity, some of it eliminated in later published revisions, but a good deal of it intrinsic, and perhaps necessary – part of the sense of a momentum, history as happening, verbal density matching the rush and confirming the involvement. Immediacy was the aim, and the effect. 'John,' Lowell writes in his sonnet to Berryman, 'we used the language as if we made it.'

Although the form is totally different from Pound's *Cantos*, the *Cantos* and Lowell's sonnet sequences have this much in common, that both employ what Pound called 'the presentative method'. Everything must be thrust at the reader unexplained, as in life itself, and with a consequent effect always of urgency, often of obscurity, and sometimes of clutter and muddle. Explanation would destroy the essential poetic quality. And just as I've argued elsewhere that the *Cantos* should be read without too much stopping to question things not understood, and that the *Annotated Index* approach undermines the very element which makes them poetry, so I would say that Lowell's sonnets are best taken at their own fast pace, and to some degree on trust – taken, as Donald Davie once said the *Cantos* should be, in 'great gulps'.

Immediacy, then, pace and density of language, all of which serve to create the feeling of a particular period of history – those are the qualities one would look at in developing an affirmative critical statement about Lowell's sonnets. The negative side, if that should be one's inclination, would most likely be technical: it would have to do with his statement (quoted above) about writing end-stopped lines. Sometimes it's almost as if he wants to make every line free-standing, distinct from every other line, so that the poem seems to fall apart like a bundle of sticks. It's true that this quality of fragmentation matches something in the air of the time which is his subject; but one can also feel it to be a reflection of his own fragmented, or fragmenting, personality.

Lowell's first intention, as he found the sequence evolving, was to write a journal of a year; and though the first published collection, *Notebook 1967–68*, is not a simple calendar aggregation, with nothing added or subtracted or rearranged, it does have a sort of chronological shape and sequence.

The second incarnation comes with the book he called *Notebook*. This is the earlier book with many revisions, and with several dozen more sonnets pushed into the frame – so the sense of its being a journal of a year is gone. Nonetheless the revisions are most often improvements, usually in the direction of greater clarity; and the sequence at this point still has unity.

More open to challenge, clearly, is what he did in 1973. Once again it's not the revisions, nor the addition of further sonnets, that creates the difficulty. It's the re-arrangement of the whole bagful into three separate books. The poems about his second wife, Elizabeth Hardwick, and their daughter Harriet, go into one collection, called *For Lizzie and Harriet*; the poems about his love affair with, and marriage to, his third wife, Lady Caroline Blackwood, go into a second, called *The Dolphin*; and all the rest, rearranged not according to the chronology of writing (which would have retained something of the sense of a journal, and of compositional process) but according to the chronology of their subjects, go into the third collection, called *History*.

In the revisions to the sonnets Lowell's talent and poetic instinct are in charge; but in the reordering and rearrangement of the sequence it could be argued that ego (Lowell as autobiographer) and intellect take over, and that the integrity of the whole as a 'process poem' is compromised.

Even more than with most poetry that seems to make major claims on us, Lowell's sonnets are likely to affect different practised and intelligent readers differently. There's going to be no single right answer to the question of how far they fulfil their own poetic ambition. I'm aware that my own reading of them has a lot to do with the time at which they appeared, and my response to the events of that time. How well they will outlast their occasions remains to be seen. In these remarks I have not offered a critical statement about them. Rather, I've tried to suggest a context in which such a statement might be framed – not only their genesis in the history of a decade, but also in a broader literary history – twentieth-century poetry's struggle to discover new forms appropriate to the times.

A Life of David Ballantyne[*]

Any New Zealand writer who thinks his or her life is, or has been, difficult, full of obstacles, unkindness and bad luck, should read this life of David Ballantyne (1924–86). I remember before I met Ballantyne hearing about him, in the late 1950s and early 1960s, from Frank Sargeson and Maurice Duggan, who offered his case as a warning to a young writer not to 'use up your material too quickly'. In his early twenties Ballantyne had published a novel, *The Cunninghams*, which was so autobiographical it was said he had nothing left to write about.

Although this seemed, and seems, a strange idea, Ballantyne himself came to believe it. He wrote constantly, but there were thirteen years before a second novel appeared, and that was a less than successful return to pretty much the same material. Further, *The Cunninghams* was published in America and, lacking a British publisher, could not be sold in New Zealand. During those years Ballantyne had to sustain his notion of himself as a literary writer on the basis of a *succès d'estime* that had occurred far from home. And for most of the rest of his career he continued to be limited by the lack of a dependable publishing industry in New Zealand.

[*] A review of *After the Fireworks* by Bryan Reid (Auckland University Press, Auckland, 2004), *Sunday Star-Times*, 2 October 2004.

When recognition did come it was from one or two isolated academics writing in small-circulation literary magazines, and from fellow journalists who respected the newspaper work which had sustained him over the years. Publishing fiction was always a problem, and his work never had the kind of support and promotion it needed. Yet his novels (*Sydney Bridge Upside Down* most notably) and his short stories are among the most individual and striking that have been written in this country.

Bryan Reid, a contemporary, friend and long-ago colleague on the *Auckland Star*, has written a sympathetic, workmanlike, no-frills account of Ballantyne's life and literary career, one which pays proper attention to his work in journalism, and which does useful service in reminding us of the very different and important role the newspapers played before television became (lamentably in New Zealand's case) the community's principal source of information. It also shows how in those days work in journalism commonly went together with heavy drinking, and what damage that conjunction did to Ballantyne and his family.

Like his exact contemporary Janet Frame, Ballantyne came from poverty; but at least Frame's father, a railwayman, was always employed. Ballantyne senior had been gassed in the First World War and his damaged lungs succumbed, after a decade or so, to tuberculosis, putting him out of the workforce. He died when David was thirteen, leaving a wife and five children. David, the oldest and by far the brightest child in the family, had had less than two years' secondary schooling when he was required to go to work to help support his siblings. Reid shows that he remained defensive and prickly about his lack of formal education, and always distrustful of academics.

Frame and Ballantyne dealt with the sense of social disadvantage in ways which were different, near opposites and (for the times in which they lived) characteristically female and male. Janet spoke with a little girl voice, adopted the submissive posture and cried for help; Dave spoke with a rasp, put on a bold front and played the tough guy, never without a cigarette and a drink. They were the Marilyn Monroe and the Humphrey Bogart of the New Zealand literature of half a century ago. Janet withdrew into mental hospitals and then found it wasn't possible to get out; Dave retreated into alcohol and likewise found escape for many years impossible.

Yet they both continued to write against the odds, with extraordinary fluency and persistence – damaged souls, one with fragmentary genius, the other with huge but baulked and frustrated talent.

In 1954, encouraged by his wife Vivienne, who believed he needed to get away from Auckland and make a new start, Ballantyne moved, with her and their son Stephen, to London. He was to remain there for twelve years, working first for the *Evening News*, then for the publisher Purnell and finally for the *Evening Standard*. He was successful as a journalist, his work was rewarding, he had two plays produced and broadcast by the BBC, bought a modest house, seemed comfortable and settled – and then (against the wishes of wife and son) yielded to the silent pull of the homeland and returned to Auckland.

In London the drinking had been significant but more or less under control. In Auckland (as Vivienne told his biographer) 'he was back on the grog from Day One'. It made no difference to the quality of his journalism. Working for the *Star* again he was full of ideas, fluent at the keyboard, met his deadlines and behaved decently in the office. Behind the scenes, however, his alcoholism was destroying family life and getting in the way of his literary career. Any spare money went down as booze and up in smoke. By the early 1970s he was going on overnight binges that continued into the following day. There were scenes, violence, blackouts.

When he returned to New Zealand Ballantyne was in his early forties and had published two novels and a collection of short stories. Another novel followed soon after, and then there was nothing for ten years. They were the years lost to alcohol.

Late in 1973, urged by friends and his employer, and with an ultimatum from his wife hanging over him, he simply gave up drinking. There were no graduated steps, no AA, no support group. He missed not only the alcoholic oblivion, the anaesthetising escapes, but also the companionship, and it must have taken the same kind of will-power he had shown in his early days when he managed to keep writing novels at night and going to work in the daytime.

But he never drank again. He became a sort of elder statesman among writers, charitable, worldly wise, quietly witty and a bit sad.

He was chairman of the Auckland Branch of PEN (now the Society of Authors) and for some years a writers' representative on the Literary Fund Advisory Committee. In 1978 came a new novel, *The Talkback Man*, about an alcoholic; and in 1980 another, *The Penfriend*.

But the years of heavy smoking had had their effect. Early in 1985 he was found to have lung cancer – an inoperable tumour. A year later he was dead.

It would be nice to be able to believe that there had been some kind of compensatory gain from all the pain – an equity which meant that, though younger writers these days have it relatively easy, helped by creative writing courses, an eager local publishing industry and money from the State, the old battlers (Maurice Duggan is another example) were enriched in their writing simply by the toughness of their lives, the difficulties they encountered, the obstacles they overcame.

In fact Ballantyne's story suggests otherwise. Reid's researches show that his papers are full of detailed sketches, plans and ideas for fiction that was never written, and drafts of novels and stories that he never found the time, or the energy, or the encouragement to revise and complete. His published fiction is only a small part of his total literary effort. The wastage was enormous.

It would be a very hard judgement that said this wastage came of personal weakness; and it would be quite wrong to think of Ballantyne as a failure. To read again some of his best short stories, as I have just done, is to be reminded of how effortlessly his prose moves, how well he manages narrative, what a sound sense of structure he had, and what an easy grasp on the peculiar flavour of everyday New Zealand life and language.

It's to be hoped that Bryan Reid's book will encourage the republication and reconsideration of Ballantyne's best work and see some of it attended to in school and university English courses on New Zealand literature.

Proust Meets Joyce (and some others)[*]

The occasion that gives this book its title was a late-night supper party which Sydney and Violet Schiff (wealthy English society host and hostess and literary lion hunters) put on in Paris on 18 May 1922 with the purpose of bringing together the two Modernists they revered most, Marcel Proust and James Joyce. Also present were Igor Stravinsky, Pablo Picasso, Serge Diaghilev and a number of less famous but important figures like the Bloomsbury art critic Clive Bell and several well-titled French aristocrats. Just six months later most of those present would gather again on the occasion of Proust's funeral.

The supper, it seems, was not a great success. Joyce came well-primed (he was embarrassed not to have the right clothes), was largely silent and at one point fell asleep and snored, which caused Bell to leave. Proust made a grand entry very late and found conversation with the Irishman difficult. Nonetheless, the story of this unique meeting was retold many times, reaching its high point in the account given by Ford Madox Ford in his wonderfully embellishing memoir, *It was the Nightingale*, in which the two great writers spoke by turns, back and forth, each referring only to his own work, which the other hadn't read, and to his own acquaintances, whom the other hadn't met, and both complaining of current ailments.

The names of Sydney and Violet Schiff are familiar to anyone who

* A review of *A Night at the Majestic* by Richard Davenport-Hines (Faber, London, 2006), *Sunday Star-Times*, 23 April 2006.

has studied Katherine Mansfield's life. She was happy to be taken up by them, liked Violet very much, but found it hard to be as enthusiastic about Proust as they seemed to require; and she went off Sydney (himself a secret writer) when he seemed to slight one of her stories. On that occasion she wrote to her husband, Jack Murry: 'As to Proust with his Morceaux de Salon . . . let him tinkle away.'

Davenport-Hines devotes his first fifty pages to the supper party, but this is only a way in to his real subject, Proust. The Schiffs vanish from the narrative, and return at the end, when we are back in the year 1922, by which time their endless flattery and attention have become at once a necessity and a torment to the ailing writer.

Not a lot happened to Proust in his half century of life, but he managed to turn it into a major work of fiction, *À la recherche du temps perdu* (In search of the lost times), of more than three thousand pages, published in eight volumes over a period of fourteen years, the last three appearing posthumously. His correspondence has been published in thirty volumes; and recent Proust biographies (there have been at least five since 1990) vary in length between 600 and a thousand pages.

Brilliant, penetrating, keenly observant, precious, snobbish, hyper-sensitive, self-pitying, neurasthenic, valetudinarian, mother-fixated, Proust was slightly bi- but mainly homo-sexual, the first novelist to use the word 'homosexual', and the first to put the experience frankly and centrally into fiction. Aged seventeen and turned down by a school friend he had propositioned, he wrote the lad a typical note during a history lesson: 'I admire your wisdom while simultaneously regretting it. I am not fatuous enough to believe that my body is so precious a treasure that it required great strength of character to renounce it.'

His own sexual experience was not, it seems, vigorous, nor even particularly rewarding; but his reflections upon it, as upon everything, were endless and fascinating. Hearing, through a partition, a married couple making noisy love and washing themselves afterwards in a hip-bath, he transferred these aural effects to the first account in his novel of sex between two men. At the same time he wrote to a friend of how extraordinary all this noise and action seemed to him, for whom sex had about the same intensity as chilled beer.

The homosexual frankness came only in the fourth part of his great work. In the early volumes it had been disguised as heterosexual – as in the famous love of the narrator for Albertine. Other French writers of the time, notably André Gide and François Mauriac, welcomed Proust's honesty and applauded his courage; but Gide, himself homosexual, regretted that the principal homosexual character, the Baron de Charlus, and everything associated with him, was so lacking in beauty or romance; and Mauriac, heterosexual and Catholic, deplored the lack of a compensating 'saintly' character, and the 'terrible absence of God' from the work.

Proust wrote in bed, in a room cork-lined for quiet, and received visitors there wearing collar and tie and white gloves; and though the gloves were probably for protection against germs, he was immensely proud, and talked about it endlessly, when he found he had caught a cold from an Englishman of ancient and noble lineage. He insisted that friendship and love were worthless shams which distracted him from the serious work of writing about them; yet Davenport-Hines quotes him saying of his 'dearest friend' Reynaldo Hahn, 'If he murdered someone I'd hide the corpse in my bedroom so that people would think I had done the deed.' And Harold Bloom brackets him with Shakespeare and Freud as the Western canon's three great experts on jealousy in love.

Proust creates a world complete in itself to which you can return on repeated visits as to a foreign country. No writer analyses with greater subtlety and precision the operations of the human psyche as it remembers and reflects on experience, and as it imagines (and fears) the future. His fictions are aggregations of wonderfully constructed sentences, vivid memories, close observation and subtle reflection. And yet, at the same time that these qualities are admired and enjoyed, it's possible to feel something oppressive and repellent about the work, as if you're trapped in the basement of a crumbling château and must at all costs escape.

A Night at the Majestic owes much to the primary research of others. Its title is something of a misrepresentation; and it has been (or so it seems to me) rather nervously dressed up by its publisher to look like a book you might want to give as a present – a 'gift book' for someone who would probably never read Proust but might enjoy being able to talk about him. Nonetheless, it is well-written, cleverly put together, and its subject is inexhaustible.

Thom Gunn – the Man in the Iron Mask[*]

Thom Gunn was first known as one of the Movement poets of the 1950s, and though, like most of those associated with it, he soon found the label and the implied associations unwelcome, he might be thought of as representative at least in the sense that his work has been chiefly noted for propriety and constraint in its use of traditional or measurable forms, or discussed in terms of its departures from them. This is partly because Gunn has proved himself skilful, inventive and various in the exercise of rhyme, measure, syllabics; but also because in his case the material beyond poetry, those recurrent parallel occasions which represent a poet's central and obsessive 'subjects', have been, at least until his most recent books, more secretive, or muted, less directly engaged, in any case less public than those of his near contemporaries. Larkin was (or pretended to be) frank where Gunn was circumspect; Hughes was rough-shod where Gunn treads delicately.

No one seriously interested in poetry could be unimpressed by the

---

[*] A review of Thom Gunn's *Collected Poems* (Faber, London, 1994), written for the *London Review of Books*, and accepted. However, the editor, Mary-Kay Wilmers, and I fell out, initially about her copy-editing. In the ensuing exchange it became clear that she disliked my remarks at the end of the review about Gunn's use of the AIDS pandemic, saying I was in effect accusing him of exploiting the subject. I didn't, and still don't, believe anything of the kind is said or implied, and I withdrew the piece and offered it to Alan Ross at the *London Magazine* where it appeared in the issue for February–March 1996.

mechanics of an early poem like 'Pierce Street', with its stanza of five ten-syllable lines rhyming a b a b c, but where the half-line of 4 rhymes with 5's terminal word – this form carried through six stanzas.

> Nobody home. Long threads of sunlight slant
> Past curtains, blind, and slat, through the warm room.
> The beams are dazzling, but, random and scant,
> Pierce where they end
> small areas of the gloom
> On curve of chair-leg or a green stalk's bend.

But it is also true that a reader who pursues the thread of sense as far as it goes will find in the end a knot, a tangle, an uncertainty, which undermines the formal control.

It is a first-person poem, and the speaker hunts through an empty house until he comes upon the object of his search, a frieze of armed figures 'twice life-size'. Here are the final two stanzas:

> A silent garrison, and always there,
> They are the soldiers of the imagination
> Produced by it to guard it everywhere.
> Bodied within
> the limits of their station
> As, also, I am bodied by my skin.

> They vigilantly preserve as they prevent
> And are the thing they guard, having some time stood
> Where the painter reached to make them permanent.
> The floorboards creak.
> The house smells of its wood.
> Those who are transitory can move and speak.

There is not quite discovery here, nor recognition, nor a poetic confidence that will rest in its moment, content to let it resonate as it may, but rather a huge effort of will and intellect towards a conclusion. Somewhere in the background lurks the paradox of the lovers on the urn who cannot kiss because they are deathless art. So the painted soldiers, unlike the 'transitory' poet and painter, cannot 'move and speak'. But what is the warrant for seeing them as possessing any kind of permanence? And isn't their being offered as 'guardians' of the imagination which produced them (apart from adding two syllables to the count of ten) only an accident of their being soldiers. Would they be guardians if they had been, let's say, milkmaids?

The problem is not that one requires of all poems a perfect prose intelligibility, but that this kind of poetry of statement requires it of itself; and the tussle that has gone on between the demands of form, and the poet's uncertainly about just what it is he wants to make it 'mean', is unresolved.

Another poem much discussed and admired from this relatively early phase of Gunn's career is 'Innocence', which traces the life of a young athlete who

> Ignorant of the past;
> Culture of guilt and guilt's vague heritage,
> Self pity and the soul

becomes part of 'the Corps', where he learns 'Courage, endurance, loyalty and skill', and so is able to stand by unmoved while a man is cruelly murdered:

> When he stood near the Russian partisan
> Being burned alive, he therefore could behold
> The ribs wear gently through the darkening skin
> And sicken only at the Northern cold,
> Could watch the fat burn with a violent flame
> And feel disgusted only at the smell,
> And judge that all pain finishes the same
> As melting quietly by his boots it fell.

My problem with this springs again from Gunn's insistent yet ambiguous push towards a moral point. Deprived of a proper schooling in 'the past', the young man is fair game for an orderly and heartless barbarism. But what precise value and effect is that 'Culture of guilt' meant to have? And the shock of the final stanzas comes, I suspect, from a contradictory apprehension that the poet is either too close to the indifference which his poem seems to deplore, or worse, that he is imaginatively complicit in the act of violence.

In this late 1950s–early 1960s phase Gunn can sometimes seem at his least confusing where sense has become so abstract it dissolves altogether into form, and one is left with an inadvertent Ashberyesque *mime* of meaning:

> Nothing remained: Nothing, the wanton name
> That nightly I rehearsed till led away
> To a dark sleep, or sleep that held one dream.
>
> In this a huge contagious absence lay,
> More space than space, over the cloud and slime,
> Defined but by the encroachments of its sway.
> Stripped to indifference by the turns of time,
> Whose end I knew, I woke without desire,
> And welcomed zero as a paradigm.

Looking back on the 1950s it seems to me it was part of the thought of the time which most young poets had to break out of, or grow out of, that a good poem, one worthy of serious attention, developed from or towards an idea that could be stated separate from the poem itself. The 'slim volume' of the time offered thirty or forty ideas, frequently moral ideas, illustrated by, or springing from, observation and/or recollection. Thought grew from occasion, or was quarried out of it in the course of the poem's making; and verses were shaped towards a conclusion in which, often, a final rhyme seemed to close the gate on the initial experience rather than opening a door to it. There was something mechanical about this process, alien to the Modernism of Pound and early Eliot, whose presence (especially Eliot's) was huge, but whose influence on the practice of poetry was much less direct and pervasive than that of Hardy and Yeats.

It was a formula that served a poet like Larkin, whose skill was to add a lot of ironic, self-abasing intelligence and a large dash of quirky personality to the mix. For others a way to break out of the mechanics had to be found, and they were American poets who most clearly offered alternatives. Gunn's early move to the American West Coast, where he has lived most of his life since, opened his eyes to William Carlos Williams, Marianne Moore and Wallace Stevens; while it was his homosexuality made him honour and attend to the morally useful but technically doubtful example of Robert Duncan. His Stanford University mentor Ivor Winters made him aware of syllabic verse – the measure and patterning of the verse line, not by metrical feet (iambic, trochaic, etc.), and not by a count of speech stresses which in the mid-century largely replaced the standard iambic measure, but by the number of syllables per line. In its arbitrariness it is, perhaps, the poetic equivalent of the twelve-note scale in music; and it proved an effective escape especially from the iambic drum which beats somewhere in the skull of every well-educated Anglophone poet. As Pound put it, 'To break the pentameter, that was the first heave.'

The question 'Why count anything?' is one poets find difficult to answer. Partly, no doubt, because 'free verse' is not of itself a barrier to the iambic measure, which can stow away unnoticed; and partly because to require that lines fit a pattern, any pattern, rather than none, can set up that slow productive tension between shape and sense, forcing the reconsideration of every word and its alternatives. 'Free verse', or the poem that shapes itself from within by an energy springing out of its occasion, is fine for those moments when, as Arnold says, 'Nature takes the pen from the poet's hand.' Every true poet may know what that means; but every serious poet knows better than to sit around waiting for it to happen.

The second half of *My Sad Captains* (1961) kicks off with a number of syllabic poems. But with characteristic anxiety, or technical overkill, Gunn decides (as in 'Pierce Street') to give them a half-rhyme as well. The first poem opens –

> The window, a wide pane in the bare
> modern wall, is crossed by colourless
> peeling trunks of the eucalyptus
> recurring against raw sky-colour.
>
> It wakes me, and my eyes rest on it,
> sharpening, and seeking merely all

of what can be seen, the substantial,
where the things themselves are adequate.

So I observe them, able to see
them as they are, the neutral sections
of trunk, spare, solid, lacking at once
disconnectedness and unity.

In terms of measure (nine-syllable lines with half-rhymes a b b a) everything here is right; in terms of poetic effect it is hardly too much to say everything is wrong. The recognition of a conventional rhyme scheme, and the *look* of tetrameters, makes it difficult not to read the lines as seriously disabled iambics; and when that problem is overcome, Gunn's tendency to abstraction, to an excess of gloss on the facts produces a quilted effect. Inside every fat man, Cyril Connolly said, there is a thin man wildly signalling to be let out; and the same is true of every fat poem:

> wide pane in the bare
> wall   crossed by colourless
> trunks of   eucalypt
>   against raw sky
> wakes me

In those opening three stanzas there is scarcely more 'poem' than these seventeen words represent; and they have been smothered at birth.

Two further stanzas insist on the primacy of 'things', and 'their fine lack of even potential meanings'. It is like a new manifesto, a confirmation of W. C. Williams's 'No ideas but in things', and of John Crowe Ransom's echoing insistence on 'things in their thinginess'. But the more Gunn's 'things', his scene, his objects-in-view, are defined, qualified, generalised, explained, the less live they are to the senses.

At times the syllabic experiment did work for him, especially where, as in the sequence 'Confessions of a Life Artist', he used a short compact line (seven syllables) and let the sense amble freely from line to line. What results then is not urgent language, but it is a plausible dramatic voice.

Parts of 'Flying above California' show this phase of Gunn at its best:

> Lean upland
> sinewed and tawny in the sun, and
>
>   valley cool with mustard, or sweet with
> loquat . . .
>   Sometimes
>
>   on fogless days by the Pacific
> there is a cold hard light without break

But the compulsion to explain, as if the raw experience would be valueless, like a signature without a witness, pushes him on past that point where addition of words becomes subtraction of effect:

> that reveals merely what it is – no more
> and no less. That limiting candour,
>
> that accuracy of the beaches,
> is part of the ultimate richness.

The central poem of Gunn's early years is 'The Byrnies', not in that it is his best, but because it is one that can be read as offering an image of the author and his work. The mythic 'heroes' of its opening advance upon an equally mythic 'forest'; their identity is generalised, and it is their outer casing that gives them definition:

> The heroes paused upon the plain.
> When one of them but swayed, ring mashed on ring:
>   Sound of the byrnies knitted chain,
> Vague evocations of a constant Thing.

Well-made iambics, alternating tetrameter and pentameter, rhyming a b a b, seem like the verse equivalent of the byrnies (chain mail). But what is the 'constant Thing' of which its sounds are 'vague evocations'? Are these 'heroes' homosexual men whose defences against a hostile world become the identity by which they are known even to themselves? To insist on such a reading would be constricting; but it is surely part of, or relevant to, the psychology that produced it. Gunn's chain mail has been his formal fashioning – the poet as mollusc.

He grew up in a world where gay men signalled their kinship privately. During his adult life has occurred the accelerating process of 'coming out'. Correspondingly, his early poems, like Auden's, were neuter, available to be understood according to the sexual preference of the reader. Retrospectively, since he has declared himself, the love poems, and his interest for example in motor-cycle boys, board riders, truckers, heroes, soldiers and black leather, have taken on a narrower but more focused meaning. There is gain and loss in this.

Gunn was too old to be quite young in the social and sexual revolution of the late 1960s, but young enough to take part in it, and his poems of that time reflect new freedoms and new experiences – rock concerts, protest, love-ins, marijuana, LSD. He has said that those 'were the fullest years of my life, crowded with discovery, both inner and outer', and that almost all the poems collected in *Moly* in one way or another reflect what he refers to as 'the acid experience'. But – and I suppose one should not be surprised – the poetry does not change radically. There is no Ginsbergian outpouring, but the same effort towards containment, with a greater, though not exclusive, use of formal iambics. The central image is of metamorphosis, and the title poem, one of his best, is its most vivid articulation.

> The pale-lashed eyes my only human feature.
> My teeth tear, tear. I am the snouted creature
>
> That bites through anything, root, wire, or can.
> If I was not afraid, I'd eat a man.
>
> Oh a man's flesh already is in mine.
> Hand and foot poised for risk. Buried in swine.

This is man become animal; but some of the lines are brutally capable of another meaning, one which, though cancelled, is not

213

altogether annulled. Already, however, the pig is rooting for the other magic herb, moly, that will return him to human limit, morals and rationality, whose force is asserted in the flow and exactness of the couplets. The strength of the poem lies not just in its technical mastery and moral implications, but more, in the density and specificity of its language. Here *dinglichkeit* is not talked about. It is achieved.

Jack Straw's Castle (1976) contains the sequence 'The Geysers', Gunn's most ambitious attempt to take his readers on a 'trip'. Rhyming pairs are an oddly formal vehicle for the journey, but they are progressively broken up and interrupted, though never lost, as the combined effects of steam and mud baths, marijuana, and human proximity and promiscuity, push poet and reader towards the climax, which is certainly striking:

> torn from the shelf
> > in which I breathed and trod
> I am
> > I am raw meat
> > I am a god.

But the title poem of the collection suggests some loss of confidence in the efficacy and ethics of these new freedoms. Jack Straw is the worthless No-man within; his castle is his house, his body, his sense of self; and he shares them with the mocking ghost of Charles Manson whose orgies and murders he inwardly re-enacts.

As if in retreat from these fears and doubts the third section of the book returns to memories of England and childhood – some of Gunn's clearest, most direct and economical poems. This section also contains 'Yoko', the poem (prefiguring Les Murray's more radical experiments in this line) spoken in the charming persona of a Newfoundland dog; and 'Breaking Ground', notable mainly because its woman subject (probably the poet's mother) comes as a relief from Gunn's oppressively all-male cast.

By the mid-1970s Gunn was a part of the poetry landscape, not quite a major figure but a significant one. There is a more relaxed confidence in his writing, less anxious rigour, not wit exactly but a new sense of humour which sometimes compacts and approximates

214

to it, and a more colloquial, energetic, less wasteful language. Distance and elapsed time seem especially to give him his most successful, least striving, tone. 'Talbot Road', his recollection of London and his friend Tony White in 1964–65, is a poem so user-friendly I can imagine its author might look at it with doubt, even alarm. But that absorption in a subject which takes the teller out of himself has pared the language down; the 'poetry' is in the stripped facts, their bareness, vividness and human warmth. It is a kind of relaxation into subject and statement quite distinct from the more recent 'An Invitation', where the casual decorum of a letter to his brother ('Well, I think / After all that, we'll need a drink') never rises beyond versifying, and probably doesn't aspire to. Poems like 'Talbot Road' are not ground-breaking, or significant as literary history. What they are, however, is *successful.*

Then came *The Man with Night Sweats* (1992), not exclusively but most notably commemorating friends and acquaintances dying or dead of AIDS. Poetry is a form of public communication, not exempt from those considerations which influence the press; and if a poet has a 'subject' which is of broad general interest and can find a way to see it in verse, there is no reason why he or she should not profit by it. In 1951, before we had got used to seeing major surgery on television, James Kirkup wrote a poem describing a heart operation in vivid and precise detail. No poem Kirkup wrote before or after attracted such intense interest. In recent years Northern Irish poets who have found ways of writing about the troubles have gained what might be thought, not undeserved, but disproportionate, or anyway not purely literary, attention. So with Gunn's poems springing from the AIDS crisis.

The problem for the critic is that it is so difficult to keep the value of that interest separate from the value of the poem as poem; and the difficulty is compounded by the now widely held, and wrong, belief that the distinction is unreal, that the aesthetic and (let's call it) political cannot be distinguished. They do of course meet and overlap; but the confusion this can cause is a reason for clearing one's mind about how they differ, not an excuse for pretending that they don't.

The confusion was well-illustrated by some of the reviews of Gunn's 1992 collection, and nowhere more clearly than by Alan Sinfield's in the *London Review of Books*. 'For the right-wing bigot', Sinfield declared, 'the AIDS pandemic was a godsend', because before it happened it was becoming clear that gay men 'were doing better [than heterosexuals] with the sex and love thing'. So the subject, and thus the poems, with their reaffirmation of the gay community and family, were seen as important almost without reference to means, to form, to the specifics of words on the page; and Sinfield's only quarrel with Gunn was on the question of why he did not accept that 'the traditional idea of poetry' had 'run its course' and write exclusively 'to reinforce a beleaguered gay subculture'.

What I think can properly be said is that Gunn, approaching and passing sixty, had reached a stage where a poet often needs a new demand on his skills and resources, one which takes him out of that self most of us grow weary of with age; and that the shocks and griefs of AIDS among the San Francisco gay community provided it for him. Further, that the subject, the preoccupation, the concern, arrived at a time when he was technically equipped to deal with them. On an imaginary graph the life of the man and that of the poet would be seen to converge in these poems, the one making precise demands which the other could precisely meet.

Knox's Kiss *

If you picked up *Billie's Kiss* knowing nothing about author or publishing history you might almost believe the date of the events – 1903 – to signal the era in which it was written; and if the events were not dated, you might even place it somewhat earlier, in the second half, but well before the end of, the nineteenth century. For myself it's as if I read this novel, not once but many times, long ago, in my teens. The flavour might be that of, for example, R. D. Blackmore's *Lorna Doone* (read 55 years ago): a Victorian romance, very good but somewhat sub-Brontë, heavily plotted, a study partly in provincial manners, with aristocrats and servants, set in a wild landscape which reflects the turmoil of the characters' emotions; and with two central characters, male and female, each with strengths which are also limitations, threatened by circumstance, and destined, the writing cleverly makes us feel, either for one another or for death. There would be things to give away that the book was not in fact Victorian – for example that a fictional kiss can involve the tongue, and that the act of sex precedes the birth of children; and the style is not florid enough, not sufficiently oblique, upholstered or subjunctified; but as fancy dress it is pretty good.

* A review of *Billie's Kiss* by Elizabeth Knox (Victoria University Press, Wellington, 2002), *Landfall* 204, November 2002.

Since we know that *Billie's Kiss* is in fact by our own remarkable Elizabeth Knox, it has to be read as very proficient pastiche. It is a late Victorian romance in much the same way that Robert Altman's movie *Gosford Park* (setting a country house-party, upstairs-downstairs plot elements, uncertainty about a central character's paternity and the victim stabbed – where else? – in the library) is a conventional British murder mystery of the 1930 or 1940s. In both cases the whole thing – scene, plot mechanics, characterisation – is contained within very large post-modern inverted commas. As a consequence the experience is double: you read *Billie's Kiss* as you would read the kind of novel it mimics, but with a detachment additional to any you would have felt had it in fact been of its time and place. The addition is the recognition that it is not what it seems, and doesn't pretend to be. That the author is not British but a New Zealander adds to the sense of deliberateness and game-playing.

This is significantly different from *Memoirs of a Peon*, where Sargeson writes a pastiche of the eighteenth-century British writers whose powerful influence he is finding ways to escape from. Sargeson signals his escape by taking charge of that style, but even more by the material he puts into it, which is exclusively, typically, and richly 'New Zealand'. Knox responds as keenly to place as Sargeson does, and makes it just as vivid; but this is British 'place' – the Western Isles, which her foreword indicates she has visited. Sargeson is of a generation that was finding ways to lay claim to its New Zealand territory – a necessary phase in our literary history. Knox is of a generation (or a time, since it is not something occurring only among one age group) laying claim to the world as its territory. What the two books have in common is their declared grounding in the history of English literature.

The fact that the novel was being written while Knox held the Menton fellowship also makes a small contribution to its material. Sisters Edith and Billie (Wilhelmina) have spent part of their childhood on the Mediterranean. There are recollections at intervals of the Ligurian coast, and the story ends on the beach at Menton. These passages, perfectly functional though hardly inevitable, read like nods to the New Zealand literary community over the heads of other readers, adding a further faint set of inverted commas.

The story begins with an explosion which sinks a ferry just arrived in the port of Stolnsay where Henry Maslen, newly appointed archivist for the island's millionaire owner, Lord Hallowhulme, is bringing his pregnant wife Edith and her sister Billie. Edith, whom dyslexic Billie loves dearly and has depended upon, is drowned, along with a number of others. Murdo Hesketh, a passenger who has noticed Billie's red hair, and been victim of her clumsiness, at first believes that she is involved in, or knew in advance about, the plan to destroy the ship. This suspicion springs from the fact that Billie, at the last moment before the explosion, was seen to rush down the gangway to the wharf; and she is not able to explain (because it is shameful) that the reason for this rush was shock at/retreat from having kissed/been kissed by her brother-in-law Henry.

The explosion is both real and symbolic, and the aftershocks and reverberations continue through a plot which decidedly 'thickens', filling out the inter-weavings of the characters' pasts, offering answers which for a long time only pose new questions. This intricacy is part of the pastiche – that artificial patterning which caused E. M. Forster (who mistook it for narrative, as if there was no other kind) to lament, 'Oh dear yes, I'm afraid the novel tells a story', and to deplore that aspect of his trade as 'low' and 'atavistic'. The realist novel and the 'slice of life' story were reactions against this kind of plotting; and the sophisticated post-modern goes back to it tongue-in-cheek, while showing how well she can do it. It is like one of Picasso's moments of 'simple' representation in the midst of innovation; or Richard Strauss writing a traditional Italian tenor lyric for the *levée* scene in *Der Rosenkavalier* – high calibre 'show-off'.

The central characters of Murdo and Billie are perfectly of their type, and excellently done. Murdo Hesketh is the romance hero, smouldering, powerful, intransigent, outwardly arrogant and inwardly self-tormenting. His prototype is Heathcliff, a name his own faintly echoes, but (mercifully) less extravagant, not quite such an extreme challenge to reason and common sense. Billie is beautiful, with Pre-Raphaelite hair, physically clumsy, socially awkward (there is a hint of autism – something which *Black Oxen* reveals Knox knows about and is interested in), but truthful, direct, redoubtable and with an intelligence that shines in her verbal responses like the hair that is made so much of. Billie's hair is like Samson's, the symbol of her strength.

And do these two, Billie and Murdo, overcome the many obstacles standing in the way of recognition of their need for one another? Are they to achieve happiness together? Who will triumph in the hand-to-hand fight to the death in the ruined tower? Reader, you will have to find out for yourself!

Knox is copious with character and event, and tends to overload the narrative. She carries so much in her head, and thinks her readers, having once been 'briefed', are carrying the same load – or ought to be. Minor characters reappear after they have been forgotten, and the reader has to go back and quarry for them. *Black Oxen* had the same fault, partly mitigated by a list of characters at the front. A good story-teller should not make this mistake; and should resist the temptation to run away up every side-track that presents itself. But the writing, as always in Knox, is dependably first rate.

This book on its own would be a puzzle, difficult to deal with, and might seem, even, for all its pleasures, a somewhat wasteful use of a very large talent. But among the variety of Knox's other work it finds an honourable and interesting place – a one-off experiment, as, perhaps, each of her novels has been; and the larger picture, the Jamesian 'figure in her carpet', is still emerging.

Billie's Kiss is also another signal that New Zealand fiction is ceasing for the most part to be simply or solely regional. Knox is a fully professional writer whose feet are on this ground, but whose work is written for an international market. There can be a down-side to this, as to most good things; but it is a development which I think on the whole must be good. If the provincial voice should find her too big for her boots, as it no doubt will from time to time, that is no longer something she has to listen to or be curbed by.

As to why you should admire *Billie's Kiss* in particular: there is an oddity here. It is to be admired as an exercise in the art of fiction; but because the fiction is so self-referential, there is a slight feeling of being inside the Barthesian literary enclosure without a door or a ladder. I am, I suppose, wanting to have it both ways: not to be that provincial and curbing voice, and yet still hopeful at the thought of what this huge talent may achieve for 'New Zealand literature'. There is an analogy (imperfect, but interesting) with the case of another Wellingtonian, Peter Jackson. In *Heavenly Creatures* Jackson showed that he was capable of making a first-rate movie that had its roots in New Zealand social realities. In *Lord of the Rings* he has proved that he is world champion at making and managing hobbits and horrors. Without in the least taking away from, or wanting to seem ungrateful for, what has been achieved so far, there is still, in both cases, a consummation devoutly to be wished, in which the technical skill, only now fully revealed, combines with the realities of New Zealand time, place and history – not to make New Zealand, in Mansfield's words, 'leap in the eyes of the Old World' (though of course that would be nice) but to make it leap in our own.

Rushdie the Clown[*]

Rumour has it that Salman Rushdie's *Shalimar the Clown*, promoted as a return to the form of *Midnight's Children* and *Shame* after recent less orderly fictions, made it down to the final eight before it was eliminated (along with Ian McEwan's *Saturday*) from the just announced Booker short-list. In the way all book awards work (sales promotions disguised as rewards for literary merit), this will serve the novel well enough. The question of whether Rushdie should have been excluded, in favour of (for example) Zadie Smith, from the final six will attract as much attention as a short-listing would have done. Commerce rules.

Incomparably commercial since an unpleasant and famous Ayatollah invited the faithful to murder him, Rushdie is also, as it happens, a writer of huge and incontinent talent. He is a mixed blessing whose early work I read with patience and respect. Latterly I find the patience, if not the respect, has begun to wear thin. His talent for large structures, his memory for fact and detail, his command of the English sentence (some in this book would rival Sir Walter Scott's), his quirky naming, his ear for comic variations of spoken English, his ability to make the real symbolic and the symbolic real – it is all still there and in good working overdrive.

* A review of Salman Rushdie's *Shalimar the Clown* (Jonathan Cape, London, 2005), *Sunday Star-Times*, 25 September 2005.

Time and the fatwa have left their mark on Rushdie. His purpose in this novel is serious. I suppose it always was; but the feeling has become darker. The cartoon quality that gave his early writing its characteristic comic distancing still works, I think, though it has a slightly dated feel about it. In places one can feel him trying to escape from it, but the escapes are into journalism and anger.

Rushdie's Kashmir in this novel is a symbol of the world at a proper human scale, beautiful and productive, where racial and religious differences can find accommodation. It is an ideal, a place of romantic memory, a Paradise (the word is used). Its story, as he tells it, is Paradise Lost – destroyed by nationalism, fundamentalism, fanaticism.

Boonyi Kaul, a Hindu dancer, and Shalimar Noman, a Muslim tightrope walker, from adjoining Kashmiri villages, fall in love at the age of fourteen. When they are revealed as lovers the two communities overcome their differences and the pair are married. Some years later their region is visited by the American ambassador to India, Max Ophuls. Ophuls, Jewish, born in Alsace, Second World War freedom fighter and hero, linguist, lover of women and general man-about-the-world, seduces, and/or is seduced by, Boonyi Kaul, who is called upon to dance for the visitor, and who sees in him a way of escape from the confines of Kashmir. Boonyi is taken to Delhi and set up as the ambassador's mistress. The openings she hopes for as a dancer don't appear, and she slides into addictions to food and drugs which destroy her beauty and talent. A child is born to her, and taken from her when she is returned to her village, where she is shamed and ostracised.

Meanwhile her cuckold husband, burning with hurt, hate and shame, has joined Kashmir's Muslim freedom fighters, but bears a secret determination that, however long it takes, he will kill Boonyi, Max Ophuls, and any child resulting from their affair.

The novel begins in Los Angeles with Shalimar cutting Max's throat on the doorstep of the house belonging to India (a.k.a. Kashmira), Max's now 24-year-old daughter to Boonyi. It then tracks back over the preceding two decades (and even further back to Max's youth and his war exploits), covering the gradual destruction of Kashmir by Indian military repression and Pakistani-backed fundamentalism. Somewhere past page 300 Shalimar decapitates Boonyi and sets off for America in pursuit of his second goal, Max's murder, with which the book opens. The final 100 pages are largely taken up with Shalimar's stalking of India (or Kashmira). Does he succeed in killing her too, or will she turn the tables on him?

Shalimar the Clown moves through a range of modes and tones – in Kashmir variously mythic, reflective, idyllic-pastoral, brutal-realist; in Los Angles electrically post-modern. It is large enough to contain such variation; and the narrative is an impressive feat of engineering. That it is not my cup of tea doesn't mean it won't be yours.

Craig Raine and History[*]

One had heard for some years about Craig Raine's 'narrative poem' before it became, upon completion, and through the intercession of literary agent David Godwin, a 'novel in verse', sold to Penguin for an advance of £60,000 after Faber's offer of £15,000 had been declined. There was talk that it might win the Booker Prize – not enough talk, perhaps, or not public enough, and it was released too late in the year to make an impression on the by-September-exhausted judges. If it had been chosen for the short-list it would have made the year's Booker debate more interesting, and I would have rejoiced for the author. Since it did not, it will do no harm if I say that *History:The Home Movie* is not a novel, and perhaps not a long poem either – by which I mean that it would be more accurate to describe it as 87 poems connected if not quite unified by a common form (loose unrhymed triplets) and style, and by common subject matter – two families, ultimately interlocking, the Russian Pasternaks and the English Raines.

High on one of the two connected family trees offered at the front of the book to assist the reader, Boris Pasternak figures; low down on the other, Craig Raine. Yet a note at the end insists, 'All characters in this book are fictitious, and any resemblance to actual persons, living or dead, is coincidental.' Relationships are changed, separate incidents are brought together in the one poem, fact and invention mixed; but

[*] *London Magazine*, February–March 1995.

the foundation in actual events and people is so clear, the denial seems worse than mendacious; it seems lazy. Some better formula should have been found.

One can see that the poet faced a problem. It must be very widely known that his wife, Ann Pasternak Slater (called Li by friends and family), is the daughter of Boris Pasternak's sister; and Raine's own writing, especially the prose passage in *Rich*, has opened his parents' household to the public. So how are we to distinguish the writer Pasternak, or the boxer and faith-healer Raine, whose 'resemblance to actual persons . . . is coincidental', from the men who bore the same names and shared the same life experiences?

Partly, I suppose, by the fact that in the book the demands of narrative and of poetic art, and not fidelity to 'what happened', determines what remains as it was, and what gets left out or changed. The book, for example, joins the Raines and the Pasternaks a generation earlier than life did, the fictitious Eliot Raine marrying Boris's sister Lydia and fathering Lisa who marries Craig – a device which has the curious effect of making the fictional Craig Raine his wife's first cousin, which the actual Craig Raine is not.*

The fact pack is shuffled and re-dealt, partly, it would seem, in ways which give events public and historical significance; so while the work remains a 'home movie' – a private family record – the word 'history' in the title keeps some suggestion of its larger meaning. But we do need to know something of the history in order to see it there; if we are ignorant it will scarcely reveal itself. And one of the oddities of the work is that it is the push towards 'history' which makes us most aware that it is fiction. We must accept, for example, that the sign-writer Jimmy Raine (Uncle Charlie of *Rich*) is watched at his work by Churchill in London in 1931 (inadvertently giving the great man an idea for a speech in the House), attends a Mosley rally in 1934, encounters Haile Selassie in Bath in 1936, and on guard duty in Gibraltar in 1942 fails to recognise General Eisenhower and arrests him. This seems a high score of encounters with great figures of our

---

* If I had read a life of Pasternak no doubt the lines between fact and fiction would be clearer to me. I notice that in my edition of *Doctor Zhivago* the final poem is translated by Lydia Slater. This must be Ann Pasternak Slater's mother; and we may suppose, therefore, that the fictitious Eliot Raine bears some relation to Ann's father.

time for an ordinary citizen in just ten years. Similarly Eliot Raine talks to Yeats in 1920 in Oxford and meets him on the stairs in Vienna in 1934, attends the London production of a play by Mussolini in 1932 when the Prince of Wales is present, marries a Pasternak, and in 1954 appears as psychiatric witness for the defence of the cousin of a royal, accused of attacking his wife with an axe.

Any of these things might have happened; but could they all? Eliot's second encounter with Yeats (the conjunction of names is awkward, but the awkwardness seems to be welcomed and exploited) occurs when both are seeking a Steinach operation for sexual rejuvenation; but Eliot Raine in that year is only thirty. And in the court case of the royal axeman, it has to be accepted that Norman Raine, the boxer and faith-healer, is both next-door neighbour to the accused, and brother to the expert witness. These improbables, this casualness about fictional plausibility, are tolerable in a sequence of poems only because the real interest lies elsewhere. If this *were* a novel, they might be serious obstacles to full engagement with the work.

But in fact this is a collection of poems before it is anything else; and though the hype which turned it into a 'novel in verse' may be to blame, to write about it, as a number of reviewers have done, as if one is dealing with it when one describes character and incident, is quite unsatisfactory.

Craig Raine's relation to the Modernist movement is interesting. It is part of his inheritance – he has absorbed it; he has also in some ways rejected it, and in others taken the by-pass road. In form his work is conservative, but (unlike, say, Larkin's, or Anthony Thwaite's) also neutral, in the sense that poetic forms do not greatly interest him – they are not for him an issue. He is famous for analogy – simile, metaphor, the conceit, the image – and that too is a conservative characteristic. Despite T. S. Eliot's 'like a patient etherized upon a table', Modernism mostly avoided simile and metaphor, I think because they tend to sound 'literary' (what Wordsworth called a 'family language of poets') and to compromise the impression that the vehicle is spoken language.

But the 'Martian' similes Raine made his name by were not usually instant and open; they were often opaque, teasing, offering the fascination of what's difficult and the pleasure of problem-solving. By this route Raine found his own intuitive way of conjoining again those apparently alien elements in Eliot's Modernism – the mysteriousness of French Symbolism and the wit of the Metaphysicals. Now he has aspired to go the next step – to offer a long poem, or poem sequence.

No sooner had the Modernist poets – those who in retrospect would be so-called – decided, or accepted from their nineteenth-century precursors, that 'the long poem is a contradiction in terms' than they began to look for ways out of the box which seemed to be a consequence. It is by that significant piece of literary history that the originator of Imagism became the author of the *Cantos*.

It had become quite clear, or at least clearly agreed, that the uniquely poetic element was something distinct from sequential narrative and logical argument. The long poem, then – and Pound had epic ambitions – could only be an aggregation of fragments ('These fragments I have shored against my ruin') which were in some sense 'pure'. What Pound called 'the presentative method' – meaning that nothing should be explained, but should be simply *there*, like an object, present to the senses – would keep the voice dramatic and the line alive. And 'history', that larger significance which epic required, would come to the reader, not as in expository or narrative prose, but by means of what he called 'the luminous detail':

> Palace in smoky light,
> Troy but a heap of smouldering boundary stones . . .
> The silver mirrors catch at the bright stones and flare.

Or again:

> The enormous tragedy of the dream in the peasant's
> bent shoulders
> Manes! Manes was tanned and stuffed,
> Thus Ben and la Clara *a Milano*
>   by the heels at Milano.

My first thought on reading the early Pasternak sections of *History: The Home Movie* was of Chekhov. My second was to dismiss the first because, after all, place and characters were Russian, and what would you expect? My third was to reinstate the first, since I was *not* reminded of Tolstoy or Dostoevsky.

Then I remembered that it was Chekhov, first in a letter to his brother, later in *The Seagull*, who said that the way to convey a moonlit night was not to write 'long and stilted descriptions'. The writer Trigorin, Treplieff explains in *The Seagull*, has done away with those. 'He writes that the neck of a broken bottle lying on the bank glittered in the moonlight, and that the shadow lay black under the mill-wheel. There you have a moonlit night before your eyes.'

Here is the likeness to Raine, and common ground with Pound. Chekhov's 'neck of a broken bottle' is Pound's 'luminous detail' – and Raine, above most poets writing English at the moment, is a master of detail.

But there is also a difference. Chekhov, like the Modernists, shunned analogy, which he saw as tarnished with literariness. Raine has made analogy so much his stock-in-trade it is almost a liability, like an especially clever trick that arouses expectation and must be endlessly repeated. His are not metaphors of the kind Chekhov complained about in a letter to Gorki – seas that breathe, skies that gaze, nature that whispers, speaks, moans; but nor does Raine satisfy, as Pound mostly does, Chekhov's preference for 'simple phrases – "The sun set", "It was dark", "It began to rain" '.

It is instructive to look at the two poets, Raine and Pound, separated by half a century, undertaking similar poetic tasks in the course of writing their long poems. Here for example are two characters in action, the first a sign-writer at work, the second a woman about to throw herself to her death from a high window:

In his hand, greatness,
laid on the mahlstick

which flattens its muslin nose
like a miniature pudding
tied up for steaming.
                    (Raine)

And she went towards the window
        the slim white stone bar
Making a double arch;
Firm even fingers held to the firm pale stone:

229

Swung for a moment,
            And the wind out of Rhodez
Caught in the full of her sleeve.
            (Pound)

Here they describe wet weather:

On the road sparks of rain,
then rain doing a rain dance.

Ski sticks, deck tennis, quoits
on the pool at Peredelkino.
Through sliding glass

the garden wavers, bleeds, runs,
a waterfall of falling greens.
            (Raine)

That day there was cloud over Zoagli
And for three days snow cloud over the sea
Banked like a line of mountains.
Snow fell. Or rain fell solid, a wall of lines
So that you could see where the air stopped open
and where the rain fell beside it.
            (Pound)

And here, the behaviour of water:

Listen, listen to the water
washing the gravel pit
like a little girl
wearing her mother's shoes.
            (Raine)

and the water flowing away from that side of the lake
is silent as ever at Sirmio
            under the arches
            (Pound)

Here they observe/remember a person/persons:

> George Craze Esq, presides,
> his hearing aid
>
> like a lost spermatozoon
> having a word in his ear.
>> (Raine)
>
>> old Ford's conversation
> consisting of *res* non *verba*,
>> despite William's anecdotes, in that Fordie
>>> never dented an opinion for the phrase's sake
> and had more humanitas.
>> (Pound)

Or they evoke Mediterranean scenes:

> All day, sunlight has divided
> like cells on the sea, and gone.
> The full Mediterranean moon
>
> is brighter than a microscope.
>> (Raine)
>
> Forked shadow falls dark on the terrace
> More black than the floating martin
>> that has no care for your presence
> His wing-print is black on the roof tiles
> And the print is gone with his cry.
>> (Pound)

It is surprising how direct, literal, unliterary Pound seems. Raine's images say 'Look at me!'; Pound's say, 'Look at the object.'

Everyone knows that Pound's faults are roughness and a tendency – an *American* tendency – to over-reach himself; but Raine, for all the richness of the human material and the boldness with which he makes use of it, does not avoid what appears a characteristic English fussiness. The cabinet maker's precision is also a limitation. So the question arises: should the temperamental minimalist have taken on the giant History? Has the flyweight wrongly entered himself in the heavyweight division?

I use the term minimalist because Raine uses it of Chekhov, clearly with no negative intent. 'Chekhov is a great minimalist', he writes in one of his essays. 'Like Jane Austen, who can create interest and comedy from a pencil stub, he makes do with very little.'

Three or four times in *History: The Home Movie* the source of all the information we are offered is given a voice – that of a spy. At the 1919 conference of the Russian Communist Party this persona tells us, 'I am here on my own account / disguised as a pencil.' In an essay on Mussolini's play (the same one attended by the Prince of Wales and the fictive Uncle Eliot) Raine discusses Nabokov's disquisition on a pencil, and adds, 'I think of historians, perhaps unfairly, as people with no time for pencils. Treaties, so to speak, are signed by fountain pens, gripped between important fingers, and overseen by famous faces.'

There is clearly a connection between Chekhov as minimalist, Jane Austen's pencil stub, the pencil which historians overlook and the spy 'disguised as a pencil'. It is being signalled that we are receiving the small man's truth, the unofficial story, history as it is lived rather than as it is subsequently written.

Since the Romantic movement turned its back on eighteenth-century generalities, insisting that the poet did, after all, number the streaks of the tulip and that the universe was to be found in a grain of sand, we have been heading down a road which, it might be argued, leads logically to *History: The Home Movie*. But if Pound believed in the efficacy of the luminous detail, he also believed in, and continued to affirm even after its defeat, 'the dream in the peasant's bent shoulders'. It might have been, in his case, an unworthy dream, or one that took an unfortunate turn; but it meant that there was a reach always beyond the immediate, and that there was a hierarchy of value, a variable scale of importance, attaching to the ways in which human beings occupied their waking hours.

Modernism, in other words, held still to one or another of the grand designs – Christianity, Communism, Fascism, or, as a last resort, to the transcendence of Art. In this sense alone, I think, Raine might be called 'post-Modern'. There is in his vision no way of apprehending a value which will hold the fragments together in a larger unity – or none that I can perceive, or feel as I read. Cleverness becomes a value in itself.

The question must be asked, even if it doesn't have to be answered, whether those who lived through the great and terrible events of the eighty years Raine's poems skip over and sometimes wade through, might be imagined protesting that if history cannot be made noble, or coherent, or even meaningful, it doesn't have to be demeaned. Rather too much has been made of the fact that Raine's male characters' masturbatory habits figure at not infrequent intervals throughout the sequence. There is no reason why they should not; but it does indicate something about the closeness of the focus.

Perhaps a better way of putting my faint and bleating protest (because that is what it amounts to) is to say that while intellectually I can't argue with Raine's vision, and even probably share it, I don't believe it is one that can sustain an epic structure. If the truth is that there is no pattern other than that which illusion provides, then it may be that the epic scale requires either illusions, or heroism.

As the nineteenth century was coming to its end Chekhov wrote, in a letter to A. S. Suvorin,

> We paint life as it is, and beyond that neither whoa! nor giddap! Whip us and we cannot go a step further. We have neither immediate nor distant aims and our souls are a yawning void. We have no politics, we don't believe in revolution, we have no god, we are not afraid of ghosts, and I personally am not afraid even of death and sightlessness. One who desires for nothing, hopes for nothing, and fears nothing, cannot be an artist.

But Chekov was an artist; and so is Craig Raine. And if, in the case of *History: The Home Movie*, architectonics does not, and cannot, match ambition, that fact should be stated and set aside. It should not be allowed to stand in the way of the pleasure and profit to be had from poems which are consistently skilful, witty, inventive, linguistically rich, and humanly interesting.

A Good War on the Inarticulate*

On the cover Les Murray is quoted recommending Gray as 'one of the contemporary masters of poetry in English'. Rather than 'mastery' I would settle for something more modest, like 'authenticity'. The personality found in Gray's work is not guileless, but it's more innocent than the ambitious strategist who plays such a large part in Murray's. Which is not of course to suggest that Gray lacks a range of skills and forms. From the succession of short, penetrating images, Japanese style, where his keen sense of what is *out there* ('The grass here is born as straw', 'The surf / is a mural of Valhalla') meshes with a talent for analogy –

> I am one of those who have watched their image in a hearth, where a fire
> was tearing itself to pieces with its nails and with its fists

– right through to the long (or longish) poem in the long line, he displays, if not the bristling armoury of a Murray, certainly one sufficient to wage a good war on the inarticulate.

---

* *Stand*, June 2000, a review of Robert Gray's *Lineations*, published by Arc in the UK (1998) and combining two books previously published in Australia, *Certain Things* (William Heinemann, Port Melbourne, 1993) and *Lineations* (Duffy and Snellgrove, Potts Point, 1996).

The long-liners especially test, measure and prove his strengths. It's as if a lexical and grammatical structure, projecting out into space, might at any moment break and fall, but holds up because the feeling that sustains it is sustained; and for me part of the interest of these poems is precisely in that apprehension, not quite of fragility, but of precariousness and of daring.

The poem in the present collection where this skill conspicuously falters is 'The Pines', and it's worth remarking on, if only as a measure of difficulties overcome elsewhere. With its allusions to Shakespeare's *Richard II*, the Brontës, Arthurian legend, the legend of the sleeping princess, its parallels with Wordsworth's 'Tintern Abbey', and its descriptive echoes of Murray, this is a poem I can imagine providing material for a first-rate academic seminar. So much to notice. So much to comment on. So many connections to be made. But what of the mechanics? Here the long lines are sustained less by passion (though passion is declared in them) than by deliberation. They sag, and the attempt to support them with half-rhyme couplets – end-fasteners to hold them up – looks make-shift.

Gray is a poet of strong feeling – passion of a low-burning, slow-release, persistent intensity. There's something mysterious about this quality. Poets so often lay claim to strong feeling as justification, and the result is very often one or another kind of posturing or poeticising. Gray's poems are coolly, unarguably and yet unassertively, passionate – as if passion can be 'matter of fact'. The tone is measured; the gaze is level; the eye is 'on the object', as Wordsworth said it should be. And indeed the Wordsworthian quality and influence are everywhere. Gray is a poet who even dares, now and then, Wordsworthian moral reflections –

> What fools we are
> by the criteria of the senses,
>
> of life. We want to be rid of everything difficult, and give up what
> is real
> as being rid of all that's dark, there is no light.

Here we have 'wisdom' baldly articulated, but without causing the reader to feel put upon, because in context it comes as so inevitable an upshot of the larger picture – a poem vividly characterising the experience of sea-travel through the southern ocean. And the point of view accords perfectly with Wordsworth (for example with the sonnet 'The world is too much with us . . .')

Elsewhere, Gray being a man of his time, these moral reflections are quite un-Wordsworthian in their import –

> . . . when shall I lie again in a landscape that is bright like satin
> with my Venus of the sweet grass, her breasts plump as quail?
> . . .
> The one perfection of this world is lust.

Something commonly overlooked in commentaries on Wordsworth is his great skill in, and management of, narrative, and Gray at times shows a similar talent.

> In one of the side streets
> of a small hot town
> off the highway
>
> I noticed the garage,
> its white boards peeling
> among the grey paling fences.
>
> There was a lone petrol pump,
> from the sixties, perhaps,
> out in the sun-blaze.

There you have the perfect economy of a story opening (or, equally, an opening shot in a movie) – so much 'place' so effortlessly on the page; though it has to be said that what follows (which has charm and interest, and contains the typical felicity of 'Elusive as music, our feelings / are blown through us') doesn't quite match the promise of those three stanzas, because not enough happens. Wordsworth would have talked to the garage man and extracted a confession about his life.

Equally atmospheric, and more complete as a poem, is 'Harmonica', a scene on a country railway station in which a small cast of characters is bodied forth, and then the focus narrows on just two:

> The man and woman hardly spoke:
> boots, jeans, sheepskin collars; his balding head;
> hers the luggage, in plastic bags.
>
> She wore his hat; he'd had a drink.
> A middle-aged girl with loose open face, the sort
> who might come on a bumpy road.
>
> She waited calmly, in the cold.
> He took out and began working on
> harmonica, and wasn't bad.

And then, a little later, 'The train simply appeared, its sound / blown away. A single light, sliding around the forest.' The man puts her on board, and we're left with some words from one of the tunes he played, 'Amazing Grace'.

What we have here, and in much of Gray's work, is the poet as observer rather than participant. He is usually more interested in telling what's out there than in talking about himself; and (perhaps consequently) he reveals more about himself than the insistently confessional poet can do, whose word is partial and self-serving. This is Wordsworth of the *Lyrical Ballads* rather than of *The Prelude*.

Tact is an element in all this – to say enough and not too much; to be there without presuming, without ego crowding out the world. (It's what makes the wide space between the good and the unsatisfactory in D. H. Lawrence.) There's an example of it in a brief and lovely poem, 'Small Hours', where the poet-persona, the 'I', gets up in the night, looks out at 'the mottled yard / . . . like itself in photocopy', and is joined for a moment, unexpectedly, by his mate. I imagine (guess) this, in the writing, to have presented the following problem: they have touched hands as if 'at the rail' of a ship, and he has said, 'Nice to meet', which characterises and focuses the strangeness of the nocturnal encounter. To write 'I said' would be to put too much self into the selfless moment. To write 'You said' was not what happened. How is this solved?

until 'Nice to meet' one of us said
who turned towards the dark wave
of our fathomless house.

Gray's poetry, like Les Murray's, is rooted in his experience of a mainly non-urban Australian landscape. Like Murray, he sees that experience as the source of whatever power he has to make a poem speak at large, with authority, with significance beyond its author and its occasion. Unlike Murray (whose books are usually dedicated 'To the glory of God') he has not offered, like a parallel text, an ideology and a faith, as if the poems need these for ultimate sanction. In this sense Gray might be described as the more serious about poetry, though not, of course, more conscientious or committed or talented. And in fact one of his epigrams might be addressed to the kind of poet Murray is:

So this is the castle
of your ideals –
now show me the dungeon.

A Life of John Mulgan[*]

The John Mulgan story as I knew it in the 1950s, picked up out of literary conversations of the time, and confirmed in the 1970s in two books by Paul Day, went in broad outline like this: Mulgan, product of a liberal-conservative, literary family, and reflecting its values, was a student at Auckland University College during the Depression. At the end of his second year, 1931, he was one of two Auckland nominees for the Rhodes Scholarship, and although he didn't get it, the Governor-General, Bledisloe, who chaired the awarding committee, indicated that he expected to see him back next year, a clear hint that his chances, when he had completed his degree, would be very good.

When the Auckland riot of 14 April 1932 occurred, in which the unemployed smashed windows and looted shops all up and down Queen Street, Mulgan enrolled, along with many other male students, as a special constable. He was drilled, issued with an armband and a baton, and went forth the next night to 'protect private property'. But 'something happened' – his 'road to Damascus' O'Sullivan calls it. He was confronted by one of the unemployed, listened, felt ashamed, and went home. Later, according to Paul Day, he 'penned an acid editorial' in the student paper, *Craccum*, declaring support for the rioters.

* A review of *Long Journey to the Border: A Life of John Mulgan* (Penguin Books, Auckland, 2003), by Vincent O'Sullivan, *New Zealand Listener*, 22 November 2003.

239

Further, when a highly charged controversy about freedom of speech blew up on the campus later in the same year, Mulgan's name was among those supporting the free-speech candidate for the University Council. These two signs that he was veering left (so the story went) cost him the Rhodes. Because of his 'outspoken espousal of the cause of free speech and social justice' (Day) he was not nominated in 1932; and despite an apparent protest about this from the Governor-General, he was not nominated the following year either.

He then went to Oxford on borrowed money, graduated well, wrote his one novel, *Man Alone*, married, worked for Oxford University Press, entered the British Army when the war began, rose to the rank of lieutenant-colonel, did heroic things behind the lines in Greece, and died, tragically and mysteriously by his own hand, in Cairo in April 1945.

Mulgan was (and remains) a heroic figure – a quality enhanced, as it must always be, by early death in circumstances of war. But there was the additional element that he was a hero of the left, one who was wronged by Auckland's reactionary professors, but who subsequently triumphed where it mattered, 'overseas', in England, in Oxford. A good deal of this (but not the Anglocentric part) I found attractive; and *Man Alone* had a special importance for me because it was the first novel I read at school which gave me simultaneously the flavours of twentieth-century literary modernity and of real New Zealand.

In the late 1970s, however, when I came to study the Mulgan story closely, I found a significant part of it questionable. In particular the idea that a wrong had been done over the Rhodes Scholarship appeared to be without foundation. The 'acid editorial' which was said to have damaged his chances turned out to be a few mild, harmlessly reflective, modestly penitent sentences, and unsigned – so it was not even possible to be sure who had written it. His support of the free-speech candidate for council consisted principally of signing (along with many others) the nomination form. And his lurch to the left was no more than a gentle half-turn – something not completed until much later in Oxford. Finally, and much more significantly, I had access to the university's records, and there were, I discovered, irrefutably sound academic reasons why the College should rate others ahead of him for the Rhodes in 1932 and '33. Mulgan's performance had been so far

240

below that of his two competitors it would have been a serious injustice for him to have received the Auckland nomination in those years.

If there was a scandal in connection with the Rhodes Scholarship it was not that the College failed to nominate Mulgan. It was that the Governor-General, whose proper place was no more than to chair a committee choosing two winners from the nominees sent to Wellington by the four Colleges, stepped so far beyond his proper role as to attempt to make Auckland change its mind; and when he failed in this, persuaded his committee not to award any scholarships for that year.

My conclusions on this question were set out in *Islands* in April 1979, in an article that covered a great deal else as well.* Critical articles in literary journals usually draw no immediate response, or at most a brief letter or two. This one drew responses that ran to fifteen pages, and more were to follow. If it had been a chorus of disagreement it might have been disconcerting; but it was more like a group of people in a room each, and simultaneously, saying something different.

What I learned from this was something one knows in general – the power of myth; but also the degree to which this man Mulgan had become an emblematic figure, at least to his own generation. He and his father each represented something distinctive about New Zealand, and the differences between them, literary and political, marked a shift in our history, really from the condition of being a colony to whatever the next step – a 'client culture' perhaps – is properly called; and my article, dealing with both father and son, touched on the delicate areas of that transition.

But the story of the leftist deprived of the Rhodes Scholarship by wicked reactionaries was too good to be easily given up. James Bertram in particular defended it. At the time, Keith Sinclair was writing his history of the University of Auckland, and Dorothea Turner, Mulgan's sister, wrote urging him to prove me wrong. In a spirit, not of competition but of proper enquiry, Keith tried. In May 1980 he reported to her that he had not been able to.

---

* This article is reprinted, along with two postcripts, 1981 and 2001, in my *Kin of Place: Essays on 20 New Zealand Writers*.

All of which is background to the book under review, and another by James McNeish, *Dance of the Peacocks*, a study of Mulgan and four others of his generation who went from New Zealand to Oxford in the 1930s. Sinclair said in his history that I had 'demythologized Mulgan'. But a strong myth can be proof against facts, especially if you choose to ignore them. Here is Humpty Dumpty back on the wall, his cracks lacquered over. He was done out of the Rhodes! He was wronged!

O'Sullivan and McNeish worked in some degree in collaboration, but they are not alike in method. Both have written fiction, but of very different kinds, and the differences are paralleled here. McNeish is always (Fairburn, Mackenzie, Lovelock) the excited, theatrical, patriotic, often indignant myth-maker. One likes him for his enthusiasm and can almost forgive his recklessness with facts. O'Sullivan is subtler – careful, measured, scholarly, low key.

So readers can now take their pick of two different but equally 'wronged' Mulgans. On that crucial second night of rioting in April 1932, for example, O'Sullivan's Mulgan was 'quietly' confronted by one of the unemployed, 'an old digger', a New Zealander. McNeish's Mulgan, on the other hand, was 'backed into a doorway' and 'harangued' by a returned soldier who was British. Whichever it was, loud Pom or quiet Kiwi, both Mulgans were ashamed. McNeish's 'went home and threw away his baton'; O'Sullivan's 'walked back to the police station, and handed it in'. McNeish's Mulgan was now the total and instant convert: 'Within a few days he was producing underground pamphlets on behalf of the unemployed'. O'Sullivan treads more warily: 'It was not in Mulgan's personality to act as an overnight convert, or to take up sudden causes.'

I offer this incident with the returned soldier simply as an example. It finds, so far as I'm aware, no corroboration anywhere in Mulgan's writing or recorded conversation, and seems to come solely from one hearsay recollection divided like the loaves and fishes among Mulgan's recorders and variously rehashed. At every point in McNeish's account of these events it's easy to see where he is inventing, over-stating, making a good story, bolstering the myth. But O'Sullivan, in his own less obvious way, can be almost as bad, offering statements which, though plausible, are entirely speculative, and which at times seem to need viola or cello accompaniment to conceal their lack of substance: 'it was as if the figure of the ex-soldier who spoke to him in Karangahape Road had become an embodiment and an icon of what must never be betrayed. The ordinary man, who might rise to extraordinary things, was increasingly his touchstone . . .'

It was as if . . .

When Auckland is left behind O'Sullivan is more dependable, but his task, though less complex than McNeish's, is in one sense harder. When the life of one of his characters becomes tedious McNeish simply jumps ship and takes up the story of another. O'Sullivan has to slog on through the boring bits; and I have to say I was surprised to find the long middle section recounting Mulgan's life in Oxford less than gripping. It would have been an excellent life to have lived, and at a very exciting period of history. If it is not a great read in O'Sullivan's telling that may be partly because 80 or 90 per cent of the material here is taken direct from Mulgan's letters to his parents, where he adopts a serious, often sententious, manner and offers the sort of account of himself that young men away from home do – detailed but selective, guarded, mainly cheerful and always proper. Did nothing wild or wayward, erratic or erotic, happen to him during these years?

With the outbreak of the war a more real person comes into focus – competent, admirable, though not always entirely likeable. Mulgan, the reader has already noticed, enjoys the company of men (but not 'intellectuals'), dislikes women who are 'too intelligent', and distrusts shows of emotion. (Earlier, when his student girl friend Jean Alison begins to tell him she is becoming fond of him, he says 'Steady on!') Writing from his posting in Ireland he tells Gabrielle, his wife, that he is happier now than he has been living with her, and that she 'mustn't mind' his saying so. He decides she and the baby must leave for the safety of Canada, and when she pleads to be allowed to stay in Oxford, where she has the support and company of her mother, he refuses to listen or discuss it. Arrangements have been made – she must go. As he becomes more content with the soldier's lot, Gabrielle's distress and uncertainty mount. He suggests in one letter that she might like to find for their child 'an acting father in my absence – I should be a lousy father anyway. Do you want one? It seems sad for you to live alone, easier for men.' And he goes on to say that many in the army will 'never want to go back to domestic life'. She asks why he married her and he says it was because 'you were young and very pretty and very nice to me and I knew that you loved me'. He doesn't say that he loved her.

He seems clumsy, insensitive, baffled in some of these exchanges, which is not, of course, to say that that is how he appeared to those who knew him well. Like many – perhaps most – biographies this one prompts more questions than can be answered. But I was reminded of the fact that it is man against landscape that makes Mulgan's only novel, *Man Alone*, remarkable. Its human relationships are wooden, as if characters interact by thought rather than feeling; and the central one, between Rua and Johnson, lacks intuitive depth or substance.

Mulgan's war of waiting and inaction was over when he was sent to North Africa, where his own British regiment fought alongside the NZDiv. He made comparisons, almost always in favour of the New Zealanders, and thought often of applying to join them. He was restless. As second in command he lodged a complaint against his commanding officer and then, when that one had been replaced, against a second. He was then offered, and accepted, a new role as a British officer with resistance fighters in occupied Greece, the most demanding and dangerous part of his war experience. Cool competence, concern for the welfare of his men, courage even to the point of personal recklessness – here he seems 'made for the job', and remarkably like that other New Zealand hero, Charles Upham.

After the European war had been won he had a brief period of rest in Cairo and then was returned to Greece to assess claims for money and assistance from Greeks who had helped the British and suffered for it – a depressing task in a country depleted by war and now riven with violent political conflict. It was during this period that he completed the draft of reflective autobiography that would be published after his death as *Report on Experience*.

When he returned to Cairo in April 1945 his part in the war was over, and he had said goodbye to Zoi, his Athens secretary to whom he had grown attached. In Cairo there was another woman friend, Christine, a Pole, who at the inquest into his death would claim he had told her he regretted his marriage. There is a suggestion that Christine may have become pregnant at this time, and had an abortion.

Everyone who has given any thought to the Mulgan story must have tried to imagine what was in his head that caused his suicide at this moment – whether it was something capable of presenting itself in a rational guise, or entirely beyond reason. Mulgan was sociable and successful, cheerful, likeable and admired; yet there was also a side to his character that was grim and secretive. Before taking the doses of morphia that would kill him he wrote to his commanding officer saying that he had throat cancer (this was untrue) and asking him to invent a cover story – that he had died of a fever, or taken the overdose by mistake. He also wrote a farewell letter to Zoi, and one to Christine. To both he repeated a phrase he had used in that reply to Gabrielle when she asked why he had married her – 'You were very nice to me.' There was nothing to Gabrielle – but that would have been because he was hoping she and his family would not be told that he had killed himself.

The contradictions and the puzzle remain; and there are passages in this book where O'Sullivan appears to hover on the brink of a disclosure, or more likely a speculation, which, however (and I suppose quite properly) he doesn't permit himself. He emphasises the melancholy, the depressive note that one finds everywhere in Mulgan's prose, and perhaps that is all there is to go on.

Part Three First Person

By way of explanation

I have many notebooks full of literary jottings. Mostly these are
ideas for current work, or for something that may be taken up in
the future; and also drafts of poems, reviews and essays. I have only
once or twice begun to keep a journal, and almost at once given up
because of a feeling of uncertainty, and consequently falsity, about
just whom I was writing for, and for what purpose. In some ways I
regret the failure to keep a record of events and encounters that are
forgotten, or only hazily remembered. But now and then during
the past ten years, usually when I have been travelling abroad,
and especially when travelling alone, I have kept 'travel notes',
often scattered among notes towards whatever fiction I have been
currently working on. Some of these follow, and then a final set of
notes kept irregularly during 2006–07 with this present book, and
its theme of the self present in and/or absent from literary-critical
writing, in mind. In my introduction I have called this section 'the
riskiest part of the venture'. I feel I am inviting strangers in. Most
of you will be pleasant, even friendly, at the very least tolerant
and polite; a few will want to spray-paint the walls and wreck the
furniture.

There is, however, one other way of looking at these notes.
Many readers these days are keen attenders of the numerous
festivals where writers read their work, appear on panels and submit
themselves to interview. Since the appetite for occasions of this
kind is large, and growing, it's reasonable to assume there will be
some interest in seeing them from the point of view of one writer: a
glimpse of what may be going on 'backstage' so to speak, either the
literal 'backstage', or the backstage in the brain.

Where persons are referred to whom a reader would not be able
to identify, or where there is anything else that might be obscure, I
have added minimal explanations in square brackets or footnotes.
In I think only one case a name has been changed, and in another
reduced to an initial.

Travel Notes, 1999

1/7/99: Hacienda Hotel, LAX: I set off yesterday (after hotel check-in) to walk to the ocean. Dim memory as I went along – 'done this before' – and I had. You walk maybe two miles down Mariposa and come to a blockage, the line of power pylons, a wide track made for them, fenced, which can't be crossed. So access to the ocean is cut. I remembered from the previous time that if you go right or left somewhere short of this blockage there's a way over or under, past oil wells. But I was too weary and turned back. I ate a large meal and watched TV – in fact slept through most of a programme about Dashiell Hammett and another about teaching kids to be good about homosexuality (the non-commercial channel), then went to bed and continued sleeping.

As you walk towards the ocean you can see away to the left (i.e. south) a big cluster of wells and storage tanks and I don't know what – metal, and oil stains, like a giant car engine. This area has been ravaged by unregulated 'development' and an alternative consciousness of 'how to behave' is still only struggling out of the egg.

I read Drusilla Modjeska's *The Orchard* on the plane because Karen Ross on the phone from the Book Council had said a book of Modjeska's is set in the Varuna Writers' Retreat in the Blue Mountains, where I'm to go in September. This book was written there, and perhaps the house and garden in the mountains, where the main character (Ettie) lives, are modelled on it. But since Modjeska is not a writer to look out much, it hardly matters. My notes jotted in the back of the book after reading the first section, 'The Adultery Factor', read:

This book is an odd mix of the true, the half-true and the false. Very much a female (one kind of female) book in that it believes in words – that you can get at the truth, or the essence, of the m/f thing by talking. It doesn't recognise the male preference for, and faith in, doing rather than saying – that doing may be the most truthful way of saying. Not 'Believe what I say', but 'Believe what I do'. (Not 'Read my lips', but 'Watch my cock' would be the negative view.) It does run on, like someone talking through the night in a strange bed when all you want to do is sleep; and it's often boring. It's full of a kind of feminist thought that has become shop-soiled. You can see it coming a mile off, the stale old trope, the stale old rhetoric, the stale old first-person plural catching 50 per cent of the world's population in its big slack net. But the reflections, though they have this weakness, obviously come out of experience and are on the whole stronger, more convincing, than the fiction, which is thin and always teetering on the edge of the fake/the dishonest. The representation of Ettie as powerful and wise strikes this reader as wishful. I don't *feel* power or *see* wisdom. It's not just that I'm not convinced; I don't even begin to believe in Ettie. She is, I suppose, what Modjeska would like to become.
At the end of this section, having the abandoned mistress, when the affair is over, in a relationship, not with another man, or alone, but with a young woman, has a floating, slightly insincere, *theoretical* feel to it. This, I would guess, is a (hurt) 'straight' woman using the gay hint (it's no more than that – she doesn't know how to develop it) for theoretical reasons, and even for practical reasons: theoretical because the lesbian is at least an *escape* from male dominance, and even a revenge; practical because of her potential readership/following.

Later I read section 2 about her problem with eyesight and a period when she thought she might go blind. Here I thought Modjeska revealed herself as a sort of crazed egotist – pretentious, demanding, humourless. I thought she would be simply insufferable to know – an alone person blaming the world, and especially its 50 per cent that is male, for all her troubles. Again I'm struck by the fact that this woman doesn't look *out* enough. I'm egotistical (of course I am), but the world and the things in it, and especially the behaviour of people, their faces, their speech, their interactions, *interest* me endlessly and make me forget self. Not fair to make this a male/female thing? No, of course not. But (on the other hand) isn't *this*, looking inward, inspecting and reporting on the self, precisely what the feminist movement has claimed for itself? This is where a Mansfield differs from a Modjeska. KM looks inward (often ruthlessly), but she is also always interested in the world out there – and not only as it relates to her. She knows how to 'get out of herself'. And she has always the saving grace of *humour*. Modjeska is humourless.

This morning after a long, interrupted, but long (and interrupted) sleep, I had muesli (a mistake in the US) and fruit followed by English muffin (as near as they get to toast here) and jam, and coffee. I will now walk for an hour, then have a snack, then check in at the Tom Bradley terminal . . . and all the rest of it. Next stop London.

3/7/99: Here I am in [daughter] Margaret's, and [son-in-law] Guy's lovely flat in Maida Vale. Kay has been here since early June. Leafy London summer. Bare uncluttered floors and space. A pity to fill it with furniture. (Wouldn't it be interesting to start again with a *tabula rasa*!) I watched Clinton on CNN – a news conference, and the first time I've seen extended coverage of him dealing with questions. I was impressed. He's hugely competent – and a nice guy.

Lovely green almost-silence. Passing cars, not traffic. Echoing voices. Kay and I had a pasta lunch somewhere nearby and retired for siesta.

4/7/99: 'Shopping' yesterday. E.g.: Looking for sandals I found a jacket. £155. Went to buy it. It was a suit. Jacket and trousers for £155! Tried on trousers. Yes, OK, but needed very slight alteration – just a centimetre lengthening. Couldn't be done until after sale – eleven days. OK I'd take them anyway and get it done elsewhere. Then the assistant whispered that they would be £85 in the sale tomorrow. Opens at 12. Jacket and trousers for £85!!! Kay thought I should strike-while-the-iron-was-hot. Guy and I thought hell no – not when half price beckons. But Marg remembered there was a plan for tomorrow – to go

251

to Oxford. I decided I would take a gamble. If they're there on Monday I get a suit for £85. If not I don't get a suit I didn't want.

I then bought sandals £20 (at a sale).

Dinner at the local Indian – with Yvonne. My shout. £80 (almost a suit!).

6/7/99: (Tuesday.) Sunday we went to Oxford, walked across the meadows for a pub lunch at the Trout, walked back across meadows, then down Walton Street, St Giles, the High; pots of tea at the Mitre; back via Banbury Road, North Parade, 91 Woodstock ('our' house), Plantation Road, Southmoor Road (where the Davins lived all those years) to the car on the edge of the meadows. All charming, but not my life. A brief taste (1996–97) was enough. But the flavour is very potent.

K and I to a dinner party that night at Beth's, with Julia and husband; also Alan Hollinghurst who brought us a copy of his latest novel [*The Spell*] inscribed.

Monday I went back to the Regent St and got the suit (Portuguese, wool, very fine and light, perfect fit after all, including trousers) for £85.

Lunch with Christopher MacLehose and Margaret. We talked about the cover for *Talking about O'Dwyer*. Back at the Harvill office we looked at pics of Oxford which Christopher wants for the jacket. There was one he likes a lot, of two elderly dons who could be [characters in the novel] Mike Newall and Bertie Winterstoke. I'm glad, because Christopher is so particular about presentation he might hold up the works if he didn't find something he liked.

6.30 a party at Christopher's to celebrate the thirtieth anniversary of the Spanish publisher Anagrama. Many notables there, including Julian Barnes, David Lodge, Vikram Seth, K. Ishiguro. Also Martin Amis, looking, I thought, tortured with anxiety, but with the new teeth he has made famous securely in place. Peter Strauss of Picador told me he loved *All Visitors Ashore*; joked, somewhat grimly, about Keri Hulme's not having produced the promised novel after so many years and such a big advance.

Pasta afterwards at M & G's local place, Raoul's.

11/7/99: We flew to Nice on the 8th, picked up a hirecar at the airport and drove to Rapallo in Italy, checked in to the Hotel Villa Cristina (Villa Vittoria in my novel of that name) – distinctly crummy, but clean, and nice enough, overlooking the little Piazzetta Ezra Pound, and the port. We were up at 6 a.m. to have breakfast and climb the *salita* up to Sant' Ambrogio, and were back in time to sail with Massimo* on *Vagabonda III*, and swim off it in the Bay. Next day we went out to Portofino and Santa Margherita on the ferry, had lunch, went up the cable car to Montallegro (Kay terrified, refusing to look down, rebuked by a bossy Englishwoman because she was 'missing the view'!); then had a drink with Angela [Massimo's wife] in town – Massimo having gone off to conference – and finally a meal at their house, looking out over Rapallo and the great sweep of the Golfo del Tigullio.

On Sunday we drove back to Menton, checked into our favourite hotel (the Edwards, less crummy than the Villa Cristina, but still very modest) and went looking for Elizabeth Knox (current Mansfield Menton Fellow) and Fergus Barrowman. We found their young Jack playing with a ball outside the Mansion we used to call Onion Towers when we rented a flat there with the children in 1977. Had dinner with them that evening.

Today Kay and I have climbed to the Annonciade (morning) and been swimming with them this afternoon. When I was in Washington with Elizabeth she wore long skirts all the time and I wondered what her legs were like – whether she was hiding them. For the record, now that I've seen her swimming: they are very good legs.

27/8/99: Kay returned to New Zealand from Melbourne and I'm now (just arrived) at Varuna, the writers' retreat in the Blue Mountains, where Eleanor Dark lived and wrote. Modjeska's Ettie in *The Orchard*

---

* Professor Massimo Bacigalupo, of the University of Genoa, a friend I met through Pound studies, is the son of Ezra Pound's doctor in Rapallo, and grandson of his local chemist. The Bacigalupos have owned three yachts called *Vagabonda I, II* and *III*. Massimo as a child met Pound often and sailed with him. Olga Rudge, Pound's mistress and the mother of his daughter Mary de Rachewiltz, lived in Sant' Ambrogio above the town of Rapallo, and Pound used to walk up the *salita* to visit her there. A few years before the visit recorded here I had met Mary in Rapallo at a Pound conference and lunched with her in the Bacigalupo's garden.

[see above], with her home and garden in the Blue Mountains, is perhaps partly based on an idea of Eleanor Dark.

I will say more about Varuna in due course; but to go back more than a month: the stay in Uzès was the usual lovely round of reading, the morning walk in from the village along the back road, through vines, fields of sunflowers, plantations of *chêne* oaks, into the woods, over the stream and past the château and the mill, and finally into the town for coffee and food shopping; then home again in the heat for lunch, siesta, swim in the river at Collias – all this interspersed with smaller swims in the pool; and finally the evening meal by the pool when the bats have replaced the swallows and the air begins to cool. We visited Ted and Joan [Sturmer – friends from student days] in Barjac (Ted making banana cakes and boozing with the Gypsies); drove over to Le Vigan to have a meal with Antonia [novelist A. S. Byatt] at her local *auberge* (where she runs up a tab that includes her nightly champagne) and swim in her pool; Margaret and Guy came to stay with us; Pat and Tony returned and, after a few days with them, we drove back to Nice, returned the car, and flew back to London. Oh and there was a solar eclipse on the drive to Nice. We watched it from a stop along the auto-route. Darkness at Noon. We were in London about a week before flying to Melbourne (an interesting stopover in Singapore) where the Festival put us up at the Grand Hyatt – and how desperately unattractive American-style 'luxury' seemed after French/ Italian crummy.

I suppose the most memorable thing that happened to us in Melbourne (this was before the Festival began, and before Kay flew on to Auckland) was a day spent with an old friend of our student days, E. E., who spent most of her childhood and youth in New Zealand, is the '*mischling*' only child of refugees from Hitler (mother Aryan, father Jewish). She's highly intelligent, with a long and prodigiously detailed memory for people, places, occasions, books; but also, it seems to me, solipsistic, and (despite children and grandchildren elsewhere in Australia) *lonely*. She took us by train to Williamstown for lunch and to walk on the beach. There was a cold wind, the lunch was awful, we were suffering jet-lag, and E, whose conversation is a monologue, usually of woes, often about the second husband who left her many years ago (she left her first for the wicked second), was not going to let

254

this opportunity be wasted. She talked and talked and *talked*, in her way which is at once astonishing, impressive, and terrifying. There is no accent (except that it's *just* perceptibly English as a second language), every sentence linguistically rich and grammatically perfect, with a beginning, a middle and an end. She's like the man in Molière who discovers '*ce qui n'est point prose, est vers*' and '*ce qui n'est point vers, est prose*', and is delighted to think that he speaks prose. That's what E does – she 'speaks prose'.

So it's quite exhausting being with her, not least because you feel immense sympathy and admiration for her; and the exhaustion is worse if you're a bit below top form and can't do her the favour, now and then, of rushing into a pause and taking a turn to speak – something which requires a determination that weakens as the hours go by. After the rigours of Williamstown in the wind, she drove us from the station to our hotel, but stopping off on the way for a 'quick look' at the Jewish Museum, something not to be taken lightly, or quickly, or at all so late in the day. Back in the car, somewhat shaken, and reaching central Melbourne, I caught sight of the Hyatt and, keen to get away, said we should jump out at once (we were stopped at a traffic light) so she wouldn't have to manoeuvre through traffic right to the hotel entrance. In my eagerness I flung the back door open just as a motor-cyclist came shooting through on the inside. She (it was a she) hit the door hard and flew off into space, landing on her back on the pavement where she lay quite still, encased in black leather from head to foot, eyes wide open staring up at the sky. I asked her whether she was all right and she didn't answer, though she appeared to be looking at me, and seeing. I thought she must be seriously hurt, and so did she, which is why she wasn't moving, not even to speak. Meanwhile cellphones were calling police and ambulance and the long slow process of an accident and its aftermath began to unwind. The ambulance took Ms Leather away. At the police station I had the impression that E had found a cop willing to hear about her second marriage, while I made a statement and waited. News came from the hospital that the victim was not seriously hurt – nothing broken, just bruises. The cops told me if I had done this in NSW it would have been OK because, there, motor-cyclists are not allowed to shoot through on the inside. In Victoria the law is different and I was in the wrong, but they wouldn't be pressing charges. E, who, on her home turf, is meticulous about cleanliness and tidiness and making everything perfect, and who might therefore have been thrown into a spin about the damage to her car, was in fact saintly and uncomplaining about it. In fact she seemed quite pleased by the whole business, as if it had 'taken her out of herself', which I suppose it had. Very late we got back to the Hyatt, and next morning I went to the airport to put Kay on her flight to Auckland.

The Melbourne Festival is big and somewhat impersonal. Toronto is big, but they keep the writers together – you dine together at a different restaurant every night, and go on expeditions together (one always to Niagara Falls), and get to know one another. In Melbourne people tend to fly in, make their appearances, and fly out again, often without even meeting.

Next day was a Saturday and I attended a panel at 10, chaired one at 12, and gave a reading at 2. For the reading I was strangely paired with the famous Oz comic writer Kathy Lette. Could an audience that came to hear her have wanted to hear me? Or vice versa? But we carried it off. She announced to the audience that she was 'an appalling reader of [her] own stuff', so she wouldn't read, just talk. What the talk consisted of was a comedy routine – lots of one-liners – first about how good it is to live in England because she doesn't have to put up with 'Aussie blokes' whose awful ways she described (graphically); then how awful it is to live in England because 'the Poms' are so disgusting; then how terrible it is to spend time in Los Angeles where everyone has had a face-lift, and every other kind of 'lift' (with anatomical details of the consequences, including to the clitoris). Finally she offered a comic/scatological disquisition on the perils of natural childbirth. In the audience her famously liberal QC husband, Geoffrey Robertson, who must have heard it all before, seemed entertained.

I can't remember now what I read after that. I didn't feel up-staged so much as that we were wrong-staged, each by the other. Propriety determined that I kept a neutral face during all this, and that she stayed awake during mine.

Next day I was on another panel, 'Whose past is it anyway?', about writing historical fiction. So often these panels don't work because each writer comes with a tightly prepared statement and reads it, or delivers it. You have A, followed by B, followed by C, followed by D, and no significant interaction. I know some people find it hard to ad lib, but they should try; should trust themselves and the audience – cast themselves on the waters and see what happens. For me one of the best moments in the Festival came from an unscripted, apparently spontaneous, beautifully articulated and penetrating reflection by Andrew Riemer in a panel on crossing language barriers. He spoke of English as his second language while the first (Hungarian, I think), spoken in infancy and lost, remains somewhere at the back of his consciousness, unavailable but alive, a ghostly grammatical structure and vocabulary.

Other memorable things in Melbourne were a restaurant meal with Michael Hulse [British/German poet] and Peter Goldsworthy [Australian poet] and Peter's tall beautiful intelligent daughter Anna, a pianist, after which Michael and I went to a play I remember only by its name, *Burnt Piano*. I'd also seen a Brecht there a few days before, *The Resistable Rise of Arturo Ui*.

28/7/99: (Continuing this at the Varuna writers' retreat). Yesterday, after disliking the huge US-style Grand Hyatt in Melbourne, I was enjoying the last of my few days in Sydney at the 'Chateau Sydney' in Potts Point. I'd done a good deal of walking – over to the Art Gallery of NSW, the Opera House, the shops. I'd done an interview with the ABC which went well, and had a nice lunch with Mel Cain and Kaye Wright of HarperCollins, the latter a great enthusiast for *The End of the Century at the End of the World*. That was at the Bayswater Brasserie where I had dinner the next night with Michael Hulse (who had also come on from Melbourne) and Australian poet Robert Gray.

This was to be the day Peter Bishop would pick me up and drive me to Varuna, and after the usual glooms and adjustments of being alone after Kay returned to Auckland I was beginning to feel back on an even keel. Potts Point is so pleasant, so full of surprising corners and backdrops. I set out to walk one last time across to the Gallery for another dose of Oz Art. The hotel lift was slow so I went through the door marked EXIT to walk down the stairs. The door closed behind me, I went down three flights, and couldn't open the door into the foyer at street level. Back up, down again, all doors locked, and no response to my knocking and hammering. I was locked in on an echoing concrete stairway. Agitation! Finally I went past a point on the stairs that said it was not to be passed except in case of fire, down a further stairway, and got out into an underground car park.

Shook myself out of my ruffles, emerged into the street and went on my way. The walk, the Gallery, the gardens were lovely. On my way back I waited where construction site workers had made a temporary street crossing. Behind me a fork lift unloaded a pile of cement into a puddle and muddy water with a fine mix of cement whooshed up my trousers and across the raincoat I was carrying. I was wet; but worse, the trousers were horribly splattered with marks that dried in brown-white stains. Back in the hotel I considered simply throwing them away. At least they were unwearable until cleaned. I changed and thought, these things come in threes, don't they? What would be next?

Peter Bishop called for me at two thirty and we set off for the mountains. He has a tentative voice, ginger whiskers, son of a Scot who came to Armidale to teach classics at the university (shortly after I left it in 1957), became professor there, and remained until retirement. Peter has been director of Varuna for about seven years. I asked what he'd done before that. He said he'd 'done some free-lance work' – about poetry, I think he implied, for the ABC, and played the piano in restaurants in Katoomba, until 'the recession' when that 'dried up'. He and his wife have three children, the youngest sixteen. This was none of my business, I was only looking to 'get the picture', and the picture forming seemed to suggest the Varuna job as a plum for someone who had not a lot to put on a CV.

I mentioned that I hoped to watch the NZ/Oz rugby test the next night. He said there was no TV at Varuna. 'We thought writers would want to talk to one another, not watch TV.' I'd been hoping there would be individual TV sets in the rooms so I wouldn't be inflicting the test on anyone who didn't want to watch it. It hadn't occurred to me there would be none in the house!

We came to Katoomba, by which time the cold (it had been 21°C and Spring in Sydney) was creeping into the car.

My first (and I suppose extreme) reaction to Varuna was to sit in my room, stunned, wondering how I could get out of the week the NZ Book Council has committed me to. I didn't especially want to come here; but at least I imagined comfort – even perhaps a little luxury.

Everyone I'd spoken to had heard it was nice, wonderful, etc. No one had actually been here. I'd thought misfortunes come in threes. Here, after being locked in a stairwell and splashed by concrete-mud, was the third.

At the end of a suburban street at the edge of Katoomba you drive up a muddy path through trees. The house is a two-storey yellow stucco 1940s-style building, a style that sprouted in my childhood (though I grew up in the gloom of an earlier style – the Redwood panelling of about 1920). Certain things have a gloomy familiarity, especially the use of ply-wood interior panelling, cupboards etc. It's as if ply-wood had just been invented (I suppose it had) and was wonderfully 'modern'. But the interior stairway is curving, concrete, with a stainless steel railing – very art deco. The plywood is painted pale yellow of course, and the upstairs bathroom is tiled in pale yellow and green. These were the pastel ('modern' – even *moderne*') colours of my childhood. The upstairs floors creak. The furniture is old and everything strikes me as ugly. There is a central heating system but it's insufficient for this big draughty house which is cold, cold, cold. The kitchen is full of unfinished business, mainly food. The laundry is a battlefield which made me think of the time when I was a student and worked as an orderly at the Auckland Hospital and was stationed for a few days at the bottom of the laundry shaft in Infectious Diseases. No, that's ridiculous; but there is a general atmosphere of hippie, or 'bohemian', squalor. Outside, the trees close on the house and the sky closes on the trees. It looks as if it ought to rain even if it doesn't.

So I sat in my room with my unopened case thinking I should just reflect for a while before doing or saying anything. It was a great comfort to be 100 pages into Arthur Miller's autobiography, with 500 pages still to go, and wanting very much to read on. Even the unfinished Proust might be a refuge. Meanwhile I would unload my first reaction on Judy Scott* whom Peter Bishop had told me was here. But when I saw her she at once, before I could speak, launched into a song of praise for Varuna. She'd had such a wonderful week, had got

---

* Rosie Scott, now an established writer in Australia. I knew her as Judy when she was a child in New Zealand and Kay and I were friends with her father, the (shall I say?) 'alternative' historian, Dick Scott, and her mother Elsie.

so much done, it was so beautiful, the walks, the bush, the mountains, the other writers . . .

Well, she is a rational being, a sensible person. That was her Varuna. I had better work on mine and keep my mouth shut.

Later I did speak to her about it, but circumspectly, explaining that I was on my way home after two months away, not working on anything, etc. I told her (but as a joke, as if I didn't mean it) that my first thought was, 'Jesus, where am I? A monastery? A fucking jail?'

30/8/99: Things get better (as how could they not?). Yesterday, having got a ticket by credit card on the phone, I took the train to Sydney to see Verdi's *Don Carlo* at the Opera House; not one I'd seen before – dramatically incoherent, but musically coherent, I thought. I liked it, and especially the conductor, Simone Young, whose movements were so expressive and graceful and who sang along with the choruses and mouthed the arias, a whole opera in herself, and all (as one saw when she came on stage to take her bow with the cast) on unbelievably high heels. How did she not fall off them? Or did she do a quick shoe change on the way from pit to stage?

That, with a two-hour train trip each way, a walk to and from Katoomba Station and from Central Station to the Opera House (all on a swollen and very sore ankle sprained on Varuna's rutty track from road to house) filled the day from about 10 until 8 when I ate Sheila's roast rack of lamb with spinach and mushrooms followed by bananas in brandy.

Sheila cooks off the premises and each night brings the meal to the house. She prides herself on endless variations and goes in for a lot of garlic, much of it raw. The first night there was something bizarre – pancakes stuffed mainly with garlic, and a tomato dish followed by cheesecake with poppy seeds. But it's not ordinary cooking, and last night's was especially good.

This morning I walked down to where the landscape takes its amazing plunge. Years ago (forty years!) I remember seeing Echo Point and the Three Sisters up here. We must have driven up with Aileen and Clem [Kay's late sister and husband]. I carried a general image of that sudden thousand-and-more-foot drop, the landscape at one level simply coming to an end, and another beginning far below, and going away for ever – but it had faded and shrunk in memory. And I'd forgotten the birds. I watched a confrontation between a warrior cockatoo and a peacenik kookaburra high in the thin leafless branches of a dead gum. My attention was drawn first by the cockatoo's screeching, even louder and uglier than the usual call which, along with the lost-child cry of the crows, is present all the time. It's a sound that rivals, and perhaps exceeds, the donkey's bray in the competition for the ugliest sound in nature.

The cockatoo (white with yellow crest and under-wings) clearly considered the dead tree its territory and was doing its best to drive the kookaburra away. As it screeched from a nearby branch it raised its crest and opened its wings, so there was a fanning of yellow-out-of-white to give visual accompaniment to the rising crescendo of the screech. When this was ignored, it flew in circles, coming in close as if to attack. The kookaburra pointed its beak – that was all – as if to say, 'If you want to run on my sword, mate, here it is, but I'd rather you didn't'. The C then landed on a nearby branch, and when further screeching and fanning-of-feathers was ignored, approached with darting pecks. Again the K just pointed its big heavy black beak, but made no aggressive motions, no sound, and showed no anxiety.

Next the C stopped screeching and tried some quiet parrot talk, intimate in-the-ear stuff: 'Listen jerk, I'm giving you one last chance . . .' etc. When the K seemed not to hear, the C did some tricks, meant to impress. It took hold of a branch with its beak, let go with its feet, and swung. It clambered up and around branches and hung upside down. 'Would anyone really want to hang around when a bird with these skills was telling him to fuck off?' – that seemed to be the message. The K didn't even watch; it stared away into the distance, marvelling at so much space, so many trees, and that any bird would care to make such a fuss about a dead one.

Some further aerial stuff followed, swooping and strafing with hideous screeching. No effect. So the C returned to the branches, tried this and that and at last hit on a new method of attack. It hung from a springy branch by its feet and lunged so the sway of the branch carried it forward, then pulled it back, then forward again, back . . . and so on. By this means it could make a rapid succession of swoops, not just one as when flying, and seemed able also to by-pass the beak. The K,

261

clearly still unharmed and unalarmed, but weary of all the fuss, simply flapped off, leisurely, elsewhere.

The C's ego was satisfied, but the K had certainly not lost face nor (I would say) suffered a defeat.

So ended the battle of the C and the K, here in the Blue Mountains on the morning of 30 August 1999, and I, both C and K, am its sole witness and military historian.*

31/8/99: Beautiful clear weather, sunny and warm by day, crisp and clear by night. This morning I did washing and then took the Irish novelist Hugo Hamilton (who arrived last evening) to see the 'drop'. We took the cliff-top walk from just below here to Echo Point and the Three Sisters – then back along the road. Then I walked into Katoomba. Hugo is an asthmatic who has developed sarcoid, a lung fungus, and is on steroids. He panted up the steep parts of the walk. He's very nice.

1/9/99: I have given up Proust. Some years ago I read vols 1 and 2 of a three-vol. set, and resolved on this trip to read vol. 3. I was some way into it, at least 100 pages, and could have gone on. It does in its way take hold. But I decided I didn't want to spend so much time with a person I didn't admire or like. I suppose the first-person narrator must be very close to Proust; one would suppose almost indistinguishable. But even if an expert should tell me that this is not so (and I would find it hard to believe) that would make no difference. Whether 'I' is Proust or another (isn't he referred to somewhere as Marcel?) and quite distinct, he is snobbish, self-enclosed, self-congratulatory, precious, humourless and boring. So what is the hold? Why does one read on? On what is the big reputation built? Is it more than the fact that the whole is very large and that there's a commitment of self in reading it all, which makes 'Pwoost' part of one's personal history?

I think one reads on because it creates a complete world, and gives a complete sense of its central consciousness; and because, even in translation, the sentences are complex and interesting, with a linguistic

---

* I think some part of this bird battle may have gone into a subsequent novel, I'm uncertain which but probably *The Secret History of Modernism* (Harvill, London, 2001).

economy and ecology all their own. I can imagine that in French, if one's French were up to it, the style would be a very large part of the appeal. But I felt almost that to go on reading was like keeping bad company.

Arthur Miller is much better company, an intelligent observer of himself and the world of the middle century, whose life is interesting in itself, and more interesting as he reflects on it. Sometimes it becomes blurred. Sometimes he's rather highfalutin, especially about Marilyn Monroe, as if he has to excuse his affair with, and marriage to, her by elevating it. But even that is deeply touching. And the way he sees his life in tandem with the politics of the times matches so nearly the way I see my own.

Of course I wronged this place (Varuna) and on the whole Judy [Rosie Scott] was right. I don't like sharing a bathroom. And it's not a beautiful house. But my first reaction was 'doing a Charlotte' [daughter] (as at the Mill house in France a couple of years back). The place is quite clean and convenient; and now that the sun has come out I can see the beauty of the garden. I also feel the romanticism of the old lefties, Eleanor Dark and her husband, Bruce (? – Doctor Dark) – their idealism, paranoia, faith. This was their house, and she wrote most of her books here, including *The Timeless Land*.

And the writers are a pleasant lot, though I find the young playwright, Herbie Greenglass,* a pain. For a couple of days I was virtually alone with him. He sat opposite me while we ate, and talked at great length, in his furry monotone, about his progress as a playwright, which seems almost entirely a story of failure. He had (he said) some good years from about 1990 to 1996, when he had Government grants (pronounced as in ants, not aunts). And in 1996 one of his plays was produced. He graduated (in theatre I suppose) from one of the big city Colleges of Art and since then has been (to put it brutally) writing things no one wants. If he goes on to great things that will seem noble. If he doesn't . . .

Herbie has a 'partner'. We all know she's Catherine, but he refers to her always as 'my partner'. She's 'a dramaturge' and, he says, everything he writes is submitted to her before it's offered anywhere

* Name changed.

else. At present he's writing something in which she pointed out (phew! – saved!) that the male characters were overbalancing the female, so he's currently writing up the female parts. She's a vegetarian and when she visits and spends a night with him Sheila cooks vegetarian. I don't mind vegetarian food at all, and wouldn't complain if I did; but I do mind that I'm not allowed meat because Herbie's 'partner' is staying the night. She is a person of immense sympathy for the underdog. He says so and so does she so it has to be true. She has a kind of charm I find faintly patronising, like a universal Nurse, the Wagnerian World Matron.

Brook Emery is a blue-jeaned poet aged fifty, yet to publish a book, not having begun to write until late, but apparently with some recent success, and his first book now accepted and due for publication soon. He was a schoolteacher for many years and then got out because he was suffering depressions. He has grey whiskers and is rather nice; seems a firm character, an orderly man, with something distinctly schoolteachery about him – the best rather than the worst of that. His marriage is currently breaking up.

Hugo Hamilton is great Irish company and no doubt very talented.

Heather Stewart is a small (early-to-middle middle aged?) Oz who hasn't published anything, I gather, but is writing a life of Christina Stead. She's slightly nervous, tentative, pleasant, with beady eyes and big specs, a pointy nose, quite a lovely mouth, pointy breasts and a somewhat stiffened body, the result of major back surgery.

Hugo and I gave a reading, preparation for reading together next week in Sydney.

9/9/99: Back in Auckland after the Sydney Spring Writers Festival, where Hugo Hamilton and I read with Evelyn Conlon, also of Dublin and equally charming.

At Varuna Heather Stewart told me she had seen me at the Sydney Poetry 'Write-in' in 1975. I met Penelope Nelson there and asked Heather if she knew her. She knew her slightly, and told me a story about her. I may not have all the details right, but it goes like this:

A person called Bob Ellis, fiction writer, poet, script writer, and sometime speech writer to Kim Beazley and other Oz Labor majesties, is currently much in the public eye because he wrote a memoir in which he said a woman now married to a senior Labor person called Abbott or Costello (both names are involved in this story, which therefore already partakes of comedy) had, as a student, recruited to the Party the man now her husband, and also the other, by taking them to bed. There was a defamation case and Ellis lost to the tune of many hundreds of thousands of dollars. It had gone to appeal, and the verdict was due any day. Ellis was also, concurrently, involved in a paternity suit, he denying paternity, saying if it were proved it would be the first recorded case of a baby conceived by oral sex.

This Ellis had earlier written a book called *The Nostradamus Kid* about his student days at Sydney Uni, and had made it into a movie. It concerns a panic that Sydney was about to be destroyed (whether because of the Cuban Missile Crisis or not I'm uncertain – if so it had also something to do with the prophesies of Nostradamus) causing him, or the character based on himself, to take off into the Blue Mountains with his girlfriend of that time. I don't know whether he names her, but the girlfriend was Penelope Nelson, and she figures as a socialite from a good school and suburb, both her parents well-known journalists. When Penny saw the movie she was moved to write her own memoir of their time together, called *Penny Dreadful*, which involved her virgin status, her loss of that to Bob Ellis, the Cuban missile crisis, and their taking her mother's car and driving up to the Mountains to escape death. After waiting about for the Big Bang they returned to find panic caused by absence of daughter and car.

Penny's father was the *Bulletin* columnist David McNicoll, and I remember once at that 1975 'Write-in' she turned over a copy of the paper and there his column was, with his picture, and she said (or did I?), 'Even here Big Daddy is watching us.'

So . . . At the Sydney Spring Festival last week I went to hear Bob Ellis, a (now) corpulent and rumpled dwarf with the remains of good looks and an extraordinarily deep voice. He is one long gossip column on short legs, clearly with some literary talent, interesting experiences in the corridors of Canberra, a stock of one-liners, an entertainer. I wondered was Penny Nelson in the audience, but if she was I didn't see, or didn't recognise, her.

And quardle oodle ardle wardle doodle the magpies said.

13/9/99: E-mail from Margaret 10/9/99 attaches one from Mel Cain in HarperCollins, Sydney, to Christopher MacLehose in Harvill, London:

RE: CKStead
He was absolutely lovely. He did a wonderful radio interview for me and then Kaye Wright and I took him to lunch and both loved him.
Mel

As Margaret says, 'clearly a PR success!'

An Interview with a Croatian Journalist[*]

Jadranka Pintarić: Your new novel *Talking about O'Dwyer*, the eighth in your rich bibliography, has been a success in New Zealand and has won you also British critics and readers.[†] Allow me to say that we too feel we have a reason to be proud of that as part of the novel takes place in Croatia and the recent war is part of the background. On the other hand, the protagonist's life is connected fatefully and in several ways with the descendants of a Croatian family in New Zealand, which is the reason he comes to Croatia. I realise most novelists hate this question, but I can't help myself: to what degree are the Croatian characters based on real people and to what degree are they your own literary creation? Further, do you really know any Croatian families in New Zealand?

CKS: As *Talking about O'Dwyer* makes clear, Croatians (Dalmatians, in particular) have had an important place in New Zealand social history, especially in the northern part of the country, so I have always known people who came, or whose forebears came, from your country. Also my wife, Kay, grew up in Henderson, west of Auckland, where the Dalmatians began what is now the New Zealand wine industry, and

---

* Published, translated into Croatian, in the Zagreb literary journal *Quorum*, 5 June 2000.
† It was published in a Croatian translation as *Makutu* in 2001. The German translation also used that title.

some of the memories in the early part of the book are hers. Because of that connection I was particularly happy to have one of my novels, *All Visitors Ashore*, chosen for translation into the Croatian language, and Kay and I were delighted by the reception we had when we came to Zagreb for the launch of the novel. As you know, I returned the following summer, and parts of *Talking about O'Dwyer* draw on those visits and the wonderful people I met.

JP: In several of your novels, including this last one, protagonists return either to their old lovers they never got over, or to an event from their childhood or early youth which they can't forget. Through the recollection of those moments their whole life is reconstructed and in the end they realise that the event was fateful, that it determined their whole life. Furthermore, in *Talking about O'Dwyer* it is suggested that a curse, cast by a Maori woman in an ancient tradition of pre-technical societies, determined the course of several lives, directly or indirectly. Do you personally believe there are events in life that determine us forever?

CKS: I think there are two answers to this. If you live long enough to be able to look back and see an evolving pattern, in retrospect there are going to be moments of chance or choice which significantly influenced, or even determined, what followed. On the other hand, novels are stories and stories need shape, so almost inevitably such moments of decision and their consequences for good or ill are going to figure more clearly, more significantly, or with a significance that is more apparent, in a narrative than in real life.

JP: In addition to the curse, what connects the lives of *Talking about O'Dwyer* is Wittgenstein's famous sentence: 'What we cannot speak about we must pass over in silence'. J. M. Coetzee said: 'In every story there is a silence, some sight concealed, some word unspoken.' What in this story is the silence you wanted to show, what is it that is not spoken about?

CKS: If it were absolutely clear to me how this question should be answered it would, I think, be equally clear that it should not be answered. Each reader must find the silence and its meaning. For the author to provide a statement of it would take away a sense that there is a discovery to be made.

JP: Someone said that you are 'an astute voyeur of human behaviour who shifts from one character to the other with ease' (a compliment of course). For the structure of the novels you write, a good knowledge of human nature is undoubtedly necessary; but not only that, since your characters are often of different ethnic, cultural, educational and social backgrounds. Does this require much research or is it just a matter of your natural talent for entering others' souls?

CKS: Research can be useful about facts, but not about the human psyche. There are two routes into this. One is observation. A novelist – or the kind of novelist I am – must be interested in the world outside self. Observing behaviour, you learn to 'read' it and understand what it signifies about the state of mind, the emotions, the thinking, of the person observed. The other route is through imagination and self-analysis. It is, I suppose, the verbal equivalent of acting. You become that character. In the end you become all the characters in your novel.

JP: The plot of your novels is never linear and simple, and in most cases it takes place in distant parts of the globe, thus indirectly incorporating some other cultures, mores, scenery, everyday life, history and mentality into the text. One might say that very subtly, discreetly, and indirectly you promote multiculturality. To what degree is that a result of the fact that you travel and research a lot yourself, and how much is it the reality of the cultural and ethnic diversity of New Zealand?

CKS: I have sometimes tried to make my novels more linear, but there is always a strong impulse to break up the time-line and to move about in time and space. It's an intuitive thing, but I have rationalised it to myself as follows: I think a novel should be an image of the human mind, and the human mind clearly exists in the present, but carrying memory, and anticipating a future. We live in past and future as well as in the present. So the linear novel simplifies too much and fails to represent the complexity of the human consciousness.

As for cultural variety, either at home or abroad: this does indeed represent my own life. New Zealand is very much my home base, but (like the whole world) it is becoming increasingly multicultural. There are our two basic cultures, Maori and Pakeha; and then, especially in recent years, there have been new settlers from a very wide range of backgrounds. Also, as you've observed, I love to travel, and during my lifetime travel has become easier. The world has shrunk, we interact more and more with different cultures, both at home and abroad.

JP: Critics have called you a 'master novelist' and an 'artist of narration', but you first entered the literary scene as a poet and got the first rewards for poetry. Only then did you turn to prose. Is that a logical order, as T. S. Eliot said, i.e. that a serious writer must sooner or later turn to prose because it is the only way to fully show his ability and talent and, above all, literary maturity? How do you feel about the relationship now, after eight published novels and eight books of poetry (coincidence?)?

CKS: I think in fact there are, to date, eleven books of poems. When I go back to writing poetry I always feel I have returned to 'first base'. It is the most demanding and the most fulfilling verbal art. But it is more esoteric, it doesn't have the wide scope of fiction, it doesn't reach out to such a wide audience, and it resists translation. There are things that fiction, or equally expository prose, can do, which are not possible in poetry. Poetry, really, is about language. Every poem in English is a celebration of the English language. Since I seem able to do both, I don't see any reason to confine myself to either one.

JP: You were the editor of a collection of New Zealand short stories and have published two books of stories yourself. In your opinion, what is the relationship of these two literary genres today? Is the short story still treated just as a foretaste of a novel (or lack of 'wind' in the author to persevere); or has it gained equality and respectability among public and critics?

CKS: I think the short story at its best can be a little nearer to poetry than a novel can be. The tradition of the short story has been very strong in New Zealand, especially because of the example and influence of Katherine Mansfield, and then of Frank Sargeson. But books of stories are hard to sell. Readers don't like having to start over and over again – so for that reason, if for no other, it lacks the status of the novel. But it is very hard to do well, and therefore (to me at least) the short story as a form is challenging and critically interesting.

JP: Each year when the Booker Prize is awarded there is at least some polemic about whether it still makes sense to limit it to the literature of the long-dead socio-political context of the Commonwealth. Does the community still exist in any sense? Your protagonist in *Talking about O'Dwyer*, when he first comes to London, says that he wonders why everyone back in New Zealand thinks of England as their true homeland. So, is English culture, and to what degree, still the common denominator of all the countries which were part of the Empire?

CKS: There are two aspects to the Commonwealth: the parts of it (like New Zealand) where the majority population are of British (English, Irish, Scots, Welsh) ethnicity, and the parts (like India) where an older culture and languages preceded, continued during, and survived, the Empire. Clearly if your ethnic inheritance is British, the Commonwealth is more important. But the broader Commonwealth still proves it has meaning by the fact that the former colonies choose to remain members and continue to meet. Part of the reason for this is the international currency of the English language; and part is the inheritance of certain British legal conventions and political institutions. Britishness becomes less important to us as time goes by; but it is not unimportant. Partly it is a protection against Americanisation, which the Canadians certainly fear, and so should we. Also – and this is the opposite of what you might expect – the authority of the British Crown is in at least one respect more important to Maori than to Pakeha in New Zealand, because the Treaty of Waitangi, which authorised British settlement and guaranteed certain rights to Maori, exists, so to speak, 'over the heads' of the Pakeha, an agreement between Maori and the Crown. This becomes a very complex issue when you try to analyse it in terms of present law, because the question of whether the authority of the Crown in New Zealand now resides in London or in Wellington comes into it, and radically alters the Treaty's original meaning. But it still has for Maori, I think, a certain emotional force.

JP: The Croatian translation of *Talking about O'Dwyer* will soon be published. Will you visit Croatia again on that occasion? It seems that your last visit was inspirational and fertile – it resulted in the novel the idea for which was conceived in Zagreb and on our coast.

CKS: I would love to come back for the launch and I do hope it will be possible.*

JP: Could you tell me something about the novel you are working on now. What is it about? Will it surprise your readers?

CKS: It begins with an elderly writer suffering writer's block. That sends him back in memory, to London at the end of the 1950s. I don't think it will surprise anyone. It's perhaps not the kind of novel that will attract a lot of attention, but it's full of subtlety and jokes and I think those who read it will be entertained, as I was in writing it.

---

* It was not, but I returned in May 2007, by which time I had three novels in print in Croatian – *All Visitors Ashore*, *Talking about O'Dwyer* and *Mansfield*, and I was invited to the Zagreb Book Fair for the launch of a fourth, *My Name was Judas*. See also p. 131.

Travel Notes, 2000

27/5/00: [London.] *Spectator* review today of *Talking about O'Dwyer* says, 'It seems incontestable to me that C. K. Stead is among the very best contemporary novelists.' Describes the novel as 'dazzling'. The review by someone called John de Falbe.

I've been re-reading Doris Lessing's *The Golden Notebook.* When I read it last, some time in the '80s, I felt it so powerfully influenced my fiction (*The End of the Century at the End of the World*) I had to fight to get out from under it, and that I should never read it, or Lessing's fiction, again. Now I feel I read it much more consciously, seeing clearly what she's done, so I feel (and hope it's not an illusion) I can use it without the kind of problem it created for me last time. I've gone back to it because the present novel [*The Secret History of Modernism*] is set mainly in the '50s and Lessing gives such a close portrait of that time in a left-political frame. What strikes me now is the way she has focused so closely and literally on real people she has known, it gives her complete confidence either in describing 'what happened', or equally in departing from it.

31/5/00: Odd that after that note above (27/5) I met Doris Lessing last evening at the launch of a novel by the Norwegian Gunnar Kopperud (with whom I read at the Hay-on-Wye Festival) and talked to her. I had met her just once before, in a lift in Wellington! She was very nice, friendly, and introduced me to Ruth Fainlight and Alan Sillitoe who were friends of Janet Frame's. I have difficulty connecting her present presence (which means appearance, I suppose) with the rather beautiful young woman of the photographs whom one connects at once with the fiction.

6/6/00: [Oxford.] Remember the swan this morning, in that area of watery woodland beyond the University Parks, so attentive while its cygnets fed in a backwater.

8/6/00: The swan (same one) in the river this morning with its cygnets and its partner. The field enclosed by willows, and what? – the *chattering* trees which I think are probably poplars. It's all so dense and beautiful in there. For me it represents the territory of *The Wind in the Willows* – the childhood reading of the not quite 'post'-colonial; the 'England' of that now defunct child.*

The Golden Notebook varies in interest but is remarkable in keeping the interest alive. The most vivid sections are the Africa ones – especially the novel-within-a-novel that ends with the White leftists bringing about disaster for the Black cook. The rest is many variations on a theme – a central character and her friend and their experiences with men. She loves, he leaves. Then many empty experiences. Then again she loves and again (after a time, even years) he leaves. I feel these are based on reality but also imagined. She is trying to come to terms with a failure which must in part be hers (though one can't be sure), and if it is, she's not able to show that it is, or how, or why, it is. All she can show is how the men fail. But why do they? Or why does she choose men who fail? (I think she asks herself this.) Or is one to take it, as the feminist movement of the '80s took it, that all men will fail all women? The All-Men-are-Beasts scenario? I think she is too subtle for that: much subtler than the uses she has been put to by feminists. (She thinks so too.) The novel, though so long, rough-hewn and repetitive, stands up awfully well. Towards the end of the Notebooks section, between Freewomen 3 and Freewomen 4, a tone

---

* See *The Secret History of Modernism*, pp. 142–3, for what became of these scenes, and the swans.

almost of madness sets in. I can see why the novel frightened Kay when she read it in the '70s in London. There is a Jewish 'lover' (I put it in inverted commas because he's impotent) and then a Ceylonese, and both veer frighteningly between seeming orderly and rational and charming, and almost insane; and in their insane phase they echo the central character's nightmares. This is the man as destroyer of the female. One would like to know more about *her* – D. L. – why life has been so dark for her.

11/7/00: (Los Angeles, en route back to New Zealand.)

I usually check out on the day of departure and either go in to Santa Monica or spend the afternoon by the hotel pool, but here (Holiday Inn) you can only get into the pool with your room key, so if you've checked out you're shut out. An extraordinary meal (how awful US cuisine is!): grilled chicken with vegetables, the chicken dried out to strings just fine enough to get into the gaps between teeth, the vegetables slices of marrow and courgettes with tough rind and dry seedy centres – all of this on a flat cow-pat of mashed potato which in turn is surrounded by a sort of cow's urine sauce, vinegar flavoured.

I spent my last evening in Oxford at the Raines [Craig Raine and his wife, Ann Pasternak Slater, known in the family as Li]. There was also a visiting Italian, and his son who is to have a holiday with Vasca [Raine] (both thirteen). At one moment, around the table, Craig and Li were trying to remember how it was that, during the War, Craig's mother didn't know what had happened to his father (the pro boxer and faith healer he writes about in *Rich*) after the father had been 'blown up'. For some months, I think they said, the mother remained in ignorance. How could this have been? In the middle of this exchange I hear Li say, 'Olive would have been preoccupied with Norma.'

I ask, 'Who is Olive?'

'Craig's mother.'

'And Norma?'

'Craig's sister.'

I explain that my mother was Olive and my sister Norma.

These dreams at intervals through the night in LA: (1) Margaret and Sophie and I are at somewhere like Hay-on-Wye. Everything is clean and spotless. There's talk of 'so clean you could eat bacon and egg off the floor'. Then it seems this is literal. We *are* to eat bacon and egg off the floor. A good atmosphere – happy.

(2) I'm with Tony Axelrad in an exotic place, not France but like it. We have to hurry and Tony is panting and having difficulty keeping up. He explains he has 'a heart condition'. I suggest I should hurry on ahead. I'm convinced Tony will die. We are sitting on the ground and a sparrow, quick and chirpy, begins to eat Tony's shirt, which is a kind of net. We all like the sparrow but I'm sure its eating the shirt has something to do with Tony's illness

(3) I'm with Margaret and Sophie again. We get off a bus with luggage. I manage to take up all of my three or four pieces, in my hands and over my shoulders. We step into Customs Street (Auckland) and Sophie says she has left one piece of luggage behind for me to carry. I say I can only just manage my own. She says I carried all of mine and one of hers before. Margaret is impatient with Sophie, who insists: 'You can do it.' All at once I say, 'This is outrageous. I'm 78 and you're a fit young woman.' Margaret goes down towards the waterfront to check our arrangements. Now Sophie and I are following. We have all our luggage, hers and mine, quite effortlessly, and I have an arm around her waist. I say affectionately, 'You are a very badly behaved Frenchwoman.'

'No,' she says, but not taking offence.

'Yes,' I insist. 'But you were so charming the night you cooked for us' – referring to the supper with Werner Forman. 'Beautiful and charming.'

We are very fond. It's one of those moments in dreams, suffused with warmth.

I woke, half woke, and went to the bathroom, going over this sequence. In the bathroom I thought, 'This is the first time I've got my age right in a dream.' Usually I dream I'm much younger and then, very slowly, as I wake, I add years, and more years, until the depressing truth is reached. My thought continued: 'In fact I added a year. I won't be 78 until October.'

I thought this in what seemed full wakefulness. Then, still in the bathroom, in the dark, I realised that far from getting it right I had *added ten years*! I am 68. But at the end of the dream age didn't matter – I suppose that was what was so nice about it.

2/9/00: [Melbourne.] It's Grand Final Day – the Final of the Australian Rules Football championship, the most popular winter sport in Victoria. The central city is blocked for a parade.

I suppose this [Writers' Festival] session on publishing poetry springs from anxiety as large firms drop poetry from their publishing lists. There used to be publishers who wanted a poetry list, not because there was money to be made, but because it represented 'class'. Democratisation comes at a cost. Now almost the sole criterion is profit, and the poets get trimmed. When I chaired a session with Hans Magnus Enzensberger in Wellington a few years back he said poetry was the only industry he could think of where the producers outnumbered the consumers. A good quip; but I suppose it's more accurate to say that for the most part the producers *are* the consumers. So poetry publishing depends on various kinds of charity, subsidy, patronage: publication by university presses, Arts Council grants, awards, private patronage, self-publication. It's important to recognise that this has always been the case. It's not new. Shakespeare's poems and sonnets seem to have been the product of patronage. Dedications were in effect bought, in the 'sure and certain hope' (as the Anglican burial service puts it with such fine ambiguity!) that art will 'outlast brass' and that to attach one's name to it is a means to a kind of Horatian eternity. They weren't published by Shakespeare but by a bookseller who must have seen a profit in it for himself. There would have been none for Shakespeare, whose reward was recognition by friends and financial support by his patron. Almost none of Donne's poems were published in his lifetime. They were circulated among friends. There have been examples of poets famous in their own lifetime, and rich from the sale of their work – Pope, I should think, and Tennyson as he got older; certainly Byron. But these examples are rare. Mostly poetry is a solitary art. Was it Milton who said he wanted 'fit audience though few'; and Keats who wanted to leave 'Great verse unto a little clan'?

Most loyalties in poetry these days tend to be local; and more regional than national. In America, West Coast poets are read on the West Coast, and East Coast poets in the East. But cutting across those loyalties at present we have also the fame phenomenon; a few poets get singled out as 'great', and most attention internationally falls on them. It's a convenient short-cut for literary editors and publishers. Seamus

Heaney from Ireland, Ted Hughes from England, John Ashbery from the US, Les Murray from Australia, Allen Curnow from New Zealand – these are the 'A-list', the Fame Club, the Nobel aspirants. There's something Koru Club about it, and inimical to poetry. It should be poems that matter, not poets. (But of course it would be nice to be one of the club!)

Young poets need one another; and they need a few good periodicals as young actors need theatres. They also need to have faith in poetry, and confidence (which will not be misplaced) that whatever happens in the big bad world of commerce, poetry will survive.

22/10/00: [Toronto Harbourfront Festival.] Pain in shoulder continues. What can I remember of getting here?

On the Ak–LA leg I watched a new Woody Allen movie in which he has cast himself, no longer as the tormented NY Jewish intellectual (i.e. himself), but as a small time crook (the movie is called *Small Time Crooks*) who is hopeless as a crook but a faithful husband. It's funny, has a 'philosophical' dimension, and one will need to see it again on a proper screen and stay awake (I dropped into a ten- to fifteen-minute black hole while watching) – but Woody should probably stick to being himself.

Los Angeles: I stayed at the Crown Plaza which is OK for an overnight (anything is) but somewhat shabby. I tried to walk to the ocean but was defeated by the volume of traffic. I had a wake-up call at 4.15 a.m. which turned out to be earlier than it need have been for a 6.26 a.m. flight. LA to Chicago I was beside a fat young woman who heaved and sighed and overlapped through four or five hours and slapped cream on her arms and legs and bosom at intervals. I could (just) stand her overlapping flesh, but not the smell of the lotion.

Toronto: The Harbourfront Festival has developed hugely since I was last here. So has Greg Gatenby [the director]. He greeted me warmly, and waxed lyrical/religious about swimming with dolphins in NZ.

I had a muted conversation this morning over the toaster with Anita Desai who now lives in Boston. I was so quiet (taking my tone from her) I think she rather hoped I might come with her on a visit to galleries, but I want to *walk blindly about* today, recovering from jet-lag and planning my reading for Tuesday, so I can go on the Niagara trip tomorrow more or less sure of what I'm going to do.

Later: Jeffrey Meyers' lecture on Orwell was headlong, gossipy. He inscribed my copy of his book 'To Karl with gratitude for help when I started out as a biographer.' Since Mansfield he has 'done' Wyndham Lewis, Hemingway, Lowell, D. H. Lawrence, Conrad, Poe, Edmund Wilson, Robert Frost, Bogart and Gary Cooper, and is now working on Errol Flynn. What a list! – but he's a pro, with energy and enthusiasm, and keeps to one possibly sound principle, that if you work on one biographical subject for more than two years you start to dislike him/her. One very odd thing: I have a distinct visual recollection of him (rather dingy) from 1976, which in no way accords with my present image of him (rather dashing). How does such a discrepancy occur? Also (and quite separately) my present thoughts about him are somewhat tarnished by my knowledge of his very public and ungentlemanly savaging of a woman who helped him professionally, and with whom he stayed, while he was working at the Turnbull Library in Wellington.

Later again: At dinner in a restaurant Greg Gatenby vacates his seat beside Kjell Espmark, Swedish poet and 'the nation's leading expert on poetic Modernism', who is also a member of the Swedish Academy and chairman of the Nobel Committee. Greg gives up his seat so Margaret Atwood can have it. Meanwhile she, 'Peg', has grande-damed her way down the room shaking everyone by the hand before arriving at the favoured place. I hear Espmark tell her how much he admires her poetry. The rumour here is that Canada considers her its leading contender for the Nobel, since the death of Robertson Davies; and Canada hasn't had the Nobel for literature. Am I in the presence of Lit Hist in the making?

Espmark goes to Gotland every summer and does the summer play with Lars Ardelius and Per Jersild.*

I've just pinned down the particular *Swedish* quality. They have charm and reserve *simultaneously*.

---

* These, Lars in particular, are Swedish friends. Kay and I have been to Gotland and seen the barn where a play is written and performed among friends each year. There are no reviewers, and no script or record is kept of it – that is part of the ritual. I wrote a poem about it, 'Gotland, Midsummer' published in *Dog* (Auckland University Press, Auckland, 2002).

23/10/00: Trip to Niagara; then a very good lunch. I talked to Robert Drewe (Australian writer) about Espmark's Nobel role and he said, 'Just as well Les Murray and David Malouf are not here – they'd be all over him.' I'd heard of Murray's Nobel ambitions, his attempts to get his poems translated into Swedish and published there. But then, on the other hand, one hears these stories always in Stockholm, where they tend rather to gloat over their proprietorship of the world's biggest and most famous set of prizes. There was the story I heard about Günter Grass treating 'a rather insignificant little man' (not Espmark, surely?) rudely until he found he was chairman of the Nobel Committee, after which he was seen walking up and down outside his hotel in the hope of intercepting him.

25/10/00: I spent most of yesterday preparing for my reading. The group dinner (each night the writers are taken to a different place) was at a Japanese restaurant. I talked to Margaret Atwood's husband, Graeme Gibson, also a novelist but possibly better known as an ornithologist. They plan to be in NZ in February and I've said I will look into locations for bird-watching, and will e-mail info. They've been once and visited Kapiti. I mentioned the albatross colony near Dunedin; also Tiritiri Matangi in the Hauraki Gulf.

My reading went well, especially the poems.

Yesterday was the J. K. Rowling event, 20,000 children in the SkyDrome, 'the largest literary reading ever', and they're looking to the *Guinness Book of Records*. Greg said she was the most nervous reader he'd ever had to deal with, and he's dealt with thousands. She vomited before going on, but then was OK. The audience, largely children, screamed and shouted – overwhelming noise. Fashion is mysterious and inexplicable. I said to Robert Drewe, 'It occurs to me she has overtaken Rushdie as the world's most famous writer.'

He said, 'Rushdie will have trouble with that.'

I said, 'So do I.'

The shoulder continues very painful. Yesterday, one way of preparing was 'walking about'. It confirmed my years-ago somewhat negative view of Toronto as the boring prototype North American city – grid-pattern skyscraper canyons on a flat plain, or plane – though the lake looks less 'dead' than it did last time. Yesterday and today have been foggy, but before that there were blue skies and sunshine, with the orange and yellow of autumn leaves and the blue of the lake. Once into the canyons, however, it's the familiar cold hard noisy non-world of North America (which is not, of course, all of North America).

I saw a Matisse exhibition at the Art Gallery of Ontario, a collection made by the two Cole sisters, friends of Gertrude Stein. They bought Matisse when he was unknown, and went on buying him right up to the 1940s. Their collection was bequeathed to the Baltimore Museum and is here on loan. It's a great cross-section, not all 'successful', or 'best' Matisse, but some that are stunning and all interesting. He is totally congenial to me, because he's working all the time towards 'art' in the sense of aesthetic enrichment/harmony/complexity/depth/pleasure; in other words, towards Beauty (which means, not sugar, but affirmation without deception, or self-deception).

This morning I walked for two hours, all the way to Bleecker Street, where I once walked at night with Miroslav Holub and Libby Brewitt,* and many years later wrote a poem about it, 'Ode to a Nightingale'.

Preparing for my reading yesterday I found a poem I'd completely forgotten, 'The Real Thing'. *No* recollection of it, though it's clearly mine! I liked it, and read it as a pair with 'The Right Thing'. It reads well. The Ukrainian I read with was drunk. He took a glass of wine to the rostrum and smiled blindly into the lights explaining that he had a cold and that the wine, which he sipped at intervals, was his medication. He read Song Number this and Song Number that. The numbers were very large – 530, 780, etc. There was a line, 'I bang my head on the eyes'. Oh, I thought, he's a surrealist. Later it was repeated of a carp in a frozen lake and I realised 'the eyes' was 'the ice'. He also had a lot about 'a woman's breeze'. Slowly one understood that 'breeze' was 'breast'. There was a good big audience, probably because the third reader was Canadian, Farley Mowat,† who has a big following

---

* This was in 1981 during an International Poetry Festival in Toronto. Holub was a famous Czechoslovak poet; Libby Brewitt was secretary to the festival organiser, Henry Beissel. The poem appears in *The Right Thing* (Auckland University Press, Auckland, 2000).

† Postscript, 2007: The marauding ship currently attacking Japanese whalers in Antarctic waters, with such reckless daring Greenpeace's tactics appear almost polite, is named after this writer – one can see why. He is very popular as a conservationist and spokesman for the Inuit, who used to be Eskimos. I'm told it's no longer proper in Canada to refer to them as Inuit. They are now Aboriginals, a term which has just become unacceptable in Australia.

here. He is a bluff snowman-showman with a big subject (the North, the Inuit) and not a lot of style.

26/10/00: I dreamed last night that Ken Smithyman had died. (In fact he's already dead.) It was full of colour. A group of students and staff of the English Department came up Grafton Road in some kind of cart wearing bright-coloured clothes and pretending to be dead. I thought one of the 'bodies' must be Kendrick but they all jumped out and he was not among them.

This morning my shoulder/neck problem had returned, worse. I discussed it with Amanda Prantera, an English novelist published by Bloomsbury who has had sporting problems with back and neck from skiing. She invited me to come with her to the Thomson Gallery – Thomson of the newspapers. The person there told us it was 'the best place to see Canadian art'. In fact it was clear that Thomson had collected only representational art and eschewed the 'modern'. There were some nineteenth-century works interesting because of their subjects; and a few of the twentieth century likewise; but it was, on the whole, a depressing collection.

On the walk back Amanda told me about her 'love affair' (which lasted ten years, and I put it in inverted commas because they never had sex) with a younger Italian (her husband is Italian, a surgeon). After it ended – i.e. he got himself another woman – he was drowned. This revelation and others (in fact she told me quite a lot about her private life) came up because somehow the subject of 'penis envy' had been mentioned. I joked that it was supposed to be something women felt of men, but I thought men felt it of other men; and she was illustrating that it was something she, as a woman, had felt – by which she seemed to mean envy of what she saw as the power and freedom of the male. She told me she had decided last night to watch pornography for the first time in her life but didn't like it, and having got it on the TV of her hotel room, doesn't know how to get rid of it. She is frightfully posh, with wonderfully thick, very curly hair. Interesting, explosive, attractive.

Greg Gatenby introduced me to A. Alvarez. When I was young Alvarez figured a lot as a literary critic and I remember I used to think (possibly unfairly) that he was one of a club, with nothing very profound to offer. Recently he has figured in the controversy that still swirls around Sylvia Plath. He was her friend, and I think protector, when Ted Hughes left her. We talked about Anne Stevenson's biography of Plath, *Bitter Fame* [1989], and about Stevenson herself whom I got to know at an academic conference in Germany in 1990, and again a year or two later at the King's Lynn Festival. I told him how I once travelled with her, on a bus from Tübingen to see the springs at Blaubeuren, and found I was on her deaf side, so was able to change sides and repeat my comments on the return journey. Alvarez thought (of course) that as a biographer she has a good ear and a deaf one. That biography put him at odds with her – he on the side of the Plath-defenders and Hughes-accusers, she a Hughes-defender. I was, not on the fringe of all that long-ago drama, but on the fringe of the fringe, because the doctor who was attending Plath at the time of her death, John Horder, was ours when we lived in the Nuffield flats on Prince Albert Road in 1965, and in that year, during the Commonwealth Festival, I got to know the Canadian poet David Wevill whose wife, Assia, had left him for Hughes. Assia subsequently killed herself, also by gas, as Plath had done but, unlike Plath, she also killed Shura, her child to Hughes. Hughes's 1970 collection, *Crow*, is dedicated 'to Assia and Shura'; and I also have Wevill's *Birth of a Shark* (1964) dedicated 'to Assia'. Eighteen Commonwealth poets were commissioned to write poems for the Festival that year, and we read them in various combinations at the Royal Court Theatre. I still have Wevill's, which I think must have been written after Assia left him but before her death. It begins

> Every man
> Carries a scandal
> At his heart.
>
> The woodpile hides
> A baby, or
> A dead wife's bones.

There is a fascinating book, *The Silent Woman*, by Janet Malcolm, which is really about literary biography and the 'after-life' of Sylvia

Plath, but which springs in the first place out of the publication of Stevenson's *Bitter Fame*, and out of Malcolm's interest in its author. Stevenson had been a year ahead of Malcolm in College (they are both Americans), an 'arty' girl, a poet, someone who seemed to Malcolm to stand out from the crowd and from the dreariness of the 1950s. Stevenson married an Englishman and moved to England, which only made her seem more mysterious and interesting to Malcolm. They were near contemporaries of Plath, and so the reading of *Bitter Fame* draws Malcolm into an intricate enquiry, partly about the famous poet and her famous absconding husband, Ted, but partly about herself, Stevenson, and the women of their generation.

27/10/00: Martin Winckler is the pseudonym of the writer described in the Festival poster as 'France's newest literary sensation. His novel, *The Case of Dr Sachs*, has sold over half a million copies and won the Prix du Livre Inter.' He's impressive – or at least agreeable – at first; but then, as he talks on and on obsessively about his sales, his success, people who loved his book and bought extra copies, people who gave a copy to their doctor . . . etc. etc., the tide runs out, the cup of goodwill is drained. He was pleased to meet me, he said, because we are published by the same Paris publisher,* and he hoped I might interest my London publisher, Harvill, in his novel, which as yet has no English-language publisher.† His novel – in French *La Maladie du Sachs* (a pun?) – has been made into a movie by Michel Deville. Winckler (pron. Vin-claire) has eight children, three from an earlier marriage, two stepchildren from second wife's earlier marriage, and three from second marriage. (Robert Drewe has seven – five from first marriage, two from second.)

I found that Barry Humphries has been through Toronto, when he gave the newspaper interview I read a few days ago. He will be back on Nov. 5, by which time I will be gone. I left a note for him at his hotel, to collect when he arrives.

---

* The publisher is POL who also publish the later work of Marguerite Duras. They published one novel of mine, *The Death of the Body*, which in the French version is *Je ne suis pas ce corps*.
† I tried, unsuccessfully, and there may still be no English-language version.

Susan Sontag, who was throwing her big hair about whe
Hay-on-Wye, is now throwing it about Harbourfront.

28/10/00: Leaving today for London. My dialogue session with Karen
Mulholland went well, I think. Good questions, better answers. It
should make an interesting archival tape, which is what they want.
Blake Morrison came; and I went to his reading with Martin Winckler
and John Banville. I enjoyed Morrison's reading but was slightly bored
by Banville's – not what I expected. There's something in-turned, in-
grown, picked-over, about Banville's writing, though there's no doubt
he writes extremely well.

Travel Notes, 2003

5/6/03: (St. Maximin/Uzès.) We got here last evening from London –
via Perpignan where we picked up our hirecar; had a meal at Suzy's in
the village. This morning did the usual walk into Uzès; this afternoon
drove to the supermarket for basic stores, and to the river for a late
swim. Margaret just rang to invite us to Sophie Henley-Price's 'non-
wedding', the wedding being off but the lunch on, at her parents'
Château near Apt on Saturday 21st.

Before coming to London I was at the Sydney Writers' Festival
and before that at a sort of retreat or bonding exercise at a place
called Eaglereach in the hills above the Hunter Valley – just six of us:
Palestinian Raja Shehadeh from Ramallah and his American wife;
Ronny Someck, an Iraqi-born Israeli Jewish poet; Ghada Karmi, a
Palestinian who has lived most of her life in London; Aminatta Forna,
Sierra Leonese from London; Marcel Beyer, a young German novelist;
and me. We were looked after by a Chinese Australian, Annette Shun
Wah. I now have books by some of these people. Kay has read two by
Shehadeh, and is now reading Ghada Karmi's. I am reading Aminatta
Forna's, *The Devil that Danced on the Water*, alternating it with *Nicholas
Nickleby*, the only major Dickens I haven't read before.

Today's river swim: water clean and running fast – deeper than
usual (i.e. very). The evidence of last September's disastrous floods
(27 killed in this region), which we were here to see, remains along

the banks. L'Enclos, one of two restaurants wrecked at the village of Collias, has been rebuilt, but we spoke to *le patron* and it seems he's locked in combat with the mayor and may not be allowed to reopen. He's very dark about this, understandably, but when you see that the flood went right over his restaurant, sweeping off its roof, it does seem a dangerous location.

6/6/03: This is the last time we'll be in this house, though I hope not the last time in St Maximin.* (Tony and Pat have bought a house right in the village and say we will be welcome to stay there.) I've been in this house at least five years in succession – possibly more. I like waking in the upstairs room with the sun behind the house shining on the valley and on the houses in front at a lower level. I think of it as 'my favourite Van Gogh' – his colours, his subject; the painting he didn't paint. The vineyards are particularly green this year, the wheat fields (if that's what they are) particularly golden. I like the 'existential' routine here. You get up, breakfast out by the pool, walk the 3 or so kms into town, walk back in the heat, lunch, siesta, swim, and finally eat by the pool after the swallows have handed over to the bats. I'm writing nothing so I'm writing this. (*Mansfield* is finished and Christopher† says he wants it but has yet to name an advance.) Even the problems with plumbing etc. have become just part of the routine. When we arrived we found the downstairs loo was blocked again, so we cut the nozzle off the hose, ran it through the house, and cleared it as we've done before.

I measured the walk in on the Uzès map. It's about 3.5 kms each way, so 7 per day if you walk it all. (Sometimes we drive part way, and park at the edge of the woods.) The river was wonderfully fresh and clear this afternoon. We ate by the pool this evening – *soupe de poissons*, salad and pasta, *tartes aux pommes*, with wine and coffee. Christopher rang offering the same deal on *Mansfield* as on *The Secret History of Modernism*. I said that would be OK. It's modest by UK standards, better than excellent by NZ standards, and will keep the English bank account respectable, which allows us to spend time outside NZ

---

* St Maximin is not the large town of that name near Aix-en-Provence, but a very small village just outside the town of Uzès.
† Christopher MacLehose of Harvill, my London publisher – more recently Harvill Secker.

without touching money at home except for fares. I tend to think to myself, 'Let the book prove itself: if it does, it/I will be rewarded; if it doesn't, I won't have taken money I/it didn't earn'.

An e-mail today to say the books short-listed for the Montana poetry award were by Glenn Colquhoun, Robert Sullivan, and someone called Jeffrey Paparoa Holman. No *Dog* [my own collection of poems, eligible and entered]. Another message said the rumour is the poetry judging was left entirely to Marilyn Waring. Could that be true? Yes, I'm afraid it could.

7/6/03: I dreamed last night that I was in a sort of motel somewhere in outback uttermost NZ – not an ordinary motel, more like an old-fashioned wooden shop building, two storeyed, with a narrowing shape, and the downstairs entrance on a corner of the street in the rounded apex. The (also narrowing) room above, looking over the street, was a tea room, as in my childhood, with cake stands and frilly white tablecloths. Elizabeth Knox was there and told me she wanted to have a 'digital orgy'. I was unsure whether this meant sex or writing and was keen to find out, but we kept missing one another. On waking I thought this catches something about la Knox – but I suppose possibly (she would say) about me too.

Another brilliant day.

8/6/03: Continuing reading – alternating – Aminatta Forna and *Nicholas Nickleby*. *NN* is not Dickens at his best. One enjoys the comic strip evils of Wackford Squeers and Dotheboys Hall; but when it comes to things like the comic strip (or fairy story) goodness of the Cheeryble twins who have recently appeared (I'm a little past page 400) it's like swimming in treacle. But of course Forna can't compete, and I don't suppose would expect to. Her book is of great interest but so far (p. 126) the personal memoir approach means that one doesn't get a clear sense of the political principles that were at stake in Sierra Leone when her father was in the thick of it. Hers is a child's view (black father, white mother) but with facts, subsequently learned, added to the story. And although she says the issue was whether Sierra Leone was to embrace Western democracy and non-violence, or a one-party state, it feels in her account more like a power struggle. The question that lingers in my mind is whether, if the other side had won and her father had not been hanged, there would have been democracy or just a different one-party state. There is also the matter of the mother's character which she skirts around. I don't mean that the mother must have been a bad woman – though she *might* have been a wild one; but there would be elements of interest there that the daughter has had to leave unexplored. The child's acceptance of whatever happened, and the sharpness of certain memories and observations, are of great interest; and she emerges as an attractive and intelligent personality – as she is in fact. (Beautiful too!)

Kay is telling me bits of Ghada Karmi's book, as she did of Raja Shehadeh's, and it's obvious that those two have the advantage of having a universally known subject – Palestinians v. Israelis – so although their books are also personal memoirs, they are directly involved in the politics and haven't (as I'm sure Aminatta did) had to learn them after the event. In person they too, like Aminatta, were immensely attractive. Shehadeh was sadly calm and contained; Karmi equally civilised, but angry, indignant. Her family were simply robbed of their home in 1948 and have never been able to regain it or return to it. She and I have Bristol in common; she graduated there, I think just a few years after I was there doing my PhD.

We didn't do our 7 km walk yesterday but drove to look at the Pont St Nicholas – completely (beautifully) restored after the *déluge* of last September which washed away the road and the upper structure. Then coffee at Arpaillargues. River swim around 6 p.m. Tonight we eat out, at *le Bistrot de Gréjac*.

9/6/03: A feeling of exhaustion this morning, probably heat as much as anything, so we drove to town, and missed out the river swim. Swam in the pool. Read and listened to music. Kay finished Ghada Karmi's book and wept. Can we talk to the Fs [Jewish friends, loyal supporters of Israel] about these books? No, I don't think we can. This evening we've been to Suzy's for a kir (white wine and cassis – which Eliz Knox introduced us to in Menton). I'm pushing on with Aminatta and Dickens. Smike has been captured again by Wackford Squeers but then escaped. Will he be lost in London? Aminatta's father has become Minister of Finance in Sierra Leone. Her parents have divorced and the mother has married a New Zealand diplomat, and now the children are being sent to live in Sierra Leone with their father and stepmother.

11/6/03: Yesterday came a message from Roger and Joselyn Morton that they are coming a day early and have to bring Mitch – their grandson – because Freddie (their daughter) and her French husband are in the throws of casting one another off and Mitch (aged I think about fourteen) has escaped to be with his grandparents. They will drive all day and reach us late tonight.

Yesterday we looked at the place Tony and Pat have bought in the village to replace this house. He wanted us to see it and let him know what we thought. I think it's quite charming – two rooms and bath/loo upstairs, two with shower/loo down, and a decent terrace – right in the middle of the jumble of roofs and walls and narrow streets that is the ancient village, and with a view from the upper level out towards the ridge of hills on the far side of the valley. (Also a bonus of wild bees on the terrace – a hive in the wall.) I wonder whether he will regret the loss of space, garden, and pool. Perhaps he thinks of the new place as their summer retreat and they will continue to live in the Hague.

The weather continues burning hot – 'flaming June' means something here. Today we went to the internet together. I did my contract business with Harvill and Kay wrote one to Charlotte. There was a nice one in from C – full of Grimshaw comedy. Conrad (aged ten) is clever at school and refuses to read *The Hobbit* which he describes as 'gay bullshit'. (It seems the word 'gay' in the schoolyard has developed a new meaning – just 'silly', 'stupid', or anything at all you really dislike.) We've had our siesta and read. I'm up to 516 with Dickens, 175 with Forna. It's almost 6 p.m. and we will now go and swim in the river. I have accepted the Harvill offer for *Mansfield*.

Later: Down at the river we looked further at the damage done by the floods last September. Some has been repaired but a lot remains. Some houses and gardens that were swept away completely won't ever be rebuilt/restored. Too dangerous/uncertain. The height the water reached is extraordinary. One has to imagine that whole deep valley simply filled almost to the treetops.

We've just had dinner by the pool and Kay is now cooking so tomorrow's meal for us and the Mortons will be ready *en avant*. Yesterday we went to *Les Collines de Bordic* and got two bottles of their 2001 Merlot and filled the *pichet* (= seven bottles) with their table white (very pleasant wine), all for 12 euros (= about $NZ24). The oleanders are flowering, it's the cherry season (all Tony's taken by a neighbour), there are still some 'Anzac' poppies, and many other wildflowers, along the roadsides – poppies in the wheatfields too. The swallows do their hurtling and chatter overhead while we're eating, and then, as it grows dark, the bats take over. It has the same feel as Crete in May.

16/6/03: The Mortons have been and gone. They brought 13-year old Mitchell, the eminently sane child of their not always dependable daughter, Freddie. Mitch's father, whom Freddie never married or lived with, is one of the Love family – possibly a grandson of the Love who commanded the Maori Battalion. Mitch is completely bilingual (French and English, with possibly still some Maori from kohanga reo), quick, observant, good company, a handsome lad with a sweet tooth that should be curbed. He says Freddie and her current French husband (father a railway worker, mother a cleaner, brother in jail, and sister dead, murdered by an Algerian serial killer who used to do in his victims on long-distance trains at night and throw their bodies out along the tracks) are talking of divorce, so Mitch has gone to Roger and Jos to have a break from them.

Roger seems anxious, almost precarious sometimes, but well-protected by Jos who is the Rock. They have sold their house in Auckland and seem to be living on the proceeds, pursuing their current dream of a life in France. They are half owners of a somewhat ruined house in the Dordogne, but have fallen out with their co-owner (who, when we knew her long ago, was the stunningly glamorous wife of P, director of the Auckland Art Gallery) and so can't get on with repairs until ownership questions are settled. They almost froze to death during the winter. They are generous, sociable, capable with their hands, enterprising and brave, and are making French friends. They will survive. They are coming back to spend the French winter in NZ's summer, partly on their yacht, which they've kept in Auckland, and partly with friends. Kay invited them to count ours among the number of Auckland roofs offering them shelter. They are quite exceptionally nice and flavoursome, good-hearted, never boring; and Roger's Auckland productions of Berkoff plays (they had worked with Berkoff during their long period of living in London) were brilliant. Roger has a mysteriously swollen leg at the moment. I fed him Dispirin in case it was DVT from the long drive here, and Kay supplied anti-inflammatories in case it was rheumatic.

Roger was treated shabbily in NZ, and there is every reason for them to feel hard-done-by. I believe that if, after all those successful years away, they had returned to our Village Capital rather than to Auckland, and done their theatre productions there, they would have been embraced, and arts funding would have been found for them. Because they came to Auckland, the Wellington arts bureaucracy ignored them.*

The lavender has come out and seems to have brought with it a wonderful assortment of butterflies and other flying insects, including one of (roughly) dark grey and white stripes with false eyes at the back of the wings and two false feelers so that it looks as if it's facing one way when in fact it's facing the other. How this helps it I can't imagine. (Must there always be a good reason for surviving mutations?) There are also the insects that look and hover-fly like humming-birds, but are not humming-birds. (And how does that help?) Hovering over the stream through the woods today there were a kind of dragonfly I haven't seen before, with four black wings. The wildflowers along the roadsides are lovely. It's surprising how much more life of every kind – animal and vegetable – there seems to be in Europe than in NZ: quite the reverse, I'm sure, of what every good Kiwi grows up believing. (And the All Blacks were beaten by the Poms at the weekend!)

Last night we saw *Dogville*, a movie by a Swedish director, with Nicole Kidman, which won an award at Cannes. It begins very boring – and in a way goes on being boring (visually); but it has a narrative grip, and moves to an extraordinary climax. It's not, as at first appears, just an abstract allegory, but really an all-out assault on America. America is Dogville. Dogville is America. America is a sentimental

---

* On this point compare the amounts granted for theatre in the main centres in 1998 listed on p. 153.

hypocritical moralistic veneer over every human frailty and failing, and, lacking depth, its logical social outcome is violence. The violence is appalling, but cleaner than the sentimentality and hypocrisy. That's more or less the message; and to leave you in no doubt that it is to be read as specific to America it ends (after the story is finished) with a song about America accompanying a whole series of stills of historical American degradation. It's an extreme movie, making an extreme point, but I was impressed. And Kidman proves again that she is not just a pretty face on long beautiful legs. She is an actress with huge talent.

18/6/03: This morning for a change we drove to Bagnols, a town a little larger than Uzès but with fewer tourists. One feels in the heart of France there. The countryside on the way alternates hillslopes of *garrigue*, left for hunting I suppose because the ground is infertile, and valleys that are beautifully planted with vines, wheatfields, olives, sunflowers, etc. I like especially the sunflowers at this stage. Later, when they have their huge golden heads, they will look wonderful. But at the moment they are well short of full height, with no colour except a green that is half way between olive and battleship grey, and with the flowers, just forming, giving the field a strange texture. Coming back from the river this evening I tried to photograph it in the slanting light.

E-mails from Rog and Jos [Morton] saying 'we are missing your smiling faces' and fighting post-holiday blues. His leg is still swollen. One from Charlotte. She has had a good reaction from Dawney (her agent) to revisions to her novel. Now waiting on the reaction from Fourth Estate. Marg phoned this morning and e-mailed instructions for getting to the 'non-wedding' on Saturday. No word from Ollie – he's living at 37 Tohunga to get on with his PhD thesis.

20/6/03: E-mail to say Roger has probable DVT – will see a specialist soon. Meanwhile he has had an injection (in the stomach, Jos said) and must lie still and wear a stocking.

An e-mail from AUPress yesterday to say *Dog* has been short-listed for the Montana for (wait for it) . . . book design! I replied to Christine asking did she suppose this would please me, when it wasn't short-listed for the poems, and when, for example, Robert Sullivan's Captain Cook book (in which, truly, I can't find much that isn't linguistically flat and intellectually predictable) was? I copied to Elizabeth. They will be shaking their heads and saying, 'There he goes again.'

Many insect rescues to be done in the pool, and even so, there are many fatalities. There has been a big wind during the past day and a half, but the temperatures remain up in the 30s. Yesterday we did the 7 kms walk and the afternoon swim.

22/6/03: Yesterday was fraught for more reasons than one, not the least of which was driving to Lacoste through Avignon's misleading signage, for Margaret's friend Sophie's 'non-wedding', the wedding planned for that day having been cancelled and the couple asunder for ever. It was in a marquee in the garden of the Henley-Price's house. Sophie is a Henley-Price, which is to say, I suspect, Price with a bit extra for effect, possibly done by her father, since her aunt, beside whom I sat, told a story about her youth in which the punch-line was someone saying to her something that began 'Well in that case Miss Price . . .' Sophie's mother is French and they are both, mother and daughter, rather bee-yoo-ti-fool and stylish and fluffy and frothy and wilful, but there is also high intelligence and a load of money. The aunt, sister of Mr H-P (certainly not Hire-Purchase), is the wife of an arch-deacon, and I did rather badly at table, I think, by being too conscientious with her, answering everything she asked ('And what about the Maoris?' – I should have answered in a voice of Peter Sellers, ' "And what about the Maori", I heah you cray') too strenuously/seriously. She's an Anglican wife and a social worker but she's a middle-class Pom too, and I think found serious talk somewhat bad taste and too exhausting in the hot weather. It was as if I had swept her around the intellectual dance floor before she'd had time to refuse.

We took Margaret and Guy to a restaurant in Apt for a meal in the evening and motored back here late, encountering only a few difficulties coming through Avignon, where the crowds at midnight were not dancing on the bridge but were pouring out of the Pope's Palace.

Latest e-mail report from Rog and Jos is that he has had a scan and there's no clot – no DVT. Just a knee injury and inflammation.

24/6/03: Yesterday we drove back to Margaret & Guy's *bastide* (once again through Avignon – once more unto the breach), had a swim in their pool. Having lunch out of doors under an awning in the village of (I think) Goult, with M & G & Joey and their friends Angus and Anneka and baby Barnaby, I was, in my out-of-doors English-speaker-in-France voice, telling how I had bored the arch-deacon's wife with serious talk, and how I had stumbled into this out of conscientiousness, because I didn't want to show by my behaviour that I would rather have been somewhere else at the table (or not at the table). At just this moment, there she was! – passing stone-faced. She didn't look at us but I was sure she had heard.

Today I've e-mailed Christopher protesting at the projected date for *Mansfield*, Spring 2005, and suggesting September 2004.

25/6/03: Christopher has e-mailed back that it will be earlier yet, May 2004. It was 'Becky Toyne's mistake'. Marg says mistakes at Harvill are never allowed to be Christopher's. As the boss, he's exempt.

The heat is excessive.

I seem to have adjusted to the French keyboard at the internet shop at least to the extent of using q when I mean a on this one. We were going to go to Maussanne les Alpilles and say hullo to Natasha Spender but mowing the lawn finished me for further effort. We go to the Sturmers tomorrow for lunch.

This morning I lay in bed (no – lay on the bed – too hot for bed-clothes, or clothes of any kind) thinking about *Dog*, which includes the King's Lynn Poetry Prize sequence, not having been short-listed for the Montana. One knows a good deal about how book prizes work everywhere, that they are a reflection of commerce and popular taste, that they belong to the moment and have little to do with enduring literary quality. (Would Henry James have won the Booker? Or James Joyce?) As for poetry: one lives with the knowledge that it's something few people understand or know how to read, despite the fact that there are (strangely) many many who aspire to write it. Poetry has to be its own reward, unless/until the recognition of excellence becomes part of common knowledge, as (after many lean years) it did for Curnow, in which case the poet wins the award because he is who he is, not because, or not necessarily because, someone has really recognised, and could articulate critically, the quality that is there on the page. All that acknowledged, however, one can still be surprised, not so much that awards often seem to go to the wrong book, but rather that they are accepted and applauded so unquestioningly. There is, especially on the New Zealand literary scene, a rather woolly and uncritical goodwill, so that these prizes become, in the short term anyway, self-fulfilling. I remember in 1985 that *All Visitors Ashore* (which has had quite a life since, both in NZ and overseas) wasn't short-listed for the Wattie Award (as it then was) and something called *Blackball 08*, which no one has heard of since, was. And then I look at these stunning overseas reviews quoted on the new Vintage paperback of *The Secret History of Modernism*, just received ('as subtle as Jane Austen and as fatalistic as Thomas Hardy . . . a minor miracle of a novel', *Irish Times*; 'Stead's writing is meticulous and elegant, packed with ideas and insights', *Daily Telegraph*; 'Stead is challenging, fun, urbane and brilliant. Read him!' *The Spectator*) and reflect that it didn't make the Montana short-list; and more, that someone, himself a novelist, often in the running for prizes, was a judge in both cases, seventeen years apart.

This, it might be said, is a line of thought one should not pursue – either bad for the character, or displaying bad character, or both. On the other hand Matthew Arnold says one must 'see life steadily and see it whole', and these facts represent one part of my literary life.

1/7/03: [London.] We have been back some days in our (i.e. Ann and Anthony Thwaite's) Paddington pad. 'And in Paddington autumn is air-borne, earth-given / Day's nimbus nearer-staring colder smoulders.' I think that's how it goes (Curnow's elegy on his father) – and of course it's not autumn; it's warm muggy mid-summer, but the temperature feels almost comfortable after Uzès. I remember when I first read those lines, I think in Lou Johnson's *NZ Poetry Yearbook* in the early 1950s, the word 'Paddington' alone seemed exciting/exotic/romantic. That was the late- (not quite post-) colonial reader, before he had ever set foot outside NZ; and it was still a time when only the rich, and soldiers in wartime, travelled 'overseas'. It was as if the NZer who had written the poem had stepped out of reality and was now sending back a message from the other side – from the world of books, where there were red pillar boxes and London bobbies and country lanes and Big Ben. He was in 'Paddington'! Imagine! A 'proper' view of this condition would be that it constituted some kind of colonial or imperial deprivation, but looked back on from now it doesn't feel like that. It has a kind of magic about it – as if one lived then in a double time-and-place which has shrunk to single dimensions. Ouch! Heresy!

I read at NZ House – at the NZ Studies day – with Emily Perkins on Saturday. Emily is nice, intelligent, lively, and read a story I thought very good. The Deputy High Commissioner, Suzanne Blumhardt, reminded me that she had offered NZ House for the launch of my next novel (*O'Dwyer* was launched there), so I told her about *Mansfield* and have secured the venue for May. Now six or so weeks stretch ahead, and I feel like high-tailing it back to France, or home. An e-mail from Charlotte today. She's been sick – chest infection. I told her to treat the laptop as a gift (she was saying they could now repay the loan) and use the money to pay for help with the children until we return.

There's nothing to report. London is London is London. The days of 'Pictures in a Gallery Undersea' when it was mysterious, dirty, dark, threatening – exotic, ecstatic, erotic, emphatic – a feather in the colonial cap and a bone in the colonial throat – a place of pilgrimage and complaint, love and hate, homage and rejection – all that intensity is long (long!) gone. 'He who is tired of London is tired of life', said Dr Johnson, who was tired of life but terrified of death and clung to London as a sort of half-way house. Anyway I saw Kiri Te Kanawa in the street today, which would once have figured as a 'London experience'. I smiled at her at two paces. She *froze*. Yuk, a fan!

5/7/03: I'm reading the US edition of Miranda Seymour's novel, *The Summer of '39*, published in the UK as *The Telling* – about the Robert Graves/Laura Riding visit to the Shuylers in America, which ended the Graves/Riding liaison and the Shuyler marriage – but with names changed. I'm reading it so I can have lunch with her with a clear conscience. And I've borrowed *A Whistling Woman* from Margaret so I can do the same with Antonia [A. S. Byatt]. Then perhaps I will read Ghada Karmi's book which at the moment I'm avoiding because I have little appetite for more fact-for-the-purpose-of-opinion reading – especially when it's an opinion I already hold. And there's Aminatta Forna's book, already read. No end of possible lunches!

I had lunch with Finola Dwyer [NZ-born movie producer] about *Villa Vittoria* and the movie: nothing changed there. Roger Donaldson still keen to make it, but money can't be raised. She's a good talker and it was a nice lunch – at the Groucho Club.

Otherwise we have been to a play at the Olivier with Yvonne, *His Girl Friday* – frenetic/funny (quite), full of shouting and bellowing, but worth it to be just a few feet (front-row sold-on-the-day seats) from Zoë Wanamaker doing her stuff. Tonight we dine with Margaret & Guy and Sophie and her (real as distinct from pretended) reason for not going ahead with the wedding – a French drama critic *qui s'appelle (je crois)* Frédéric.*

13/7/03: Frédéric proved to be good company in that energetic French intellectual way – serious good fun and a pleasure. But that was a long time ago. Next night we went to Bill Gavin's dinner party which included some of the cast of *Whale Rider* passing through London, and a Kiwi expat called Peter Walker who wrote *The Fox Boy* about a Maori child abducted, or somehow acquired, after a battle in 1869, and adopted by Prime Minister Fox to be brought up as 'an English gentleman'. Walker was for a time foreign editor of the *Independent on Sunday* and is now free-lance, dealing, I think, with an overworked liver – a great talker, a very interesting man, who swims in the ponds at Hampstead Heath. (Ghastly thought!)

Monday we went to the *Le Cercle Rouge*, a noir classic at the National Film Theatre. Tuesday Graeme Brown brought the sheets for me to sign for the fifty hardback signed and numbered copies of *King's Lynn & the Pacific*,† after which he and I had a pub lunch. That evening Kay was at Margaret's, and Anthony Thwaite and I went with Peter

---

* Frédéric Ferney, front man for the TV book programme on France 5, *Le Bateau Livre*.
† In 2001 I won the King's Lynn Poetry Award (£1000). The conditions require the winner to write poems about King's Lynn, linking it with some other port or region it traded with in the past, and then return to the festival the following year and read them. Mine linked the port of King's Lynn with the Pacific through King's Lynn-born explorers James Burney and George Vancouver who sailed with Cook. That was the opening sequence in *Dog*.

Porter* to the local Indian, 'Spices', an evening of exceptionally good book-talk.

On Wednesday we went to the Kirchner exhibition at the RA (Kay had been once already) – loved it, having known next to nothing of his work.

Thursday was Helen Clark's lecture at Chatham House – nicely judged, intelligent as always, and diplomatic. At question time she held her ground on Iraq and effortlessly batted away a few journalists (one in particular from the *Telegraph*) who set traps for her. Then got takeaways and watched the Larkin Programme at M & G's (they had videoed it).

Friday we went by train up to Low Tharston for lunch with the Thwaites, followed by a walk, out-doors table tennis, and (best) punting on their mill stream – idyllic in the summer heat, trailing through reeds and under willows, followed part way, and then waited for, by their tame family of ducks, parents and children.

I finished the Seymour novel, which builds to a pretty strong and horrifying climax, and I'm now reading the fourth of Antonia's Frederica Potter quartet, *A Whistling Woman*, which is her usual (but more than usual) mix of compelling succinctness in dealing with character and human action (*such* intelligent prose), and an overload (I often feel) of academic 'content' that seems to burst out of the fictional mould. The novel as badly packed parcel. Antonia has said publicly that J. K. Rowling's work is a heap of horse shit and for this has been applauded in some quarters (including *chez nous*) and derided in others. The *Sun* has described her as the 'snooty' author of a 'relatively unknown' Booker Prize-winning novel, *Possession*. 'Relatively unknown' in the offices of the *Sun*, no doubt!

Not a bad week, though these days I still find London a stressful and unlovely environment. I've booked for us to go back to France for

---

* Thwaite and Porter are both much published poets, and figures on the British literary scene. Porter is Brisbane-born but has been in London since the 1950s. Thwaite is English, formerly literary editor of the *Listener*, then co-editor of *Encounter*, and now literary executor of Philip Larkin's estate and editor of his letters. He and his wife Ann (biographer of A. A. Milne, Frances Hodgson Burnett, the Gosses, father and son, and others) live in a mill house in Low Tharston, Norfolk. It is their Paddington flat we often 'borrow' when in London, and were occupying at this time.

five days – to Menton – at the end of the month, after a party M & G are putting on for us.

18/7/03: In the intolerably hot weekend we lay about in the parks with Marg and Joey (Guy was in New York) and I received a liberal award of J's cold bugs. Marg also, and we have both been in bed, Kay going over to help M each day.

On the Monday we went to *Jumpers* (Stoppard) at the NT, and realised we had seen it in 1984. I'm sure it must have influenced the writing of *The Death of the Body*, which I stayed on in London to write a first draft of after Kay and the girls had gone home. I find it fascinating to recognise forgotten influences like that – as I did when I re-read the last pages of *Les Travailleurs de la Mer.* *

Tony Blair has just given a speech to a joint session of Senate and Congress. Seventeen – or was it nineteen? – standing ovations.

21/7/03: Tony Blair's triumph was short-lived. On the plane from Washington to Tokyo came the news that Dr Kelly, a former weapons inspector in Iraq who had given a story to the BBC about Downing Street's dodgy use of 'intelligence' material in the lead-up to the war, had taken himself off to a wood and killed himself – cut his wrists. The nineteen standing ovations were at once wiped from the pages of the Press, and the spotlight was back on the war and the legitimising of reasons given for it, which has not been subsequently justified by the discovery of any Weapons of Mass Destruction. Flat on my back with 'flu I have spent the past few days combing the papers and feel I have the probable story behind the story. It is (no one has quite said this, but it must be so I think) that the weapons inspectors really believed their findings were going to be significant – a determinant of war or peace – and have gradually had to realise that they were not significant at all; they were just a front. The war was going to happen, and their findings would only be useful and used if they promoted the war, not otherwise. So they are pissed off. Even the fanatical Oz, Richard Butler, has turned against the Bush, Blair, Howard trio and said they have lied. So I think Kelly must have approached the BBC

---

* See 'The Sweetshop Window', pp. 59–60.

in the same spirit, given his story, then been tracked down by his masters in the Ministry of Defence. It was said he had approached his boss to confess he'd talked to the BBC (I don't believe that) and was being very leniently treated, given 'a mild reprimand'; but I read in one report that he had been 'interrogated', possibly for some days, in a safe house! He will have minimised what he told the BBC, and been instructed to stick to that. Then I think the intention has been to discredit the BBC report by exposing Kelly while pretending his name got out by accident. He was called to give evidence to a Select Committee and acknowledged (almost inaudibly) having talked to the BBC. Asked if he had talked to more than one journalist he declined to answer, and (most interestingly) said it would be for the MOD to answer that. Asked if he was the source of the BBC story he said he couldn't be the sole source. This didn't quite fit Downing Street's scenario. They wanted him the sole source, NOT having said all that was reported. Then the BBC's reporter, Andrew Gilligan, would be guilty of exaggeration, and would be discredited. On the Friday afternoon Gilligan was being called again to appear before the Committee, this time in secret session, and Kelly went off to an Oxfordshire wood, took some painkillers, and very efficiently cut his left wrist and bled to death. Now the BBC has admitted he was their source, and that they were protecting him while he was alive, and Downing Street is trying again to make it seem that Gilligan exaggerated what Kelly told him – which puts the BBC in the position of having to say, or imply, that the poor dead man lied, or didn't tell the full truth, to the Select Committee. What a dirty little war it has been. How grubby and inglorious. Worthy of the unworthy Bush, and the grinning Blair who seemed to promise so much and has proved to be a Man of Straw (backed by the boy of Straw, Jack, who in his younger days, they say, was an anti-Vietnam war protester.)

22/7/03: More or less recovered from 'flu. Dinner at Susan Butler's (a friend of Bill Gavin's) where we met an extraordinary Russian pianist, Olga Thomas (age 42) – beautiful, but more than beautiful – in some peculiar way *radiant*. Towards the end of the evening she played Ravel and Debussy on a slightly tinny piano, and then (at Bill's insistence) did her party trick which consisted of playing the Harry Lime theme from the movie *The Third Man* with two hands and the stiletto heel of her right foot.

23/7/03: The launch of Anthony Thwaite's latest collection of poems, *A Move in the Weather*, at the Art Workers Guild in Queen's Square. Last year Anthony told me he was going to call the collection *Senior Moments*. I don't know how many apart from myself recommended against that, but I'm glad we were listened to.

24/7/03: Miranda Seymour rang to say her husband, Anthony Gottlieb, has 'dumped her' and that she will come to our party alone.

5/8/03: Some days have gone by since the last entry. 25th was the party which was a huge success – a mix of our friends and Margaret's & Guy's. That was a Friday. On the Sunday morning we got up just after 3 a.m. and caught the 4.30 bus from Marble Arch to Luton, flew EasyJet to Nice, and took the bus along to Menton and the Hôtel Edwards, noisy and plain as ever, and still with its generous French breakfast in the garden. We had five days there, swimming, walking about, sweltering. We scored tickets for one of the concerts in the music festival – the Mahler Chamber Orchestra, I think from Germany. There's an extraordinary effect there of the sky becoming a deep and intensely *blue* blue as it darkens (the concerts start at 9.30 p.m.) The houses and two churches which enclose the square become two-dimensional, as if they are a stage set painted conscientiously to look three-dimensional when really one can see that they are not. And the sky itself looks like cyclorama – quite unreal. Nothing in Nature, you would think if you saw it in a theatre or movie, was ever *so* blue! I.e. it's a stage set in which the real is made (by Nature – though it's also man-made) to look unreal – stylised, and intensely beautiful.

We visited the olive grove, looked from there into our (1972) flat in the Garavan Palace [where we lived for eight months with our three small children]; went by bus up to St Agnes; took Tessa Duder (current Mansfield Menton Fellow) out for a meal – & etc. Had a very good time, with much swimming, walking, remembering and nostalgia.

6/8/03: An enquiry into Kelly's death is about to begin. He's to be buried (belatedly) today. Meanwhile Downing Street has at last given up (after many days of trying) its attempt to discredit Gilligan and the BBC.* It has become clear that Kelly spoke to two – possibly more – BBC journalists, that one taped him, and that the message was always the same: Downing Street was using intelligence reports only to make a case for the war, and since the reports were not in the least compelling, they exaggerated them ('sexed them up'). Also that the chief sexer upper was Alistair Campbell, the PM's spin doctor. This is what Kelly was telling the BBC in his secret meetings with them. So now Downing Street has been trying to plant the idea that Kelly himself was untrustworthy, saying 'off the record', that he was a 'Walter Mitty', a fantasist who made himself more important than he really was. This line was plugged in an unofficial briefing by another Kelly (Tom), a spokesperson for the PM. But the *Independent* ran it as a news story, saying this description of the still unburied Kelly (Dr David), came from Downing Street. This was denied (twice), then had to be acknowledged – and Kelly (Tom) has had to take the blame and apologise for blacking the reputation of Kelly (Dr David).

8/8/03: On Friday 1 August I had lunch with Christopher MacLehose to conclude the deal for *Mansfield* – and just to have lunch together. Great company in his absurdly pukka way. That evening Kay and I went to a reading by two young novelists, Adam Thirlwell (Craig Raine's assistant on *Areté*) and Ben Rice, after which we had a meal at the Polish Club in Kensington with Craig and Li, Christopher Logue† and Rosemary Hill – Logue wonderfully and outrageously and loudly rude about Blair, making Craig (who seems, like Ian McEwan, equivocal about the Iraq adventure) uneasy.

Saturday was *Richard II* at the Globe. 'For God's sake let us sit upon the ground and tell sad stories of the death of kings . . .' 'This royal throne of kings, this sceptred isle, / This throne of majesty, this seat

---

* Postscript, 2007: This was premature. Downing Street didn't give up until it had thoroughly bullied the BBC and produced 'judicial reviews' which seemed to blame the Corporation and absolve the Government. The passage of time has worked to tarnish these coats of official whitewash, but in the interim the BBC has seemed distinctly cowed and cowardly.

† Logue, whose collection *Songs* I read and greatly admired in the 1960s, has become famous in recent years for his stage versions of Homer, in which he performs with astonishing power.

of Mars, /This fortress built by Nature for herself / Against infection and the hand of war . . .' It's all there in my head somewhere because I lectured on it for several years. Bushy and Green [Bush and Blair] 'the caterpillars of the Commonwealth'. 'He is come to open the purple testament of bleeding war.'

> Cover your heads and mock not flesh and blood
> With solemn reverence; throw away respect,
> Tradition form and ceremonious duty;
> For you have but mistook me all this while.
> I live with bread like you, feel want,
> Taste grief, need friends. Subjected thus
> How can you say to me I am a king?

It was well done, with an all-male cast, and Mark Rylance a first-rate Richard. But I must say something about tears. (Richard says a lot about them too – he's the most lachrymose by far, surely, of Shakespeare's heroes, but that is not my point.) I seldom weep in theatres or movies. Kay weeps a lot. Some do, some don't – it demonstrates nothing, good or bad, any more than the colour of the eyes that weep, or don't. But the first time we were at the Globe – that was last year – I wept. It was *A Midsummer Night's Dream*, so clearly it wasn't because it (or I) was sad. It was because it was beautiful – that and the sense one is in the place (perfect replica of the place) the plays were written for. A sense of Shakespeare's presence, nearness. This time I hadn't been able to get three seats together so Kay and I and Margaret sat apart. When we converged at the end in the place where the groundlings stand we were all wet-faced. I think Kay had wept mainly because of the tragedy – the death of Richard. For me, although it was moving, it wouldn't have been enough. When Richard is in prison and hears music and comments on it, Rylance had him do a few steps of a formal Elizabethan dance. At the end, when the cast came out to take their bows, they formed up and, accompanied by the musicians in the 'heavens', did this same dance. It went on and on, becoming more and more vigorous. The audience clapped in unison. It was a brilliant idea (and goes back to Elizabethan theatre practice, I think) because the whole audience are drawn more closely into the experience. We are participants, cast and audience 'dancing' in spirit together. Again for me I think it was simply beauty – BEAUTY – that made me shed tears. Outside of opera it was my most moving experience in the theatre.

What else? On Sunday we went to Ghada Karmi's for dinner (she's the Palestinian woman I met at Eaglereach in Australia during the Sydney Festival). She had invited the lovely Aminatta Forna (who also came to our party at Margaret's) and her husband, Simon.

On Monday evening we had supper at Yvonne's and watched the Larkin video – *Love Again*. Tuesday evening we had drinks with Finola Dwyer and her friend Louise Chun and Margaret & Guy, and then supper at Raoul's (M & G's 'local').

Wednesday we went to a play, *Vincent in Brixton* (about Van Gogh), in which too many cups of tea were made and too much stage business done. Not without interest – but forgettable, and I did doze for a moment in the extreme heat.

Yesterday I had lunch with Miranda Seymour who told me a lot about her break-up with [second husband] Anthony. As a fiction writer I shouldn't forget her image of him sitting up in bed, 'tight in his pyjamas', listing all the things she had done wrong or failed to do during their marriage, none of which he had ever complained of before. One was that she spent too much on clothes – 'he,' she said, 'who has eighty pairs of shoes!' She told me again about her late father's obsession with a young man – a layabout, hobo, mainly gay, smelly moron (by her account) – which went on for, I think she said, eighteen years, at the end of which he stole her father's gun, went back to London and shot himself, and the father died five months later.* She also talked about Thrumpton, the park and the country house (the family seat – it has the gift of a church 'living'), and the behaviour of foxes and of gamekeepers, and seemed more eccentrically aristocratic than ever before.†

Today Kay is over 'hanging out with M' and I have done the washing and hoovered the floor. M cooks for us tonight and Sunday we depart.

* Postscript, 2007: All this has since been told in her remarkable book, *In my Father's House*, Simon and Schuster, London, 2007 (see p. XXX). And Miranda has remarried.
† Her book reveals indeed an extraordinary set of forebears on both sides, including earls and lords, and a direct line back to one of the Stuart kings on the wrong side of the blanket.

A War Story[*]

Her name is Ingrid, she comes from Malmö in southern Sweden, a widow (once, long ago, married to a Frenchman) aged 78 who might pass for 58. Every year since 1970 she has come for a few months of the summer to this little rural village in the Languedoc where she has a house. She has a French daughter and a Swedish daughter, grandchildren and great-grandchildren. She is handsome, energetic, enthusiastic, warm-hearted and smokes cigarettes which she rolls from French tobacco with a machine. Recently, when the village celebrated *quatorze juillet*, she sang karaoke in the square and danced with M. le Maire. She is our neighbour here and we have become friends.

From time to time we have drinks together in the evening, or dine at Chez Suzy, the little café-restaurant in the square. She tells stories of the village thirty years ago, when there were still donkeys to carry loads up and down the narrow streets, horses to plough and harrow the surrounding fields and pull loads in the vineyards; when there was a *boulangerie*, an *alimentation*, and, two or three times a week, a visiting butcher's cart, a fish cart, a cheese cart. Those were the days (she tells us) when what is now Chez Suzy was a café where the locals met. It

---

[*] *New Zealand Listener*, 5 March 2005. This is written as a story, but is (obviously) closely based on a real person recounting real events, though with names and small details changed – so I let it stand, here, as 'faction'.

was run by a woman said to have made her small fortune as a prostitute in Marseilles and retired, with her husband, to respectability in the provinces. Now there are no little shops, no visiting carts, no donkeys in the village or horses in the fields, just a supermarket ten minutes drive away – and Chez Suzy is full of tourists.

'Like us,' we say.

'Like you,' she says, grabbing our hands across the table, squeezing them and smiling, dismissing nostalgia. 'How lucky I am to have met you.'

We (husband and wife) tell her we are the lucky ones. Our conversations are like that, full of small explosions of good feeling. Her English is halting as is our French, and we go back and forth constantly between the two languages.

She talks often about the fact that I am a writer, that she has many stories, that she should have written hers but will never do it now. One night when we are sitting, the three of us, having eaten an excellent meal and drunk a little too much wine, as the twice-over clock in the *mairie* strikes its second ten (the last it will sound until seven in the morning), she grasps me by the wrist. 'I will tell you a story.' There is something breathy in the way she says this, a catch in the throat. 'It happened more than fifty years ago and I have only ever told it once – to my grand-daughter.'

It was 1946. Ingrid, a schoolteacher aged 21, was engaged to a Dane but wanted, before she married and 'settled down', to see something of the world that had been closed to her during the war. She persuaded a girlfriend to come with her. They travelled *auto stop* – hitch hiking – and headed for Paris, which she remembers now as if recalling one of the French black and white movies of that time, full of drama and romance, accordion music, poverty and noble sentiments. When their money was almost gone and it was time to return home, she knew she would have to find a way to come back. Her appetite for France was aroused, not satisfied. Her planned future, teaching small Swedes, marriage to a Dane, the life of a conventional housewife, seemed remote and unromantic.

They had seen nothing of occupied Germany and thought they might return via Hamburg and Kiel. No one was permitted to cross into that country without special papers, but a truck driver hid them in his cab and got them over the border. Their next pick-up was with two American soldiers who said they would take them to Hamburg. As the afternoon wore on they seemed to be taking more and more remote roads. It began to get dark. The Swedes were nervous, the Americans silent.

They came to a village or small town and in the half light could see that, like so much they passed through, it was in ruins. One of the soldiers, the driver, whose name was Chase, was large, loud and strongly built. 'Here,' he said, 'we'll introduce you to a nice family. Good Germans – you'll see. They'll give us something to eat.'

The four climbed a steep stair. The apartment they came to was scarcely more than one large room. There were a young husband and wife and two small children. Like all Germans at that time they looked strained and undernourished; but they offered food to the travellers – dark bread, cheese and a little dish of cabbage. The Americans gave them chocolates and cartons of cigarettes which were at once hidden away; also a stack of tins of food, army rations. Cigarettes and chocolates, Ingrid knew, were used as a dependable currency.

Not much was said. The children were awake but unnaturally round-eyed and unnaturally silent. The German woman looked uneasy; her husband seemed kind, but he too was anxious, and there was something desperate, avid, about the way he watched the gifts being unpacked and hidden away. There were halting exchanges in English and in German, but no warmth. It was all a transaction.

When they returned to the car the German man came too. Ingrid thought he had come down to say goodbye, but he took the wheel.

'Let's go,' Chase said. As they drove, he sang songs of that time, some with strange words that didn't sound to Ingrid like English or anything else – 'Mairzy dotes and dozy dotes' and 'Chattanooga Choo Choo'. He sang tunelessly and without enthusiasm, as if to fill the silence.

She was squeezed between him and the German. In the back her friend sat with the other American. It was dark now, and they seemed not to travel on major roads. But what was a major road in ruined Germany?

She felt fear taking hold of her. 'Where are we going?' she asked. Her own voice sounded weak, child-like.

'Honey,' Chase replied, 'we are goin' to Hamburg aren't we?' And he laughed as if she too should enjoy the joke.

She gripped the driver's thigh. His face had been reassuring. It was as if she knew him – enough to be sure he was a good man. She spoke to him in German, which she knew much better than English. 'Please help us.' She said it quietly but urgently, leaning towards him. 'I'm afraid.'

He didn't reply, except with the faintest shake of his head.

After a time she appealed again. 'Please, help us' – squeezing his leg so hard he flinched and nudged her away.

They turned off one dark road into another, even darker. The silence in the car was terrifying. Ingrid began to appeal once more, again in German. She was stopped by a sharp blow to the face.

'That's enough,' Chase said. 'Stow it.'

Her nose bled. Her eyes filled with tears – not weeping tears, but the kind that spring from pain. She was beyond fear now. Shock had put her into what she later thought of as 'survival mode' (though she didn't expect to survive) – a kind of stillness.

'I'm crazy because of the war,' Chase said. He spoke fiercely. 'You understand?'

Through tears and blood she told him that, yes, she understood.

'Good,' he said. 'So let's get on with it.' He gave her a cigarette, lit it, and lit one for himself.

In a village that seemed more than half destroyed and entirely deserted they stopped outside a building. 'Come with us,' Chase said.

Ingrid made one last appeal to the driver. 'Please . . .'

'Go with them,' he replied in German. He kept his hands on the wheels and his eyes ahead. 'You won't be hurt,' he said.

She took this to mean they would not be murdered, and she believed him. She and her friend went into the dark building. On dank mattresses they were raped. Later they were dropped in a small town, not far from a railway station, and the army car sped off into the dark.

At the station they were told there would be no trains until morning. They found a hotel nearby and told the man on the desk what had happened. 'He gave us a room,' Ingrid said, 'and water. He charged us nothing. In the morning we caught a train to Kiel.'

And afterwards?

'Afterwards,' she said, 'my friend and I were the same. We went together to see a doctor. We had tests. We were not pregnant and we had caught no disease. It was over. We spoke of it to no one – not even to one another. It had not happened.'

'And yet, after all this time . . .'

'Nearly sixty years,' she confirmed.

'You remember.'

'Oh but of course. I remember. Especially the fear.'

'And you told your grand-daughter . . . As a warning?'

She thought about that, looking up from the terrace into the sky that still, even in darkness, managed to be blue. 'No I don't think so. Not so much . . . It was a little gift – that's all. And a gift to you also. It's a story, isn't it? You can write it.'

I had to think about how to ask my next question. 'If you wrote it yourself . . . would there be a point?'

'It was war, you mean? Or had been war . . .' She tailed off for a moment, then began again. 'Yes. Yes, it was the German. That is the point. I was so convinced he was a good man, that he would not . . .'

'Allow you to be murdered?'

'He loved his wife and children. For him, you see, I think it was a calculation. We would suffer and survive, as they were suffering and surviving. That's all. They needed those things – the cigarettes, the chocolates, the tins of food.'

'And the Americans?'

'Oh, the Americans.' She shrugged, dismissing them. 'Well, they had won the war.'

At Home and Abroad, 2006

7/9/06: Since finishing *The Black River* (insofar as a collection of poems is ever finished) I've been writing the Hocken Lecture (now the Michael King Memorial Hocken Lecture) to be given in October. The subject was triggered by Margaret Scott, who is currently transcribing Charles Brasch's journals, e-mailing on some minor questions about Brasch and Frank Sargeson, causing me to think about first meetings, with Brasch in particular. So the subject is to be 'Fifty Years Ago', and the help I got as a young poet from three older writers, Brasch, Sargeson and Curnow. In the samples Margaret has e-mailed from the Brasch journals I'm astonished at how he seems to live in a world predominantly, sometimes entirely, composed of visual impressions, in which his reactions are hypersensitive, largely aesthetic (sometimes aesthetic/snobbish), often extreme and faintly ridiculous; and I find it interesting that being so much of, and for, the eye, these reactions seem very largely to lack 'observation'. He *sees* so exclusively, and his seeing is so full of shudders and ecstasies, he fails to *observe*, to read signs and between the lines, to interpret, to understand. That will be one implication, a minor one and not spelled out, of what I have to say in my lecture.

Work on this lecture has also set me re-reading Sargeson's three-volume memoir with the marvellous titles, *Once is Enough, More than Enough* and *Never Enough*, books which are these days neglected, as is all of Sargeson except the early stories. There are wonderful passages of writing in all of them, and at the same time passages which reveal certain strange and (to me at least) even distasteful preoccupations and obsessions – with his own body when it wasn't functioning properly (wounds, pus, skin problems, dressings, mouth ulcers), and with the bodies of others, real and fictional. I noticed the same thing when I re-read and wrote about *Memoirs of a Peon*.

But it's so interesting to trace the development of his style – and he *is* above all a stylist. There's such an abrupt change in mid-career. First (or first published) came the twentieth-century Modernist, the cut-down style of the early stories, where he did what Twain did for America and Henry Lawson for Australia – domesticated and regionalised the language of fiction, gave our own talk back to us instead of the faded language of middle-class English fiction. Then there was the abrupt change to the Mandarin style (as he liked to call it, meaning elaborate, even ornate) of the later stories and novels. But then there is, I think, a third phase: through the three vols of autobiography, and on into the novella, *En Route*, you can see him working his way, not back, but onward, to something which is neither the cut-down working-man's lingo/argot/talk of the early stories (itself a slightly faux ventriloquial act, but brilliant) to a new energised language which mimics the rapid, almost breathless speech of an articulate, loquacious, bookish person (himself in fact) under the pressure of events. Unfortunately he reached this point almost (though not entirely) too late, in the sense that one feels there are the beginnings of a loss of grip on his own mind, though still with some wonderful passages, right to the last.

The other thing that's notable is the extent to which his auto-biographies are really works of fiction. In some respects – especially his relationship with his homosexual lover, Harry – they tell the story as he would like it to have been rather than as it was. There's that passage, I think in *More than Enough*, where he says Harry moved in with him and in effect for the next 35 years never left. In fact Harry was hardly ever there – as you can detect if you read the narrative and look for him. And when he did move in, during the last few years of his life, when an extra room had been built on for him, I don't think Frank handled it very well or patiently; and finally shuffled him off, protesting, into an old folks' home where he died, neglected by Frank, who didn't go to his funeral. Somehow Frank does and doesn't deal with all this, but mostly between the lines. It's there as much in the denials as in the claims. And yet of course the feeling was real, and the love for Harry, which I think went largely unrequited.

I don't think when I knew him I recognised how tormented he was in the decade of his fifties by the feeling of having made such a big thing of devoting his life to writing and having produced so little. By the time he's writing *Never Enough* there has been the productivity of his sixties, and the relief to his puritan conscience is enormous. And on p. 116 comes this extraordinary admission:

> . . . through too many thin and sterile years of my fifties I suffered a paralysis of will, a failure of nerve [. . .] And I added my own special brand of folly to the dilemma: I exhausted myself in search for excuses: there was my tuberculosis, my dermatitis, my poverty, housekeeping chores were wearing me down: there was . . . but I could recite a whole string whenever it suited me.

Before I came to this brave confession I had been noticing (not for the first time) how his ailments and difficulties are exaggerated and dwelt upon. And I remember writing somewhere* that Frank was less than honest about his income and determined in 'keeping up indigent appearances'. Yet these excuses have continued through the three books of autobiography. It's as though he has this moment of complete clarity about himself, but it doesn't cause him to look for it elsewhere in the book he's working on, and revise accordingly.

8/9/06: I thought a day or so ago of how much traffic goes back and forth by e-mail and is not kept as letters once were. So I printed out and stapled together the messages of just 24 hours, as a sample. They included exchanges with jazz-singer Mahinarangi Tocker who is setting my poem 'Black River Blues' to music (she's there in the e-mail in-box three and four times a day); with Margaret Scott about Brasch; with

---

* *The Writer at Work*, University of Otago Press, Dunedin, 2000, p. 58. See also p. 1 of my novel *All Visitors Ashore* (Harvill, London, 1984) where Melior Farbro, the character based partly on Frank, is described as being 'in good shape despite his limp and his endless complaints about corns, piles, tinea, peptic ulcers, migraine'.

Sophie and Frédéric in Paris who have just met up with Charlotte and her family; with Michele Hewitson who has seen my new novel referred to as *My Name was Judith*; with Dr J. E. Bennett who is requesting permission to use remarks by Sargeson I'd quoted to Margaret Scott about the Parker-Hulme murder trial of 1954; with Gerri Kimber, whom I met at the NZ Studies conference in Paris in June, about her Mansfield researches; with a young poet about his collection of poems turned down by AUPress [and later accepted]; with Elizabeth Caffin, editing *The Black River*; with Tanya Wilkinson at the Corban Estate Arts Centre who thanks me for my talk there on Monday evening; with Michael Schmidt at Carcanet about poems of mine for *PN Review*; and a message to contributors from Encyclopaedia Britannica. That's all in one day!

One subject that has emerged from my doing the Hocken lecture is the version of Racine's *Andromaque* in a modern setting which I wrote while an MA student. It impressed Frank Sargeson and was much discussed by him and Brasch. I have now found the typescript and have wondered whether something could be made of it. The verse doesn't work but that could be repaired. The real problem, as I recognised even at the time, is that the obsessive and irrational loves which the plot demands – of Oreste for Hermione, of Hermione for Pyrrhus, of Pyrrhus for Andromache – could never be made plausible in a modern setting. One such, perhaps; but three – never! And yet I find myself twitching towards it, wanting to try. Then I thought of two versions, one modern (but retaining the ancient names, which in my 1955 version I modernised); the other not only as Racine wrote it – i.e. a translation – but rhymed as his was.

I even began this (latter) mad scheme, thinking if I could do about four to ten lines per day it would soon be achieved. But I've forced myself to stop: first, because Racine's verse is distinguished French whereas regular rhyme in English, unless written by a master when such was the mode, is only a substitute for distinction (see below!). Also it sets up bad habits; one begins to hear everything in iambic pentameters, and in rhyme. Someone (not me) should try it in English using not only rhyme, but Alexandrines (iambic hexameters) with the French caesura – now *that* would be worth the effort; because there's no doubt (and this is what fascinated me as a student) the play has a wonderful dramatic structure, if you could just make its 'givens' plausible. Here's as far as I got with it (and anyone who checks will see that in order to achieve the rhyme I had to make the translation one of the general sense of each passage rather than of the exact meanings line by line):

Orestes

So now the wrath of Fortune's at an end
Or so it seems, when here I find my friend –
You, Pylades, lost to me half a year –
How should I think to find you waiting here
To greet me in this place I dreaded most,
The court of Pyrrhus on this alien coast?

Pylades

I thank the heavens that seemed to shut the gate
And keep me here, complaining of my fate.
Six months I've languished since the storm that tore
Our fleet in two, in sight of Epirus' shore,
Fearing what you might suffer, or that, surviving,
Your melancholy in some hovel thriving,
Lacking the friend I know you need, might tell you
To end the life which you so little value.
But here you are, my Lord, and with such train
Of horse and men I know you don't again
Come courting death.

Orestes

              Alas, my friend, who knows
What fate is signalled by these outward shows.
Love brings me here, whether to live or die
I leave to chance and cold Hermione.

Pylades

No friend, you cannot mean it! – let *her* decide
Your fate and fortune? Where is that steely pride
Which sprang in Sparta out of the soil of shame
And made you say you hated even the name
Of her so heartless? Did you then deceive me?

Orestes

As I deceived myself. Can you receive me
As friend, my friend, in pity as before
For one who never hid his heart, but wore
It fondly on his sleeve? You saw me suffer
As Menelaus promised his only daughter
To conquering Pyrrhus. Yes, you saw the pain
I dragged from shore to shore, my anchor chain,
Yet stood beside me showing a steady hand,
Cooling my rage, who could alone command
Reason to wake in me and recognise
That I was mad, that she had only eyes,
Had arms, had lips for him. So then I swore
I would forget her, called her 'Sparta's whore',
Renounced her, wiped her cleanly from my slate –
Or so I told myself. Just then our State
Threatened, called on its men. I rushed to join,
Hoping that war and glory would consign
All thought of love to their ferocious fire,
And I, regaining fame, would lose desire.
Now listen and admire how Fate, by seeming
To free me, trapped me . . .

Still listening? Well, sorry but I stopped there, and won't take it up again (I promise!).

12/9/06: Elizabeth Caffin, editing *The Black River*, is anxious that the poem 'Kentucky 1853' might give offence. I expected this – would have preferred to leave it mysterious but have agreed to put an explanatory note. The arrival of that poem, coming as it did, title and all, in a dream, was for me an interesting 'event'. I don't think it arrived quite complete in words, but rather as a set of events and characters, and as a narrative structure. But there must have been words too, since even the title was provided by the dream. Did anything that might account for it indeed happen in Kentucky in 1853? I have no idea. Here's the note:

> Kentucky 1853: More than one reader has said he/she feels as if this is familiar territory but can't quite 'place' it. I feel the same. The whole

poem, including the very specific title, was a dream – and there was that notebook by my bed to dash it down before it was lost. I feel sure it must have some buried source in my childhood reading, not available to conscious memory – Harriet Beecher Stowe, Mark Twain, Brer Rabbit, the songs of Stephen Foster, or something else of that kind – or an amalgam. This causes me to reflect that the reading of my childhood, though 'Dominion' status hadn't quite got us out of the colonial frying pan, was not entirely British. I'm aware that the kind of 'Darkie-talk' used in the poem – though it must derive from attempts by those Classic American writers to reproduce the actual sounds of English as spoken by Black slaves – is unacceptable these days. But the process by which the poem arrived, its peculiarity and particularity, I find interesting – and especially the fact that there is a whole possible (and terrible) fiction potential in it; the sense of a knife-edge being walked by the Black man.

15/9/06: An item in the *Herald* this morning says the University of Auckland is to cut fifty academic jobs. One doesn't like to concede anything to the Tory blue shade of Kingsley Amis, but he said of the universities long ago, 'More means worse', and in many ways that has proved to be true. I don't know about Science faculties, but Arts (and this is long ago) used to ensure that you graduated Bachelor with a basic (essentially historical) knowledge of the subject you majored in. Then at MA, and beyond if there was a beyond, you became a specialist. That meant everyone on the staff had to do some basic bread-and-butter teaching; and that was good – you learn so much so quickly when you have to teach a subject. (My knowledge of Shakespeare comes much more from teaching than from student years.) Then, gradually, as students clamoured for subjects they were 'interested in', or considered 'relevant' (a big word in the 1960s), and as lecturers demanded the right to offer courses in whatever they'd done post-graduate work on (however remote), the idea of giving undergraduates an *education* in their field faded, and was replaced by randomness – a bit of this, a bit of that, a bit of the other and you had a degree! I remember in the '60s being appalled that students coming from the seventh form no longer knew where Pope came in relation to Wordsworth, or Tennyson in relation to Donne. Now I don't think you could count on even senior students knowing those basic facts.

They might or they might not, depending on what they had or hadn't taken courses on. (But they would be very kind, and look them up for you on the internet!) There's no overview, no 'big picture', no history as on-going continuous narrative. Partly this must be one result of giving universities money for the number of students they attract and retain, rather than for the quality of what they teach. Universities now advertise for students, try to offer appetising courses, protect their 'market share' and are afraid of failing anyone. (We used to be quite proud of our high failure rate at Stage One: it meant our standards were high!)

History is history and can't be 'corrected', so it's only ever useful, or practical, to start from the *now* and move forward. But one reaches an age where, possessing an overview, one does inevitably speculate about what might have been if alternatives had been chosen; and in that frame of mind I can't quite resist the reflection that the Universities should have held on to the idea* that they were small- to moderate-sized, élite institutions, demanding a lot from their students, and producing graduates deserving of respect; and left the doubtful and peripheral stuff to the Polytechs, Institutes, Training Colleges, Wanangas and Whatevers. Instead, they went after money, expansion, the commercial model and fashion, and belong, alas, where they are now, just another lump in the New Zealand educational porridge.

20/9/06: Our difference with the Fs [Jewish friends] over Israel has broken out again, despite the efforts all four of us make not to let it darken an old friendship. It came out of an exchange in a coffee shop about the Don Brash revelation (having an affair with a Business Roundtable blonde) during which it became apparent that the Fs no longer support Labour because of Helen Clark's and Phil Goff's position on Israel. Later a stinging e-mail came in from him. Mine back tried to sort out the (as I saw it) element of misunderstanding; but on Israel and the Palestinians I didn't see any way of concealing what I felt, that it has become now an issue on the scale of those twentieth-century cruxes – Hitler and the Jews, the Spanish Civil War, Vietnam,

---

* Which (dare one say it?) persists in Oxford, and I suppose also in Cambridge and other top British universities like London, Edinburgh and Bristol.

South Africa – where every serious person has a responsibility to take a stand, bear witness, speak out. My final para reads:

> On the Middle East, of course we differ. I remember hearing during the 1981 Springbok tour days that one wasn't permitted an opinion about South Africa because one hadn't been there, and now you are saying the same about Israel. You have been there, now and then, but one can read accounts by people who have lived there all their lives – and are still there. Kay has just read (for example) a book, *The Other Side of Israel*, by Susan Nathan, a British Jew who went there with high hopes and has chosen to live among Palestinians because she is so appalled by what the Jewish state inflicts on them, and because she wants, as a responsible and moral Jew, to bear witness and speak out. Our friend E in Melbourne also takes that view of Israel's current brutalities. And so (though not a Jew) do I. I think anyone who wants the Jewish state to survive (as I do) should realise that making your neighbours hate you, imposing your will on them, bullying them with superior weaponry, while simultaneously thinking that wrongs done to you in the past justify this, is simply storing up hatred for the future and won't facilitate survival in the long term. The loyalty of the Diaspora is not necessarily doing Israel any favours.

I came out of a shop yesterday and ran into him. He greeted me. I said, 'Did you get my message?' 'I did – of course.' 'Well . . .' I said, not knowing where to go next. He said, 'I think we'll leave it there' – and we passed on. [A day or so later came a totally conciliatory e-mail from her.]

22/9/06: Paul Millar, who is writing a biography of Bill Pearson,* e-mails thanking me for a copy of the poem I wrote about Bill, which appeared in the *Listener* a couple of months ago, and asking me to identify three men with Bill in a photo captioned 'The Bachelor's Club 1957'. I recognise Jack Golson (distinguished anthropologist, now in Australia) and Dick Shannon (biographer of Gladstone, now in the UK). Kay thinks the third might be Bill Mandle (History Department.

---

* Former colleague in the Auckland University English Department, and best known as author of the novel *Coal Flat*.

Now where?). Paul has recorded a memory of Bill's, of having written me a drunken letter, from Sydney, in which he made up many different insulting variations on the name Shadbolt (Shotbolt, Hotshit etc.), to which he received no response. Do I remember this? (I don't) and do I have letters from Bill? I know I have many letters, but (remembering how long it took me to extract the Curnow correspondence for Terry Sturm and the Turnbull Library) I know it would take a week I can't spare to go right through and find them all. However I know there's a file of correspondence relating to my editing of the *Oxford NZ Short Stories: Second Series*, which contains letters from Bill. I go hunting for it. It takes me only an hour or so to find, and there sure enough are not one but two such letters from Bill, one from Auckland (I was in London), the second from Sydney, and a number of other letters (some six, eight, one even ten, pages long) from that period 1964–65 when, first, he was away on leave and then I was. Bill talked into his letters – rambled on at length; I would have said a lonely man's letters, and yet when we are leaving for London at the end of 1964, and he is about to return from leave, he bombards me with addresses of people I should see – all people he has visited, and none of whom I could, in the year that followed, overcome my normal social reticence sufficiently to approach, except Davin, whom I knew already, and Dave Ballantyne. Paul asked did I ever see Bill the worse for alcohol. Here's my reply:

> As to alcohol: well yes, one saw Bill pretty much the worse for booze from time to time, until he seemed to cut back or go off drinking altogether. But I also had the impression that he was one of those people who get drunk very quickly. I could never decide whether this was because there was already a lot of alcohol in the bloodstream, and it just needed a top-up to send him over the limit, or whether he was susceptible to very little. But I never saw him raving or fighting or falling over. I thought of him as the windmill. He widened his arms out and seemed to sway from side to side – sort of rolled along like a sailor in high seas (half-seas over). Obviously sloshed, but harmlessly and inoffensively so.

23/9/06: Paul Millar replies,

> I imagine you won't be surprised to know that Bill had greater ambivalence towards you than any other of his colleagues (except Betty

[Sheppard] of course). On the one hand a deep and abiding respect for your intellect, your forthrightness, and your critical and creative achievements. He mentioned to me a number of occasions when he was grateful to have you in his corner. On the other hand an unease that strengthened at times towards fear of what he imagined you might be capable of should you get to a position of authority over him. He was by inclination anti-authoritarian, but I think he may have envied (perhaps subconsciously) your certainty of purpose, your ambition, and what he saw as your freedom to defend your position passionately and publicly. He'd spent a lifetime schooling himself, for obvious reasons [Bill was a closet homosexual], to keep a low profile.

Paul then asks what my response would be to the following comment Bill made in 'a discussion about promotions and his chagrin that you'd leapfrogged over him' [he was ten years my senior]:

C. K. Stead had been appointed as a lecturer in 1959 and duly applied for promotion at every stage where he was eligible to do so. (Looking back on his career I see that he was a young man in a hurry and that his aim was to climb as high in power and income as he could, so that he could afford to retire early and be a full-time writer.)

My reply is as follows:

The quotation is typical Bill. The criticism is implied, as if my applications were bad form – but then comes the honest and fair Bill in the parenthesis, but with a little of the paranoid Bill in the word 'power'. I never sought power. When Musgrove retired the whole Department was canvassed by the VC and on the basis of that I was offered the headship. I declined. But it's true I had dependants to think of and at the same time was positioning myself to get out as soon as I could.

24/9/06: Out to Karekare – lovely out there. It feels like spring, and I think about swimming but Kay talks me out of it because I have to give a public lecture soon and will be annoyed if I catch cold. Here (Tohunga Cres.) we've had the white plum blossom, and now have the green leaf. And buds just beginning to form into leaf on the grape vine.

25/9/06: A cat we have named Ticket has adopted us. It's well fed so we don't feed it. It's hungry for company, not food. I've never known such an aggressively touchy-feely cat. It climbs on board when I'm lying reading on the couch and pushes its face into mine, between me and the page, rubbing against the roughness of my 5 o'clock shadow, and finally sleeps curled like a large scarf around my neck.

Dentist: decay under the crown on a 'pre-molar'. I feel slightly panicky, not at the prospect of more dental work so much as at the thought that it might disable me just when I have to give my Hocken lecture in Dunedin.

Charlotte and the kids back this morning (Paul back a week earlier) from what seems to have been a triumphantly successful trip to London and France (including Menton, where C. started school in 1972). We will bring them Thai takeaways this evening before they crash off to sleep with jet-lag.

26/9/06: Fiona Farrell e-mailed the other day to ask whether I had any short stories for next year's *Best NZ Stories* which she is to edit, taking over from the other Fiona, the Dame, Kidman. I sent one I had offered the Dame, who declined it on the grounds that stories in these collections are supposed to be around 5000 words. Fiona F. has read it, likes and will use it – is not fussed about the length requirement which she sees as flexible.

This has put Fiona Kidman back into my thoughts – particularly the memory of seeing her at a reception at the NZ Embassy in Paris in July after I had given the opening keynote address to the NZ Studies Association's annual conference there. Kidman is this year's Menton Fellow, and had said, on accepting it, that it was 'a lifelong dream come true' – this from the woman who had mounted an attack (along with Lauris Edmond, Vincent O'Sullivan, Tony Simpson, Owen Marshall, Maurice Gee [who later deeply regretted it], Patricia Grace, and cohort) on the London flat for NZ writers,* arguing that they had

---

* The flat, purchased by the Hon. Michael Bassett, Minister for the Arts, as part of the spending authorised out of Lotto Funds for the 1990 sesqui-centenary celebrations, was a gift from the Labour Government to our writers, and probably the most generous single gesture ever made by a Government to the NZ literary community. The flat, with a lease of 75 years remaining, cost £132,000 and would now be worth not less than £500,000.

not been consulted, and that the purchase of a flat there represented a now irrelevant Euro-centric obsession with the 'Mother Country'. This attack was so ferocious, politically ill-judged and sustained, that when the Government changed the new Minister, Doug Graham, felt free to sell something which, he was able to say, writers appeared not to want. The same writers then made another fuss, describing the sale as 'an attack on the literary community'. And here she was, now 'Dame Fiona', at the Paris reception, anxieties about Europhilia lost in the mists of her past, smiling with pleasure and enthusiasm when it was announced that a Centre for NZ Studies was about to be established, based at the University of London Senate House and affiliated to Birkbeck College. I thought, 'If only the London writers' flat hadn't been sold, a fellowship to this NZ Studies Centre could have provided accommodation as well!' I said nothing. But I ask myself once again, how was it that Kidman was made a Dame 'for Services to NZ Literature'?

Which reminds me in turn that Bill Pearson, all that long time ago, was inventing insulting names for Shadbolt (see above) because S. had written in the Sydney *Bulletin* that *Coal Flat* was boring, admired only by Pearson's friends and a few academics; and I (then, or very soon after) would have been in agreement with his (Bill's) feelings, especially because Shadbolt lampooned me as the boring balding (a sensitive point to a young man!) unintelligible academic D. K. Flinders, brother of the tearaway-narrator, Nick, in *Among the Cinders*. But after many years of ups and downs in my relationship with Shadbolt, when it came to the London flat fiasco, we found ourselves allies. He resigned as chairman of PEN, and wrote to the paper deploring the damage done in particular by that 'graceless and garrulous pair' Edmond and Kidman. Roger Hall was also distressed by the whole business, and wrote to the *Listener*, in answer to a letter by Tony Simpson,

Tony Simpson, Fiona Kidman, etc decided that if some writers couldn't use the London flat then none should. They and a few others arrogantly decided that they represented the interests of *all* writers and flung the minister's gift back in his face.

Over the next 70-odd years, very many writers would have used the London flat. From his own selfish viewpoint, Mr Simpson might not consider it a loss, but many writers would bitterly disagree with him and his actions.

27/9/06: I find the Pearson correspondence interesting. Bill was not embarrassed (as I think I might have been if the roles had been reversed) in asking me (21 July '64) to consider his stories:

> Allen has told me that you are editing a second series of NZ stories for Oxford and I was pleased to hear this because I can think of no one less likely to be influenced by the personal considerations that operate so frequently among the prose writers. [. . .] Now I am writing to ask you that my few stories should not be overlooked. If you see them and reject them it won't offend me; it's that I don't want them to be passed by through not being seen.

He then gives details of his stories and where they can be found in periodicals. In my reply (28 July '64) I wrote,

> I was very pleased to have your letter but I couldn't help wondering whether you suspected (as Frank did) that I wouldn't be conscientious and thorough in doing this NZ Short Stories. Anyway I'd like you to know that I had your stories in mind; that I've already read and decided against 'Social Catharsis' and 'Uncle 52'; and that I knew of your stories in a Paris magazine and intended to track them down. Your letter makes my job easier – but it would have been done. I would like to have you in the book because I admire *Coal Flat* so much.

I must have written in more detail later about why I thought the rejected stories unsuccessful – and persuasively, because Bill wrote (2 May '65),

> I was glad to have your comments on those stories [. . .] it enabled me to see them in a new light [. . .]: what I mean is that it had never occurred to me that why if I read those stories they still get me in a way C[oal] F[lat] wouldn't is that they are as you say too personal. [. . .] What I thought was objective and non-personal was really a vivid projection, ?subjective-correlative? of a paranoia. Anyway I think I know now where they stand and can forget them and not see them as neglected unjustly. It is the first tangible criticism I have had of [them].

I might have felt uneasy looking back on all this i
that I did find a story of his, 'At the Leicesters
good and which went into the collection. I've j
in forty years) and it stands up well – E. M.
during the war, an image of end of Empire de
of two middle-class English expatriate wom..
keep up colonial appearances against the tide of time.

28/9/06: Looking at what I wrote a couple of days ago about the London flat I can see it's not enough and that I should really one day set out the whole thing, making use of the very full file I kept at the time. Two things upset me:

One was my fellow writers' political clumsiness – blindness – which caused the loss of a great asset, never likely to be offered again, and which was no encouragement to Ministers in the future to indulge in generous acts to the literary community. The decision to purchase a flat there had nothing at all to do with Euro-centric habits of mind, nor with old-fashioned loyalty to the 'Mother Country'. It was simply a recognition that NZ writers like opportunities to get away, to widen their horizons, to make literary friends and publishing contacts outside NZ; that London is a very important centre for such contacts; and that, far more than the cost of travel, the cost of accommodation there is prohibitive. The Frontline programme which suggested 'Bloomsbury' (where the flat was located) was chosen because of its literary connections with Virginia Woolf and her set was simply wrong. It was chosen because it's central; because you can walk from Ridgmount Gardens, where the flat was located, to most of the theatres and libraries, museums and galleries of the West End.

The second thing that upset me – and still does when I think of it (very seldom) – was that my motives were impugned. It was suggested I was doing this for myself; even that Bassett and I were old mates doing it for ourselves. The truth is that I knew Bassett only as well as I know many former colleagues who taught in the Arts Faculty at the University of Auckland. We got on well as colleagues, but it was not a close friendship, and there was nothing self-serving about the flat. I had been in the habit of going to London almost every year (something that has continued). I had my own friends, academic and literary

ere, and accommodation (often in those days at London
Mecklenburgh Square) was, for me, never a problem. But
er New Zealand writers without such connections it would be,
the flat was for them.

It was said there was no consultation; yet the whole thing kicked off
with a meeting in the Minister's office, with Fiona Kidman present, to
discuss her proposal that a house on an island in the Ohiwa Harbour
near Whakatane (accessible only by dinghy or motor-boat), belonging
to her friend, be purchased as a writers' retreat. Those present (senior
PEN members) were invited to canvas opinion among the writing
community about this proposal and alternatives, without going public
about it in case nothing came of it, or complaints about the cost were
raised by those unsympathetic to such expenditures on the Arts.

I found no one, either in the eighteen members of the PEN National
Executive with whom I discussed the proposal, nor among writers
in Auckland, who wanted a writers' retreat on the island favoured
by Fiona. Most liked the idea of something offshore – Sydney, or
London if that didn't seem too extravagant. I don't know what Fiona
and the others reported back, but on the basis of those reports Bassett
settled on Sydney first, and sent me there to look at prospects. Then
he decided to 'think big', and sent me to London. I travelled economy
class, stayed in the cheapest B&B hotels, and kept the most meticulous
reports of everything I looked at, including material from estate agents
and my own photographs of interiors and exteriors. In London I
worked only and always in collaboration with the High Commissioner
of the time, Bryce Harland, and was never free (nor wanted to be)
to make decisions. I was scrupulous in the extreme. Yet when the
Frontline programme was made it was shown that I had offered to be
first to occupy the flat, as if this proved the whole enterprise had been
self-serving. What I had said in fact was that someone would have to
occupy the flat and buy what was needed there (cutlery, plates, pots
and pans, table-cloths, kitchen equipment, bedding, towels, and so
on) and that I would be in London soon and was willing to do this.
After the row blew up and I withdrew, the Government had to pay
someone to do what I would have done for nothing.

So what was the fuss based on? I think it was an example of the
element of competition/envy/suspicion/paranoia that is always a part

– only a small part, but potentially a poisonous one – of every literary and artistic community. I'm not pretending to be exempt from this; but this was a particularly bad case. Fiona Kidman was always volatile, suspicious, inclined even to be obsessive; and once she had floated the idea of the house on the island, and it was rejected, she took it personally and invented evil reasons for how and why it had come about. She engaged Lauris Edmond (an entertaining companion but a foolish and mendacious person) on her side, and then Vince O'Sullivan, and the whole thing built a momentum of its own in Wellington, to a point that was ridiculous, embarrassing, and to me personally deeply hurtful. I had been very active in the literary community (chairman of the Literary Fund Advisory Committee, later of the Authors' Fund Advisory Committee, national vice president of PEN, etc.) and withdrew from all such activities, and have never gone back to PEN (now the NZ Society of Authors). A Big Sulk, if you like, but also a Nice Rest.

I don't know what Bassett feels but if he wasn't hurt he must be a saint. His was an extraordinarily grand – unprecedented – gesture on behalf of New Zealand's writers, 27 of whom showed their appreciation by issuing a public statement dissociating themselves from PEN's expression of gratitude to the Minister.

There is a fashion these days for recording names of 'famous' people on plaques and walkways, as in the Hollywood Boulevard 'Walk of Fame' – large stars set in the sidewalk each recording the name of a movie actor. Sydney has had its Writers' Walk at Circular Quay long enough to demonstrate that the choices made frequently prove, in the long term, odd or inexplicable. Dunedin began the fashion in New Zealand, and Wellington is following suit. I think somewhere – perhaps beginning on Lambton Quay and tracing a path up to Vincent O'Sullivan's office at Victoria University where the Frontline programme showed them gathering – or alternatively going from the dinghy-landing up to the house on that island in the Ohiwa Harbour – there should be a walkway recording the names of those 27 signatories.

PS to the above: I have now looked up my file on this matter and a note there suggests (something I had forgotten) that it had been Mike Bassett's intention to make NZPEN (now the NZ Society of Authors) owners of the title. (And, although it was a lease – on which 75 years remained – it was also a title, so the lease was renewable.) When our authors seemed to react unfavourably, Bassett left the title with the Government (I suppose with Internal Affairs). If this note is correct, the opponents, who were later to complain of the sale of the flat by the incoming National Government, had made it possible by their own actions. If they had said thank you rather than complaining, writers collectively would still be owners of that asset; or could have sold it and put the money to other uses.

In a letter to the *TLS* about this affair (21/1/91) Fiona Kidman told British readers that in New Zealand '[Stead] is widely considered to have disgraced himself over the purchase', the cost of which, she went on, represented 'nearly one third of the annual [Government] allocation for literature'. In fact it did not make any difference at all to that allocation. All the money came from funds set aside by the Lottery Board for the 1990 celebrations.

When it was announced that the flat was to be sold, the *Listener* of 7/1/91 published an editorial by Alexander Fry, which paid tribute to how much our writers contributed to the nation and went on, 'It is astonishing, then, that the new government should be so out of touch with the country it governs as to *take back* the nation's 1990 gift to its writers! Yet that is what they did when Arts and Culture Minister Doug Graham, and the Internal Affairs Minister Graeme Lee, jointly announced their intention to sell the Bloomsbury flat purchased by the previous government.' Describing the writers' original reaction to the gift as 'graceless', Fry went on,

> In schoolyard terms, of course, the writers 'asked for' such miserable treatment. Their reaction to the gift when it was made, in January 1990, was, to say the least, mixed. Some resented the fact that the decision on a London flat was not 'democratically arrived at'. Some demanded to know why an earlier suggestion for a writer's workplace – an island off our coast – had been by-passed. Some determinedly 'New Zealish' writers thought London effete and Bloomsbury downright decadent [. . .] All of these dissenters gave tongue, while the flat's donors (the government), the writers who would love to use it, and the huge and well-disposed reading public, writhed in embarrassment [. . .]

The trouble would have subsided fairly quickly; indeed, most of us thought it already had. As the 27 applicants [to use the flat]* attest, [it] would have been in continuous use. Like the Mansfield room in Menton (in *France* of all places!) it would have given the stimulus of foreign residence to writers who might not otherwise have been able to afford it. It would no doubt have been as productive of good writing as Menton has been. And it could well have attracted from an increasingly cultured business fraternity the kind of travel and sustenance support they give to other arts.

The realisation also seems to be dawning that New Zealand writers do not have much trouble finding quiet places in New Zealand to write. At least two such retreats exist here already [. . .]

Writers are a disputatious lot; they may not 'deserve' such largesse. But the most popular of them earn scarcely as much as a counterhand or a bus-driver; most a great deal less. And they bring us such riches! If the Ministers have not already sold that bargain of a London flat ($343,000 for a 75-year lease), it would be magnanimous to reverse their decision.

It was a good try by the *Listener*, but the damage had been done, and the flat was sold.

29/9/06: Plums already appearing, very tiny, enamel-green. I didn't think they arrived quite so immediately. When the blossom was there I watched to see that the bees were doing their job. There weren't many, but some, and now it looks as if it will be a moderate-to-good crop, if the winds don't come up too vigorously between now and Christmas.

30/9/06: I have just learned from a book called *Paris to the Moon* by Adam Gopnik, that, of the two famous Paris cafés, the Café Flore on the boulevard Saint-Germain, and its neighbour Les Deux Magots, the Flore is now the fashionable one, the Deux Magots, by comparison, *passé*. The Deux Magots has associations with Oscar Wilde and James Joyce, Hemingway and F. Scott Fitzgerald, Jean-Paul Sartre and Simone de Beauvoir, Camus and Existentialism. How could it have

---

* By an odd coincidence, there were the same number of applicants in that first round as there had been complainers the year before.

become unfashionable? Gopnik has a theory – a rather complicated one – but do shifts in fashion need explaining? They are like the Trinity and the ways of God, mysterious, inexplicable.

I went to Les Deux Magots only once, but it was for me a highly charged (in two senses) and even mysterious occasion. One of the film stars of my youth was the Swede, Mai Zetterling, who appeared from time to time in the post-war British movies that for a few years seemed to hold their own against Hollywood. I thought then that she was stunningly beautiful. Many years later, some time, I think, in the late 1980s after she had long since vanished into the mists of post-stardom, I had a message from her. She was thinking of making a movie about Katherine Mansfield and had heard that I might be a person able to assist her. I was coming to Europe and at her suggestion we met at Les Deux Magots and talked about Mansfield. I must have been heading for sixty, and she the same, or perhaps a year or two older. Nothing came of the Mansfield project. I remember little of what was said, and nothing of what we ate or drank. I remember the occasion, not because it was memorable in itself, but because it was 'Les Deux Magots' and because she was 'Mai Zetterling' – two separate legends from my youth coming together. There was for me something unreal about it, like a meeting of ghosts.

1/10/06: News that nine members of the committee that makes the Marsden Fund awards for academic and science research have granted themselves $6 million out of annual awards totalling $38 million: I know how these problems can arise – the same people who are expert in a field, and therefore called upon to adjudicate such awards, are also among those who apply for them. It's one of the problems of a small population, and happens also in the Arts. But this seems a particularly bad case – at the very least, 'a bad look'. When I was appointed to the Arts Council (Creative New Zealand) in 1999 I argued very strongly at my first meeting that the money available for the Authors' Fund (money paid to authors for use of their books in libraries) should be increased. You could say that as a recipient of money from that Fund I had no right to speak on the matter; but I saw myself as a member (the only one at that time on the full Council) chosen partly to represent the writing community; and the issue was particularly contentious because PEN, representing New Zealand's writers, had accepted that the Authors' Fund should become part of the Arts Council budget only on a promise that the Fund would be kept up at least with the rate of inflation. This was not happening and the payout to authors had been dropping year by year. My advocacy got nowhere, and I felt so bad about the refusal of the Council to increase the fund at all that year, I was thinking of resigning. Then the Chairman of the Council rang and told me my publisher (Penguin at that time) had applied for a grant to assist publication of my next novel, and that, since I was a member of the Council, there was a conflict of interest and the application would be declined. This put an end to my hesitation about resigning after only one meeting. I did it immediately, which caused a good deal of surprise and incurred some (no doubt deserved) criticism.

It was probably the right thing to do; but in fact the Arts Council would not really have made the decision for or against Penguin's application – it would have acted on a recommendation from a quite separate literary panel. (I found later that the Chairman took legal advice on this matter and was told there would have been no conflict of interest.) I felt the Penguin application was used to get rid of me – and in a way I was quite glad of to be got rid of. I'd had enough of committees, and had only agreed to become a member out of a (quite misplaced, even pompous) sense of duty. My mistake, and where I deserved to be criticised, had been in accepting the appointment in the first place.

The Council of Creative NZ at that time certainly used the term 'conflict of interest' only when it suited them, and turned a blind eye when it didn't. On the morning of that first, and what was to be my only, meeting of the Council, I found myself part of what was called its 'Audit and Remuneration Committee', which met before the full Council assembled, and had only two items on its agenda: (1) to review the performance of the CEO and agree his bonus for six months; and (2) to receive a paper from the CEO on progress towards introducing a new employment contract for all staff. The CEO withdrew from the room while the Chairman proposed we award him a bonus of $15,000 (his annual salary was $120,000) for the six months. There was no discussion (I had no grounds for an opinion) and it was agreed. The CEO then came back into the room and presented his report.

This charade was then followed by the meeting of the full Council. It was the same chairman who subsequently suggested that Penguin's application on behalf of my novel constituted a 'conflict of interest'!

4/10/06: Launch last evening of *My Name was Judas*. Mac Jackson gave a brilliant ten-minute speech – such genuine enthusiasm and such intelligent commentary. I read the bit about the boys visiting the Temple and doing 'the Boy's Sacrifice', and Jaweh telling Jesus 'Let my pigeon go'. But it was Mac who sold the book (a lot were bought). I wish I could take him with me to London and have him say it all again there. All the Auckland whanau were represented, including Ollie (V and the kids in Hawkes Bay), the Grimshaws, Guys, Lauries and Restalls. We took Charlotte, with Bill Gavin and Diana Heka, to Oh Calcutta afterwards. I feel jaded this morning, but pleased.

5/10/06: I've agreed to do two or three blogs for NZ Book Month. Part of the latest went as follows:

> Leaf is appearing on the grape vine and the first bunches are just forming; and already tiny green plums can be seen on our only fruit tree. I.e. it's spring and I have to think about when/whether to begin swimming again – possibly to be avoided since I'm about to fly to London for the launch of my new novel, *My Name was Judas*, at New Zealand House in the Strand, and to do whatever interviews are necessary to go along with that.
>
> Today an e-mail came asking whether I would agree to have my full name on the French edition, Christian Karlson Stead, rather than the usual C. K. Stead. This message was signed Claire de Robespierre – not a name to be argued with! In recent years I've often regretted that I'm stuck with 'C. K. Stead' – three monosyllables, which I think make me sound like an old commissar – V. I. Lenin, for example.
>
> I'm often asked about this, but there's no puzzle. In the early 1950s, when I was first publishing poems in periodicals, the three great names in English language poetry were W. B. Yeats, T. S. Eliot and W. H. Auden. They weren't Willie and Tom and Wystan, except to their friends and family – and I followed that precedent. It was common enough here too – Fairburn was A. R. D., Mason was R. A. K., though it was beginning to change (Frank Sargeson, Allen Curnow, Denis Glover). There was also

the problem that I was known to friends and family by
Karlson, which gradually got shortened to Karl. I wa[s]
Swedish grandfather, Christian Karlson, and it woul[d]
me to use the whole thing together with Stead. But [it]
decided this for me, and I quite look forward to see[ing my]
self in print. The Gospel of Judas by a different kind of Christian
believer.

On Saturday morning I have an interview on National Radio with
Kim Hill (always a dangerous undertaking) and then, next week, I go to
Dunedin to give the annual Michael King Memorial Hocken Lecture.

PS on writers' names: what about J. K. Rowling? Will she bring initials
back into favour? And Kay reminds me we still have V. S. Naipaul and
A. S. Byatt.

15/10/06: Here is my third and final blog for NZ Book Month:

First a PS to my last. NZ House in London is in the Haymarket, not the
Strand. Saying 'NZ House in the Strand' was a back-flip to the 1950s! – a
sign of my great age. This week (the 17th) I will be 74. The 17th is also
Ian Wedde's birthday (Happy Birthday, Ian!) and Les Murray's (Happy
Birthday, Les!) and Arthur Miller's (but I think he died recently).

Dunedin, where I gave the Hocken/Michael King lecture, was cold one
day, with hail and blasts from the Pole, less cold the next, and turning mild
the day after. A challenging climate. I was fighting off a throat bug and
terrified my voice wouldn't last the hour, but it did. My lecture consisted
mainly of reminiscences of being a young poet, half a century ago, helped
in different ways by Charles Brasch, Allen Curnow and Frank Sargeson.
A good audience, perhaps 300 – after which I was taken to an excellent
restaurant somewhere down on the waterfront by a group of academics
and librarians.

I was in Dunedin long enough to have a look over the Hocken Library
and admire its splendid resources for research; and also to see the
new Otago University Library, which must surely be the finest library
architecture in New Zealand. The Dunedin City Art Gallery, which
moved a few years ago right into the Octagon, is another fine space with
interesting displays, including at the moment the John and Mary Barr
Collection on loan from Wellington. And I watched there a Zen monk

g a sand sculpture. The Botanic Gardens in spring are stunning,
beautifully kept. Dunedin is always flavoursome, though it looks as
if it would be improved by a population boost and the capital that would
bring.

Back in Auckland Kay and I were in charge of three grandchildren
while daughter Charlotte Grimshaw and her husband went to Wellington
where her winning the BNZ Katherine Mansfield Short Story Award was
announced and the prize presented. Because I had won it 45 years before,
I was included in the publicity.

And now, Saturday morning, the *Herald* has a big interview with her,
and a review of my Judas novel, just released. So father and daughter
are, briefly, tripping over and around one another. I'm delighted for her.
She gets $10,000. I think when I won it, it might have been one hundred
guineas.

16/10/06: NZ reviews thus far of *My Name was Judas* – two big pluses
and one grudgy minus. Elizabeth Alley, *Dom Post*, 'Provocative and
compulsive, this is a small gem, perhaps as durable as the myth that
occasioned it.' Michele Hewitson, *NZ Herald*, 'This is a great novel
. . . . It is so simply told, with clarity and wit. It is certainly one of
the best pieces of writing I've read about friendship and faith . . . . It
will no doubt be controversial but it shouldn't be read for that reason;
it should be read because it is brilliant.' But Philip Matthews in the
Listener bridles at the idea that there might have been farting jokes in
what he calls the Holy Family (only Holy if Jesus is divine, which in my
book he's not) and concludes it is 'interesting but oddly mundane'. He
wonders why I make Mary Magdalene a prostitute when the Vatican
has recently ruled differently on this.

17/10/06: My birthday, 74, that is a bigger number than I ever thought
I would reach. I'm on breakfast TV about Judas. Then breakfast
(mushrooms and toast, coffee) on the waterfront with Harriet and
Sarah from Random House.

21/10/06: [Radisson Hotel, Los Angeles. 5 a.m. after some hectic sleep.]
On the way over I watched a Robert Altman film, *The Prairie Home
Companion,* based on the fiction that the famous radio show is being

closed down by a tycoon who has bought it. The 'story' is the last show, front- and backstage, Meryl Streep as one of a pair of singing sisters. Garrison Keillor as himself. An angel in a white raincoat glides about backstage. The show has been her favourite and she has driven off the road and been killed while listening. She wants to hear the end of a joke she missed and Keillor tells it, but somehow (did I drop off for a moment, or was there an announcement?) I missed it. She arranges for the tycoon to 'vanish' but the show is still sold.

Radio NZ sometimes plays *The Prairie Home Companion* over the Christmas period. Keillor has a wonderful, inimitable voice – singing, but just speaking too, he can make poetry or comedy or pathos of anything at all. Recently I had a request from the show to use a poem – 'You' (my poem to Kay). They paid me $US100. I would have paid *them* to have it read by that voice, which I now have on a disc they sent me.

Last evening we took a taxi to Italy's Little Kitchen, near the Furama Hotel, remembered from an earlier transit, where we had (surprisingly, because food here is usually so ghastly) as good a seafood linguini I've ever had, preceded by minestrone, and accompanied by á (not very nice) Californian pinot grigio. We listened in while a middle-aged man with a military haircut droned on endlessly about weapons – phosphorous bombs, cluster bombs, armour-penetrating shells, GPS-guided rockets, also automatics and hand-guns. He said 'warfare has advanced so far in three years'. Before that we'd watched some local politics on TV. Republicans in retreat everywhere in the country. Let's hope so!

22/10/06: [London.] I finished Julian Barnes's *Arthur and George* on the way over. E-mail from Charlotte this morning to say that the Judas novel has moved from eighth to second on Dymocks' best-seller list. And one from Margaret Scott reporting a good review by Sarah Quigley in the *Christchurch Press*. Also the first UK review – Alan Massie in *The Scotsman* is entirely positive.

24/10/06: Panel discussion last evening about NZ film at the newly established Centre for New Zealand Studies in the Senate House [University of London]. A very good atmosphere of confidence without assertiveness – a mix of expatriates, and home-based Kiwis on the move between festivals. A lot of relaxed talk about multi-culturalism. The confidence comes, I suppose, with success in the film business. I don't think I've met before, or not abroad, quite that sense of *ease* in New Zealandness. Panelists included Toa Fraser (*No. 2*), Roger Donaldson and Kerry Fox. Didn't feel I could manage the wine and cheese, but I invited Roger and Kerry to the Judas launch.

27/10/06: Still suffering jet-lag. Crash from 10 p.m. to 2 a.m., then either drug myself or lie awake until morning. I'm always surprised how long it lasts. Up to p. 75 of Martin Amis's new novel, *The House of Meetings*. The writing brilliant, the material repellant. The gulag as subject allows Amis to indulge his appetite for/obsession with, squalor. It licenses what is really a quirk of taste and personality. But the prose is compelling.

28/10/06: Up to Oxford yesterday – stayed in a Fawlty Towers hotel on Banbury Road. Nostalgic walks past 'our' house on the corner of Woodstock and Plantation Roads – such a very good house, with so much space, and a lovely walled garden at the back. I wrote some good poems there, and later set part of *Talking about O'Dwyer* there. Supper with Craig and Li Raine, and three of their four children – Vaska, and playwrights (as they now are) Nina and Moses. Also the children's godparents, Julian Barnes and Pat Kavanagh. Champagne and caviar first, upstairs in the room with the Pasternak paintings (by Boris's brother; Li is the niece), including the portrait of Einstein. Then downstairs to the kitchen where Li had cooked a wonderful 'English' meal – steak and kidney with dumplings and baked potato pieces, followed by a salad (not quite 'English'?), then baked apple with raisins and sour cream, and finally three cheeses and fruit.

Craig, warm and enthusiastic as ever, though possibly a little tetchy with me still at my letter taking him to task over Ian McEwan's novel *Saturday* in the *TLS*. He had said in his *TLS* Christmas Books offering (this was last December) that there had been two reasons why McEwan had failed to win the Booker for *Saturday* – 'envy, and envy'. I wrote suggesting that this was absurd, and defending the winner, *The Sea* by John Banville. I think I did this as much as anything because McEwan's

novel, (though it has two typically brilliant long set piece[s]
he's ever done), had struck me, in its presentation of th[e]
an epitome of middle-class complacency; and more, beca[use]
think it was honest about the Iraq war. It all takes place on the Saturday
of the great London march against the war, when the whole argument
for the invasion, just about to take place, was based on 'intelligence'
that Saddam Hussein had 'weapons of mass destruction' which he
could launch, even on British targets, within 45 minutes. By the time
the novel was being written, or being revised and finished, it must have
been apparent that this was a lie peddled by Bush and Blair to justify
what they had long since agreed they were going to do anyway. But
instead of having his principal character (who defends the invasion
against the protesters and his daughter) cite, as he would have done
then, these 'weapons of mass destruction', McEwan has him advance
other arguments, chiefly that Saddam tortures his opponents. So, it
seems to me, the novelist shifts the ground to protect his character
from looking, retrospectively, foolish or ill-informed. None of this was
said in my letter, but it was discussed around the table, where it was
acknowledged that McEwan had shifted his ground on the subject of
the war, pretending now that he had been '50/50' about the invasion,
whereas both Craig and Julian remembered that he had said publicly
he was 60/40 in favour. It became apparent that Julian and Pat see the
war as an ill-judged and entirely illegal adventure which has turned out
precisely the disaster its opponents said it would; whereas Craig seems
still to defend it from, I suppose, a Christopher Hitchens position,
though moderated by an amount of the common sense and sobriety
'the Hitch' is no longer capable of.

Julian was somewhat diplomatic on that subject; but not on the
subject of Martin Amis, about whom he's clearly unforgiving. (There
was a very public falling out between Amis and Barnes some years
back when I think 'Mart', as they call him, dropped Pat as his agent in
favour of Godwin – whom Pat now refers to as 'Dogwin'.)

I said I thought *The House of Meetings* was Amis back to his best
writing form. Julian, though prepared to concede the writing might
well be first class, was scathing about the novel. He thought the idea
of sitting (as Amis does) in his wife's millionaire *estancia* in Uruguay
writing about sufferings in the Soviet Gulag was essentially absurd. (I

uppose yes it is, but tend to think the imagination has to be free to go wherever it will from wherever it finds itself.)

Pat, whom I hadn't met before, is small, pretty, very deliberate (to good effect) in dress, hair, makeup – quiet but quick; and I thought one would find real warmth there if one knew her better. The Raines are lovely as a group – warm, loving, clever, original, peculiar. Julian has great charm and intelligence and is rather moral/responsible/ conscientious without being a moraliser. We walked with him and Pat back to our respective hotels on Banbury Road, he explaining, almost protectively, that the Raine family was 'essentially non-political'.

29/10/06: Last night we went to *Jenufa* (Janáček) at the E.N.O. Jet-lag not over yet and I cat-napped briefly, once in Act 1, again in Act 2. Although it seemed an intimate opera wrongly pitched to fill that huge auditorium, I was engaged – even absorbed and moved by the final act. Some great voices and a lot of enthusiasm from audience and cast at the end because it was the last night, the soprano leaping in the air and running about the stage in triumphal ecstasy.

I'm at p. 136 of *The House of Meetings*, and encountering a bad patch. But 'My aim was to get my hangover drunk' – there's a flash of the old, funny Amis.

Later: the novel recovers and finishes well, I think.

31/10/06: I did an interview this morning on London Christian Radio – 9.30 to 10, live broadcast. Quite good because it was not simply bland, and I respond better when challenged. There's an e-mail this evening to say I'm invited back for some kind of panel discussion on the subject of Judas. Then it was on for 10.30, to record an interview for BBC Radio Kent. Next came Goldsboro Books to sign 200 copies. They have a book club and *My Name was Judas* is their book of the month. After that Louise, my minder at Harvill Secker, took me and the Goldsboro Books man to lunch at Brown's. The GB man told us he decided aged nine that he wanted to join the Catholic church. His Protestant parents said no but he persisted – got himself sent to a Catholic school, decided there that he had a vocation, and subsequently trained for the priesthood. He was a star pupil, a case, it seemed, of a genuine 'call from God' to one who was outside the

Church. As a young man he dined with Cardinal Hulme, head of the RC church in the UK, and seemed destined for great things – then fell out with the church over the ordination of married High Church Anglican converts. This relaxation of the rule of celibacy didn't please His Strictness. But then (which I suppose explains a good deal) he discovered he was homosexual. Now he has a Spanish boyfriend, and is no longer sure what he believes, but is still fascinated by the whole subject and found my novel both exciting and a challenge. He was the one who chose it as their book of the month – hence my signing 200 copies, a task which sees your real signature slowly vanish, replaced by a hardly recognisable, erratic forgery.

3/11/06: 1 Nov. was the launch of *My Name was Judas* – a great party, it was, at NZ House in the Haymarket (where *Talking about O'Dwyer* and *Mansfield* were also launched). I was nervous in advance but it all passed off effortlessly, including the speeches. Jonathan Hunt [High Commissioner] was flattering and conveyed greetings from the P.M. Whanau assured me my speech was 'brilliant'. Miranda Seymour was there arrayed like Solomon in all her glory (something she manages without seeming to try) and looking tall and aristocratic (as indeed she is) with her new (third) husband, the New York taxi driver. Ann and Anthony Thwaite were there with Peter Porter. Craig and Li arrived late, Craig still possibly bristling slightly about Iraq, but full of beans, full of bounce. Roger Donaldson came with M.; Aminatta Forna looking lovely (her face is so open, so unclouded and she moves so elegantly), whom I introduced to Tony Ellis so he could invite her to the King's Lynn Festival; Alan Hollinghurst also looking elegant in an Indian-style jacket. I'd thought of him as much bigger than he is, I suppose because he has such a big (rich and fruity) voice; Christopher MacLehose and Koukla, Christopher towering, wearing his IMPEACH THEM badge with a little Cuban flag on his lapel where Bush, Cheney et al. wear their US flag-badges; John and Valerie Kingman [Sir John, former VC of Bristol University, and Valerie Cromwell, former official Historian of the British Parliament] – she has finished her stint as High Sheriff of Bristol and he has retired from Cambridge and they are now settled in Bristol. All the lovely Harvill young women were there, Margaret's old work-mates, Sophie,

Katerina, Maggie (now pregnant at 45, her first), Vicky (pregnant, also her first) – all now mothers or about to be. What a skill MacLehose had for discovering beauty and talent in single packages; Ewan Cameron reading my Judas with enjoyment and a devout Catholic's consequent trepidation – a lovely man; Tom Aitken who told me he has reviewed it for the *TLS*; John de Falbe who had tried to get it for review from the *Daily Telegraph* and the *Spectator*, but it had gone from both to other reviewers; Michele Hewitson from the *NZ Herald*, who teased Jonathan Hunt for saying in his speech that he'd read six of my novels – 'Only *six*!' – which I thought unkind because Jonathan doesn't understand jokes and thought she meant it; Steve Braunias from the *Sunday Star-Times*, currently in Cambridge on a fellowship writing a book on birds; Barbara Ewing, who kept urging me to read from the novel, as if challenging me to do it – something I had no intention of *not* doing when it came to the speeches. Roger and Joselyn Morton had come over from France, where he is having great success with an exhibition of photographs he took when he was here in London in the 1970s and '80s. And many more. After the launch Geoff Mulligan, head of Harvill Secker, took Kay and me, with Margaret and Guy, and four from the firm, to a Spanish restaurant in Charlotte Street, where Monique Corless told me Brazilian rights for Judas have been sold; also that a Croatian edition of *Mansfield* has appeared. Home at midnight, I was asleep at 12.30 and awake at 4.30, wide awake, and that was the end of sleeping, which meant I wasn't at my most lucid when Gerri Kimber arrived, as arranged, at 9.30, with breakfast goodies from Baker & Spice, and her new recording device, to do a two-hour interview for BRONZS (*British Review of New Zealand Studies*). We were just getting started when Charlotte rang from NZ to say there was a letter offering me the ONZ, the one limited to only about twenty members. General astonishment, not out of modesty so much as from my (and Kay's) thinking that all such public honours were over for me, the copybook having been so variously blotted since my CBE in 1985. (One of Gerri Kimber's questions was to be 'What was meant by the Stephen Stratford title to his *Metro* article years ago, "Why the Literati hate C K Stead"?') Anyway, great pleasure; and Gerri will make the arrival of that news a way into her interview/article – but we are meanwhile enjoined to silence about it until the public announcement,

Waitangi Day '07. I was exhausted by the end of the interview. We then shoved all our stuff into bags and took a taxi to Paddington where we will occupy the Gloucester Terrace flat of Ann and Anthony Thwaite. They gave us lunch and then headed home to Norfolk, and a taxi came to take me for another BBC interview about Judas.

4/11/06: Beautiful clear sunny day – but *cold* – the air colder than it ever gets in Auckland except on a rare frosty night. So now I can quote the Curnow lines again and they're apposite: 'And in Paddington autumn is air-borne, earth-given, / Day's nimbus nearer-staring, colder smoulders' – *strenuous* Curnow, but atmospheric. Last night was *La Traviata*: we got on the tube at Paddington and sat while the carriage filled and announcements of 'severe delays' came over. Did we risk waiting, or risk a taxi? Made a dash for the latter – a long queue, though moving fast. Told the woman driver (grey hair, very middle-class accent) that our opera started at 7.30. She drove like the wind, changing lanes, taking us through back streets, over cobbles and traffic humps (through Seven Dials) – got us there with five minutes to spare. Fare £11.40 – I paid 15. Guy waiting, on his cellphone to Margaret also caught on the Bakerloo line. She arrived late but was allowed in at the back until the first scene break.

La Traviata is redolent of one's romantic youth. But really the great scene with the most wonderful music is the one between Violetta and old Germont. The last act is static and was badly staged. To me, one of the most extraordinary things about the opera is that you're given, in the Overture, but quite long and emphatically enough to establish it in your consciousness, a very beautiful theme; and then, when it comes again (not until the third act) from Violetta – 'Love me, Alfredo' – it lasts about thirty seconds, a passionate, desperate, heart-rending appeal, and is gone! Think what Wagner would have made of it – hinting, approaching it, giving a glimpse (what is the aural equivalent of a glimpse?), developing it, releasing it, unleashing its full force – and then recycling it, a leitmotif. Did Verdi not quite recognise its beauty and power? Or was there some artistic instinct that this parsimony, leaving us longing for more, would be more effective? It's impossible for one such as I, a sensitive but technically ignorant ear, to know. I remember that when it was all over between me and D (both aged about twenty) I gave her a recording of the Overture (a 78rpm of course) with a message saying that the beginning was now the end. Very romantic, very deeply felt.

6/11/06: Veuve Clicquot and canapés with M and G to celebrate the incipient or putative or indeed impending ONZ, followed by All Blacks match at Twickers on TV, then takeaways. I forgot to mention that at the supper after the launch a taxi driver returned to the restaurant with a typescript left in his cab by James of Harvill Secker, who received it without alarm or celebration. Just another MS written in blood – like a Stage One examination script to a weary professor, or a bobby calf to a freezing worker on time-and-a-half.

9/11/06: Last night we took Anthony Thwaite, Margaret, and Peter and Christine Porter to the local Thai restaurant that has replaced the Indian, Spices. The usual great evening of literary talk. Kay described the conversation she'd overheard in Byzantium coffee shop, her favourite, on Moscow Road, about Clive James, Helen Gardner, T. S. Eliot (just 'T.S.' – no surname), Germaine Greer ('silly, but not stupid') etc. and described the two she'd overheard whom Anthony then identified from her description as George Watson and John Gross.

One anecdote of Peter Porter's: His first encounter with Allen Curnow was on a festival panel in Australia and a questioner asked Allen, 'Have you been influenced at all by that brilliant New Zealand poet, James K. Baxter?' Allen went rigid and dark: '*Influenced* by Baxter? I *created* him.'

In the street afterwards we said goodbye to Margaret, then to Peter and Christine, and walked back to the flat with Anthony who was to spend the night there with us. Indoors, and at the top of the stairs, he appeared to miss his footing and tumbled like a movie stunt-man all the long way to the bottom where he cracked his head, loud and hard, against the skirting board and lay unconscious for about a minute. As he came around I asked him the usual questions. He knew he was Anthony Thwaite. Asked who I was he stared for a moment and then said, 'Yes. You're . . .' (face screwed up with the effort – and then triumphant, as if answering a quiz question) 'You're . . . *C. K. Stead!*' But he didn't know what day it was, nor where we'd been, nor with

342

whom. Kay had dialled 999 and been told he shouldn't move – just kept warm until the ambulance came. I asked him a couple of times more what day it was and he fished in his pocket for his book, saying 'Stop asking me what day it is. I'll tell you . . .' (Flicking through the pages.) 'We're somewhere in November.' He insisted on climbing upstairs to the flat where he was sitting on the couch when the ambulance people arrived, still a bit confused, but improving. He's 76, two years my senior, and they insisted on taking him in for assessment. We went to bed, not expecting to see him again that night, but at 2.30 or 3 a.m. we heard his key in the lock and called out to him. He'd checked himself out against the hospital's advice, saying he was perfectly well. This morning I tapped timidly on his door half-expecting he might be dead, but he was sitting on his bed, dressed, very bright, waiting for us to wake. He seems fine, and insists we are not to tell Ann who will think he fell because he was drunk. He wasn't. We drank three bottles among six, the men drinking quite a bit more than the women, so I think he'd had two thirds of a bottle, as I and Peter had, over several hours and many courses.

12/11/06: Since the above I've spoken to Peter who tells me that once when they were dining together Anthony blacked out and fell forward on to the table, so completely unconscious Peter thought he was dead; and that next morning Peter had a hangover but Anthony was up and about like a Regimental Sergeant Major. So that, of course, explains the tumble, the beautifully relaxed way of it – no grasping at banisters to save himself, which would probably have prevented him going all the way to the bottom, but might equally have meant harder bumps and broken bones. He must have blacked out as he reached the top of the stairs.

Last Sunday (to go back a few days) Saddam Hussein was found guilty and sentenced to death – Victor's Justice of course (why were Bush and Blair not in the dock for war crimes?) – but who could believe other than that the verdicts were timed for two days before the US mid-term elections in the hope of giving Bush, and therefore the Republicans, a boost? Malcolm Rifkind, a Tory, even said so publicly. But to no effect. (Praise be to Allah!) On Tuesday the Democrats routed the Republicans, taking both Congress and Senate. Now all the architects of the Iraq war are gone (Aznar, Berlusconi) or discredited and politically neutered (Bush, Blair) – except, I suppose, little Johnny Howard, the man who thrives on lies.

On Thursday I did an interview with the BBC World Service for The Ticket (their Arts and Entertainment programme), signed books at Foyles, Borders, Hatchards, Waterstones and the LRB Bookshop. Then lunch with Kay and Peter Walker at the Groucho Club. Friday I had lunch with Miranda Seymour and we swapped suggestions about agents and movie rights – apart from which there was the usual warm enthusiastic chat.

Yesterday was the dedication of the New Zealand memorial at Hyde Park Corner, a very striking piece of public statuary in a very conspicuous location – sixteen bronze shafts, or posts, angled skyward with various inscriptions and symbols when you're up close and can see detail. The detail is somewhat random and even kitschy, but the large impression is bold and striking. The occasion was rather like that – collective strength. The conventional element was strong – bands, the military, the Royals – but the NZ element managed to predominate and not to embarrass. The Royals were there in full force (Q, Princes Philip, Charles and William, Princess Anne, Camilla P-B and a Royal Duke), together with Tony and Cherie Blair. Helen Clark spoke well. Blair spoke of how NZ and UK had fought together over the years but for the present was only able to mention Afghanistan, not Iraq – a triumph for New Zealand, and especially for the Labour Government, that it wasn't possible to name us as part of the 'coalition of the willing'. Q made the dedication speech. For me, the only embarrassing item was Dave Dobbyn singing 'Welcome Home', sounding like Bob Dylan on a bad day with feeble lyrics. Hayley Westenra (a fine natural voice – is it being wasted?) and the NZ Defence Force cultural group led the singing of the national anthems. It ended with a tremendous haka. Then the Royals left and the invited guests were allowed to wander about inspecting the monument. A London Maori group formed a circle and sang 'How great thou art' in Maori, and it was one of those moments (they don't happen often these days) when I found my voice again and sang too – I mean *could* sing, not just that I *did*. Russell Marshall had just finished Judas and loved it. Cath Tizard too – a big hug from her. Roger Donaldson was there, Don Brash, Judith Tizard,

Paul East, Mark Burton, Paul Reeves, Kerry Fox, Sean Fitzpatrick – we were all wandering about in the evening half-light, tripping over and greeting one another. At the reception afterwards, just along Piccadilly in the RAF Club, I talked to Fleur Adcock, back from six weeks in NZ and swearing she would never return – ever. (I've heard that from her before.) Judith Tizard said Helen had brought two RNZAF plane-loads of vets, army, navy, airforce, a band, politicians and civic leaders to make it a real NZ occasion. It was. Helen's speech at the reception was brief, spontaneous, fluent and funny. The food and wine were good. We went on to M and G's, where we learned that the West End had been brought almost to a standstill by the security precautions necessitated by having such a feast of Royal targets assembled in one place, and that consequently Margaret had been caught up in one of those French tragi-comedies her friend Sophie creates at intervals, involving Sophie trying to reach the airport for Paris while keeping up, on her cellphone, a running commentary of curses, despairs and blame.

Our plan with M and G had been takeaways and the All Blacks v France. We had the takeaways but couldn't get the match on TV. Guy kept checking on line for the score which, last heard, was 47–3 to the ABs with only a few minutes to play.

A strange review of *My Name was Judas* in Friday's *Independent* makes it sound interesting ('pleasingly unpredictable') but concludes that 'on the key question of whether or not [Jesus] was truly divine, Stead, through Judas, enters an open verdict'. Did the reviewer (Peter Stanford, who has written a book about Lord Longford) not read the final page, the final lines of the last poem?

> Our friend was
> not the Messiah, nor
> will there be one.
>
> This is the truth
> I write. It will not
> hurt you. Grasp it!

A brief review in *City A.M.* concludes 'a tremendously well-paced, moving narrative'.

20/11/06: [Auckland.] We flew straight through (via Hong Kong) – with the usual jet-lag and viral consequences. I crash at 9 or 10 p.m., wake at 3 a.m., and lie awake telling myself to be patient while the night insists on having every minute it's owed by the clock. At 6 a.m. I get the *Herald* in from the gate. A lovely pic this morning of the annual cross-harbour swim setting off from Devonport with the city skyline ahead. I would love to do that. We haven't swum yet – I'm waiting for the cold and sore throat to pass. Many e-mails during the past few days, including,

Dear Karl,
It was lovely to see you whilst you were in London – and I hope your long journey home went okay!

There was a lovely review in the *Daily Telegraph* on Saturday:

'Stead's timing in publishing this novel is exquisite . . . Stead's book delights in subtle comedy and takes care to puncture all kinds of minor myths . . . Making Judas an agnostic is a brilliant stroke that allows Stead to offer rational explanations for all the miracles . . . While everyone knows the events, Stead confounds expectations at each turn, offering a subtly changed interpretation of every occurrence . . . Written with glowing simplicity and rich in delicate humour . . . Stead's deft marshalling of the language, the way he gets words to do his bidding without ever being obvious or showing off, only adds to the pleasure of reading this thought-provoking, witty and highly topical novel'.

Well done – this is an absolutely glowing review! I shall send you a copy. I am expecting the *Sunday Times* review to run next weekend, and I shall keep you updated with more news.
Best wishes,
Louise

I'm especially pleased by this review because it's by James Wood, whom I've often said is the best UK reviewer of fiction at the moment. Gerri Kimber is hard at work on the interview. I'm invited to Venezuela, all travel and accommodation and fees paid, but the dates coincide with the Auckland Writers & Readers Week so I will have to say no. But Fernando Rendón is inviting me to Medellín (Colombia) in July and this time I might say yes – even though I would rather go to Hugo Chavez's 'Bolivarian Republic of Venezuela'. In Colombia I will probably be kidnapped by a drug baron or shot in the street.

Big protest developing against the waterfront stadium Trevor Mallard seems determined to inflict on Auckland. I hope it (the protest) succeeds. Three *Herald* columnists all spoke of 'vision' on Saturday, supporting the waterfront stadium which its designers represent as drifting in a halo of white light. My 'vision' is of a wall between city and harbour, a vast space locked to the public 90 per cent of the time, and 60,000 rarely filled seats surrounded by a structure decaying while Council and Government argue about who owns its mounting debts.

30/11/06: Too much happening. Can't keep up this journal for the moment. The campaign to scotch the waterfront stadium was successful. Review just in of the Judas novel from the London *Sunday Times* by someone called David Grylls: 'a subtly potent revisionist account of the life of Jesus' – accompanied by a rather good cartoon, in bright colours, of Jesus, Judas, and . . . me.

Swimming has begun and I hope to reach the yellow buoy again before Christmas.

Interview with Gerri Kimber*

My Name was Judas

Gerri Kimber: *This book is a tremendous tour de force, receiving particularly favourable reviews. What made you decide to choose this subject for a novel?*

C. K. Stead: It arrived as an idea when I was writing my novel *Mansfield*. I was talking to someone about [D. H.] Lawrence's messianic character, saying he was so different from myself I could only represent him from the outside – through Jack's eyes, or through Katherine's; or in the chapter specific to the Lawrences, through Frieda's. I said, 'It would be like writing about Jesus. How would I do that? It would have to be through the eyes of one of the disciples – Judas, I suppose, the one perceived to be least sycophantic.' So the idea was planted and it just wouldn't go away. I decided I would want the Judas character to be like myself, a sceptic, a rational man who doesn't believe that people walk on water or rise from the dead. The next problem was just how you would have that kind of person become a disciple? It presented itself as a narrative problem – a challenge; and the solution was to begin the story with their boyhood together, Jesus and Judas, followed by a crisis

---

* Published in the *British Review of New Zealand Studies*, April 2007.

in the life of Judas which would explain his going with Jesus as an adult. I was thinking all these things out, and at the same time I was telling myself this was NOT a subject for a person of my temperament; that I was wasting mental energy. But the imagination was set in motion and couldn't leave it alone. It was then I had, by chance, my conversation with Paul Morris [professor of religious studies at Victoria University], when he said to me, 'These are our stories. They must be constantly retold.' A wonderfully liberating statement! That was the sequence by which I arrived at doing something which on the face of it seems so out of character.

Would you call yourself an atheist?

I resist the word atheist and prefer to call myself a non-theist. There's an essay I wrote in a collection called *The Writer at Work*, entitled 'What I Believe'. There I explain that to say, in answer to the question 'Do you believe in God?', 'No, I don't,' implies that you know what 'God' is. 'God' is a word with too many meanings to be meaningful or useful. So I prefer to call myself a non-theist – but if people think that's just a quibble, then atheist will do. The important point for me personally is that our society's ubiquitous Christian theism constitutes a set of ideas acquired in childhood which I've come to see as myths from a pre-scientific age, with no foundation in reality.

Some people go the other way as they get older.

Yes. And that's usually out of fear.

Why do you finish each chapter with a poem? They appear like refrains at the end of every section of prose, giving the writing a lyrical quality.

I wrote the first draft without the poems, and then felt the novel lacked something I wanted it to have. And once the poems were in, I felt that what had been missing had been supplied. There are some things which are purely instinctive for an artist and you must follow what they tell you to do. In this case, it was particularly strong. One reason might be that this is a novel which denies religion, but it doesn't want to deny everything that's beyond the prosaic, the real, the factual, the mundane. It wants to acknowledge something 'higher' – an element of the ideal if you like. Therefore, making Judas a poet and presenting his poems, which are not simply a repetition of ideas in the chapter but something more, seemed to give the whole book a lift and imbue it with a special resonance. For me, the arts – music and poetry in particular, but the arts in general – are, in my life, what religion is in other people's lives. So it has to be for my Judas. On the subject of the poems, I noticed in the *Literary Review* that the reviewer said they were 'modern' poems that would never have been written that way at that time; that they were anachronisms. Well, I would say that if you were to translate poems from that period you might well choose to use modern forms. Why not? He also said they had no scansion. It's true they don't have conventional scansion; but they are in fact syllabic poems – thirteen-syllable triplets. It's like a little code hidden there. I did at one point think of giving the clue at the beginning of the book in the form of one of those triplets:

> Thirteen syllables
> because there were
> thirteen of us.

But then I decided, No, it's a code for the clever reader to crack. The magic number, said to be the unlucky one – twelve disciples plus Jesus: thirteen. Every one of those 150 stanzas in the book has thirteen syllables – no more, no less.

You are pulling together two of the strands which most define you as a creative writer – your work as a novelist and your work as a poet – and intertwining them.

Yes! It was only when I began to write them I realised that for the first time I'd found a way of being both fiction writer and poet in a single work.

The beginning of the book and the discussion of universal questions, some of which still perplex us today, launches the reader into the great unknown at the very outset.

I wanted to indicate at once that Judas was a man who had set super-natural explanations aside and was trying to proceed by observation and common sense – what we'd now call a 'scientific' approach, insofar as that was possible at the time. That's what he and his Greek brother-in-law were doing. And that's partly why I made him a man who had moved away from his Jewish origins and immersed himself in the tradition of Greek thought, to which the Middle Eastern monotheisms seem alien and non-rational.

How much research was needed to write the book? It reads like an historically accurate version of events, which is obviously the effect you intended.

I did a lot of research. First I had to go back and reread the Gospels. I took a lot of notes because I wanted to see how the four accounts coincide and how they differ – and they do differ, quite considerably. I also read the Acts of the Apostles and other relevant biblical texts; and then, too, a number of biblical and theological works, mostly historical but also interpretive. Also some of the Gospels which were rejected by the early church from the Bible as we have it – the Gospel of Thomas, for example, from which comes (I think this is right) the incident in Chapter Sixteen of Jesus requiring the disciples to find a way of describing him as *like* something else – a game which, in my version, Judas declines to play. I read some history of the Roman empire in that area at that time. And I tried to get a proper visual sense of the terrain, because it's the first time I've ever written about a place without having been there.

So you did not make an exploratory trip to the Middle East?

I intended to, but then I began writing and it all happened too fast. But I was anxious about that. I've always said I would never write about a place I hadn't been to. I broke my own rule, and I still wish there had been time to go there first. Location, the particulars, the texture, of place, is a very important element in my writing. But once the writing had begun it didn't seem safe to stop.

You can't tell from reading the book!

That's good to know! I got some contemporary photographic works from Jewish friends, to give me a sense of the terrain as it is now. And a very useful source was a late nineteenth-century travel book* by a man and his friend travelling through the Holy Land, as it was called then, with one writing the prose and the other painting water colours. In those days very little had changed, visually, from biblical times and it gave me a good pictorial sense of my subject. For example, the colours of the landscapes, and how they alter, I took directly from those watercolours and the accompanying notes which give the time of day when the picture was painted and details such as which way the wind was blowing at the time.

You have certainly portrayed the Roman occupiers in an historically accurate way, but also in an inimitable Steadian way too with the 'slap, slap, slap' sound of the Roman platoon entering Jerusalem (p. 55).

Well, as I say, I did read a lot and then of course you reach a point where, when you've enough material, your imagination does the rest.

How much licence did you initially decide to take with historical fact and especially with the biblical character of Judas?

I decided immediately that he was going to be a person roughly as old as myself, which meant he had to have survived long after the death of Jesus. In the Gospels, of course, he hangs himself. In the Acts of the Apostles he falls down in a field and is disembowelled. So you could say, well, if one is wrong, they could both be wrong.

They both sound like wishful thinking on the part of his contemporaries to me, which means there was good chance he did survive!

I didn't want him to be the betrayer as represented in the Gospels. I must have decided that very early on I think.

---

* *The Holy Land Painted by John Fulleylove Described by John Kelman*, Adam and Charles Black, London, 1902.

You don't mention anywhere that Jesus was descended from the line of David and therefore could literally be described as the King of the Jews. Your Jesus comes from a very humble, ordinary background, with no mention of any royal blood at all.

I may be less than clear or secure on this question. On the one hand, because of the tradition of the Virgin Birth, Joseph is not actually Jesus' father – in which case it's irrelevant if Joseph was descended from David, because by that account (and, in a different way, by mine) Jesus was not of Joseph's line. And I've never heard it suggested that Mary was descended from David. In one story a blind man calls out to him, 'Son of David', but I've taken that to be merely a symbolic title.

You paint a very unsettling portrait of Mary, the mother of Jesus: 'The mother he couldn't abide' (125). What made you decide to do this?

Yes, I suppose that's the part most likely to give offence, especially to Catholics, for whom Mary is particularly revered. Well, there are just a few encounters between Jesus and his mother in the Bible, and he's always unpleasant, or cold, to her. He says more or less, 'Woman, what have I to do with you? Go away!' There is no occasion in the Gospels where Jesus is nice to her. As a fiction writer you have to develop the larger picture out of small hints. So I could say I took my line on the mother from the son!

The last description of Mary appears on p. 179, some seventy pages before the book ends. You have really made her a minor character.

There is a tradition of Mary being at the crucifixion – and of course the ensuing artistic portrayals of this, the mother with the body of her son, the *pietà*. But she is only actually depicted as being present in *one* of the four Gospels – John – which is believed to have been written some time after the others and to contain the most invented material. So, three to one, the Gospel writers seem to say she wasn't there. And since there are some indicators that Jesus didn't encourage her, and even drove her away, it's reasonable to take the view that she would not have been in Jerusalem at the time of the crucifixion.

In this novel Jesus is 'demystified'. You show how his power and magnetism are earthly in origin – not divine (149–50). The miracles are not miracles at all (169). Did you set out to give a 'fundamentalist' mindset to Jesus and most of his followers? You actually mention the word 'suicide' (216) – which has connotations with today's suicide bombers. Is this the effect you intended?

No, this doesn't quite fit with the way I thought about it. I tried to represent Jesus as charismatic, a wonderful preacher, very clever, but almost too successful for his own good. The idea that he might be the Messiah comes first from his followers. As in the Bible, he doesn't begin by asserting that he's the Son of God; but by the end he's asserting it emphatically, to the exclusion of everything else. I thought of him as a great man, but really on the edge of sanity – not quite like the suicide bomber, who believes in a power outside himself which will sanction what he does and reward him for it. Jesus comes to believe he *is* the power. I see him as a tragic figure. By the end, however, I agree, he has become fanatical, suicidal, and hard to like. He seems to set aside, or forget, his own early teachings about the needs of the poor, the hungry and the dispossessed. In those final days his message has boiled down to, 'Believe in me or burn in Hell.'

When you think of all the many millions of people who have died in his name – for me it's another way in which the book seems relevant to the world we live in today and the mindset of the fundamentalist, of whichever religion.

Certainly, the fundamentalist slant is not irrelevant to the novel.

You call in question (in effect) so many tenets of the Christian faith: the miracles, the Last Supper, the betrayal by Judas, the Resurrection, the Ascension. There's nothing left for your average Christian to hang his hat on in this book!

I set out to tell a story which I, or a person of my temperament and intellectual disposition, could believe. I don't mean to say literally, historically, 'This is what happened' – because how can we know? But if this *was* a 'Gospel', I could believe it, whereas I can't, I'm afraid, believe the story as we have it in the Bible. I did think at one stage of calling the book 'The Gospel According to Judas'.

That might have made it even more controversial.

Yes, perhaps. I did intend naming each chapter in a similar way to the Gospels, i.e. Judas One, Judas Two, etc. [At this point Stead picks up a copy of the book lying on the table next to the microphone and flicks through]. How strange! I intended to do that but it appears to have been dropped. I don't remember changing my mind. Maybe I sent a wrong copy!*

Are we meant to perceive Bartholomew as gay?

Yes.

And Andreas? I thought he came over as quite camp.

He's certainly camp. I didn't however want him to seem like a paedophile. He's half in love with the boy Jesus – which is why he becomes his tutor without payment.

So was there a particular motive in making Bartholomew, one of the Apostles, gay?

No particular motive, but it suited the character as I imagined him. And surely, one of any twelve is likely to be gay. It hasn't got any meaning beyond itself. But you know, there's a very curious incident in one of the Gospels – in Mark. Jesus and his disciples are in the Garden of Gethsemane, and as the arresting group made up of Roman soldiers and temple authorities arrive, a naked youth runs from the garden. It's part of the story, and a few academic interpreters of the

---

* I have since checked and found that my copy, the one that was sent to the publisher, had chapter headings Judas, Chapter One, Judas, Chapter Two etc. This must have been removed by a busy-fingered copy editor and I, carelessly, failed to notice.

Gospels touch on it rather nervously suggesting it has some symbolic import – for example that the youth escaping naked, leaving only his loin cloth behind, is an image of Jesus' escape from death. I, of course (ever the realist!), deal with it as a real event with an entirely natural explanation.

Are you suggesting that the Garden of Gethsemane may have been the Hampstead Heath of its day?!

I can imagine a lot of people reading the novel, thinking this is an element I've invented for titillation. Whereas it's something that's there in the biblical story and the novelist wants to make narrative sense of it. I've checked with friends who are fairly serious Christians and found they had no recollection of such an incident – because of course you're hardly likely to get Sunday sermons on 'The Naked Youth in the Garden of Gethsemane'.

The final stanzas of the novel sent shivers down my spine when I read them:

> *Our friend was*
> *not the Messiah, nor*
> *will there be one.*
>
> *This is the truth*
> *I write. It will not*
> *hurt you. Grasp it!* (244)

Is this what you believe? Is this the essence of the Gospel according to C. K. Stead?

Yes. In the final two stanzas C. K. Stead and Judas become one – the voices become one voice. There is a lot of myself in the character of Judas.

C. K. Stead the Poet

You are the only author to win the New Zealand Book Award for both poetry and fiction.* How important has your poetic career been to you in your life?

It's primary. I started off my career writing poetry and when I go back to writing poems – and there have been long periods in my life when I haven't been able to – it gives me more satisfaction than anything else. It's also relevant to say that the best work I've done as a literary critic has been based on my own experience as a poet – on my knowledge of the practice, the process. So my poetry is fundamental – more important than anything else. However, there are a lot of things you can't do in poetry, and a lot of people you can't reach. You can reach out much further with fiction.

If you had to be remembered for only one aspect of your long career would it be as a novelist, literary critic, poet, essayist, short-story writer or teacher/ academic?

I would most like to be remembered for half a dozen poems.

This may surprise people.

Literary people in New Zealand probably wouldn't be surprised. Outside New Zealand I'm best known as a critic and now, more recently, as a novelist.

How important for you is the role of the poet in society?

I think I'm fairly realistic about this and recognise that poetry is a minority art. There are rare periods when one or another poet becomes a household name, but those are not necessarily the best poets. Byron was known throughout Europe during his lifetime, but he's not the best English-language poet of his period. But poetry puts such demands

---

* I suspect this might be true also of Ian Wedde.

357

on both the writer and the reader, you just have to accept that a lot of people are not sophisticated enough to deal with it. It can be too demanding.

In The New Poetic *you write:'The poet is a man with a store of creative energy, which in part he commits and in part commits him, to a function which must be in one way or another a social function'. Do you see your poetry as having a social function?*

Every human being ought to be politically and socially responsible. Writers have a greater responsibility only in the sense that they have a public, and that what they say and do is noticed more. I don't like the idea of poetry as a vehicle for ideas or propaganda. I think that's confusing and destructive to the poetic urge. You can put your political and social consciousness into poems only insofar as they become part of your emotional life; but as soon as you try to make a poem a vehicle for ideology, or an instrument of persuasion, then the poetic impulse is compromised. Poetry does have a social responsibility indirectly, however, in that it should represent the very best use of the language. Pound says somewhere that poets are the voltmeters and steam-gauges of society. He means that if you look at poetry at one place or time and see that what's applauded and rewarded is full of clichés and sentimental writing, then that's often an indicator of a broader social failure. That's the primary sense in which poetry has a social function. The poet's responsibility is to the language.

So when you're being political, you are not trying to convert others to your point of view. You're just informing your readers . . .

I'm trying to make something, make art, of my feelings at that moment in history. Often those poems are deeply felt; often angry. But they're not – or they shouldn't be! – trying to persuade. That is a very important difference.

Your poems are often political, for example 'A Small Registry of Births and Deaths'. They are frequently highly personal as in 'With a Pen-Knife'. Would the latter go into your 'Desert Island' selection of poems?

Well, it wouldn't get into my top ten. It might go into my top two or three dozen.

Would you be prepared to tell us which of your poems would make it into your top ten list?

I can tell you some of them. 'Pictures in a Gallery Undersea' – even though it owes so much to Eliot, I think it's still very much my own poem. And it's one of those poems that just happened in an inexplicable way. Maybe 'Whether the Will is Free'. Definitely the whole 'Quesada' sequence. Some of the Catullus poems. The sequence called 'Paris'; and also there's a shorter poem called 'Paris: The End of a Story', which I quite like as well. And then I would have to make a small anthology of shorter ones, including quite a number from the last four books (that's counting a new one just about to appear).

There are so many classical references in your poetry, for example in the collection Crossing the Bar. *Why do you feel this need for a classical input?*

It's strange isn't it, because I have so little classical education. I've found in the Latin poets (read, I should make clear, in translation, or in the original but with accompanying English texts) a certain tough objective quality, which I admire and want to emulate, particularly, but not exclusively, in the poems of Catullus. Catullus has given me a way of writing which is neither autobiographical nor fictional, but somewhere in between. I can write in the first person, write in a persona very close to my own and yet not my own. It's not quite Catullus either, and there's no way that any one reading those poems is going to be able to tell which bit is autobiographical and which is fiction. I can use at one moment something that happened to me, and the next it can be entirely invented, and I'm in the same protected area. Which means then that all the thought, all the stylistic instinct, goes where it belongs, into the art of poetry, not into making a public image for myself. It's a release from ego, really. And then the Latin poets have also helped me with the political aspects of my life – for example in those poems you mention in *Crossing the Bar*. Washington becomes Rome, while I adopt a voice that speaks from some outpost of the Empire, far from the centre of power.

The New Zealand landscape is obviously very important to you creatively, and yet, for example in 'Paris' you write:

> *Here there is nothing but the spite of choked passages*
> *and green bananas, nothing but the spirit of Palmerston North*
> *going to bed in lambskins. Paris summon me to your table.*

Would it be too obvious to say that you have a real love/hate relationship with your homeland?

No, that would be true enough, I think. The example you quote would have come out of something particular, but it's on-going. Maybe New Zealand is beginning to forgive me and accept me, but I've had a lot of conflict; and I suppose I can't just say it's everybody's fault but mine! I certainly haven't had a smooth ride in my home country and there have been periods when I've felt I was *persona non grata* there. At those times I've been awfully grateful that I have some kind of identity outside New Zealand; that I've had an 'escape'.

Are people in New Zealand aware that you have felt this sense of alienation?

Oh yes, I think so – and I suppose it's sometimes resented. One is supposed to be 'loyal'. It's surprising, in a small country with a small literary community, how intense the positive and negative feelings can be.

In In the Glass Case *you write: 'There is in most literature a regional element' and [on James K. Baxter] 'No poetry moved me in quite the same way, at so profound a level, as our own' (217).*

That was true when I was young and just discovering New Zealand poets. Yeats and Eliot, Pound, Keats, the classical English-language poets right back to Donne and Shakespeare, were immensely – immeasurably – important to me. But then there was a special sense in which certain poems by Curnow, Fairburn, Glover and Baxter hit me absolutely between the eyes, because of the local element. They were turning what I knew at first hand into poetry. That was very important.

There are lots of poetic experiments in your work but frequently you turn your back on them to return to a coherent personal narrative. Would you agree with this analysis?

Yes and no. The way you've put it might suggest that the experiments are not part of the personal narrative. I do think the whole poetic oeuvre is my life, central to my life; but the experimental poetry is as much part of that as anything else.

Many of your poems stress the need in life to be yourself – not to falsify your personality in order to accommodate others, as in 'Putting it straight in London'.

There's a lot of comic exaggeration in that poem of course. It's not true, for example, that 'I read two novels before puberty. Read one of them twice.' [Laughs] Or that I went to school without shoes. It's really exaggerating the differences for effect. So you might say it's a poem about rejecting false selves which nonetheless, in part, creates a false self. Nothing is simple!

Do you feel your poetry has changed much over the years?

When you're young you begin with imitation and influence. That's how it should be. As you get older you merge into what is just yourself. So you're still reading other people's poetry but it doesn't make such a visible mark on you.

And yet, as we discussed earlier, your influences are always with you.

Yes. If you're a poet and not just a versifier, you can't do it on your own. You need the help of the poets who've gone before. That's the nature of art. You're not just born miraculously an artist. You've got to know, and have access to, a tradition, and in various ways that debt should be acknowledged and signalled. It's disconcerting when you meet young people who think they can 'be a poet' without reading poetry.

Your country has accorded you many honours but not that of poet laureate.

In New Zealand the poet laureate changes every year and is actually sponsored by a wine company – not the same as in the UK at all.

Even so, would you want to be New Zealand's poet laureate?

Yes, for the wine, not for the honour. Poets laureate, here or there, don't have a great retrospective history for being well chosen, do they?

C. K. Stead the Literary Critic

In your role as literary critic you are described thus on the New Zealand Book Council website: 'His literary criticism [. . .] [is] writerly, accessible, little theorised [. . .] in a prose of ease and clarity'. You yourself say 'I am not interested in arcane dialogue. I would like, where possible, to be understood.'

A couple of decades ago, when the fashion for literary theory was at its height, there was a lot of deliberate obfuscation. People seemed afraid that if they said things simply and directly, they wouldn't be taken seriously.

But if you can't read the code, you can't access the message.

That's right. With literary theory came a whole terminology only available to people who had studied literary theory! I think the important things to be said in literary criticism are often difficult to formulate because they contain both subtleties and complexities. These complexities shouldn't be fudged and the subtleties must

362

be respected. But you should always try very hard to intelligible. Otherwise what are you in the business for? Just people! Fashions wash over the academic world. Usually there are few initiators who are really doing something original, interesting and worthwhile, and then a hoard of imitators. But intelligibility seems to me to be something one should strive for even though one might not always achieve it. It's a courtesy to your readers.

To my mind it is also the measure of a greater intellect – those people who are able to achieve accessibility and intelligibility for complex theories.

Fashion is very powerful, and it's interesting how it moves on. Terry Eagleton used to be the great proponent of literary theory. Recently I've noticed he's started to refer to it, not only as though it was needless and wrong-headed, but almost as though he never had anything to do with it.

In your introduction to In the Glass Case *you write: 'Many critics fail because they allow their own truest, innermost responses, which may initially be faint, to be contradicted by some doctrinaire requirement, or by the knowledge of what others have said' (9).*

I learned that very early. When I was young there was a way of dealing with T. S. Eliot which one can say now was simply wrong. It was partly a result of the way Eliot had presented himself – as a 'classicist in literature', who had no interest in, or acquaintance with, romantic 'inspiration'. Writing poetry was 'frightful toil' (his phrase). And though there were difficulties in reading his poetry, this was simply because there were gaps, or missing 'links in the chain' (again his own phrase). You had only to put those links in, yourself, and it all came together in a beautiful coherent lucid sequence. Critics – Cleanth Brooks for example – would perform this exercise. Well, I read *The Waste Land* as an undergraduate, and then read its interpreters, and I thought, 'It's not that sort of poetry at all. It comes from the gut not from the intellect.' So one of the things I did in *The New Poetic* (which was my PhD thesis from Bristol) was to read his criticism in a way no one had thought of doing before, looking for any and every indicator of what the actual experience of writing poetry had been for him. The indicators were there, sure enough, and I was able to use them as justification for a completely different kind of reading of *The Waste Land.*

What was so interesting was that around the time *The New Poetic* came out, it seemed the perception of Eliot changed. I don't mean that my book achieved this, although no doubt it helped. What I mean is that the book came at the right time. It said things people were ready to hear. And then the manuscripts of *The Waste Land* were found and published a few years later, and there wasn't much room for argument. That was one of the reasons why *The New Poetic* was so immensely successful. My later book, *Pound, Yeats, Eliot and the Modernist Movement,* was more sophisticated, subtler, fuller – probably better literary criticism, but nobody particularly *needed* that book, whereas somebody needed to say the things that were said in *The New Poetic.* It went on for several decades being used in universities over here. In fact the latest of many re-issues was just last year, from Continuum, 41 years after first publication.

My point in all this is that fashion has a lot to answer for. We're all in some degree slaves to it. You might think literary criticism would be quite different from clothes and furnishings, but it's not.

You continue in that introduction: 'For me, the act of literary criticism has never been unconnected with my own practice as a writer. If I find myself with fresh perceptions about the nature of fiction or poetry, they almost always come in part from the experience of writing in these genres' (12).

Yes, that's true. And growing up in the age of T. S. Eliot meant that for me there was no disjunction between, for example, 'being a poet' and 'being a critic'. They went together quite naturally.

But I've always been aware that I have different identities in different places and at different times. So, there was a time in New Zealand when I was very well known for a novel called *Smith's Dream,* a political fantasy which was never published elsewhere, but became Roger Donaldson's (and also Sam Neill's) first movie, *Sleeping Dogs;* while in England I was known as the author of *The New Poetic.* It was as if these were two completely different people; and then there was the third person in between who wrote poems, and was known only to the few who read poetry. So I learned that insofar as one has a public identity, it's likely to be partial, even inaccurate. Or multiple and contradictory. I've often felt that my own public persona was fragmented, though within myself there is a single and continuous – what? 'Man of letters' I suppose.

C. K. Stead the Writer

Your introduction to In the Glass Case *also states: 'One of the problems of writing criticism in New Zealand is the smallness of the literary and intellectual community' (11). Do you still think this?*

Yes.

In April 1990, Stephen Stratford wrote an article in Metro: 'Blaspheming against the Pieties: Why the Literati hate C K Stead'. Why do the literati hate C. K. Stead?

I'm wondering now whether they do! Especially with the phone call this morning!* All is forgiven! But for a while, that was so; or seemed so. I was accused, among other things, of being racist and sexist. That wasn't true, but the truth didn't seem to make any difference. The questions I'd raised were to do with difficult and delicate issues. For example, favouring people on the basis of race or sex. If you insist on favouring writers – as happened especially, but not only, in the 1980s – because they're Maori or because they're women, isn't this in itself racist and sexist? I always recognised there were arguments on both sides. I thought I dealt with the matter quite delicately. The problem, however, was that I'd had an image of belonging to the liberal

---

* As the interview was about to begin the phone had rung. It was a call from Stead's daughter in New Zealand with news of a letter saying he was to be made a member of the Order of New Zealand on Waitangi Day, 2007. This is New Zealand's highest award, limited to about twenty living members. Allen Curnow and Janet Frame were members. Margaret Mahy is currently the only other writer with this award.

left, which is still where I'm sure I belong. I'd been known as an anti-Vietnam War protester, right in the thick of that movement. I was arrested during the Springbok tour on the field at Hamilton when the Test match was stopped – my one criminal conviction, of which I'm still proud. So, as I say, I had an image; and then I started questioning bits of the liberal package, and it was as though I'd suddenly become a fascist overnight! A turn-coat. An apostate. Actually, I didn't feel I'd changed; just that I was testing rationally and questioning whether everything in the package was sound. The consequences for me in New Zealand for a while were quite dire. It affected the way my work was reviewed, and possibly still does to some extent. That was the period when I felt glad I had half a foot somewhere else. There were times when I thought I was mad to have gone back to New Zealand when I was young. I could have had my whole academic and literary career here in the UK. There'd been no reason to go home. It was a kind of literary nationalism and idealism that took me back. I had moments of questioning that decision.*

In recent years you have been accorded some of the highest awards a writer can achieve – CBE (1985), Fellow of the Royal Society of Literature (1995), Honorary Doctorate from the University of Bristol (2001) and now, it seems, the Order of New Zealand. Do these accolades matter to you?

I regard the whole business of awards, especially literary prizes – putting one work of art up against another and ranking them – as a nonsense. But they exist, and when your book is nominated, you want it to win. If you're on a short-list and a book you don't respect wins, it's hard to feel cheerful about it. And those award ceremonies can feel like a kind of ritual humiliation, even for the winner. I try to cultivate detachment but for an average egotist it's not easy.

As for public awards and royal honours, well, I'm just like any other human being. I think it's shameful to be pleased, but when we were just getting started this morning and that phone call came, you could see, I'm sure – I was delighted. I remind myself that these things are not important. And ultimately of course they're not. My real life still

---

* See the postscript at the end of this interview for further remarks on this question.

comes down to whether I go out to the little office I have in the garden and whether my writing there is going well or badly. I am the person who has to be satisfied, no one else. I'm my own awarder of good marks and bad. That, ultimately, and my family and friends, are what matter to me. The pleasures associated with the ego are fleeting. But yes, they're real enough.

Do you think it is accurate to call yourself – as so many critics have done – a 'confessional' writer?

No. No, because to me that term is associated with a particular kind of poetry of the 1960s and 1970s: Robert Lowell, John Berryman, Ann Sexton, Sylvia Plath, for example. They not only bared everything but also had very disordered lives. They had something to bare! If you weren't alcoholic, or mad, what did you have to confess? There are certainly autobiographical elements in my work, but as I said when we discussed, for example, my use of classical personae, I've developed ways, precisely, of avoiding confessional writing. There are personal elements, yes. But 'confessional'? – I would say no.

Your writing has also been called metafictional. Is this a conscious style?

There are certainly metafictional elements present in various degrees in my work – for example, *All Visitors Ashore* and especially *The Death of the Body* are I think metafictions. And yes, it's conscious. I usually make decisions about structure, and related technical matters. At the same time – for example, in movements back and forward in time, which I do a lot – I never plot those in advance. The stylistic decision is a conscious one, but *when* I move backwards and forwards – that just happens in the course of the telling. It's an intuitive part of the process. I'm sometimes asked why I complicate things, especially to do with time. Again, it's an intuitive thing, not the result of any theory. But the way I've rationalised it to myself is as follows: The human mind doesn't exist in a continuous present. You're carrying in your consciousness, memory – the past is an operational force, so to speak. And you're also carrying anticipations of, and even intentions for, the future – where you're going, what you're doing and how it relates to what you will be

u're living in triplicate; and insofar as fiction is an
an mind, then the closer it can get to that triple time
earer it gets to a representation of consciousness; of
to be human. That's why I often find narratives which
ological, and go from A to B to C to D, boring to write
and unrewarding to read. They don't have the feel of the real. 'Felt life'
– wasn't that the old Leavisite touchstone? We used to mock it when I
was a graduate student at Bristol, but it makes a point. So perhaps (and
surprisingly) my rationale for metafiction is that I'm a Realist. In some
degree the 'real' requires it!

*Finally, it must give you great personal satisfaction that one of your children,
Charlotte Grimshaw, has become the latest recipient of the Bank of New
Zealand Katherine Mansfield Award for Short Fiction, an award won by
yourself as a young writer.*

It's great. Charlotte's a very good fiction writer. She's published three
novels and she has a collection of short stories about to come out,
so winning the Katherine Mansfield award will help promote those
stories. I have great faith in her talent. In fact the achievements of all
three of our children are immensely pleasing to us both.

Postscript, 2007:

My answer to the question about 'Why the Literati hate C. K. Stead'
was somewhat inadequate, partly because I was far from home and I
do forget, as time goes by, what the arguments were about; and partly
because I was reluctant to wash New Zealand dirty linen in London.

I should explain that the behaviour that got me into trouble from
time to time springs partly from temperament and partly from family
culture. I grew up in a political household where social and political
ideas were constantly debated. One of my earliest memories is the
sound of my father, J. W. A. Stead, who was a senior official in the
Labour Party in Auckland, a trade union secretary, and for some years
president of the LRC, talking, sometimes arguing, with A. S. Richards,
MP for Roskill and a member of the first Labour cabinet, both of
them hammering the table in their excitement and breaking off for

violent fits of smoker's coughing – all this racket coming through the wall to me where I was supposed to be sleeping. My mother was also involved in Labour politics; both my parents were members of the Fabian Society; and my grandmother, who lived with us, was an old-fashioned militant Socialist whose contributions to discussion consisted mainly of slogans such as that religion was 'the opium of the people', that conscript soldiers were 'the Capitalists' canon fodder', and that employers enjoyed 'grinding the faces of the poor'. Being intellectually engaged in the daily affairs of one's city, one's nation, and the world, knowing what was going on, having liberal opinions and sharing and defending them – all of that was what one did, and what I have gone on doing. So as I became at once a writer and an academic, one of my research interests was poetry and politics; how these do and don't mix; how they can be made to work together, and the ways in which they are opposites and inimical.

For a long time none of this had any contrary effect on my literary career. A generally 'progressive' outlook predominates among the literary community, and I blended into that background. But around the age of fifty I found myself (as I explained in answer to Gerri Kimber) questioning some aspects of 'the liberal package', especially the anti-sexism anti-racism campaigns which seemed to me, as they became more radicalised, to become themselves racist and sexist. I still saw myself as a person committed to the political left, but that was not how others saw me. To them I had become (much worse than a conservative) a renegade, an apostate – one on whom it should have been possible to count and who was letting down the side.

I still have not been able to track down the Stephen Stratford article, 'Why the Literati hate C. K. Stead', but I do have a later one, 'Talkin' 'bout my generation' in which he defends me against 'politically correct liberals' whom he describes as 'the New Conservatives' and who had decided, he says, that I was 'an incorrigible reactionary'. Quoting something Mark Williams had written, implying that I was engaging in public argument only to attract a larger middle-class readership for my fiction, Stratford wrote

There is no engagement with [Stead's] argument, simply abuse. It is enough to portray Stead as aligned to *Metro*'s supposedly socially ambitious middle class readers – all 378,000 of you – to dismiss whatever he might say about education, politics, language, literature.

In fact, if the earlier Stratford article was bad from my point of view (and I can't be sure that it was) there was one that was much worse in a magazine he edited in the early 1990s. This was by Nigel Cox in *Quote Unquote* (both – author and magazine – now deceased) in which Cox more or less wrote my literary obituary, suggesting that since leaving the university my poetry had dried up, my novels were 'forgettable', and that, apart from causing upset by continuing to voice illiberal opinions, there was nothing left for me as a writer but 'the dying of the light'.

The matters that caused ill-feeling were often delicate. As an example: I questioned the inclusion of poems in Maori (with English translations) in the Wedde, McQueen *Penguin Book of New Zealand Verse*. After pointing out that neither of the editors knew Maori, and so were 'choosing blind', I quoted six, as it seemed to me, very banal examples of Maori poems in their English translation. I then commented:

> It may be that the Maori behind these verses, and many like them, is fine, striking, noble, inventive or beautiful. If it is, the translations have not done justice to the originals. On the other hand, if the translations do match the quality of the originals then they might be better left unexposed to comparison. Either way the loss is to the mana of Maori.

I thought I dealt with the matter quite sensitively – but not sensitively enough, it seems, to satisfy in those days militant Michael King, who told his readers in *Metro* that I had advocated 'the ethnic cleansing of New Zealand literature'.

Another example: I called the Treaty of Waitangi an 'informal and expedient document, made to serve the needs of a time long gone and a situation no longer pertaining', and questioned (criticised) the willingness of politicians, bureaucrats, and especially our highest Court, to give it an authority it had never previously possessed.* This

---

* See 'The Treaty and the Emperor's Clothes', *The Writer at Work*, p. 211.

questioning of our revered 'founding document' gave offence – and I'm afraid I also mocked it in a poem.* The impulse here was not so much a desire to make waves as a quite genuine (whether misplaced or not) irritation at what I felt to be Pakeha false piety and self-abasing cant in so much of the Treaty talk that went on at that time. There was, after all, also a Pakeha view of our history, and the only people who were making any attempt to put it were red-necks and racists. I thought that point of view should be put by a reasonable person who was neither.

I felt the same about males during the height of 1980s feminism. This was a time when, as I recall, the journalist Denis Welch, standing for Parliament I think for the Values Party, apologised publicly for being male; and the young academic, Kai Jenson, went about in a dress as a declaration (he explained) of solidarity with women. In this climate I tried to give the male point of view a voice which was distinct, intellectual, reasonable, and not sexist – for example:

> A radical change is occurring in our social organization, chiefly, I suppose, because effective birth control has freed women from constraints which, though social in effect, were biological in origin. Even if I feel – and I do – that there is some loss (and I mean loss to both women and men) as well as great gains in the changes, I wouldn't want to resist them in the least. What I resist, and many good strong independent women resist, is the rewriting of history, the shifting of Marxist class terminology into the area of gender, making men simply oppressors and women the oppressed, and bringing that forward as a 'fact' into the present. At present the suicide rate among young males in New Zealand is four times that among females; the rate of male admissions to mental hospitals is higher – but we are told females are oppressed. Clearly liberals – those good people with whom I went to the barricades in 1981 – are selective in the use they make of statistics. The huge disproportion of Maori in our jails is said to be (and no doubt is, at least in part) a sign that they are oppressed and disadvantaged. No one offers the even greater disproportion of males over females in jail as a sign that males are oppressed and disadvantaged.

---

* 'Treasure Island', *Straw into Gold: Poems New and Selected*, Auckland University Press, Auckland, 1997, p. 151.

I am not saying they are – only that statistics are being used, or ignored, according to their convenience.*

And from the same essay, another example:

> Women writers continue to insist that they are neglected or unfairly treated by the patriarchy which once ruled the literary roost. A common story is that of the woman in late-flowering middle age whose creativity was held back in her younger days by domestic responsibility. We have heard this with varying degrees of emphasis from many women writers in New Zealand. I have never doubted that what they said was true. I only wonder about the husbands whose creativity was not merely held back – it was crushed altogether – by the parallel necessity to earn a living and support wife and family.

Insult was added to injury when I published a novel called *The Death of the Body* about a professor of philosophy whose academic specialty is the mind/body problem, and who has an affair with one of his students which gets him into trouble with his department's 'Women's Collective'.† This came in the wake of the scandal, in the Auckland University English Department, when the head of its Drama Department, the playwright Mervyn Thompson, was kidnapped by radical feminists, tied to a tree, declared to be a rapist and threatened with castration. The events in my novel were not so melodramatic, but a connection was made in reviews. Here I suspect my offence, insofar as any was given, or taken, lay not in any rational analysis of the issues (which I would have thought belonged in an essay, not a novel) but in a sort of witty insouciance about them. If a statement, a 'position' on these issues, was implied by the novel, it could only have been that for me, as a writer and as a human being, the relations between the sexes

---

* From 'The New Victorians', *Answering to the Language*, Auckland University Press, Auckland, 1989.

† This (I think in some ways my cleverest novel) was not (of course) short-listed for the Wattie Award, but it was subsequently written about (with considerable brilliance, I think) by Reginald Berry in *Landfall* 163, Sept. 1987, and by Mark Williams in *Leaving the Highway: Six Contemporary New Zealand Novelists*, Auckland University Press, Auckland, 1990. Published in the UK in 1986, it was reissued there in 1991 and 1999, and has been translated into French, Portuguese, German and Swedish.

were fit subject for tragedy or for comedy, but not for politics. There are some things, I think the novel implies, too subtle, and too precious, for politicisation.

This was an intellectual position which, at that time, put me at odds – though subtly, because none of it came to open debate – with radical feminists; and it was during this period that my nomination was successfully opposed in Parliament, once for the position of chairman of the National Library, and a second time for some role (I've forgotten what it was) in the Arts Council, by women MPs whose reasons were never explained but seemed not to surprise anyone. One of these was Marilyn Waring (Nat), the other the Hon. Margaret Shields (Lab).

Another matter that set me at odds with the literary community was the London flat for writers, but that is covered in some detail on pp. 273–7 above.

Finally, to this list of my offences, I have to admit to having been consistently conservative in matters of the teaching of English in schools, and about the framing of the English syllabus; and as a professor of English, and later professor emeritus, I saw it as my role to say so, and say why. I displeased some of the teaching profession with those commentaries, which I stand by.*

---

* 'On teaching English' in the present collection is a typical example. Other examples are 'English in our Schools' and 'English in our Universities', *The Writer at Work*; and 'Teaching English', *Answering to the Language*.

373

At Home, 2007

22/1/07: Margaret and Guy and the children have been for Christmas and are now back in London. I have now swum to the yellow buoy 25 times this summer. (On this date last year the score was nine.) There has been much publicity about Jeffrey Archer's PR machine announcing that his next novel, to be published in March, will be a Gospel according to Judas. Here is *Private Eye* on the subject:

> Last year the distinguished New Zealand novelist C. K. Stead published *My name Was Judas*, a fictionalised memoir in which Judas Iscariot defended himself against the charge that he betrayed Jesus for 30 pieces of silver. In Stead's version, Judas didn't kill himself after the crucifixion but lived to a ripe old age and with a clear conscience.
>
> Now, with a loud fanfare, Jeffrey Archer reveals the startlingly original premise of *his* next book. *The Gospel According To Judas Iscariot* is, er, a fictionalised memoir dictated by Judas Iscariot to his son, defending him against the charge that he betrayed Jesus for 30 pieces of silver. In Archer's version, Judas didn't hang himself after the crucifixion but lived to a ripe old age and with a clear conscience.
>
> Another triumph for the master story-teller!

There has been a similar piece in the Independent by Boyd Tonkin, the literary editor; a very good review of *My Name was Judas* in another Scottish paper, the *Scotland on Sunday* ('Ironically, within these pages it is Judas himself who raises Jesus from the dead'); and a very negative (hurt Catholic?) one from Eileen Battersby in the Dublin *Irish Times*. Alan Massie in the *Scotsman* included it among his best books for 2006. And I've had enquiries from an Oz called David Reeves, who, it seems, wrote a musical called *Cyrano* and wants to come over and talk to me about turning my Judas into a musical. I will be all ears. But I am weary of Judas, and would like to write another novel like *The Secret History of Modernism* which only very literary people will hear about or read.

This is not the first time I have found my name linked with the dreadful Jeffrey Archer's (who seems to have been permitted to keep his Lordship despite his stint in Belmarsh for perjury). The very first review I received of *All Visitors Ashore* in 1984, by Norman Shrapnel in the *Guardian*, bracketed my novel with three British political novels, including Archer's *First Among Equals*.*

Craig Raine has sent me his new book on T. S. Eliot, which at a quick skim seems to have all his intelligence and originality and liveliness, and in its final chapter, defending Eliot against the charge of anti-semitism, all the blind stubbornness of his loyalty – loyalty, I suppose, to Faber, where he worked for some years as poetry editor (Eliot's own role); but more, probably, to the widow, Valerie Eliot, of whom he's very fond. I find it puzzling, because the anti-semitism is so glaringly *there*, it's not worth arguing.

And Miranda Seymour has sent me her new book, *In My Father's House*, about her father, and the great house he fell in love with and contrived, ultimately, to own (and to leave to her); and his late-in-life fourteen-year passion for a young man who became a hanger-on layabout leech in the family until he shot himself, whereupon the father wept more or less continuously for five months until he, too, died – an extraordinary book, rich material beautifully handled – the movement back and forward in time, the hints dropped to arouse anticipation and to be taken up later, and the use of her mother's voice as a counterpoint/ counterweight to her own strongly (yet ambiguously) negative view of her father. It's masterly.

---

* 'Yet it seems ironical that for sheer immediacy, for that annihilation of distance between writer and reader, we should have to turn to a novel located on the New Zealand waterfront 30 years ago.' *Guardian*, 5 July 1984.

5/2/07: Yellow buoy score is now 37.

Much publicity, interviews etc. about the ONZ which is to be announced tomorrow. Mundane questions, mostly. A slightly Aunt Daisy atmosphere. ('How do you feel about this award?') But I mention each time that since Allen Curnow and Janet Frame died, that has left Margaret Mahy as the only writer with the ONZ, so there's a gap to be filled. I don't say that it's a big surprise (though it is) because that too might be construed as false modesty. But I am pleased, and grateful to whoever has done this. And then, in addition, there's an altogether other feeling, which certainly can't be expressed, or even hinted at, but would need a little poem with a title like 'Catullus receives the ONZ'. That thought is really an off-shoot from two or three weeks in which I've been reading in and around Catullus with the idea of doing something with his longer poems – the ones I've so far avoided because they present difficulties I haven't encountered with the shorter ones – contradictions of tone, strange mixings of formal (even stagey) and informal, complexities, obscurities. I've tried to do a version of no. 68, and decided it's a failure and that I can't do it; even that it can't be done. It can be 'translated', and has been many times, but never producing a good poem in English. Either there's something untranslatable there; or something wrong with it as a poem in Latin – probably the latter, meaning that what we have must surely be an imperfect text. What I did was follow pretty closely the sequence of statement and meaning in the original, but cutting them right down, especially the long deviation in the second part about Laodamia which slides into a repeat of the first part's lament about the death of his brother in Troy. The effect of this was to make the tangled knot in the middle of the second part of the poem smaller, but didn't alter the fact that it was a tangled knot.

Catullus 68

Storm-tossed, shipwrecked, even at Death's door,
so you seem, Manlius, and indeed tell me you are,
begging for a poem, for words that might console
a sleepless man abandoned by Venus and the Muse.
Your letter comes as a seal of friendship and trust,
and were I not myself shipwrecked, storm-tossed,

you would have from me all that the Muse and Venus
(those twins whose careless clients once we were
in the green season of youth) chose to bestow.
But with my brother's death, believe me friend,
died poetry also and the pursuit of love,
laughter, and the high hopes of my clan.
So when you ask me why I live alone
here in Verona, where good folk go to bed
early and mostly alone, keeping company
only with my box of books, I tell you truly
that grief has robbed me of the gift of giving
and taking pleasure like a robust Roman.
Yes Rome is 'home', but when the soul is homeless
one must wander with it, even at the expense of friends.

II

And yet, and yet . . . How will silence serve
except to hide in the tomb's webby darkness
the name of Manlius and the good he did me,
which you, Muses, may if you choose record
for eyes as yet unseeing, ears unborn.
My struggle with Venus is well-known to you.
How brutally she forced me into the fires
of insane love, my sweat-stained verses relate,
but not how, when the torture was extreme,
my friend brought me relief. He it was
offered a house where we, as on a stage,
could play our parts, she my radiant goddess,
her sandal on the threshold of my dream
as famous Laodamia came to her husband,
he destined to die in Troy and she to die
sooner than live without him – Troy that seems
destroyer of dreams, where my own brother lies
in unblessed soil far from our family tombs.
The snow-white dove, symbol of unbridled passion
was Laodamia, and so was my Clodia
as Cupid hovered in his saffron cape
and she and I played lovers under the moon.

So if she must have other lovers, Muse,
let me remember Juno's tolerance
of wandering Jove, and let me not forget
she came to me, not from a father's hand,
but from a husband's bed on a brilliant night
of stars and comets. And if the nights that were mine
are marked in her diary with a secret sign
let that suffice.
                    To you, Manlius, I offer
these lines, the best your stricken friend could manage.
May you be happy and your house prosper –
but before even you, dear friend, may she be blessed
whose life alone shines light upon this page.

If I'm to use Catullus 68 at all it will have to be something even further, much further, removed from a translation; not even a 'version' – just one of those poems which skim, pick and choose, the poet/translator as 'snapper up of unconsidered trifles', like Autolycus in *The Winter's Tale*.

6/2/07: Big easterly blowing. As we went down to the water at Kohi one of the High Tide Club, David, came out, shook my hand and said 'Congratulations, well done!' Kay urged him to tell me not to go out to the yellow buoy. He said, 'Don't, Karl, not today, or yours will be shortest membership of the ONZ ever' – so I went around the white buoys, which was quite a battle, but very refreshing. Then we had coffee and read the papers, including the *Dom Post* and the *Press*. Four new ONZes – the other three already knights, and the largest space going to All Black and rugby administrator Brian Lochore who coached the All Blacks when NZ won the World Cup in 1985. Then Paul Reeves, sometime archbishop and former Gov. Gen.; Owen Woodhouse, venerable jurist; and CKS. E-mail messages coming in hourly and I'm replying at once, to be sure they're all answered.

I've written declining after all to do this year's University of the Waikato Sargeson lecture, but before deciding this I went through a great deal of Sargeson's correspondence during the years 1955–56 and a bit beyond. I was interested in how he wrote about Janet Frame, how conscientious he was in trying to help her to get away overseas, and how ambiguous this was – partly a feeling that she should get away to advance herself as a writer, and partly (with accompanying pangs of guilt) a desire, a determination even, to get the weight of her presence off his own back, even though he thought there was a very high chance that she would not survive – that it would be Robin Hyde all over again. He speaks of her so warmly, always with immense admiration for her talent and intelligence. But it's quite different from the way he wrote about Renate Prince who had occupied the hut before Janet, and of whom he always spoke with unqualified affection. What he writes about Janet is full of ambiguities. He never deviates from describing her as 'mad', and says that as he understands more and more about her, what he feels is 'blank despair'. He even has a theory, which he seems to have derived from her, and which is almost the reverse of the story she tells in her autobiography, where she says she read about schizophrenia and simulated the symptoms in order to attract attention, and thus inadvertently brought about her own wrong diagnosis. Frank's idea (this is in a letter to Charles Brasch) is that Janet was so exceptionally intelligent she was able to simulate sanity, in order to get herself released. She could imitate sane behaviour even though not really sane. He says there are times when he can't listen any more to 'fantastic misinterpretations, accounts of nightmares, and unceasing talk of death'. And apart from that there is the emotional burden of feeling responsible for looking after her.

One detail in the letters to Brasch fascinates and puzzles me. He describes how, as 'a farewell expedition with the Steads', the four of us had taken a bus from Takapuna and gone 'swimming under the cliffs up the coast, a perfect day, with nobody else about'. I've written about this expedition myself, more than once, and think I introduced it into a novel – possibly *The End of the Century at the End of the World* – describing it as a kind of idyll, interrupted, but not (or not as far as I knew) spoiled, by artillery guns going off on the headland above us, causing Janet to panic. This was the day when Frank wreathed himself in seaweed, took a driftwood stick as a pipe, and did a pan-dance in the shallows – completely charming. 'But, Janet', Frank tells Charles, 'apparently enjoying herself, was collecting misinterpretations and minor traumas to last her for several days afterwards. There is nothing I can do.' This casts a new, or an extra, light on the strange case of her story, 'The progress of poetry', which gave such gratuitous insult and offence to Kay and me; light also, perhaps, on my strange encounter with her in the army hut, which I describe in *All Visitors Ashore* (pp. 76–78), and which Michael King refers to and quotes.* I had no inkling of the (for Janet) negative aspects to that idyllic day swimming until a couple of months ago when I read Frank's letter to Charles; but how interesting it would have been if Frank had spelled out in more detail the kinds of things Janet said to him, in particular what form these 'misinterpretations' took. It would have offered a better insight than anyone has had – or has put on record – into the workings of that strange mind. He also said more than once, to me and to others, that Janet had threatened his life. Of course he liked drama, and liked the idea that people were 'mad'. (In a letter to me in Australia he records with relish that 'young Jowsey' is showing signs of Janet's problem – which must have been wishful rather than true.) It's true, as I've recorded elsewhere, that when Janet's doctor at the Maudsley Hospital in London asked me whether I thought she was 'mad', I said no – and I meant it. I think it's right to see 'sanity' as a spectrum, up and down which we all move, with a norm that is like the norms for body temperature, or blood pressure. There must be some who are permanently so far off the scale of 'normality' that they can't function socially at all, but Janet was not one of those. Even acknowledging all that, however, it remains true that there was something very strange about her – shyness, hypersensitivity, timidity, fear, to the point of morbidity, certainly; but even beyond all that, something intangible I felt very strongly, with a sort of animal apprehension when we were young; something that expressed itself physically, in her body language, her clothes, her shoes, but in the body itself, neck, skin, hair. In *All Visitors Ashore* Cecelia Skyways is Janet idealised, without any of that. It doesn't, and wasn't meant to, accord exactly with the Janet known to me, though it is partly based on her. But who knows that that

---

* *Wrestling with the Angel* (Viking, Auckland, 2000), p. 126, King quotes the passage from *All Visitors Ashore* and says I went along to this meeting 'not averse to hints of a dangerous adventure'. In fact I went in all innocence, thinking I was there to read and comment on her poems. If I had been 'not averse' to an adventure there would almost certainly have been one. King and I fell out publicly about this in the correspondence pages of the *Listener* in April 2001.

– the fiction – is not a better, deeper, truer apprehension of the 'real', the interior, the magical Janet Frame?

10/2/07: Congratulating e-mails, letters and cards continue to come in, many from old friends, but a lot from public figures, politicians especially, who see it as their role, I suppose. Some seem extraordinarily remote: for example congratulations from the chairman, councillors and staff of Environment Canterbury! But there's a sense in which all are welcome, and I'm trying to answer politely. There are far more cards than at Christmas. I will have to decide at a certain point that it's Twelfth Night. Also in the post another cluster of reviews from the UK including one from the *Sunday Express*, 24 Dec. '06, by Roger Lewis, which begins,

> Sooner or later most great writers get around to reinterpreting the story of Jesus. None can quite compare, however, with the brilliance and plausibility of C. K. Stead – an elderly and obscure New Zealand author who – on the basis of *My Name was Judas*, must surely be a prime candidate for the Nobel Prize.

How's that for even-handed!

22/2/07: I read Vince O'Sullivan's book, *Nice morning for it, Adam*, with some effort, and conceived an essay, which I probably won't write, about a style I would call 'Wellington Pedestrian', with O'Sullivan, Lauris Edmond and Louis Johnson as the chief exponents. It would be partly about semi-*official* art; the art of a provincial capital – rather like a medieval European city state. Vince is the best brain of the three. None of them, I think, aspires to 'music'; and none is much interested in, or more than basically competent in, matters of poetic form. Each poem is the expression, sometimes indirect but often quite direct, of an idea. It's a vehicle, a conveyance. Lauris (who in reality was quite raunchy, and could be good company) used to adopt a special 'naice' voice for reading; and the most damning thing one can say (and it's true) is that the voice suited the poems exactly; they were made for one another. Lou was an old-fashioned journo and made a feature of being a bit dashing, a bit wild, a bit louche, something which his lubricious reading voice suited. Vince's stock-in-trade is exactly represented by his title – the language of the 'ordinary Kiwi joker', the 'decent bloke' (heard in the slightly raspy voice of his readings) but with the little 'thrill' or shock of surprise – 'Nice morning for it . . . *Adam?*' My God, we're in the *Bible*! In the Garden of Eden! His poems are often quite hard work to read. And then there's the inexplicable streak of gratuitous malice, as in 'The boy who invented pastiche'.

23/2/07: This morning's swim was my 47th time this summer to the yellow buoy at Kohimarama. Getting close to count of fifty when, I've promised Lorna (aged 91, and looking a very well-preserved seventy), I will shout the High Tide Club champagne. I had a premolar out on the 14th. It gave the dentist a lot of trouble – brittle tooth, which shattered, and the root deep in the bone. I was on Chris Laidlaw's Sunday morning programme on the 18th about the new collection of poems, *The Black River*. The dentist told me, when he did his check on Wednesday, that he'd listened and could tell my tooth was not giving me any trouble. Margaret Scott has sent me another entry from Charles Brasch's journal after I had stayed with him in Dunedin in 1966. There is the usual pictorial description. I am like El Greco's Grand Inquisitor. I am also 'an intellectual's intellectual' – to which he adds, 'but he can't really be like that, I reflect, & wonder if I have any notion of what it is like to be Karl?' In my reply to Margaret I tell her,

> I was undercover with Charles – hiding from him. I always felt I was false with him, so I disliked him on reflection as if it was his fault. I suppose I felt he wouldn't have liked the real me, or would have liked the real me for the wrong reason, or in the wrong way, so I hid.

25/2/07: Elizabeth Caffin launched the book of poems very movingly. This was on her Birkenhead deck on Saturday afternoon. I mentioned that the last time I had spoken there was March 2001 when I launched Allen Curnow's last book, on a date which I'd been able to calculate was fifty years almost to the day since I'd first seen him, walking up through Albert Park (recognised from published pics). That was in enrolment week 1951, my first year as a student and his first as a lecturer. I then explained what I've recently learned about the ONZ – that the medal has to be returned post mortem whereupon it passes in due course to another. I'm to get the one that passed from Allen to Hugh Kawharu, who died recently.

I read 'Talking to Bill' and 'C.K.' Afterwards, we went with Charlotte and Paul, and Don and Jill Smith to Oh Calcutta (Indian restaurant).

Oliver has promised to e-mail me a photo he has from Paul Tapsell of Hugh Kawharu's grandchild sucking on the precious medal I'm to receive.

26/2/07: Yesterday I battled breeze and chop to the yellow buoy, the fiftieth time this summer, and as promised to Lorna, Kay and I then supplied champagne (not French, only Lindauer, brought in a chilly bin) and nibbles to the High Tide Club. It seemed almost all of them were there and it turned very jolly. Lorna came out of the water having had (she said) a 'vision' that the same thing would happen on April 19, her 92nd birthday. There was talk of possibly making it a barbecue. I'd felt embarrassed in advance but needn't have worried. A lot of hugs and handshakes, partly for fifty times to the buoy, partly also for the ONZ, partly just for the pleasure of hugs and handshakes.

15/3/06: A few days ago came a fax from the Thwaites to say the interview has appeared in the *Guardian* at last, a full page with the pic of me right down the middle looking (Ann says) 'severe and rumpled'. The paper seems to have waited for *The Black River* so both it and *My Name was Judas* could be included. A lot of minor inaccuracies, but a lot of space – and entirely positive, the Judas novel described as 'one of the critical successes of the last part of 2006'. Ann and Anthony were at the King's Lynn Festival where Miranda Seymour was interviewed about *In My Father's House* 'which has been getting marvellous reviews' (Ann goes on) 'and mentioned the support and sympathy of one Karl Stead at a previous festival when she was having problems with the writing of this book'. A couple of days later came an e-mail from Antonia about the Guardian piece in which she says I look 'splendidly belligerent and durable'.

Margaret has sent an excellent *Observer* interview with Miranda in which she discloses that since her book has been published she has had confirmation that her father was indeed actively gay (a question she leaves just slightly open in the book), and that this information upset her terribly – this despite the fact that no reader of her book would, I think, have guessed otherwise. It's not that she can't 'take' homosexuality; just can't take it in her father – and anyway the whole subject is fraught for her, involving his emotional cruelty to her and her mother, and her feeling as a child that she was not loved by her father as he loved his boyfriends, whose loss he wept over copiously.

Antonia's e-mail is very touching. She is being persecuted, half way into her new novel, by the noise of builders next door (the Proustian nightmare). She finishes:

> You are much better at living the literary life than I am. When I was young I imagined having groups of writerly friends but the truth is if you choose to have 4 children and be a woman and write very long books you don't treat friends properly and don't deserve them. And at school I only existed in solitude, and there is still a residuum of that.

I thought about this and (apart from the obvious fact that writing is inevitably a solitary business) it occurred to me that, these days, the literary friends I had for many years at home were mostly older and are mostly dead – Sargeson and Curnow (thirty and twenty years older); then Sinclair, Duggan, Smithyman, Bill Pearson, Dave Ballantyne, Frame, Baxter (six to ten years older):

> They were my close companions many a year,
> A portion of my mind and life, as it were,
> And now their breathless faces seem to look
> Out of some old picture book;
> I am accustomed to their lack of breath.

(That's Yeats, clumsy but heart-felt.) Then there are the contemporaries, Doyle (now in Canada), Bland (comes and goes between 'here' and 'there') – neither of them well. There was always Shadbolt of course, but that was a very thorny relationship, with plenty of fault on both sides, I'm sure. Kevin Ireland spent most of his and my working life out of the country, and Maurice Gee outside Auckland. As a friend, the most durable of my literary contemporaries here in New Zealand has been Marilyn Duckworth. There is also the fact that one's family, as it extends, becomes a very large part of one's social life; and that for many years my university colleagues were at least half of it, and the most important of those friendships continue.

Further, the literary (or literary/social) life is full of marvellous surprises, like meeting, at Jan Kemp's party, a visiting lecturer, Professor Anna Wirz-Justice (a scientist, expert on sleep, whom I had met once before, briefly, at the Hay-on-Wye Festival) and receiving later the following message:

Dear Karl

It was a pleasure to meet you at Jan's party yesterday, for more than the two minutes in a dark corridor of the Manor at Hay-on-Wye. I stayed overnight (so I could continue drinking and talking), and as I laid myself to sleep there was a book of poems of yours on the table. The Red Tram. Of course curiosity opens the book, and by chance at the page Rapallo. Well, small world, Massimo Bacigalupo [to whom the poem is dedicated] is a very good friend of mine since 40 years, since my parents re-emigrated from NZ to live in Rapallo in the 60s, and Massimo's parents were their good friends and Massimo became mine. He made groovy sixties films (in the which I stroll in the long grasses). It was so lovely and surprising to read not only a lovely poem (I have reached the age of 'Look hard. Live as well as you can.'), but to KNOW the joys of sailing out in the Vagabonda into the horseshoe bay, climbing the salita to Sant'Ambrogio (where we scattered my father's ashes under the olive trees and vines – he loved that view), walking along the Via Aurelia among the cypresses, and indeed in later years staying in the Villa Cristina. Ha!

So we should meet next time in Rapallo, and eat that marvellous fresh pasta with the walnut salsa.

Thank you for that.

Best

Anna*

---

* Postscript: There was a sequel to this later in the year when I was back in London, at Covent Garden, watching Wagner's Ring Cycle. At the interval I overheard a nurse and research scientist, previously unknown to one another, talking about melatonin as a cure for jet-lag. I joined in, saying I had heard a sleep expert say melatonin could be effective, but only if you took it at the right time, and I had forgotten what that was. The scientist confirmed this, told me how and when to take it, and asked the name of the sleep expert. I told him it was Professor Anna Wirz-Justice. He said he knew her well, and told me she was the child of Jewish refugees who had emigrated to New Zealand and then returned to Europe after the war.

The *Listener* reviewer of *The Black River*, Hugh Roberts, describes some of the poems as 'self-pitying' and 'schizophrenic'. Glenn Colquhoun's poems are dismissed in the same review as 'nerveless, slack and underthought'.

19/3/07: Copies arrived today of the French translation of my Judas novel, *Mon nom était Judas*, by (on the title page, though not on the cover) 'Christian Karlson Stead'. The book looks heavy and biblical in a French ecclesiastical way, which is a puzzling way to present it.

Then there was a meeting in the Waitakere City mayor's office, to meet a visiting 'Professor of World Cultures' from California, Peter Sellars, whose hair had been trained to stand on end – permanently, it seemed. He was fluent and spoke harsh truths about America which were clearly deeply felt. This has been my first duty as an 'Arts Laureate of Waitakere City'.*

3/4/07: I paid provisional tax a month ago and now have to pay terminal tax. 'Terminal' is an appropriate word. The King Fellowship (though I'm very grateful, and glad to have had it) is something of a trap. You get a lot of money, spend most of it, declare it, and then get taxed for it after it's gone. But there's worse: I gave a plumber (how could I be so stupid?) $2,380 advance, which he said he needed to buy materials, to renew the back part of our roof. He cashed the cheque and didn't come when he'd said he would, and neither did the materials. When I rang he said he was going to his grandmother's funeral (not a brilliantly original story) in Taranaki; then, in the days that followed, that he was still at his grandmother's funeral (answering his cellphone there); and finally didn't answer at all or respond to messages. Soon his answerphone mailbox was declaring itself full. This morning Kay went around to the address on his invoice. No plumber there – just a panel beater. Kay spoke to two workmen who said Oh yes, the dodgy plumber was the panel beater's disowned son, who is 'into drugs'.

* I received this by virtue of owning a bach on Lone Kauri Road, Karekare, though I live in Parnell which is part of Auckland City.

5/4/07: I was Onzed yesterday at Government House Auckland by the very charming Gov. Gen. the Hon. Anand Satyanand, who, I'm told by Bernard Brown, was a student of mine when I was a young lecturer, and who, as a judge, used to be known to the legal fraternity as 'Satch'. In the evening we took O & V, and C & P, and Frances and Louis [younger sister and husband], to Antoine's. We hadn't been there since Penguin launched my Mansfield *Letters & Journals* in 1977 (something that would never happen now). It has become (perhaps always was) pretentious and ridiculously over-priced (not including GST in the price on the menu is pretty close to fraud) – but we had a nice time.

I forgot to record the funeral on 30 March of Vivienne Ballantyne [widow of novelist David]. Her son, Stephen, decided she should have a proper socialist send-off, so it was at the Trades Hall, she on trestles in a plywood coffin handpainted with flowers. We sang the Internationale, then Stephen and others spoke about her, then sang the Red Flag, followed by further reminiscence, and finally Blake's Jerusalem. Stephen told how, when they were living in England, she was a member of the Labour Party, and was summoned to answer questions about herself because the party was purging itself of Trotskyites. As a schoolboy he went with her, and listened. After considering her answers the officials told her she was expelled. 'Unfair,' Stephen assured us. 'She was never a Trotskyite. She was a *Stalinist.*' A lovely atmosphere of irony and nostalgia for the good old lost cause!

12/4/07: Review of the reviews: here *The Black River* has been well-received, with the single exception of the *Listener*. Outside NZ, the *Guardian* used it as the kick-off point for their full-page interview. And the Melbourne *Age*: 'Many poets have tried to write their own elegy, but none I suggest with Stead's touch . . . a crystal-clear poet and his lines, with perfect air between them, make the poem feel like something on a piano.'

15/4/07: I listened to Alistair Campbell (interviewed by Kim Hill) on the car radio as I drove out to Henderson to fulfil my duty as a 'Waitakere City Arts Laureate' – and parked and listened when I got there. Mournful, he was. Spoke of depressions and continuing medication.

Not quite my contemporary – I think about eight years older. Diane gave me the beautiful first edition of his first book, *Mine Eyes Dazzle*, for my twentieth (which was her nineteenth – same day) birthday. I liked it then, but some years later, when he had reissued it in several revised forms, I gave it an unfriendly review for which he didn't forgive me for many years. His story is a sad one – the Polynesian orphan concealing, or trying to conceal, his race – but on the other hand he reclaimed it, adding Te Ariki to his name, at a time when there was nothing to lose and everything to gain by the reclamation; and his description of himself as 'beautiful', one who 'broke too many hearts', seemed naïve, especially when Kim suggested he was just doing what poets did in those days, and cited Baxter, and he responded as if competitively, saying he thought Baxter exaggerated his successes with women.

What does an Arts Laureate do? Well, on this occasion we were convened to discuss that very question – and how, and by how many, to increase our number, and for what benefit to Waitakere Eco City; after which we had a very nice lunch with wine, and were joined by city councillors, to discuss our morning's discussions, until 3 p.m. when I drove back to Parnell, and then to Kohimarama with Kay, and swam to the yellow buoy (number 84 for the summer – and getting cooler) to recover. The whole day's proceeding seemed slightly tainted by its *procedures*, which were so much in the commercial mould – a 'branding' exercise; and yet how could one quarrel with a mayor and council who are working hard and with complete sincerity to make the Arts an important, even a primary, part of their city's identity? And it was nice to be sitting for a whole morning beside Niki Caro (film-maker, fellow Arts Laureate – and so beautiful) who told me she remembers being 'picked on', with Charlotte, at Parnell School, whereupon the two of them ran home to our house and spent the rest of the school day there.

The night before – Friday – we had Greg O'Brien and Jenny Bornholdt, up from Wgtn, for dinner, with Mac and Nicki Jackson and Jan Kemp and Dieter Riemenschneider. As they were coming in from the street Greg and Jenny saw the mural I commissioned from him twenty years ago and they went upstairs to look at it; then out to the Lockwood (my workplace) at the back where there is one of his paintings given to me by the English Department when I left the university. By that time Jan and Dieter had arrived and joined us out there, where Jan found, on the board over my desk (on which many writer and family photographs are randomly pinned), one of herself making a typically emphatic gesture in conversation with me at a party (a photo taken by Michael King), one of Greg painting the mural, and one of my creative writing class a year after Greg was in it, with Andrew Johnston and Tim Wilson (the latter now TV One's correspondent in New York).

It was our best dinner party for a long time – a good combination; and Greg gave us his new book, *News of the Swimmer Reaches Shore*, which I'm now reading and enjoying very much – a series of meditations, and literary and artistic wanderings, around their time in Menton when Jenny had the Mansfield fellowship. It's a sort of travel book in which the travel is as much intellectual as physical. Greg is especially good at random, slightly quirky, connection-making.

My new fiction idea still lurks, neither advancing nor retreating.

Êtes-vous content? It depends on where in the 24 hours the question is asked. I woke in the night in my 'bad' state – a kind of morbid embarrassment which looks for a reason and of course always finds one – something, *anything*, that will serve as its occasion. I seldom feel guilt, but very often shame, and they are close cousins. But I see such moods, these days, as a form of depression; a lowering of the vital spirits. And it's true one loses the irrepressible bounce of youth, which no amount of Onzing can alter.

25/4/07: A good dinner this week with the Roddicks, up from Dunedin, and the Smiths. On Saturday 21st I reached the yellow buoy for the ninetieth time this summer and have now stopped, though still swimming between the whites. It seemed too cold to be in the water half an hour, which is what it's now taking me to get out and back – though last year (when my score reached seventy) I was still going out there until early May. Today the High Tide Club at Kohi are having a barbecue, winding up for the summer I suppose, though some will go on a long time yet. I had promised champagne again if I got to 100, but it will have to be next year.

Tonight on radio is Dean Parker's play which rewrites NZ history in relation to the wars of the twentieth century, with Kim Hill, Marilyn

Duckworth and me playing our (fictional) selves, 'experts' talking about Parker's (also fictional) anti-war poet, Rufus Dewar, who brought about the end of our subservience to Empire militarism – quite a subversive thing to run on Anzac Day.

The grapes are over at last – I picked a great bowl of them this morning and removed the net.

Part Four Lit Crit and Lit Hist

The Actor and the Man of Action

Andrew Marvell's 'An Horatian Ode Upon Cromwell's Return from Ireland'*

I

It is difficult to recover one's first impression of the Ode but probably for most readers the following description would cover it: The poem celebrates Cromwell's victory in Ireland and looks forward to future greatness for England, but in passing pays a beautiful tribute to the dignity of Charles, whose death was the necessary and unfortunate precursor of the present happy state of affairs.

Very quickly, however, as we give more attention to the poem, we discover an undertone qualifying this first impression. The tribute to Charles remains static; but Charles is not the subject of the poem. Cromwell is; and Cromwell alters as our focus narrows on him. He has '[ruined] the great Work of time'. He is 'Fate' over-ruling 'Justice' and 'the antient Rights'. His Government is 'the forced Pow'r', achieved by the destruction of the 'helpless Right' of Charles. There can be

* *Critical Survey*, Vol. 3, no. 3, Winter 1967.

no reasonable argument which denies that these aspects qualify the celebration; but it will be relevant to the latter part of my discussion to describe at this point how, some years ago, I misread the poem by giving my attention exclusively to them. 'And if we would speak true / Much to the Man is due.' Yes, much indeed! – the ruining of the great Work of Time, the ultimate vandalism. That was the tone of voice I concluded belonged to the poem, and I was able to extend it even into lines 73 to 112, in which Cromwell's recent and forthcoming triumphs are presented. The lines on the Irish were no obstacle.

> They can affirm his Praises best,
> And have, though overcome, confest
>> How good he is, how just
>> And fit for highest trust.

It was easy (though wrong, I now believe) to read as sarcasm this tribute put into the mouths of a people who still speak of 'the Curse of Cromwell'. And with a little ingenuity I was able to extend sarcasm into the passages that follow. I had soon persuaded myself that the Ode was a strongly Royalist poem thinly veiled (probably for the extra pleasure friends of that persuasion would have in seeing through it) as a tribute to Cromwell. Cleanth Brooks* was right but had not gone far enough.

Returning to the Ode some time later, having recovered from the exercise, I was surprised (and chastened) to find it the poem I had first read: a celebration of Cromwell. Further readings restored some (not all) of what Brooks calls 'dissenting ambiguities'. But the sarcasm, the veiled Royalist assault on Cromwell, were not there. I was left with two problems: Why had I so misread the poem? And why has it occasioned so much argument among scholars and critics who yet do not seem in any fundamental sense to disagree?

---

* 'Criticism and Literary History: Marvell's Horatian Ode', *Sewanee Review*, LX, 1952.

II

A poem addressing the Cavalier Lovelace as 'His Noble Friend';
an elegy on a young nobleman, Francis Villiers, killed in a skirmish
with Parliamentary forces; an elegy on 'My Lord General Hastings';
and finally 'Tom May's Death', a virulent attack on the reputation
of the poet and translator who had gone over from the Royalist to
the Parliamentary side – 'turned chronicler to Spartacus': four poems
during the years 1647 to 1650 indicating in one way or another
Royalist connections or Royalist sympathy. Cromwell returned from
Ireland in May 1650 and marched on Scotland in July. Tom May died
in November. If we are to date the poems by the events that occasioned
them it seems necessary to conclude that six months after writing the
Ode Marvell still had no intention of putting his poetic gifts to the
service of the Parliamentarians, and no sense of already having done
so. I might therefore, at the time when I read the Ode as a veiled attack
on Cromwell, have adduced these poems in support of my reading.

I am not sure how far it has helped our reading of the Ode that it
should have been the ground over which the academic empires of
LIT CRIT and LIT HIST have made charge and counter-charge.*
But whatever we decide about the poem, Brooks is right in the general
terms of the argument: whether we conceive of ourselves as critics
or historians, it is the same poem. The critic's text must also be the
historian's *primary* document. The historian no less than the critic
must prove that he can read it. Only the text can determine the
relevance of any information we may choose to import from outside
it; and the recognition of relevance (or irrelevance) is itself a critical
discrimination. To demonstrate, if such a thing were possible, that
Marvell was in some degree 'Royalist' and 'anti-Cromwell' before and
after writing the Ode is not the same as demonstrating that the Ode is
Royalist and anti-Cromwell. Yet again, if the Ode is a celebration of
Cromwell, 'Tom May's Death' coming six months later is a problem.

---

* The article by Cleanth Brooks cited above, and 'Marvell's Horatian Ode', Douglas Bush,
Sewanee Review, LX, 1952 (an answer to Brooks). Brooks answers Bush in the same
journal, LXI, 1953. Also relevant is Pierre Legouis, 'Marvell and the New Critics', *Review
of English Studies*, 1957, viii. Bush's summing up that the poem is a portrait of Cromwell
'warts and all' seems to me a breezy evasion of all the problems.

III

Marvell came of the middle class and from Hull. There was something in him of the tough-minded, hard-working, no-nonsense provincial, the man of action, capable at times of a certain crudeness and brutality. (It is not surprising to learn the author of the satires engaged in fist fights.) Yet his best-known poetry reveals a mind as sophisticated and subtle, capable of as much delicacy of thought and feeling, as that of any poet in English. Probably he discovered himself as a poet among men of superior rank; certainly in the early years of his life poetry was an art that seemed in the possession of Royalists, whether of Lovelace's class or of Cleveland's.

It is clear that Marvell regretted the execution and pitied Charles. But he nowhere reveals the mystical faith in kingship that belongs to the true Royalist. His background, his personality, and his later life, all suggest a man who – whatever his reservations and regrets – might have found something exhilarating in the triumph of the Parliamentary side. I am suggesting that Marvell's Royalist sympathies were literary rather than political.

The occasion of the Ode is important. The reported success of Cromwell's armies in Ireland was something which seemed to many Englishmen to ratify the victory of Parliament over the King. God was not displeased. Success was evidence of His approval. Anxieties about the consequences of regicide were allayed and patriotism satisfied. England could look forward to power, perhaps even to an Empire. This feeling is part of the Ode's texture. I anticipate at this point to say it was Marvell's *intention* to express that feeling. He set out to celebrate Cromwell, and by accident found himself celebrating (and lamenting) the triumph in himself of the man of action over the poet.

IV

Early in 1651 he is established at Nunappleton House as tutor to Mary Fairfax, daughter of the Parliamentary General whose death 'Fame' hopes for in the Francis Villiers elegy, and of the lady who shouted 'Oliver Cromwell is a traitor' during the trial of Charles.

(Mary was later to marry Francis Villiers' brother George, second Duke of Buckingham, a marriage which protected Buckingham before the Restoration and Fairfax after it.) Fairfax had resigned his Parliamentary Generalship because he would not sanction the campaign against Scotland which Cromwell returned from Ireland to conduct – the same campaign that is enthusiastically heralded in the Ode. The affiliations could scarcely be more complicated. If Nunappleton was the 'garden state' it nonetheless reflected all the significant elements of the civil conflict. There, it seems, Marvell wrote a good deal of the poetry for which he is remembered. But already in 1652 the 'forward' 29 year old was ready to 'forsake his Muses dear'. At the same time that he was praising Fairfax for weeding ambition and tilling conscience he was seeking to attach himself to Cromwell's Government. Milton's support failed to secure him the secretaryship he sought, but in 1653 he went to Eton as tutor to Cromwell's ward. From that time on he is unequivocally Cromwellian. The brief flowering of the 'Metaphysical' talent most of us mean when we speak of 'Marvell' belongs almost certainly to the period when (I am assuming) his political and literary personalities were in conflict. Once that element of contradiction within himself is dispelled, the poetry declines. Marvell's later celebrations of Cromwell (though the poem on the Protector's death is a moving personal tribute) lack the conflict in which his best poetry was generated. In the post-Restoration satires there is conflict of the will with external circumstances. 'We make out of the quarrel with others rhetoric; out of the quarrel with ourselves, poetry.' Yeats's dictum may not fit every kind of poet, but it fits Marvell.

V

The will destroying the sensibility; the sensibility coming to perfection as it dies: that (an over-dramatising and contentious short-hand) might be one way of rendering the brief life of Marvell the poet – after which Marvell the satirist, Marvell the Parliamentarian, Marvell the whatever-else, lived on. It may also be a way of describing the vision contained in the first 72 lines of the Ode. But if that is so, it seems to have been arrived at by accident. Not intending it, Marvell, we may venture, did not recognise what he had done. Lines 73 to 112 do not accord with that vision, on which the Ode's greatness depends, because they do little more than fulfil the original intention.

How can one speak confidently of Marvell's 'intention'? There is one large clue – it amounts, indeed, to a declaration. This is 'An Horatian Ode'.

There is one characteristic of Marvell's lyric poetry above all others which helps us to think of him in conjunction with Donne rather than Milton. He could cast himself into a role. He could adopt in one poem the voice of the puritan soul, in another that of the frustrated lover urging sexual need, in a third that of the voluptuary yet disembodied imagination. It does not occur to us to say he is 'inconsistent' in these poems. Each implies a dramatic situation and is governed by that.

In the Ode he casts himself in the role of Horace celebrating the victories of Caesar. We do not need to consider – though Marvell must have thought of it – that Horace had taken Brutus's side against Caesar at Philippi, and had later come to accept and praise him. What is important is that Marvell is experimenting with a point of view. That, perhaps, helps to explain how another and more personal of Marvell's voices – that of the satirist – could castigate Tom May six months later as 'chronicler to Spartacus'.

Charles need not have entered the poem. Nor need the various 'arts of peace' that seem to attach themselves to his side of the argument. That they do, and the way in which they do, indicates that to take up the Horatian role a certain violence had to be done within Marvell himself. It is expressed in the violence done to Charles. There is a Cromwell in Marvell and there is a Charles. The first 72 lines act out the victory of Cromwell over Charles that was necessary if the victory in Ireland was to be celebrated. The will is working against the sensibility, and the internal conflict is projected out on to society and made to represent it. The intended heroic poem begins at line 73. But by that time we are already in possession of another – the tragic poem we value.

Cromwell triumphs at home. If he embodies 'inevitable Fate', if his freedom is only 'the consciousness of Necessity', the freedom to 'urge' his 'active Star' in the direction it will take in any case, then there can be no return to the gardens where once he 'liv'd reserved and austere'.

He must triumph abroad. Ireland is only a beginning. Next there will be victory in Scotland, and beyond –

> A Caesar he ere long to Gaul
> To Italy an Hannibal.

Marvell is experiencing in imagination, 'living it out' with relish and alarm, the boundless moral confidence, the triumph of the will to action. That is what gives the poem its extra dimension and urgency. If the 'forward youth' should forsake his books and his 'Muses dear', whatever drives him to it will not relent. 'The same Arts that did gain / A Pow'r must it maintain.'

VI

Active and passive principles are set in opposition, the active eroding and destroying the passive. Energy becomes self-sufficient. Form is destroyed. The 'forward youth', wishing to 'appear', must oil his armour and go forth. The 'inglorious arts of peace' – poetry, learning, gardening, acting – are abandoned. The Muses are forsaken, Numbers languish in the shadow, books lie in dust, planting ceases. Rest, contemplation, reservation and austerity are replaced by restlessness, industry, violence and valour. Mars commands, Venus is neglected. The laurel goes, not to the poet, but to the warrior. The 'plot' is no longer the garden plot but the political intrigue, the military manoeuvre, even the plot of the play in which the 'Royal Actor' is to die. Lightning has broken from the cloud, cutting through the soft side that nurtured it to burn and rend 'Palaces and Temples', to 'ruine the great Work of Time'. 'Justice' and the 'antient Rights' 'complain' and 'plead', but Fate rules. The weak are broken, the strong hold; lesser spirits give way to greater.

Cromwell represents this release of new energy, and neither justice nor blame is attached to him. He is as much a part of an inevitable process as Charles is. Cromwell's 'art' is that of the hunter; Charles's is that of the tragic actor whose role is to die with good grace. Charles knows ''Tis Madness to resist or blame'. He dies passively and beautifully. He does nothing mean, common or vulgar –

> But bow'd his comely Head
> Down as upon a Bed.

He accepts his fate as Cromwell *urges* his. The actor is swept aside by the man of action. As the king who read from Sidney's *Arcadia* on the night before his execution dies, so symbolically do decorum, style, and hence poetry itself. Poetry (as Auden says) 'makes nothing happen'. It too is a kind of acting, unreal compared to the energy that can transform the world.

But the Muses were 'dear': Charles's head was 'comely'. The Ode is a celebration of Energy, and a lament for the dignity and decorum that are lost when it achieves its full freedom.

VII

To see the lines on the Irish as sarcasm was an instructive mistake. Cleanth Brooks denies the possibility of sarcasm, but finds in them a 'grim irony'. Harold Toliver* remarks that the lines 'cannot be taken ironically without totally inverting the eulogy'. He means they must either be sarcasm or eulogy, and I agree. They do not admit of the middle possibility proposed by Brooks. Either Marvell means what he says (that the Irish have admitted Cromwell's fitness for trust), or he means the opposite. To read these lines as sarcasm one must assume, first, that Marvell would have known exactly what Cromwell's armies had done in Ireland, and how they were received there; and second (as Douglas Bush points out) that Marvell was in possession of a modern liberal conscience that could extend its humane concerns to the traditional enemies of his own country. To read them that way is to lose sight of the poem as a whole, its title and primary rhetorical force.

So we may ask now, why has the Ode occasioned so much argument? Part of the confusion I think arises from an element of contradiction in the poem itself. We have been so charmed by the rich

---

* *Marvell's Ironic Vision*, Harold E. Toliver, Yale University Press, New Haven and London, 1965, pp. 183–91.

duality of those opening 72 lines, we have tended to invent duality in what follows. But after line 72, duality is gone. In fact there is a sense in which the quality of the poem declines; but this is not easy to recognise, because the verse, simply as verse, keeps up, and continues to be served by Marvell's wit:

> The Pict no shelter now shall find
> Within his party-coloured Mind;
>> But from this Valour sad
>> Shrink underneath the Plad;
> Happy if in the tufted brake
> The English hunter him mistake;
>> Nor lay his Hounds in near
>> The Caledonian Deer.

The lines are supple, the wit is operating, and yet the decline is real. It can be shown most simply by the fact that the poem begins to contradict itself. Cromwell, the man whom it was worse to 'inclose' than to 'oppose', is now the one who 'can so well obey'. He is the falcon who always returns to the falconer's wrist. His victories are no longer the work of pure energy, 'angry Heavens' flame', but duties meekly carried out by a servant of the English 'Publick'. The instrument of Fate is now the reasonable mortal 'that does both act *and know*'.

This middle section fulfils what seems to have been Marvell's original intention – a celebration. But feelings outside that intention have entered the poem before this point has been reached. The delicate balance of attributes represented by Charles and Cromwell has achieved a tragic rather than a heroic quality. Lines 73 to 112 represent a decline, not because the heroic mode is itself unworthy, but because it cannot accord with or measure up to what has gone before.

The poem recovers, however. It has taken into its texture a number of references to the various arts; and it has described the breath-taking political circumstances which are in effect destroying these by rendering them irrelevant, 'inglorious'. That theme returns in the final lines and, with it, the tragic duality. The tone of unqualified excitement in which Cromwell's victories, past and future, were described, gives way to something more measured. Cromwell is once again the embodiment of violence and fate:

> But thou the War's and Fortune's Son
> March indefatigably on,
>> And for the last effect
>> Still keep the Sword erect.

Whatever Marvell intended by that 'last effect' it cannot avoid a suggestion of death. There must be an end even to Cromwell's marching. In our final view of him he is once again Energy, but Energy seeming to lack an object. There is no longer a decorum for him to work against. All has been swept aside. He moves away from us, advancing against nameless shadows, a robot maintaining his old direction and posture because he cannot do otherwise. And so the final couplet, intending perhaps only to encourage Cromwell in his campaigns against Scotland and beyond, regains the duality of the tragic vision. The poem which began with the 'forward youth' casting aside the pen, concludes with the aging warrior still bearing the sword. The sword is undoubtedly mightier, but is there not the hint of a reminder that he who lives by it will die by it?

> The same Arts that did gain
> A Pow'r must it maintain.

Marvell's Ode may be imperfect but it is rich and strange, powerful, unique.

Eugene Lee-Hamilton, Nineteenth-century Sonneteer[*]

In his 'Epilogue to these Sonnets', Eugene Lee-Hamilton says 'I know not in what metal I have wrought'; but he adds that if the poems should be lost 'beneath the clods and later rediscovered, and if the metal should prove to be gold, they will not have tarnished'. It is a tough test that is postulated. If a poet's best work is not 'gold' exactly, iron is surely not the only alternative.

Poets, especially important but minor ones, usually acquire contemporary reputations, not only by publishing, but by becoming presences on a literary scene. They need to be known to their contemporaries, approved by some, perhaps attacked by others, part of an on-going literary history. It is difficult to become a presence from one's bed; even more difficult if the bed is in Florence and the scene on which the initial impression is to be made is London.

Browning, who was perhaps Lee-Hamilton's first master, had made Florence his home for a period; but those were the years when

[*] This was the preface to Professor MacDonald P. Jackson's edition of *Selected Poems of Eugene Lee-Hamilton (1845–1907): A Victorian Craftsman Rediscovered*, Studies in British Literature 63, The Edwin Mellen Press, New York, 2002.

he was famous as the minor poet who had eloped with the major one, Elizabeth Barrett. It was not until her death and his return to London that Browning became the great Victorian.

G. K. Chesterton said of Browning's poetry that it was full of 'a charity that went man-hunting'. Without possessing Browning's range or energy in the hunt for his human subjects, Eugene Lee-Hamilton was a parallel case. Though both were heirs to Romanticism, there is little in either's work of the Romantic confessional, the Shelleyan first person, the Wordsworthian 'egotistical sublime'. Their own stories were told, if at all, indirectly. Italy provided them with many of their subjects – landscapes and people, history and the works of art which represented it. Like Browning, Lee-Hamilton had an impressive command of traditional verse forms, a talent for story-telling and a capacity for dramatic monologue. But there is also a morbidity, a tendency to the weakness of victim-fancy (if it was not Sadism), which Browning's imagination would have cast out. Lee-Hamilton is lucid where Browning is often less than clear; but he is also earth-bound where Browning takes flight.

If our poet, far from the centre of things, is not to appear in the principal text of literary history (and Lee-Hamilton does not) there is often a special pleasure in finding him in the footnotes. Among Henry James's reminiscences of travels in Italy are any number of sentences and paragraphs that bring to pictorial life the world which English literary exiles like Lee-Hamilton and his half-sister, who wrote as Vernon Lee, occupied:

> What a tranquil, contented life it seemed, with romantic beauty as a part of its daily texture! – that sunny terrace with its tangled *podere* beneath it; the bright grey olives beneath the bright blue sky; the long, serene, horizontal lines of other villas, flanked by their upward cypresses, disposed upon the neighbouring hills; the richest little city in the world in a softly scooped hollow at one's feet, and beyond it the most appealing views, the most majestic, yet the most familiar.

I like especially to imagine Henry James's visit to the Paget household in Florence (ten years after he wrote the passage above), his conversation with Lee-Hamilton interrupted by the visit of the

Countess Gamba, whose husband was the nephew of Byron's Italian mistress, and who shocked the company by mentioning that she possessed and would not relinquish certain of Byron's letters, and had even burned one she considered particularly discreditable. This led (perhaps after the Countess's departure) to Lee-Hamilton's telling the story of Claire Clairmont, sister-in-law of Shelley and mother of Byron's Allegra, spending her last years in Florence and being battened upon by an American sea-captain and passionate Shelleyan, Edward Silsbee, who hoped to acquire literary relics after her death.

James's journal entry of 12 January 1887, recording this visit, shows how immediately he seized upon the story, seeing in it the outlines of what became his novella *The Aspern Papers*. So our poet ('H' in James's journal entry), steps for a moment into literary history, forming a link between major figures of Romanticism and Modernism.

Lee-Hamilton is not one of those writers who points through literature to a larger, teeming world. He points, rather, from literature to literature. He is a poet's poet, a scholar-historian's poet. His sonnets speak, one after another, in the voice of a character from history. But he adds something new to the dramatic monologue: that in almost every case not only the speaker is identified but also the person or object addressed. Alexander Selkirk, alone on his island, addresses, not the reader, but his own shadow; Napoleon on Saint Helena addresses a leaf. By this device we are removed even further from involvement in the drama; made to view it as outsiders, non-participants, voyeurs. That, it seems to me, gives many of his poems their strange and tragic quality. It is as if we are watching life through a glass, unable to reach out to it. In this, perhaps, his frustrations at the restrictions his health had imposed find oblique but intense expression.

As Professor Jackson explains, Lee-Hamilton spent two invalid decades horizontal in Florence, suffering an illness for which any diagnosis at this distance can only be speculative. Was it physical or psychosomatic, heart failure or (as he once suggested to his sister) 'funk'? Was the unpleasant but appealing old party right when she said, 'Light a fire under his bed and he'll get up'? That the ailment mysteriously cured itself only adds to the doubt. Whatever the explanation, these were the decades when all his best poems were written, composed in his head and dictated to his sister; and much of their 'subject matter' seems to spring indirectly from his condition of perceived helplessness.

In one of his many 'confinement' poems, Lee-Hamilton has Philip IV tell his barber that a king is as 'free' as a Turkish felon, buried alive 'all save his head / For passing dogs to sniff at'. 'Sniff at' shrinks from the reality and undermines its force. Twenty-five years later Yeats, also in a sonnet, perhaps remembering this one and even echoing a phrase, was to complain of a world in which 'all my priceless things / Are but a post the passing dogs defile'. Not just the choice of the apposite word, but the unstraining alliteration and the extraordinary tightness of the sonnet form as Yeats uses it there, confirm 'gold' to Lee-Hamilton's silver. We are not, in other words, here considering the work of a great poet. But he is certainly a very good one, whose best work, long buried, has not tarnished and deserves more readers and more attention than it has had in recent decades. Every serious reader will be grateful to Professor Jackson for his good taste in making the selection, and for meticulous and unobtrusive scholarship in the presentation of his texts.

From Wystan to Carlos

Modern and Modernism in New Zealand Poetry*

> . . . it would seem to be a truism that [. . .] what *creates* the artist-writer is
> not the ideas (experiences, perceptions) he has nor the fact that he has
> them but the fact that he gives them form in writing. [. . .] The butcher, the
> baker and the candlestick maker (after all) have ideas and experiences too.
> – Ian Wedde, *New Zealand Universities Arts Festival Yearbook*, 1968

In so far as the discussion of New Zealand poetry has had any critical
structure, it has come from Allen Curnow's introductions to his two
anthologies and from the counter-statements these elicited. What I
propose to do in the present lecture is to enquire whether we can't
discover another set of terms – not because there's anything wrong
with the ones we have, but because a new point of observation is likely
to alter the picture, and it is surely time for a change.

Before I depart from it, however, a word about Curnow's critical
viewpoint. It was very much a product of the literary thinking of the
1930s. It placed great emphasis on 'truth' and 'reality'; and Curnow

---

* An address to the Writers' Conference, Victoria University of Wellington, August 1979.
 Previously published in *In the Glass Case: Essays on New Zealand Literature*, Auckland
 University Press/Oxford University Press, Auckland, 1981, and revised for the present book.

added a regional element by implying that in our case the 'reality' laid bare by the poem might be expected to be recognisably 'New Zealand'. As a general expectation this was not unreasonable. But was it also, as some poets felt, prescriptive? Certainly Curnow himself could not have written some of the best of his recent work if he had stuck exclusively to what he called, in his 1963 lecture on this subject, 'the New Zealand referent'.*

It was something in the literature of the 1940s and 1950s that called itself 'international' that Curnow particularly set himself against – a provincialism (as he saw it) which tried in effect to by-pass the limitations of the region by excluding regional reference and making the poem look as if it might have been written anywhere. I agreed with Curnow that strategy – the attempt positively to evade the features of the region – was bound to be self-defeating. (And it was Allen Tate, not Allen Curnow, who called Internationalism 'the New Provincialism'.) But there is another kind of internationalism which is in no sense an evasion of those local responsibilities Ian Cross urged upon us in his opening address. Let's concede with Curnow that most good writing is likely to have regional features. Nevertheless the language we use – the English language – is in some degree international, and this is something to be thankful for. Imagine if, here in the South Pacific, we spoke Danish or Dutch or Swedish – how exclusively it would throw us upon ourselves, and consequently outward upon the homeland for relief from our own provinciality. Or worse, how locked in we would feel if we spoke a language exclusively our own – Maori, for example.

Let's propose, then, that we take the international fact of the English language as our basis and consider our poetry historically, as part of the broad development of poetries in English during this century – not in the provincial spirit that we must subserviently follow what's happening 'Overseas', but rather in the spirit of an affirmation, recognising that we are part of the community of the English language and that this is something that gives us considerable freedom of choice and action. Such an approach will inevitably direct our attention to technical questions, questions of poetic strategy and poetic form,

* 'New Zealand Literature: The Case for a Working Definition', *Essays on New Zealand Literature*, ed. Wystan Curnow, Heinemann Educational Books, Auckland, 1973, p. 149.

rather than towards 'the New Zealand referent'. It is, after all, about nine years since Murray Edmond suggested in *Freed* 3 that it was time 'to construct a poetic rather than to name them hills and construct a national consciousness', but I don't see much sign that anyone has followed his suggestion.

I said a moment ago that Curnow's critical position, with its emphasis on 'truth' or 'reality', was very much a product of the thinking of the 1930s. If we go back further, to the period of the First World War, we find English poetry divided between Georgians and Modernists – a conflict which, by 1930, it seemed the Modernists had won, so that for a long time 'Georgian' became a term with dismissive overtones. But within the Georgian movement there had been in fact a variety of talents and directions. There were indeed literary sentimentalists who wanted to versify bluebells and cottages and country lanes; but there were also truth-tellers and realists who wanted to write of life as they found it, including poverty, urban ugliness, social injustice and consequent suffering. These realists became the war poets we remember and honour. Most notable among them was Wilfred Owen who declared 'the true poets must be truthful', and 'the poetry is in the pity'.

The poets of the 1930s I think inherited this strand of Georgianism – the realism, the truth-telling, the sense of public responsibility. Their poetry was committed to uncovering the ugly truths about society which conventional literary sentimentality had conspired to hide; and from this, it was hoped, might spring the seeds of political revolution, or at least of social change. So English poetry in the 1930s was harnessed to something beyond itself. It became an instrument for change.

Since the term Georgian was out of favour, and since the young poets of the 1930s – Auden, Spender, Day Lewis, MacNeice – admired Eliot and *The Waste Land*, it seemed at the time, and has seemed to literary historians since, that they were the inheritors of Modernism. In fact they were not – and I will show in a moment why they were not. In England poetic Modernism had no inheritors. Eliot's *The Waste Land* and Pound's *Cantos* have no direct or significant offspring in Britain except perhaps the work of Basil Bunting. The line of development out of early Modernism occurs in America. In his 1960 anthology *The New American Poets* Donald M. Allen was able to trace four post-war poetic movements, the Beats, the Black Mountain poets, the 'San Francisco Renaissance' and the New York Group, all back to a common point of origin in Pound and Carlos Williams. This is a very broad and variable stream, but the poets have enough fundamentally in common for it to be regarded as a single stream. Of course British poetry learned something from early Eliot, and even a little from Pound; but Auden – the dominant figure of the 1930s and 1940s in British poetry – is really the inheritor of what I'm calling the Georgian realist tradition, not of Modernism.

Pound, and Eliot in *The Waste Land*, had made a breakthrough in poetic form parallel to that made in the same period by Webern, Berg and Stravinsky in music, and by Picasso and Braque in painting. They had created what can be called 'open form' – let's not try for the moment to say what it is. Auden returned British poetry to closed forms. He acquired a certain surface liberation – he engaged in tricks and fireworks of various kinds – but in the very fundamentals of poetic form Auden was conservative. He took British poetry back more or less to where it had been before the American invasion; and there, for better and worse, it remained. The line of development for example that runs from Hardy through Owen to Auden, and on to Philip Larkin, Ted Hughes and Seamus Heaney, is more real than anything one might trace in British poetry out of Pound and Eliot.

I state these as historical facts. They haven't often been acknowledged as such, but they are confirmed in a rather surprising place, Stephen Spender's book *The Thirties and After*:

To be modern meant in the thirties to interpret the poet's individual experiences of lived history in the light of some kind of Marxist analysis. In relation to the modernist movement in the arts which began at the end of the [nineteenth] century and continued in the works of Eliot and Pound, this was regressive. For the essence of the modern[ist] movement was that it created art which was centred on itself and not anything outside it; neither on some ideology projected nor on the projection of the poet's feelings and personality. One might say that the moment the thirties writing became illustrative of Marxist texts or reaction to 'history' – and to the extent it did these things – it ceased to be part of the modern movement.

A little further on Spender says, 'We were putting the subject back into poetry'. This is true and not true, because 'putting the subject back into poetry' is much the same as taking the subject out of it. 'Subject' in either case has become something distinct from the poem, like the load on the donkey's back. For the young writers of the 1930s that load – that subject – was 'truth' or 'reality' (we are back with Curnow's terms), and the more of it you could get on to your donkey the better. It is arguable however that nothing is so 'true' or so 'real' as the donkey itself. (Ian Wedde, in the introduction I have cited in my epigraph, quotes Howard Nemerov asking, 'When you look at a cow, do you see the form or the content of the cow?') The Marxism of the 1930s, in other words, combined with that Georgian realism of the period just before, to reinforce a distinction between the poem and its subject, the language and its 'content', the donkey and its load, which Modernist theory had tried to dispense with. It is on that point that the British and American traditions have tended to split. And because New Zealand in those years tended to be more Britain-oriented than it has been since, our own poetry followed the British example. The young New Zealand poets of those years would have read everything of Eliot and probably something of Pound – just as their British contemporaries did. But the theoretical basis of the Modernist experiment was certainly not understood in those years, even perhaps by those who made it. Eliot's criticism hardly explains the success of *The Waste Land* – how could it when the final form of the poem was as much Pound's doing as Eliot's? And in any case, from 1926 to 1939 the Modernists were themselves confused by the economic and political *Zeitgeist*. Pound went crazy on Social Credit theory, so that vast stretches of the middle *Cantos* – right up to *The Pisan Cantos* – are as loaded with ballast as any Marxist could wish. It just happens from the Marxist viewpoint to be the wrong ballast. Eliot went away into his own brand of right-wing religio-politicking, which infected his later poetry and which I think impaired it.* No

---

* 'T. S. Eliot, himself the outstanding modernist poet, through his later work helped to deflect modernism and its acceptance in Britain.' Michael Schmidt, *An Introduction to Fifty Modern British Poets*, Pan Books, London, 1979, p. 8.

one, it seems, was exempt in those years; and we would hardly expect – or want – our own poets to have been unaffected by the pressures of the age.

I'm suggesting, then, a distinction between poetry which was simply 'modern', and the poetry of the Modernist movement. Owen and Auden were distinctly modern poets in their time, but they were not Modernists. The Modernist movement was initiated around the time of the First World War – its great texts were *The Waste Land*, the best of the *Cantos*, perhaps also the work of William Carlos Williams and Wallace Stevens – and it bore fruit in poetic developments that followed in America. The distinction – again very broadly – is that for the Modernists a poem was not a vehicle; it was a work of art whose material was language – language in action, language at maximum energy, resonance, intensity. The realist tradition, by contrast, tended always towards using the poem as a vehicle. You could decorate the vehicle; but the critic who inspected it would want to know what it contained, and what value the content had beyond the values of art. Did it promote the Revolution, or national consciousness, or God, or morals, or 'values'?

Is the distinction I'm proposing here between moderns and Modernist really one between moralists and aesthetes, roundheads and cavaliers? It has I suppose, or it has developed, something of that character, at least in its broad outlines. As Spender said in my earlier quotation, the Modernist movement 'created art which was centred on itself', whereas the new poets of the 1930s saw themselves as 'putting the subject back into poetry'. But the Modernists would not have conceded that the pure poem, the poem as pure work of art, told less truth than the poem as vehicle. In fact, Pound would have argued that the truth which can be lifted out of the poem is less true than the truth which is indissoluble from it – because insofar as a statement can be removed from its 'vehicle', precisely in that degree it fails to partake of the truth of imagination. And it is perfectly respectable to argue that the truths of the poetic imagination are less vulnerable, more durable, more comprehensive, subtler – in fact *truer* – than the truths of politics, morals, philosophy, or whatever abstractable 'content' the poet as moralist or realist propounds. At this point there are a number of resonant statements by Keats that might be called up

411

in support; but I will quote instead the short poem by William Carlos Williams that many will know:

> so much depends
> upon
>
> a red wheel
> barrow
>
> glazed with rain
> water
>
> beside the white
> chickens.

Why so much depends upon a red wheelbarrow, *what* depends upon it, the poet hasn't permitted himself to say. What he has ensured is that we have seen the barrow – in fact we've *imagined* it – noted its colour brightened by the glaze of rain and set against the whiteness of the chickens, and encouraged us to ask ourselves why such experience is important. It's important of course because it's hardly possible to abstract from it. It's what might be called primary living as distinct from the compulsive interpretations of living which occupy so much of our waking life. It's not enough; but it is the staple diet of consciousness beside which all intellectualisation is cake and cream. Imagination depends upon a red wheelbarrow; I would say sanity depends upon it – and so does the truth of poetry.

If I'm making myself understood you will have noticed that I'm beginning to take sides, and that's something I don't want to do. I have a preference at the moment for Modernist poetics; but it would be ridiculous to use that as a measure for the worth of particular poems. Clearly very bad poems are written every day according to Modernist principles; and the whole history of English poetry up to the twentieth century got on perfectly well without them. But there is just one thing to be said in favour of my preference. If one looks at developments in the arts from an historical perspective it does seem there is a certain flow of the tide. You can swim against it if you want to, and you might swim brilliantly. What you can't do is turn it back. It's conceivable for example that some poets might have written polished heroic couplets in the manner of Pope after 1790, but it's not conceivable that by doing they would have made any appreciable difference to the onset of the Romantic Movement. They would have been swimming against the tide of literary history.

Let me go back now to the 1930s. It was a decade in which politics bore in on everything. Modern poets were dedicated to 'truth' – the truths of urban squalor and depression, and the hope for radical political change and economic reform. Poetry became responsible and public, and the most influential new voice in Britain, and surely here too, was W. H. Auden's. So in New Zealand we find poets as different as Fairburn, Curnow and Glover in revolt against Georgian sentimentalism, influenced strongly by what I've called the Georgian realist tradition, believing (in Owen's phrase) 'the true poets must be truthful', confronting economic, political, social, historical realities which had previously been evaded in New Zealand letters. Instead of God's own country, a land of milk and honey, a South Seas Paradise, the land of 'Kowhai Gold' and Christmas under the pohutukawa, we're presented with a land of mean cities and mortgaged farms, 'a land of settlers /With never a soul at home'; with Glover's

> But all the beautiful crops soon went
> > To the mortgage-man instead
> And *Quardle oodle ardle wardle doodle*
> > The magpie said;

or Curnow's

> The pilgrim dream pricked by a cold dawn died
> Among the chemical farmers, the fresh towns; among
> Miners, not husbandmen, who piercing the side
> Let the land's life;

or Fairburn's

> This is our paper city, built
> on the rock of debt, held fast
> against all winds by the paperweight of debt.

These are the true poets being truthful to social history and political reality. The workers are celebrated; our economic and cultural subservience to Britain is deplored; the beginnings of national consciousness are discovered in our history and in our relation to soil and sea.

All this must have been exciting while it was happening and it's still exciting to look back on. There's a freshness in the writing that comes of a happy conjunction of talent with the times. The public themes are broadened beyond the purely political to express a regional awareness and a national consciousness. Curnow in particular, but also Glover, wrote public poetry which had none of that hollow official flavour, none of the thumbs-in-braces bombast that had characterised Edwardian poetry for public occasions. It was a fortunate moment for New Zealand literature.

There are times when external forces provide so much of the energy needed in the arts it seems all the artist needs to do is hang on and steer. But when that momentum of the 1930s and 1940s died away, what was left? I would say an uncertainty about the fundamental techniques and purposes of poetry. There were bound to be new poets after the war, and surely no one ought to have expected them to go on repeating what the Curnow generation had done.

The new New Zealand poets in the early 1950s seemed to gather around Louis Johnson, and one of the things they proposed to do was to 'people the New Zealand landscape'. They were going to write urban poetry, where they felt the staple of their predecessors had been images of rural life and of untamed land- and seascape. But this, on the face of it perfectly reasonable, project only made more obvious the limitations of the realist tradition. It was all very well to want to deal with human material rather than images of unpeopled landscape; but in practice it seemed to entail taking on the role of the fiction writer with inadequate means – summing up the neurosis of a suburban housewife, the poverty of spirit of a wealthy merchant, the craving for love under the exercise of political power – in a few glib verses, just as Auden had wrapped up the life of characters, some fictional, many historical, in a single sonnet or a dozen four-line stanzas. Louis Johnson was an able entrepreneur, and an able and encouraging editor. But it was going to take more than discontent with Curnow's anthologies (there was a lot of that), and camaraderie among the poets, if New

Zealand poetry was to find a new direction. What was needed was a movement which would have deeper implications for the practice of poetry itself.

In the 1960s, I think it can be argued, such a movement occurred. A new wave of young New Zealand poets discovered what I'm calling the Modernist tradition. They found it partly in Pound and Carlos Williams; they found it even more in the post-war American poets who, as I said earlier, constitute a broad development out of Modernism.* Ian Wedde was the first of these poets to make a strong impression. His poems began appearing in student publications in the middle 1960s, and I'm sure his presence must have helped to trigger the slightly more radical movement represented by the periodical *Freed* which ran through five issues from 1969 to 1972. I don't have the chronology exact, but I'm conscious that in the space of just a few years Wedde, David Mitchell, Murray Edmond, Alan Brunton and Jan Kemp – together with Russell Haley and Riemke Ensing who were quite a few years older – had arrived on the Auckland scene. Six of the seven I've named graduated from the Auckland University English Department where, among other significant influences, a number of them took Roger Horrocks's American Poetry course and, one or two, Allen Curnow's course on Wallace Stevens. All of them were published in *Freed*, along with Bob Orr, Bill Manhire, Rhys Pasley, Arthur Bates (later Baysting), and others. Some of them were to appear later in Baysting's anthology, *The Young New Zealand Poets.*

Freed was not the beginning of the new movement, but it was the strongest and clearest single assertion that the new poets of the decade were not taking the path of their predecessors, and that they were interested in matters of poetic theory. We have all learned, and rightly, to be respectful about the advent of *Phoenix* at Auckland University College in the early 1930s – the periodical in which modern New Zealand poetry had its beginnings. I wonder whether a proper

---

* The various discriminations possible within the Modernist (and Post-Modern) movement, are no doubt important, or considered so by the followers of this or that school. Such subtleties and refinements of allegiance are best left to others. My own concerns are 'broad brush'.

perspective might not teach students of our literature to see the advent of *Freed* in the late 1960s as an event of comparable significance.

It's time now to attempt to say what is meant by 'open form'. My terms will be broad, omitting fine distinctions – an approach which may not satisfy the purist, but useful if it should teach some of our reviewers to avoid the kind of mistake Ida Baker made when she was living in France with Katherine Mansfield and asked how much milk cost per metre.

Closed form might suggest formal measures, stanzas, rhymes – and in the case of Yeats or Auden it most often does. 'Open form' might suggest 'free verse' – and again, in the case of Pound or Williams it does. But in fact the distinction is more fundamental than that. It comes back to the question raised by the Spender quotation, whether you can distinguish a poem from its subject. It comes back to our conventional social distinctions between one compartment of life and another – literature as distinct from politics, politics as distinct from philosophy, thought as distinct from feeling, and all of these distinct from the governing personality. Far from being an aesthete who wants to distinguish literature from life, the Modernist poet, the open form poet, wants literature to invade life, to absorb life, almost to become indistinguishable from it, collapsing conceptual distinctions. Life does *not* order itself into narrative, or into logical argument; so in the degree to which the poem organises itself in that way, it falsifies. Life does *not* explain itself or point a moral; so in the degree to which a poem does these things, it is artificial. That is one aspect of open form – an openness to experience *as it occurs*, not a bringing of experience to be judged at the bar of previously formulated ideas or ideals; an attempt to get nearer to the true feel of experience; a preference for the inherent actual as against the organised abstraction.

As far back as the nineteenth century there had been a movement against those organisational abstractions on which long poems had traditionally been constructed. Indeed the idea got about that there could be no such thing as a long poem; that a long poem was a contradiction in terms, because the structure which held it together was essentially non-poetic. In the 1890s poetry was effectively reduced

416

to the lyric, because only the lyric was 'all poetry', free of the un-poetic superstructure on which long poems were hung. Imagism, around the time of the First World War, was a further effort towards purification. Not only was the superstructure removed; the artificialities of rhyme and stanzas went too. But Imagism tended to be visual and static, and Pound move quickly to Vorticism. The poetic moment became, not the static image, but the moment of maximum linguistic energy. Again this was a moment that couldn't be sustained, so the long poem continued to seem an impossibility.

Yeats wrote a few narrative poems; but on the whole he never departed from the poetics of the 1890s which taught that true poetry was the lyric – the short poem – and it was lyric poems he wrote all his life. Pound, on the other hand, had an epic ambition. He wanted to write a long poem – a poem (as he said) containing history. But how could you write a long poem if both narrative and logical structures were artificial, non-poetic? I'm not sure whether Pound ever articulated how he solved this problem, but he did it by a principle that can be described as accretion, or aggregation. Whether your basic poetic unit is the image, or the vortex, or both – insofar as the units are pure, and come from one personality at one phase of his or her life, they will be found to cohere,* to have a natural unity, without artificial (narrative or logical) linking. The broad interests, the recurring emotional concerns, the quirks of personality, the individual tricks of speech and ways of looking at the world, all these, I think, constitute what American poets (most notably Robert Duncan) called the 'Field' – and it is the Field that gives such unity and coherence as the work requires. These are the components of what has sometimes been called 'the process poem' – Modernism's solution to the problem of the long poem.

Poetry, then, is not a form but a quality. Achieve the quality, one might almost say, and the form will look after itself. So the *Cantos* – the best of the *Cantos*† – or equally a poem like *The Waste Land*, and many

---

* It is interesting that, late in life, when Pound despaired of ever pulling the whole of the *Cantos* together into unity, he said only (he was mainly silent in his last years) 'I cannot make it cohere'.
† It can't be stressed too heavily that the good and the bad in the *Cantos* are poles apart in quality. I have tried to spell this wide disparity out as clearly as possible in the chapters on Pound in my *Pound, Yeats, Eliot and the Modernist Movement*.

Modernist poems since, are built up of these radioactive fragments, without logical or narrative linking. In this way the long poem becomes possible again, while the purity of poetry is maintained. And I repeat that by 'purity' here is not meant the aesthete's detachment from life but, on the contrary, immersion in life, likeness to life – life-likeness in the very absence of those structures which life as we live it moment by moment doesn't have. And to get even nearer to veracity, to the linguistic re-enactment of experience moment by moment, there is an attempt to exploit, as the basic material, those natural speech patterns, the runs and pauses, the interweaving of breathing and vocalising, which constitute the poet's own individual manner of speaking. As Michael Harlow said in a recent review, 'the poet is listening to his own speech and scoring it on the page spatially and semantically'. The word 'scoring' is important because it reminds us of the underlying aural – I would tend to say 'musical' – structure of Modernist poetry. And this emphasis on spoken language can be seen indirectly to enforce a permanent regional element wherever Modernist principles are applied. Poets may derive their theory from the French and the Americans, but it requires them to use the language of the tribe, the local language as they hear themselves speak it.

'The true poets must be truthful', Owen said – and now perhaps we can all agree he was right, but with the proviso that you must choose your truth. And as I said earlier, it is quite as responsible and respectable to take the view that political, or economic, or national, or moral truths are themselves simplifications; and that the poet trying to get inside the very skin of experience is a greater truth-teller, a more profound realist, than the poet who sets out to improve the world. 'An artist', Keats wrote to Shelley 'must have "self-concentration", selfishness perhaps.' And he went on, 'You I am sure will forgive me for sincerely remarking that you might curb your magnanimity and be more of an artist.'

The staple book of poems of the 1950s contained thirty poems, each of a page or page and a half. Look at the products of the Caxton Press for the twenty years from the end the Second World War and you'll see what I mean. Each poem has a subject and works its way towards a statement – usually a moral statement – which one not infrequently felt carried no great conviction but was an artistic device for rounding things off. My own 'Night Watch in the Tararuas',* which went into Curnow's Penguin anthology, is a pretty fair sample of the type – the scene (with its symbolic overtones) set, the problem elaborated, the conclusion drawn:

> And know that though death breeds in love's strange bones,
> Its failing flesh lives warmer than the stones.

It was a poetic strategy I had learned especially from early Baxter. Of course plenty of good poems were written in that mode – a mode that goes back, I suppose, to Wordsworth's 'Tintern Abbey' and Gray's 'Elegy written in a country churchyard'. But if you had no ambition to be a moralist, if in fact you believed that moral pronouncements tend as much to falsify as to illuminate, and if you didn't want your final lines to shut the gate on the experience which was the occasion of the poem, then you found yourself looking for some other structural principle. Modernism provided one – a mimetic, as distinct from a didactic, principle.

The thirty-poem book was the staple for the 1950s; but some of the older poets had already tried to expand into longer forms. Fairburn's *Dominion* (1937) had offered one attempt – and one could see in it evidence of some awareness of Pound and Eliot. But *Dominion* was basically a heavy-handed piece of economic and political didacticism. And when Fairburn added two further long poems in the 1950s, 'To a Friend in the Wilderness' and 'The Voyage', they were both verse elaborations of very simple moral propositions – so simple, the elaboration comes to seem, not a vehicle for an idea so much as an excuse for 'poetry'. Even Glover's 'Arawata Bill' sequence of the same period, which ought to have stood on its own feet as a piece of scene-setting and characterisation, had to be rounded off with a bit of conventional high sentence:

---

* I took an example of my own here, to avoid the accusation of picking on someone else.

R.I.P. where no gold lies
But in your own questing soul
Rich in faith and a wild surmise.

You should have been told
Only in you was the gold.

And as for Charles Brasch in his long poem, 'The Estate' – re-reading it recently I was reminded of Matthew Arnold's complaint about 'the modern English habit (too much encouraged by Wordsworth) of using poetry as a channel for thinking aloud instead of making anything'.*　Brasch does a great deal of 'thinking aloud' in 'The Estate'. Fairburn was actually anxious at this time about what he called 'aestheticism', and the spirit of John Keats, creeping into our poetry. In fact he needn't have worried. It was Wordsworth, not Keats, who still presided.

James K. Baxter enunciated what was to be the predominant literary attitude of the 1950s when he said, in his celebrated address to the 1951 Writers' Conference in Christchurch, that a poet must be 'a cell of good living in a corrupt society'; and he concluded, 'I have dealt with the development of ideas rather than the development of verse-forms; mainly because to me verse-form seems a tool for sharpening ideas.' There you have that separation of form and content – 'verse-form' on the one hand, 'ideas' on the other – which had been characteristic of the 1930s. Nothing had changed. There was still the donkey and the load – but agreement about what the load should be was going to become more and more difficult.

During the 1960s, however, a change occurred which Baxter himself exemplified as clearly as anyone, and it was something which nothing in his 1951 address could account for. By the end of the 1950s his simple poetics of 'ideas sharpened by the tool of verse-form' had run him into the turgidities of his 1959 collection *In Fires of no Return*. And he perhaps perceived, in the twilight way Baxter did perceive such matters, that there wasn't a poetic vocation to be made out of

---

* *Unpublished Letters of Matthew Arnold*, ed. Arnold Whitridge, Yale University Press, New Haven, 1923, pp. 15–16. Arnold's complaint exactly accords with the observation by Ian Wedde which I have used as my epigraph.

cheap fiction in verse. He needed a new start, and he made one by putting himself (or *a* self) squarely into the centre of the poems. This was a development that owed a great deal to recent American poetry, (particularly Lowell, and perhaps Berryman) – partly but not exclusively to what I've been calling the Modernist tradition. The best of Baxter's work I think is represented by the late sonnet sequences, and there you can see him using what I've called accretion, or aggregation, to achieve a longer poem. The individual units – those radioactive fragments – are not entirely 'open'. The continual shaping of experience to fourteen lines is a considerable restriction, even though rhyme and five-stress lines have been dispensed with. There is also the linking element of the persona – the self at the centre, speaking and acting throughout. He continues to be a moralist too, or at least to engage in moral reflection. But the moralising is absorbed into the persona – it becomes an aspect of character, a way of projecting the living body of the self. The result is a considerable freeing-up of his poetry, a shaking off of that formula of the 1950s, where the final statement had the effect of banging shut on the imagination. There is a more vivid sense of reality, a less structured approach to experience, a freer and more flexible interaction between the language of the poem and the world beyond, and a richer sense of a living presence:

> Yesterday I planted garlic,
> Today, sunflowers – 'the non-essentials first'
>
> Is a good motto – but these I planted in honour of
> The Archangel Michael and my earthly friend
>
> Illingworth, Michael also, who gave me the seeds –
> And they will turn their wild pure golden discs
>
> Outside my bedroom, following Te Ra
> Who carries fire for us in His terrible wings
>
> (Heresy, man!) – and if He wanted only
> For me to live and die in this old cottage

It would be enough, for the angels who keep
The very stars in place resemble most

These green brides of the sun, hopelessly in love
With their Master and Maker, drunkards of the sky.

Baxter's talent, or genius, finds its fullest expression in these late sequences. And there is another characteristic they have in common with Modernism, if not derived from it directly: that is that the forward movement, the momentum of expression, is more important than the *mot juste*, or the polished phrase, or the brilliant image. That is where Baxter divides most clearly from Curnow. Curnow is all perfection of phrase; Baxter deals in beautifully judged approximations; and while one admires, indeed can be left breathless and spellbound by Curnow's lines and phrases, it's also true I think that it's the perfections which shut readers out, rendering us spectators, while the approximations (*when* beautifully judged) can seem to draw us in, inviting us to share in the poetic task.

So I have arrived by this comparison at another aspect of Modernism, and it's one that goes right back to Mallarmé and the French Symbolists. Perhaps the most fundamental sense in which the Modernist poem is 'open' is in never quite completing the statement, never closing the account. It is 'open' in reaching out and engaging the reader's imagination.

Words are the poet's material, just as the sculptor's is clay, the painter's is pigment, the composer's is sound. And here a delicate balance is called for to maintain the freedom of poetry against the realist, the seriousness of poetry against the surrealist, and the particularity of poetry against the idealist. The realist, as we've observed, often tries to make poetry serve something beyond poetry – morals, politics, a programme, a cause. The surrealist tends to deplete the language by diminishing meaningful reference, thus turning poetry into verbal play and whimsy. While the idealist's direction is always away from particulars into Rilkean or Platonic abstraction.

I come back to the red wheelbarrow: it is a fact (there is, in Curnow's phrase, a 'reality prior to the poem'), and the fact is *imagined*. The barrow is the meeting point of subjective and objective. The words 'red', 'wheel' and 'barrow', the words 'rain', 'water' and chickens', have sound values and associations. They have textures of their own; and in the poem they have syntactical and grammatical connections. But they also *mean* – they *refer*; and the art of poetry is to exploit, to the full, every potential the words which are its material have. So I find the 'surrealist' strand in Modernism the least satisfactory, though useful on occasions for deflating pomposities. Even in the work of someone as clever as Alan Brunton, there is a thinness in the language because the poet has let invention supersede perception. The language is showing us the mind of Brunton rather than a world as it appears to the mind of Brunton. It's in this sense I would argue poetry should be 'public': not in making moral, or political, or religious, or philosophical pronouncements (though it may want to find ways of doing any of these things), but in *not* being private. At its best it will be – has always been – one person's vision of a shared world.

When I chose my title – 'From Wystan to Carlos' – I had in mind that Allen Curnow had called his first-born Wystan; and that Ian Wedde, about 35 years later, had called his first-born Carlos. And though I don't know, and haven't enquired, whether either was actually naming a child after a poet, Curnow in 1939 can't have been unaware that Auden's first name was Wystan, any more than Wedde can have forgotten that W. C. Williams's middle name was Carlos. (And I might, in passing, bring Pound in here by mentioning that Bob Orr, one of the *Freed* poets, called his first child Ezra.) So I use the names to suggest the road New Zealand poetry has travelled during these decades. By a strange irony W. C. Williams was born a couple of decades before Auden; but Williams in this lecture has been one of the poets representing Modernism, and Auden something more conservative; and the change from Wystan to Carlos represents, not poetry getting 'better', but poetry becoming more radical in relation to what went before. It represents an expansion of possibilities, which I think had to happen if our poetry was not to settle into a staple of polite middle-class writing – accomplished, but prone to the deadening effect that occurs when the absence of stylistic vices becomes more important than the presence of virtues. There are all kinds of folly associated with the experiments and expansions of the 1960s and 1970s, but these needn't detain our historical overview if it can be seen that, in the best work of the time, distinct gains were made.

If I should discuss these matters with Allen Curnow I'm sure he would tell me that if you have talent you don't need to worry about literary history; and if you don't, it won't help you. But it doesn't seem to me irrelevant to ask what happened to Curnow's poetic career between 1957 and 1972, and to point out that during those fifteen years he published only one poem. One man's career can illustrate literary history without his being aware of it; and it seems to me that Curnow's silence at the end of the 1950s illustrates that the movement in which he began had run its course. When he reappeared in 1972 his poetry had assumed at least some of the features I've suggested characterise Modernism. And perhaps the most interesting point for my purposes is to recognise that of all the poems in his most recent books, the longest, 'Moro Assassinato', is the freest, the most 'open' in form, as if the pressure of the events which the poem relates, together with the knowledge that they had, built into them, a beginning, a middle and an end, released the poet from his usual anxieties about shaping, and so released the language to find its own form, making it his most nearly Modernist poem, the one that deals least in those finalities of phrasing I've suggested can make the reader spectator rather than participant in the process.

Curnow's example is a reminder – Kendrick Smithyman is another – that it's important to avoid the sort of stylistic Puritanism (Alan Loney is an obvious example) that says you're either Modernist (or Post-Modern) – or Old Hat. There is an either/or syndrome – a mild paranoia – that goes with avant-garde developments in the arts, and that is far from liberating. The ampersand, the oblique stroke, the spelling yr for your and th for the – these for a time became signals of virtue, of membership of the club, and a poor substitute for poetic perception and originality.

Kendrick Smithyman is probably the best case of a poet very much grounded in what I've called the realist tradition of the 1930s, and with no inclination to alter the basic pattern of his poetry, who nevertheless has read very widely in the whole Modernist tradition, including the American poets of the 1960s and 1970s, as a result of which his forms have become more flexible and his use of the vernacular freer and more inventive. Smithyman is like Baxter in having adapted the practice of American poets to purposes very much his own.

Of course there's no possibility of being comprehensive, but other poets whose work could be discussed in these terms include Hone Tuwhare, Alistair Paterson and Janet Frame – Tuwhare because of his adaptation of free forms to the use of a very Kiwi, and sometimes very Maori, vernacular; Paterson, who began as one of the 'school of Johnson', and has sought deliberately for models and precedents that might take him beyond it; Frame for almost the opposite reason – because a combination of great natural talent with an inability to take herself quite seriously as a poet results in what seems a casual or accidental (and sometimes careless) opening out into free forms.

Of the group of poets who began appearing during the 1960s Alan Brunton, Murray Edmond, Riemke Ensing, Jan Kemp, Alan Loney, David Mitchell, Bill Manhire, Bob Orr and Ian Wedde seem the most notable, and I'm going to conclude with a brief word about Mitchell and Wedde.

David Mitchell has been silent since *Pipe Dreams in Ponsonby* (1972),* although one used to be always hearing that there was new work 'almost ready' for publication. Of the group I've named, Mitchell may be the one most vulnerable to a cold critical eye; the easiest to dismiss from your mind when you don't have the poems open on the page in front of you. I think of him as the most instinctive of the group, the least conscious in practice, the one who had least theory to fall back on. But he is also the one most likely to take you by surprise when you go back and rediscover just how good he can be. Recently I rediscovered my copy of *Freed* 3 in which his poem 'The Singing Bread' appeared, and I was struck again by the fact that he could write something stuffed with all the old claptrap of the 1960s, full of echoes of Ginsberg and Henry Miller, the totally

---

* Postscript, 2006: More than twenty years since this lecture was delivered he is still silent, indeed vanished from the scene. News of him would be welcome!

predictable *soixant-neuf* Paris poem, and yet to my ear a magical exercise, sustained with only minor subsidences for almost 300 lines, carried forward on no recognisable framework except what I've suggested is the aggregation of fragments within a 'Field'. Only the Modernist tradition could account for such a poem, and before 1960 no one in New Zealand could have done it.

When I reviewed Arthur Baysting's anthology *The Young New Zealand Poets* I tried to describe the strange effect Ian Wedde's poetry had on me by saying I found it agitating, like watching someone trying to thread a needle. It still often affects me in that way, and I think this must be something to do with the kind of high energy that animates the writing and is transmitted through it. Wedde's temperament is affirmative – very different from the dourness of Loney and the bleakness of Murray Edmond – nearer, I suppose, to Mitchell's lyricism, but with a more obvious backbone. Wedde tends to be expansive, rhapsodic, apostrophising, ecstatic – even an exclamatory poet; and an unsympathetic view might illustrate that description by counting up the number of times oh! and ah! occur in *Sonnets for Carlos*, and the number of different ways he has of spelling them. Far from finding myself unsympathetic, however, I want to say he comes through to me as a splendid and original poet, occupying dangerous ground where the celebratory may at any moment pitch over into the effusive and sentimental – the same ground occupied by Keats.

Yeats has a theory somewhere that nations throw up their anti-type in the form of their best writers – the dissolute Burns affronting puritan Scotland, the uncommitted Synge offending political Ireland. By that theory I think dour undemonstrative New Zealand must be affronted by Wedde's vitality, by his expansive energy, by (to use the phrase Arnold used of Keats) 'that indescribable *gusto* in the voice'. Wedde has assimilated the poetic development I've spoken about in order to give fuller expression to that forward rush of feeling which is native to himself. There is a momentum in his poetry which is fresh and exhilarating; and at the same time there is density of reference – objects, scenes, talk, people – so that there is never the sense that this is merely a mindscape. Even when he writes in tightly organised form, as he does in his *Sonnets for Carlos*, he still manages to keep the poem open* in most of the senses I've attached to the term; and in particular, whereas Baxter tailors experience to fourteen-line rough-hewn off-cuts, Wedde measures his lines, but keeps the poem moving, flowing like water, spilling over from one sonnet to the next:

44

& what's better to do than celebrate
the fact? Look
               the dark bloom's left your eyes
spring's ripe   the horizon   the blue sky
the air pours towards you   the bean flower's sweet
again   the fucking ferryman grates
his rowlocks in mid-channel again   high
clouds are spinning like tops again and I
couldn't ever have enough of all that

& you again & again & again:
waking, quickening, travelling through one
world after another   through all the weird
stations of the earthly paradise named
for one impossible diamond-backed dream
or another, as though no one else cared

45

or could care
         in all the wide
               world or worlds . . . !
Oh well.
           I wanted to write poems about
spring, and you 'Primavera', about
the nagging dream of solitude

* See my *Kin of Place: Essays on 20 New Zealand Writers*, p. 347, for further discussion on the question of just how appropriate the word 'open' is as a description of Wedde's sequence, which is in fact rhymed and syllabic. There I acknowledge that the degree to which the sequence is *organised* was insufficiently noticed (by me), and explain how and why I think it, and Wedde, nevertheless belong where I have placed them in this piece of literary history.

427

into which you break like a beanshoot curled
upon itself. But the shoot's put out

its sexy flower, you've got up, I'm late
again, Carlos is almost a year old . . .

can I ever catch up? do I want to?
turning for one last look back: that beacon,
that weird station, the lovely confusion
of the trip, your memory breaking through
to bless the present summer sojourn,
to soothe love's forever healing burn.

In tracing the development 'from Wystan to Carlos' I have not been
trying to lay down prescriptions poets should follow, and I have not
offered a measure by which poems can be judged better or worse. I
have tried to recount a piece of our literary history and to suggest that
there has been, in recent years, an expansion of poetic possibilities.
In particular I suggest that the change in Baxter's poetry during the
last decade, the continuing (and more relaxed) fluency of Kendrick
Smithyman, and the re-emergence of Allen Curnow as a major voice,
together with the appearance of a group of younger poets of whom
Ian Wedde seems at present the most energetic and versatile, are all
explicable in a set of terms which must include a proper understanding
of the Modernist movement as a variable and powerful force operating
on the practice of poetry.* Without that Modernist element, our poetry
would have been less confident, with a narrower range of possibilities
and an uncertain future.

---

* A further implication was clearly that Curnow's nationalist, or regionalist (his emphasis
  varied), approach to the discussion of New Zealand poetry, though always worth very
  careful attention, had distinct limitations, and failed to deal with important technical and
  historical questions.

Index

Page ranges in **bold** denote whole essays.

430

435